Discussing Hitler

Advisers of U.S. Diplomacy in Central Europe

1934–1941

*John Flournoy Montgomery, U. S. minister to Hungary
(1933–1941)*

Discussing Hitler

Advisers of U.S. Diplomacy in Central Europe
1934–1941

Edited and introduced by

Tibor FRANK

CEU PRESS

Central Eurepean University Press

Budapest New York

©2003 by Tibor Frank

Introductory chapter
Read by Pál Pritz,
Translated by Rudolf Fischer

Revised by
Geoffrey Heller

English edition published in 2003 by
Central European University Press

An imprint of the
Central European University Share Company
Nádor utca 11, H-1051 Budapest, Hungary
Tel: +36-1-327-3138 or 327-3000
Fax: +36-1-327-3183
E-mail: ceupress@ceu.hu
Website: www.ceupress.com

400 West 59th Street, New York NY 10019, USA
Tel: +1-212-547-6932
Fax: +1-212-548-4607
E-mail: mgreenwald@sorosny.org

ISBN 963 9241 56 3 cloth

Library of Congress Cataloging-in-Publication Data
Discussing Hitler: advisers of U.S. diplomacy in Central Europe,
1934–1941 / edited and introduced by Tibor Frank.
    p.cm.
1. Montgomery, John Flournoy, 1878–1954. 2. Diplomats—United States—
Biography—Sources. 3. United States—Foreign relations—1933–1945 Sources.
4. Hungary—Foreign relations—1918–1945—Sources. 5. Europe—Foreign
relations—1918–1945—Sources. 6. Hitler, Adolf, 1889–1945. I. Frank, Tibor. II. Title.
    E748.M66D57 2003
    327.73043'09'043–dc21
    2003010043

Printed in Hungary by
Akadémia Nyomda, Martonvásár

CONTENTS

ACKNOWLEDGMENTS

My thanks go to the family of John Flournoy Montgomery, particularly his daughter, Ms. Jean Montgomery-Riddell, and his granddaughter Ms. Sally Arthur, for their generosity in making available to me the papers of the late U.S. minister to Budapest and for granting permission to publish them. The subsequent donation of these papers to the Hungarian National Széchényi Library will benefit future researchers.

I also thank Ms. Ilona Bowden, née Countess Edelsheim Gyulai, the widow of István Horthy, who kindly read an earlier version of the introductory chapter to this volume and contributed very useful comments. She also generously consented to the use of her own correspondence with John F. Montgomery, material now in the custody of the Hungarian National Museum.

I am grateful to Professor Pál Pritz of the Hungarian Academy of Sciences who also read my introducton and provided learned advice.

The Hungarian National Széchényi Library, particularly directors Géza Poprády and István Monok and deputy director Ferenc Rády, secured unrestricted access to the documents in their possession.

Pictures in this volume come partly from the minister's own photo album and partly from photographs in the collection of the Hungarian National Museum.

I am grateful to Mr. Rudolf Fischer for his graceful translation into English of the introductory chapter and to Mr. Geoffrey Heller as well as to Ms. Patricia F. Howell for revising the language of the book.

I also thank Ms. Erzsébet Bíró and Ms. Éva Eszter Szabó who assisted me in keyboarding Minister Montgomery's typewritten original material.

I am indebted to my wife and son for their unfailing support and patience, and to Thomas B. Robertson and István Bart for their enthusiasm and initiative.

FOREWORD

I

    As a visiting professor of history, I taught at the University of California, Santa Barbara, on and off for the ten years between 1987 and 1997. Perhaps the most memorable experience of those years was *Hungarian Spring 1991*, a major cultural festival focusing on intellectual and artistic achievements in the early decades of the 20th century. Assisted by a group of local enthusiasts, I organized the festival as a symbol of Hungary's spiritual renewal after long decades of Soviet domination, by way of remembering the rich 20th century spring in Hungary's cultural history. Excellent people such as Yehudi Menuhin came together for the occasion to remind the world of what Hungarian culture had been and could possibly become again. Some twenty-eight events were organized, exhibitions, concerts, conferences, and as a Fulbright visiting professor I also offered university courses on Hungary. Santa Barbara's main street boasted of fifty-eight Hungarian national flags, each sponsored by a different person or family.

    It was there and then that I met Ms. Sally Arthur. "My grandfather was U.S. minister to Hungary," she said, "he was fond of Hungary so very much." "Do you have his papers?" I asked eagerly, as I had been attempting to find Minister Montgomery's papers for many years. "I think my mother may have some of them; she lives in Washington, D.C. and in Vermont in the summer. Why don't you write her — I will also talk to her" — she responded encouragingly.

    By the time I could make all the necessary arrangements to meet Jean Montgomery-Riddell, Montgomery's daughter, it was January 1993. After some correspondence back and forth, she graciously invited me to her lovely apartment in the Watergate complex in Washington, D.C. She was a fine, elderly lady who remembered Hungary vividly. "My mother was often sick and stayed at home in the U.S. I frequently stood in for her in an effort to help my father and it was there, at the Budapest legation, that I met my future husband who served as my father's secretary. I spent memorable years at Lovas út 32." She pronounced the address of the former legation in perfect Hungarian. Ms. Montgomery-Riddell was extremely helpful: she had located her father's papers long stored in Vermont and brought them to Washington for me to see. "How would you like to use them?" she asked. I told her about my ongoing research concerning U.S.-Hungarian relations and my future plans. Cautiously I asked "How could I study these and perhaps make copies?" "Here they are, why don't you take them along?" — she replied. Her generosity and openness amazed me. I was almost frightened of the ease and immediacy of my fortune as a researcher. "Would you want me to transfer them to the Hungarian National Széchényi Library in Budapest?" — I suggested. "I am sure they would be more than happy to include them into their vast collection of *Hungarica*. "Why not?" — came the answer, quickly. "My father loved Budapest."

This is how it happened. I saw her once more, a year later. I had studied the papers in the meantime and we had a lengthy discussion about her memories. She spoke of her father and of her experiences as a youth in Budapest. Of her father's conviction that Hungary got into World War II unwillingly. That Hungary never liked the Nazis. She spoke of Regent Horthy who had personally disciplined the extreme right wing demonstrators on Hungary's national holiday in 1939 when she was with her father at the Budapest Opera House. She remembered that her father regularly organized the support of the regent after the war via a small group of Hungarian exiles with whom he was associated. She spoke randomly and enthusiastically of pre-war Hungary, a bygone world, Atlantis. It was only upon departing at the metro station near the Watergate building that I came to realize: her father had arrived in Hungary exactly sixty years earlier.

It took months to read all the papers she gave me, though her father had meticulously arranged most of them in neatly bound volumes. It took further time to complete them through the collection at the Sterling Memorial Library in Yale University, an opportunity made possible by my stay in New York City as a visiting professor of history at Columbia University in the ominous fall of 2001.

It was a lurid feeling to be looking ever more deeply into the history and making of World War II in the menacing atmosphere of New York after the attack on the Twin Towers. I came to understand the essence of fear and agony, both from my research and my daily life in a strangely parallel experience.

Corvina Publishers in Budapest wanted the Hungarian version of this book and published it in 2002. I am happy that it now also becomes available for the English-speaking reader. I hope it was the right choice to begin by publishing the confidential conversations of Minister Montgomery with Hungarian statesmen and international diplomats in pre-World War II Budapest. I also plan to publish his rich correspondence, further expanding our knowledge of Hungary's tragic wavering between Hitler's Germany and the West, a dilemma made easier to understand by the hitherto unpublished papers of this crucial eye-witness.

II

One part of the Montgomery Papers was donated to the Sterling Memorial Library of Yale University after the minister's death in 1954. The family, however, retained the confidential part of the papers, and this was the collection that I obtained from Ms. Montgomery-Riddell for the Hungarian National Széchényi Library.

It was among these papers that I found the typewritten "Conversations" which I judge to be the only existing copy. This was bound and indexed by the minister who had also numbered the pages of the two volumes. The "Conversations" were recorded by the minister immediately after they had taken place. He customarily hurried back to his legation and dictated to his secretary "hot off" his memories; the secretary later transformed his own shorthand into a typewritten version. There are a few handwritten corrections in the otherwise polished text. The series goes from late 1934 to early 1941. The minister used the material of these conversations for his official reports to Washington, D.C. as well as for his 1947 book, *Hungary, the Unwilling Satellite.*[1] The minister himself was integral to most of the conversations, though sometimes legation secretaries Howard K. Travers and Garret G. Ackerson participated in his stead.

Most dates refer to the actual dates of the conversations; sometimes, however, they refer to the days when they were recorded. The order of the texts follows Montgomery's original, except when I found mistakes in an otherwise strictly chronological sequence.

---

[1] The regular use of the conversations in Montgomery's reports to Washington, D.C. is very well documented in Thomas Sakmyster's pioneering biography of Miklós Horthy, *Hungary's Admiral on Horseback: Miklós Horthy, 1918–1944* (New York: Columbia University Press, 1994). See e.g. Montgomery, Conversations, Apor, November 30, 1937, cf. National Archives, United States State Department, 864.00/882, quoted by Sakmyster, 200 (note #99 on 428); Montgomery, Conversations, Eckhardt, November 16, 1938, cf. National Archives Microcopy, M1206/1/886 and M1206/1/1091, quoted by Sakmyster, 214 (notes #24 and 25 on 430); Montgomery, Conversations, Eckhardt, November 30, 1938, cf. NAM, M1206/1/1125-36, quoted by Sakmyster, 224 (note #61 on 431). — Montgomery's *Hungary, the Unwilling Satellite* (New York: Devin-Adair, 1947; Morristown: Vista Books, 1993), was based to a very large extent on his conversations. The second Hungarian edition *(Magyarország, a vonakodó csatlós,* Budapest: Zrínyi, 2003) is just being published by the present editor, with the links between the 1947 text and the underlying conversations fully documented.

Montgomery's original text rarely included the proper diacritical marks in Hungarian, Slavic, Romanian, or German names. For authenticity, his spelling was left intact in the conversations but corrected in my own introduction, comments, and notes. A few typing errors in Montgomery's manuscript have been also corrected.

I have added notes to the conversations as well as relevant information in the Appendix. Considering the desirable size of the present volume, I refrained from detailed comments about the political background and credibility of each and every piece of news (or rumor) mentioned in the conversations.

Tibor FRANK

A VERMONT YANKEE IN REGENT HORTHY'S COURT: THE HUNGARIAN WORLD OF A U.S. DIPLOMAT

According to *Who Was Who in America*, John Flournoy Montgomery, formerly U.S. Minister to Hungary, was born on September 20, 1878, in Sedalia, Missouri. The Montgomerys were Presbyterian and Anglo-Irish and claimed Norman and Huguenot descent. The minister was educated locally, graduating from the Ramsdell Academy in Sedalia. All his working life, apart from the years *en poste* in Budapest, was spent in the condensed milk industry. Between 1925 and 1933, and then again after 1941, he was the president of the International Milk Co. He was a Freemason.[1] He lived in Vermont, in a large home, with his wife, two daughters, and numerous domestics. He was not a career diplomat: he was appointed to his post as a result of the Democratic victory in the 1932 presidential election, as a reward for loyal and lasting services to his party, which included financial support.

For many decades he had not missed a single convention.[2] Most of his friends were old Democrats, whose support went back to President Wilson's time. One such was Montgomery's "closest personal friend" George Creel (1876–1953), an author and editor who, as the chairman of the Committee on Public Information (1917–1919), had been responsible for propaganda during the Great War;[3] another, Homer Stillé Cummings (1870–1956), chairman of the National Committee of the Democratic Party and attorney general under President Franklin D. Roosevelt (1933–1939),[4] as well as William Gibbs McAdoo (1863–1941), Woodrow Wilson's son-in-law and U.S. treasurer (1913–1918), himself repeatedly a candidate for the presidency, but losing the presidential nomination three times; a senator between 1933 and 1939.[5] Joseph Edward Davies (1876–1956) was a friend and rival who

1 *Who Was Who in America* (Chicago: Marquis — Who's Who, 1960), 3:610.
2 Montgomery to George S. Messersmith, July 16, 1936. J. F. Montgomery Papers, MGN 353, Vol. III.
3 *Who Was Who in America* (Chicago: Marquis — Who's Who, 1960), 3:194; Montgomery to F. C. Rota, September 10, 1937, J. F. Montgomery Papers, No. 353, Vol. VIII, Box 4.
4 Ibid., 201.

*J. F. Montgomery with Joseph Davies, U.S. ambassador to Moscow,
on board of S.S. Washington, June 1938*

continuously irritated Montgomery, the rich Ambassador Davies, author of
the international bestseller *Mission to Moscow* (a prize exhibit of Stalinist
propaganda) who had shown himself both blind and deaf as a star guest at
the Moscow trials.[6]

Montgomery believed in the Democratic party and was confident of its
success. As one friend put it, after the 1934 mid-term elections to Congress:
"I am writing this letter to you on the day following the clean sweep of the
New Deal in the elections. I can imagine that the result will be a matter of
considerable satisfaction to you. Every man likes to see his prophecies come
true, and you certainly prophesied this."[7] George Creel pressured him to make
a financial contribution, and Montgomery is known to have donated $5,000,
a far from insignificant sum at the time, to campaign funds for the 1939 presidential elections.[8] Presumably, there were many other such occasions as well.

After the Democrats won in 1932, Montgomery threw in his hat for a

---

5 Ibid., 1:795.

6 Ibid., 3:210. Cf. Joseph E. Davies, *Mission to Moscow* (New York: Simon and Schuster,
1941), Hungarian translation: *Moszkvai jelentés* (Budapest: Anonymus, 1945).

7 Frank W. Chambers to Montgomery, November 7, 1934. J. F. Montgomery Papers,
No. 353, Vol. VII, Box 4.

8 Jerome Politzer to Montgomery, August 13, 1936. J. F. Montgomery Papers, No. 353,
Vol. VIII, Box 4.

post abroad. If it had been up to him, he would not have chosen Budapest. At first The Hague was mentioned, but Montgomery was not in a position to accept.[9] He would have liked to go to Vienna, but FDR's team chose Budapest for him (the announcement was made at a White House press conference).[10] Montgomery was appointed on June 13, 1933, and sworn in at the State Department in Washington, D.C. two days later.[11] In 1935 a translation to Eire was seriously considered[12] and in 1939 he would have liked to move to Canada, but as things worked out he spent all his time in the Foreign Service in Budapest. For this, as for most other things, his wife Hedwig and her poor state of health were largely responsible. The fact is that both husband and wife were happy to be in Budapest. "We like it here very much and hope to remain on this job for some years longer,"[13] he wrote early in 1937.

Montgomery was never one of FDR's cronies. By the look of things, they first met at the time of his appointment to the Foreign Service, for which Homer Cummings, as a Democratic power broker, was chiefly responsible. The president received him before he took up his post and asked Montgomery to address reports to him personally, too, when he saw fit. The first such was in 1934, at the time of the *Röhm Putsch* in Nazi Germany.[14] The antipathy with which Montgomery described Hitler was so much to FDR's liking — he loathed the Fuehrer — that he read it out aloud at a meeting of his senior advisors. Montgomery wrote several similar reports, but this should not be accorded too great an importance since FDR asked many to keep him informed in that way.

Montgomery tried to make sure of seeing FDR at least once a year, but he did not always manage to do so. Even when he did, FDR seldom allowed Montgomery to have his say, only to relate at the most if he carried a message from the regent or some other important personage. Montgomery was dissatisfied with his president. "...none of my talks with him personally or by letter have ever given me any reason to believe that he had any thorough knowledge of the subjects which he discussed or that he had much interest

---

9 Montgomery, „Footnotes" to a series of articles on „Personalities." Miscellaneous articles, J.F. Montgomery Collection.

10 Edgar B. Nixon, ed., *Franklin D. Roosevelt and Foreign Affairs* (Cambridge, Mass.: Harvard University Press, 1969), I:219.

11 Ibid., 220, J. F. Montgomery, Diary, 1.

12 Montgomery, Diary, January 22-23, 1935.

13 Montgomery to Frederic C. Fletcher, January 4, 1937. J. F. Montgomery Papers, MGN 353, Vol. VII, Box 4.

14 Montgomery visited Berlin on October 19–20, 1934, the Röhm *Putsch* took place between June 30 and July 2, 1934.

in getting information. He seemed to me half-baked and to have no real knowledge of his subjects. He has ideas of his own and that is sufficient."[15]

Montgomery naturally considered it his duty to popularize President Roosevelt in Hungary and to argue in support of the New Deal. It surprised him how much sympathy he found for Roosevelt and for the U.S. as such in the Hungarian ruling elite, which was generally reputed to be conservative and pro-German. As he proudly wrote to his friend, Attorney General Homer Cummings:

> After being in Republican Vermont all summer, it was very refreshing to come back to Democratic Hungary. I say Democratic, because everybody here from the Regent down seems to be an enthusiastic Democrat. I haven't met a soul since I came here who did not express great interest in the campaign, and who was not anxious for the President to be re-elected. The Prime Minister went so far as to request me to telegraph the President election day of his ardent hope for his success, which is going a long way. Since the election, I have been receiving congratulations on all sides, and judging from the papers, the result is most pleasing to the Hungarian people;...[16]

Montgomery justifiably thought that credit was due to him personally for FDR's popularity in Hungary, especially considering the damage done by his predecessor, Nicholas Roosevelt, obviously a Republican appointment but FDR's kinsman. Montgomery suggested that President Roosevelt would play a part in a peaceful settling of Central European disputes, and he attributed FDR's popularity in Hungary to this fact.

> While the Hungarians are belligerent as far as revision is concerned, they are not for war, because they are unarmed, and they know that if there should be a war, this country would be one of the principal battle grounds. They believe that President Roosevelt will have an immense influence in a peaceful settlement of the world's difficulties, and they felt quite sure that Mr. Landon would not. I honestly believe that if the Hungarians could have voted in the last election, the President would have had as great a victory here as he had in America."[17]

---

15 Reports to the President. Text of a lecture, n. d. Miscellaneous articles, J. F. Montgomery Collection.

16 Montgomery to Homer Cummings, November 7, 1936. Strictly Personal Correspondence, 1933–1937, J. F. Montgomery Collection.

17 Ibid. — Alfred Landon was the Republican candidate in the presidential elections of 1936.

President F. D. Roosevelt with his mother and wife
Hyde Park, N.Y., November 1938

Montgomery met the president on September 22, 1937, and told him:

> It is my opinion that the Danubian countries will during the next few
> years settle their difficulties and that this will have an important bearing
> on the political situation in Europe. I reported this spring a conversation
> with Minister de Kanya which showed his ambition to bring about such a
> settlement, and everything that I have heard since that time indicates that
> everything is moving slowly in that direction.[18]

Montgomery repeatedly endeavored to bring about some sort of personal relationship between President Roosevelt and Admiral Horthy, and he
thought he found a link in their shared interest in seafaring. Horthy repeatedly referred to the president, and on one occasion (December 16, 1937) he
went as far as expressing, once again, "his admiration for the President and
told me that I should write the President that he sends his love. He said we
were very lucky to have a sailor for a President, that he had seen a movie
lately of our fleet and it was wonderful and that this was the result of having someone for President who knew something about ships."[19]

---

18 Montgomery to Homer Cummings, September 10, 1937. Strictly Personal Correspondence, 1933-1937, J. F. Montgomery Collection.
19 Montgomery, Conversations, Horthy, December 16, 1937.

When Montgomery called on Horthy on May 25, 1940, "[t]he Regent was very much pleased when I presented him the picture of the President, which he opened at once as well as the letter. He said he would reply to it. His pleasure was evident, and he said again and again that he was very proud."[20] Thomas Sakmyster, however, has rightly observed in his biography of Horthy, that "[i]t was Montgomery who had persuaded Roosevelt to send an autographed photograph to the Hungarian Regent in 1940. There is no evidence, however, that Roosevelt had any special sympathy for Horthy, and the latter's belief that he was on good terms with the American President was clearly an illusion."[21] Montgomery's desire to act as an enthusiastic broker was not backed by Roosevelt and hence met with scant success.

Horthy, on his part, was keen to obtain FDR's sympathy and he could count on Montgomery's support in this respect. In his *Hungary, the Unwilling Satellite* Montgomery quoted Italian admiral Paolo Thaon di Revel[22] who said to FDR in 1918 that the Austro-Hungarian navy in World War I, though "much weaker than his own ... had excellent hiding places in the Dalmatian Islands. 'Apart from that,' he added, 'they have a daredevil commander, Admiral Horthy, who will swoop out and attack on the most unexpected occasions."[23] "The President played cleverly on Horthy's leanings," Montgomery continued, by addressing him as from sailor to sailor, and the Admiral was very responsive. In 1940, after Roosevelt's re-election, he asked me to inform the President by cable of his delight. Thinking that this might be made public in America and cause the Regent some embarrassment, I told him it would be rather risky because the Germans might be decoding our messages. He said he did not care if they did: He would like to have me send it; and I did.[24]

---

20 Montgomery, Conversations, Horthy, May 25, 1940.

21 Thomas Sakmyster, *Hungary's Admiral on Horseback: Miklós Horthy, 1918–1944*, 321.

22 Paolo Thaon di Revel, Italian admiral, chief of staff of the Italian navy, whom Roosevelt, as U.S. assistant secretary of the navy, met during his visit to Rome on August 9–11, 1918. Montgomery mistakenly refers to di Revel as minister of the navy, as the minister was actually Alberto del Bono.

23 Montgomery, *Hungary, the Unwilling Satellite*, 45-46. Cf. Admiral Nicholas Horthy, *Memoirs* (London: Hutchinson, 1956; New York: Robert Speller and Sons, 1957) 87.

24 Ibid., 46.

Minister Montgomery with members of the legation, Budapest, March 1, 1940

Lovas út 32

The American Legation was originally in Árpád (today: Steindl Imre) utca in downtown Budapest, in the 5th District. It was during Montgomery's tenure of office, early in 1934, that they moved to Szabadság tér,[25] where the U.S. Embassy is still located. Budapest was reckoned a minor post, with a staff of twenty-seven in 1939; by comparison, seventy were stationed at the consulate general in Vienna, not even counting secretarial staff.[26] The residence, home of the Montgomery family, was in Buda, at Lovas út 32.

25 Montgomery, Diary, January 19, 1934.
26 Montgomery to George Creel, May 22, 1939. Strictly Personal Correspondence, 1938–1939, J. F. Montgomery Collection. — The comparison with the consulate general in Vienna might be misleading, as in 1939 this wasn't a simple consulate general but the successor of the U.S. legation in annexed Austria. Many of the staff would have been employed to deal with refugee or immigration matters, and also with Jewish property in which U.S. citizens had an interest.

Montgomery looked on his position as an observation post. He spent much of his time collecting information.[27] He made a surprisingly large number of contacts in his time in Budapest, the majority of which he carefully nursed. He reveled in the social life, as shown by the implied joy with which he complained to his friends. "Socially, everything is very lively here, and I am kept very busy with luncheons, dinners, teas, and goodness knows what. It gets very tiresome but it is necessary and in this business you have to keep in touch with your contacts all the time."[28] Further evidence is offered by his diplomatic reports, the care he took in dictating records of his confidential political conversations, a huge correspondence, a journal he kept for two years, and a book and articles he published later. He was not an original thinker; he represented tradition, established customs, rules, and regulations. He managed his office carefully, with a bureaucratic sense of duty that bordered on pedantry. Budapest made him into a competent diplomatist.

Even more eloquent is a permanent protocol list containing the names of nearly seven hundred persons and their spouses invited to lunch, afternoon tea, dinner, and his regular Wednesday concerts, a list which Montgomery compiled himself and kept up to date. The methodology would put many a modern *Who's Who* to shame.[29] Since most of the entries covered both husband and wife, well over a thousand people were involved.

It was an extensive yet closed world. The protocol list faithfully mirrors the odd, semi-feudal establishment of Hungary between the two world wars. Montgomery's contacts were primarily official, ministers and high-ranking civil servants, and of course senior diplomats accredited to Budapest.[30] More than half the list, however, is made up of members of the Hungarian aristocracy, headed by Habsburgs resident in Hungary, including every archduke and archduchess. The extraordinarily high number of the Count Károlyis, Széchényis, Telekis, and Zichys catches the eye. Montgomery was impressed by old names, by family trees rooted in medieval obscurity, by ceremonially dressed magnates and ancient chateaux, even if some of them now housed tenants. Montgomery also took note of the decline of one or another ancient family, such as the Apponyis and Perényis.[31] He was so impressed that after

---

27 Montgomery, *Hungary, the Unwilling Satellite,* 11.
28 Montgomery to A. S. Fedde, January 17, 1935. J. F. Montgomery Papers, MGN 353, Vol. VII, Box 4.
29 Montgomery to Robert English, May 23, 1938. Robert English to Montgomery, June 13 and July 26, 1938. Montgomery to Robert English, July 25, 1938. J. F. Montgomery Papers, MGN 353, Vol. V, Box 3.
30 Cf. the Appendix.
31 Montgomery, Diary, June 2, 1934.

J. F. Montgomery with diplomats in Budapest (in the middle, with top hat)

a few years he was prompted to genealogical studies of his own, with the assistance of his daughter, and he was overjoyed by discovering what amounted to his ancient past in America.[32]

He spent much time in the company of Hungarian financiers, the owners and executives of industrial enterprises and banks, members of the Budai Goldberger, Weiss, and Chorin families, the successive chairmen, directors, and managing directors of the Hungarian National Bank, the Hungarian General Credit bank, the Federation of Savings Banks and Banks,[33] and the Post Office Savings Bank. Early on he still kept up with his own trade and visited the Center of the Hungarian National Dairy Federation. He was not impressed by what he saw, but "[r]egardless of my real feelings I told them that they had a lovely plant"[34] He enjoyed the company of — as a rule conservative — celebrities of the world of art, such as Ernst von Dohnányi, then the prince of Hungarian music, Imre Waldbauer and Jenő Kerpely (of the String Quartet), Gusztáv Oláh, the designer of operatic sets, or, amongst the authors, Ferenc Herczeg, Lili Hatvany, and Ferenc Körmendi; the sculptor Zsigmond Kisfaludi Strobl, or the painters Cézár Kunwald and Ferenc Hatvany, the journalists and editors József Balogh (*The Hungarian Quarterly*

---

32 Montgomery to Jean (Mrs Richard J.) Riddell correspondence 1938–39, Strictly Personal Correspondence, 1938–1939, J. F. Montgomery Collection.

33 Takarékpénztárak és Bankok Egyesülete (TÉBE)

34 Montgomery, Diary, November 21, 1933.

and *La Nouvelle Revue de Hongrie*), György Ottlik *(Pester Lloyd)*, József Vészi and the Baroness Lily Doblhoff. A number of eminent Budapest university professors such as Baron Sándor Korányi, Zoltán Magyary, and Lajos Nékám, as well as Ferenc Deák of Columbia University, were also occasional guests at his table. His self-made "Protocol," this incomparable survey of the people he met in Budapest, suggests thorough familiarity with the Hungarian upper ten thousand. It bears witness to a sound knowledge not only of kinship relations, of offices held in the present or past, but also of political or denominational commitment, and indeed of hobbies and sometimes even of the skeletons in the cupboard. In the case of all important families, divorced spouses or those living apart, the children of every marriage, their spouses, and, separately, all the adopted children, were listed. In addition, or rather in first place, the crux of the matter was noted, that is, his judgment of the person and of the desirability of maintaining contact, all classified as A, B, C, or D. With justifiable political caution and prudence, the protocol book indicated the select few who "can be invited to Little Entente Parties," or "can be invited to Soviet Parties."[35] I cannot imagine that any other comparative classification of Hungarian high society between the wars existed. If Montgomery, getting ready for an evening function, wished to know what he could ask or say (or not say) to whom, a glance at his own list sufficed.

For Minister Montgomery golf came first, bridge second, and music a somewhat poorer third. Golf and bridge were veritable passions, at home in Vermont, too. His friendships at home and abroad, and his diplomatic contacts, were mostly based on the golf links and the card table.

Every weekend and day off found him out on the links; often enough he spent the odd free afternoon in the company of fellow golfers in the diplomatic corps. He favored the Hungarian Golf Club on the *Svábhegy* but he put his trust in the promise of the municipal authorities that there would be links on the more temperate Margaret Island, suitable for the cold and snowy season.[36] The promise was kept, but it was a disappointment since the course was too small and not what a golfer of his standard required.[37] Sir Patrick Ramsay, His Majesty's minister to Hungary, was a favored partner of his early years in Budapest. The Prince of Wales, later King Edward VIII and later still the Duke of Windsor, on a brief visit to Budapest, made

---

35 Montgomery, Protocol, [3].
36 Montgomery to Stanley B. Ineson, November 24, 1934. J. F. Montgomery Papers, MGN 353, Vol. VII, Box 4.
37 I am grateful to Mr. Tibor Szlávy, general secretary of the Hungarian Golf Federation for offering advice and comments (August 2002).

In the golf club: J. F. Montgomery (r) with British minister Sir Patrick Ramsay (middle) and golf pro Malcolm Goodwillie (l)

enquiries about which diplomats *en poste* played golf, and that impressed Montgomery.[38] Unfortunately, most of the senior diplomats were fonder of talking about golf than of playing it, and junior staff found it difficult to make the time. Getting a foursome or even a threesome together was not easy.[39] At times like that, Montgomery played with Malcolm Goodwillie, the pro. Sometimes he felt old, occasionally his arm ached,[40] he dreamt of a

38 Montgomery to O. B. Keeler, Budapest, October 28, 1936. John F. Montgomery Papers, MGN 353, Vol. VII, Box 4.

39 Montgomery to Alvin M. Owsley, May 12, 1939. J. F. Montgomery Papers, MGN 353, Vol. VI, Box 3.

40 Montgomery to Malcolm Goodwillie, Manchester, September 7, 1937. J. F. Montgomery Papers, MGN 353, Vol. VII, Box 4; Montgomery to Alvin M. Owsley, March 19, 1938. J. F. Montgomery Papers, MGN 353, Vol. VI, Box 3.

*With French minister Count Dampierre
at the railway station, Budapest, September 3, 1940*

hole in one[41] which he never managed in his long years as a golfer,[42] but in any event he could relax in the bracing air on the Buda hills and concentrate on touchy questions of diplomacy much better here than anywhere else in busy Budapest.

Whenever he had a free evening, he played bridge with Hungarian friends and fellow members of the diplomatic corps. The regent and Prime Minister Gyula Gömbös were his bridge partners already in 1934.[43] He criticized his partners and precisely remembered what hands he had played. His memory made him a first-class player both at the card table and in the diplomatic game.

Wednesday was chamber music night on Lovas út ("our usual concert," "our usual recital," "our regular musical [or musicale]," as the minister liked to put it in his 1933–35 diary).[44] The Melles Quartet frequently appeared,

---

41 To hole the ball in one stroke, a very rare achievement in golf. Cf. Laszlo Gyuru, *Easy Way to Learn Golf Basic Rules* (Keszthely: Litográf, 1998), 85; Steve Eubanks és Whitney Crouse, *Golfozni jó* (Budapest: Glória, 1999), 110.

42 Montgomery to Alvin M. Owsley, May 12, 1938. J. F. Montgomery Papers, MGN 353, Vol. VI, Box 3.

43 Montgomery, Diary, January 9, April 6 and 19, 1934.

44 Cf., e.g. the diary entries of November 1, 8, 15, 22, 29, December 12, 20, 1933; January 3, 10, 17, 24, 31, February 7, 14, 21, 28, March 14, 21, 28, April 4, 11, 18, 25, May 2, 13, December 5, 1934; January 3, 16, 30, February 13, 1935. Montgomery, Diary.

mostly playing the Viennese classics (first and foremost Beethoven, in keeping with the tastes of the time), but also Brahms and Debussy. Some Hungarian works, too, figured on the program, typically Dohnányi, occasionally a work by Carl Goldmark, Zoltán Kodály, Leo Weiner (his Coolidge Prize-winning string quartet), or house-composer Sándor Reschofsky, whose piano quintet and "Operetta" were both dedicated to Mr. and Mrs. Montgomery.[45] The musical soirées were attended by a select group of family, members of the legation, fellow diplomats, and closer friends such as the children of Baron Frigyes Korányi (daughters and a son) who had American relations by marriage. In the nature of things, contacts were close with acquaintances that had connections in the U.S. Sometimes there were guests from America lured by the promise of a night out on the town in exciting Budapest. "All I can say is that you will find Budapest more interesting in every way — night clubs and everything you want — than anything else you will see so you had better come as quickly as you can,"[46] the minister wrote to a friend in the summer of 1935.

The huge circle assembled by Montgomery was, however, somewhat misleading. It would seem that he provided himself with a comprehensive picture of Hungarian society. Being, however, a monoglot English speaker, he was forced to confine his contacts to English speakers, and this imposed

*Hedwig (Mrs. J.F.) Montgomery and Countess Mária Eugénia Zichy
in their box in the Budapest Opera House
(with the Brazilian and the Italian ministers in the background)*

---

45 Diary entries of January 10, April 18, May 13, 1934; February 13, 1935. Montgomery, Diary.

46 Montgomery to David Boody, June 26, 1935. John F. Montgomery Papers, MGN 353, Vol. VII, Box 4.

severe limitations, even though he employed interpreters on occasion. This decisively influenced his image of Hungary and of Hungarian society. His direct sources could only be the select few who in the Hungary of the time had learnt English, indeed those who were in a position to do so. This explains the large number of aristocrats in his circle, and his friendship with Anglo-phile politicians, primarily Tibor Eckhardt, the leader of the Smallholders' Party; hence his good relationship with Regent Horthy (a polyglot who once studied English as a young naval officer), with Kálmán Kánya, the foreign minister, and his deputy, Baron Apor, with the prime minister, Count Pál Teleki, and an earlier prime minister, Gyula Gömbös, all of whom spoke good English, just like Leon Orłowski, who headed the Polish legation. Many Hungarian public figures (Antal Ullein-Reviczky, Baron Zsigmond Perényi, Jr., Count Antal Sigray, Count László Széchenyi, János Pelényi) had English or American wives. But even those who spoke English well did not always understand Montgomery. His strong mid-western accent troubled even Kálmán Kánya, the foreign minister.[47]

Montgomery had a tremendous capacity for work and was only moderately handicapped by recurrent chronic illness. What perhaps handicapped him more in his social contacts was his highly critical attitude. In his letters, reports, journal entries,[48] and confidential notes, he constantly harps at, criticizes, and attacks the Hungarian Habsburgs, the regent's wife, Imrédy, the Nazis, fellow heads of mission, the Arrowcross, the Hungarian foreign minister and the U.S. secretary of state, President Roosevelt, his friend Joseph Davies, and, finally, even his confidant Tibor Eckhardt. All this is done wittily; humor is characteristic of all of his private correspondence. It certainly tempers the edge of his criticism.

His snide drawing-room anti-Semitism, antipathies toward Budapest — or New York — Jewish "society" expressed *entre nous* but frequently, established links with the selective "upper class" anti-Semitism of flourishing Horthyism (and of the regent personally).[49] Sometimes Montgomery's anti-Semitism did not seem all that upper class. The key was more that of a 1938 Budapest waiting for Arrowcross leader Ferenc Szálasi to appear. In May 1938 he wrote to the U.S. minister in Copenhagen: "…the Jews are so scared and they have such wonderful imagination they turn out the most beautiful assortment of stories you ever heard and one keeps thinking some of them must be true."[50] That has a snide edge but it also shows some sym-

---

47 András Hory, *Bukaresttől Varsóig,* ed. Pál Pritz (Budapest: Gondolat, 1987), 403. On Gömbös's English see Montgomery's surprised entry of January 17, 1934 in his Diary.
48 Montgomery, Diary, Personal and Confidential.
49 Montgomery, Diary, January 23, March 8, April 6, May 30, June 20, 1934.
50 Montgomery to Alvin M. Owsley, May 12, 1938. J. F. Montgomery Papers, MGN 353, Vol. VI, Box 3.

pathy. A few months later, apropos an article by Emil Ludwig, a prominent journalist and best-selling political author of the time, his tone is openly anti-Semitic: "Edmil Ludwig is a Jew, and Jews as a class are radicals. History has shown that when things are going down the Jews as a class are going up. If you go into the poorest country you can find conditions where every gentile is broke and the Jews as rich as cream. That is true here, it is true in Rumania, and it is true anywhere in the world, and has been true since the establishment of records."[51] It is as if he had not woken up to the fact in time that what, on occasion, could be reckoned as merely a controversial witticism had turned into a dangerous ideology and would soon become murderous politics.

The Hungarian Archdukes

Montgomery's judgment of Horthy depended on three factors and thus went through three stages. First, like his predecessors, Montgomery judged the regent's political and human qualities in the context of the Habsburgs. The United States, like the other Great Powers, consistently opposed a Habsburg restoration and therefore at the start backed "the man of law and order." General Bandholtz, who represented the United States on the Inter-Allied Military Mission in 1919–20, had already referred to the "Hungarian" Habsburgs[52] in a dismissive way. General Bandholtz's situation reports after the fall of the Hungarian Republic of Councils probably contributed to the international recognition of Horthy's election to the regency. In American eyes Horthy happily combined the good qualities of the old Emperor Franz Joseph in the absence of the anachronistic vacuity, even ridiculousness, of the archdukes. General Bandholtz's Budapest journal was published in the U.S. just about at the time when Montgomery, soon after his arrival, gave his first dinner with Horthy as guest of honor. They engaged in a long conversation and the recently published book was one of their subjects. "In discussing General Bandholtz book he told me he had not read it but excpected to do so. I told him there were several things in the book

---

51 Montgomery to Alvin M. Owsley, October 29, 1938. J. F. Montgomery Papers, MGN 353, Vol. VI, Box 3.
52 I have kept Minister Montgomery's usage when referring to members of the Habsburg house as "archdukes" and "archduchesses," though in Hungary they officially received the title "royal prince" and "royal princess." In reality most people kept referring to them in Hungarian as *főhercegek* (archdukes) and *főhercegnők* (archduchesses).

which I regretted and told him it referred to the calling of the Archdukes as 'Archie' and 'Archducklet.' He said, 'that's just what they are.'"[53]

The Habsburg context of any judgment of Horthy was obvious. The regent had been the last commander-in-chief of the Austro-Hungarian fleet; the foreign minister had once represented the Austro-Hungarian Monarchy, one of the Great Powers, in Mexico; the spirit and, on occasion, the arrogance of the old Ballhausplatz in Vienna lived on in the Hungarian foreign ministry on Dísz tér in Buda Castle. The majority of Hungarian diplomats had been trained in the *Konsularakademie* in Vienna. In the Budapest of the 1930s Montgomery chanced upon the complete stage of a kingdom *sans* Habsburgs where the decorative admiral stood in for the king, with an active parliament (albeit not elected by universal secret suffrage). This reminded the somewhat naïve and certainly inexperienced U.S. minister of an England which he found attractive.

Not long after getting to Budapest, Montgomery attended a Christmas party where Archduke József Ferenc and Archduchess Anna were fellow guests. The Habsburgs arrived fifty minutes late, something that was adversely commented on, but Montgomery nevertheless thought their manners superior to those of the regent's wife. His unpublished journal still shows him to be an admirer of the Habsburgs, although this may be the fruit of Yankee naivete or perhaps snobbishness:

> The noticeable thing to me about the Archdukes and Archduchesses is how much more gracious they are than those not born to the purple. They know just how to do it and go out of their way to be nice to everyone and do not overlook a soul. I have met other people here and elsewhere whose position was similar, and who I thought they were nice but after I have met the Hapsburg Archdukes and Archduchesses I have discovered a difference. Mme. Horthy, for instance, at her tea party illustrates the difference. We all sat around in a circle and she spoke to you only when you arrived and when you left and made no conversation with anyone but those sitting close to her, or those she knew. She did not converse with me at all although I was a newly arrived Minister. With the Hapsburg Archdukes it is different. Everyone in the party get attention. They even talk to the musicians and they originate and keep alive the entire conversation. It is an art that they seemed to be trained to. If they moved over to

---

53 Montgomery, Diary, April 6, 1934. cf. Maj. Gen. Harry Hill Bandholtz, *An Undiplomatic Diary.* Ed. Fritz-Konrad Krüger (New York: Columbia University Press, 1933), 193, 205-08, 273, 278. Bandholtz in fact used a variety of phrases such as "Archie Duke," "Archie Dukelet," "Archdukelet," "Archie," "Dukelet," "archduchesslets."

the United States they would do well in politics providing they could get over the habit of arriving late. I am afraid if they came to a political meeting fifty minutes late at home they might not like it.[54]

On another occasion, in the spring of 1934, Montgomery writes about a reception given by Archduke József in Buda Castle. The tone is reminiscent of General Bandholtz's earlier satirical observations. The diplomatic corps had expected supper, but in the event all they were offered was undrinkable tea and biscuits.

> We were afraid that if we left we would insult the Archduke and the whole House of Hapsburg but knew if we stayed we wouldn't get any-thing to eat and none of us had had any dinner. We argued the matter pro and con for sometime and finally the Greek Minister, Yugoslavian Minister, Jean and myself took the bull by the horns and left. I never heard how long the rest of them stayed. We went down to the Island and had dinner and were very happy to be out of it. It was about the worst managed affair I had ever seen, and how they expected the little dabs of food to go around in all that multitude I don't know. I don't think they will get many diplomats to come back if they have any more.[55]

Yet, in spite of everything, the small-town American, not really used to royal company, was charmed by the Hungarian Habsburgs to such a degree that he did not notice that there were not only archdukes (and occasionally their mothers such as Princess Izabella, Albrecht's ambitious mother) who had their eye on the Hungarian crown but that Archduke Albrecht (from his residence at Esterházy utca 24), looked for support in Nazi Germany, of all places. Albrecht was one of the U.S. minister's regular guests, and Montgomery even valued him as a source of information.[56] At Albrecht's Pannon-halma wedding Montgomery was one of the very few guests of some stand-ing; the others were a handful of misguided aristocrats. Albrecht married *en deuxième noces* and once again not *standesgemäß*. Montgomery assiduous-ly took photographs of the gold plate, unaware of Albrecht's imminent Ger-man contacts, of his close financial and political links with Béla Imrédy's party, and of the fact that in 1941, already from a German address and at a Nazi suggestion, he would be hard at work on establishing unity amongst

---

54 Montgomery, Diary, December 14, 1933.
55 Montgomery, Diary, May 12, 1934. Margaret Island was meant.
56 Montgomery, Conversations, Albrecht, March 12, 1936.

Hungarian National Socialists.[57] Montgomery, who was, in general, well-informed, appeared to be ignorant of this even after his return home, although he kept track of much lesser fry amongst Hitler's Hungarian friends. At the same time, he was shocked to hear that, though the United States did not support a Habsburg restoration, Roosevelt had received Archduke Otto in the White House, what is more at the suggestion of the U.S. ambassador to France.[58] Later, in America, Montgomery himself met Otto, who made a much better impression on him than he had expected.

Relatively many Hungarians were legitimists — that is they favored a Habsburg king — but few in government circles. The prime minister, Count Teleki, expressed himself unambiguously to Montgomery: "Hungary had no desire to go into another Austro-Hungarian Empire, nor to have a Hapsburg King. There was no possibility of a Hapsburg king in Hungary if it depended on the will of the people. One might be forced on them but he couldn't believe his throne would be secure."[59] That was straight talk.

The Regent

In John Flournoy Montgomery's eyes, Horthy's was an imposing presence. True, Montgomery, with his Missouri background, was born into a good family, and he had married well, but it was in Hungary that he first experienced the sort of pomp and splendor that emanated from Buda Castle.

A sober businessman, Montgomery was captivated by the reflected light of Habsburg times. Budapest between the wars was one of the most beautiful cities in Europe, and in what the historian Gyula Szekfű termed (with pejorative intent) the Neo-Baroque Age[59a] the magic of the Austro-Hungarian Monarchy lit up once again, and for the last time.

The regent Miklós Horthy, a landowner and naval officer, who had received his political education as naval aide to Emperor-King Franz Joseph, himself lived under the spell of the imperial court. "Even after his death," Horthy wrote of the emperor-king in his memoirs, "I continued to trust in his wisdom, and I have never regretted that I retained so many of his

57 Miklós Lackó, *Nyilasok, nemzetiszocialisták 1935–1944* (Budapest: Kossuth, 1966), 264–265.
58 Cf. the conversation with Kálmán Kánya and its footnotes. Montgomery, Conversations, Kánya, March 22, 1940. See Montgomery's article on Otto in miscellaneous articles, J. F. Montgomery Collection.
59 Montgomery, Conversations, Teleki, December 11, 1939.
59a *Három nemzedék és ami utána következik* (Budapest: Egyetemi Nyomda, [1934]), 402–415.

*István Bárczy, deputy lord-lieutenant László Endre and István Horthy
in the procession of St. Stephen's Day (August 20, 1940)*

arrangements, tested by centuries of use, in dealing with Hungarian problems."[60] Nicholas Roosevelt, himself a U.S. minister to Budapest before Montgomery, remembered that "the admiral several times told me of the admiration, respect and affection which he had for the old man…"[61] All that he had observed and learnt in thus serving his old master in the Hofburg in Vienna was miniaturized in Buda Castle. Horthy was spellbound by Franz Joseph, and Montgomery admired the admiral. He was enchanted by the changing of the guard, by levées for diplomats in the castle, by a mass for the diplomatic corps celebrated on the occasion of the anniversary of the enthronement of the pope, by nights at the Opera House on December 6, Horthy's name-day, by military parades, by cocktail and garden parties, by soirées given by the Habsburg archdukes resident in Hungary, and by news of the Saint Stephen's Day procession on August 20 (which he missed since he spent his summers in America), and by other processions too, with ceremonially accountred dignitaries, sparkling decorations, grand crosses and their ribbons, the rag-and-bone shop of a world that has had its day. Horthy's

---

60 Horthy, *Memoirs*, 152–53.
61 Nicholas Roosevelt, "Introduction," in Horthy, *Memoirs*, 8.

*Arrival of the king and queen of Italy in Mussolini Square, today: Oktogon,
Budapest, May 19, 1937*

Hungary continued as a kingdom; thus members of orders continued to use
their titles and to bear their insignia. Horthy's military bearing, disarming
graciousness, and irresistible charm impressed Montgomery. To the end of
his life he remembered him as "a very fine person and a very wonderful
man."[62]

The U.S. minister delighted in the performance. Compared to the archdukes, the head of state was the soul of punctuality. The reliable admiral, an
emphatically hierarchical government structure, and a foreign ministry that
operated with a routine that seemed dependable all suggested to him that
the country was in good hands.

The state visit by King Victor Emanuel III of Italy and his consort on
May 19 and 20, 1937 — banquet, ball, illuminations and all — was one of
the highlights of Montgomery's life.

> The return call of Italy's little king and his tall wife is in my memory
> like a grand theatrical event. The Hungarians as host were at their best.

---

62 Montgomery to Mrs. Guy [Ilona] Bowden, August 18, 1954. Hungarian National
Museum.

Hungarian dignitaries at the reception of the king and queen of Italy
1 General Vilmos Rőder, minister of defense, 2 Tihamér Fabinyi, minister of
finance, 3 Andor Lázár, minister of justice, 4 Angelo Rotta, papal nuntio

Some five hundred or more people attended the dinner in the grand ball-room of Franz Josef's palace under a ceiling of heavy silver, and a larger number attended the dance given the following night in the same room. Strict formality was observed at both events. The Hungarians wore their traditional uniforms to the dance, so it was extremely colorful.

After dinner, the party left the ballroom and went up into the old palace which looked out on the Danube and Pest. Budapest had a very fine system of illuminating public buildings and bridges. As we looked out, we saw not only the city as it normally was, but all of the illumina-tion, even up on the hills. It was extraordinary. The old palace itself was lit by candles, thousands of them in a long row of rooms, possibly a dozen, opening one on the other so that it made a long vista.[63]

---

63 Montgomery, *Hungary, the Unwilling Satellite*, 84-85. Cf. Horthy, *Memoirs*, 153–55.

*Ball in the Royal Palace in honor of the king and queen of Italy
Budapest, March 20, 1937.
Archduchess Auguszta, Miklós Horthy, the queen of Italy and the king,
Mrs. Miklós Horthy, Archduke József, Archduchess Magdolna,
Archduke József Ferenc on the platform*

He must have been aware that no other ruler visited Horthy, nor was Horthy invited to visit other kings, but the performance nevertheless enchanted him. Everything that he knew, comprehended, and valued of Hungary appeared in emblematic condensation. A country worthy of love and admiration, with a great history, joy of life, and a political culture dreaming of an independence with which he could truly sympathize was resplendent in the light of a thousand candles and an illuminated capitol. Fifteen long years later Montgomery wrote to Horthy's daughter-in-law, "I will never forget the King of Italy and the dance and dinner which was given at the Royal Palace when they were in Budapest."[64]

In the beginning, the relationship between Montgomery and Horthy did not go beyond what was prescribed by protocol.

The regent held a levée for the diplomatic corps every year, in January. Not only heads of mission attended but also every one of secretarial rank,

---

64 J. F. Montgomery to Mme Ilona Horthy, October 24, 1951. Hungarian National Museum.

Garden party honoring the king and queen of Italy, May 21, 1937

and all the attachés. The regent spoke briefly to every head of mission and all new secretaries and attachés, shook hands all round, and moved on.

In his self-made protocol book,[65] Montgomery laid down prescriptions for the arrangement of functions held at his residence. Four lines were devoted to a dinner to which the prime minister was invited, but four pages if Horthy was to be the guest. Though Montgomery was well aware of Horthy's relatively restrained role in the daily business of politics, he nevertheless felt that the functions of the Hungarian regent more closely corresponded to those of the U.S. president than did the functions of the prime minister. Montgomery must also have been aware that the constitutional powers of the regent were extended (just during Montgomery's years in Budapest) to correspond more to those of a traditional constitutional monarch or a "powerful" president of a republic.[66]

Preparation for a dinner in honor of the regent given by the legation started with a call by the legation secretary on the head of Horthy's private office. They agreed on one of the three or four days proposed for the dinner and drew up a list of thirty or forty suggested guests for a dinner of twenty,

---

65 J. F. Montgomery, Protocol, 15–18.
66 Ignác Romsics, *Hungary in the Twentieth Century* (Budapest: Corvina-Osiris, 1999), 187.

Horthy at a garden party in the Royal Palace, Budapest, 1937

which the regent himself personally approved. The list of those accepting the invitation had to be sent to the head of the private office a week before the event.

The regent's office decided on seating arrangements. All guests were given a number, which regulated their entry into the dining room. The legation notified the police and provided them with a list of servants on duty on the given night.

Guests were invited to be present fifteen minutes before the expected arrival of the regent. Five minutes before Horthy's arrival, legation staff assembled facing the front door. Both wings of the door were opened wide for his arrival and departure. (Archduchess Auguszta, Franz Joseph's granddaughter, the "majestic amazon" in author Sándor Márai's words, insisted that both wings of the front door be opened for her arrival as well.)[67]

The wives of legation secretaries and such guests as had not previously met the regent assembled at the drawing room door where the introductions took place when the regent and his wife entered. The ladies were required to curtsey.

The regent, who chose his own bridge partner, preferred to move to the card table as soon as dinner was over.

What Montgomery expected in his residence fitted in perfectly with the regent's style and habits. One may note that Montgomery, the small-town

---

67 Montgomery's article on the archdukes. Miscellaneous articles, J. F. Montgomery Collection. Cf. Sándor Márai, *Csutora* (Budapest: Pantheon, n.d.)

American businessman, was more impressed by Horthy's quarterdeck precision than by the relaxed graciousness which the Hungarian Habsburgs displayed in their hospitality.[68]

Horthy and Hitler — Through American Eyes

Horthy and his entourage were anti-Nazi. With increasing frequency they endeavored to convey their growing anxieties concerning the führer to the Americans' "man in Budapest." As Hungary increasingly drifted toward Nazi Germany,[69] these people made more and more use of Montgomery as a messenger for their real or pretended anti-Nazi sentiments. What was probably at work in Horthy was a disdain for the likes of Hitler and Nazi methods natural in a Hungarian gentleman and naval officer who had learnt his politics at the feet of Franz Joseph, as well as a desire for reinsurance at a future peace conference should, contrary to expectations, Germany be defeated in the war. Montgomery happily listened to Horthy's repeated promises concerning the "de-nazification" of the Hungarian parliament. It gave him satisfaction to observe signs that the extreme right was kept in check, through, for example, the repeated arrest of their leader Szálasi and, later, the dismissal of Béla Imrédy, the pro-Nazi prime minister of 1938–39.

In the course of the thirties, the expansion of National Socialism steadily dwarfed the threat of a Habsburg restoration. Admiral Horthy, as the defender of Hungarian national independence, appeared, to this American, as someone who opposed Hitler and despised the Nazis. Horthy and his circle, however, may indeed have opposed the Nazis, but not necessarily the Germans. For an American, the Hungarian regent seemed to be preferable to Nazi Germany just as, earlier, he had appeared preferable to the Habsburgs — that is, inasmuch as little Hungary could maintain the appearance of independence. What's more, Hitler and Horthy had both been obsessed by Communism from the start. U.S. Minister Nicholas Roosevelt remembered his farewell visit to the regent in 1933, when "he spoke with passionate earnestness about his conviction that Russia was the greatest threat not only to Hungary but to the western world. For years this subject had been an

---

68 The rules of conduct in Horthy's court were well-known to contemporaries; they were also made available in *Művelt és udvarias ember a XX. században* (Budapest: Pesti Napló, é.n.) 45–47, published by the popular paper *Pesti Napló*.

69 Gyula Juhász, *Magyarország külpolitikája 1919–1945*, 3rd ed. (Budapest: Kossuth, 1988), 136–256; Mária Ormos, *Magyarország a két világháború korában* (Debrecen: Csokonai, 1998), 147–230; Ignác Romsics, *Hungary in the Twentieth Century*, 193–204.

obsessions of his — so much so, in fact, that the members of the diplomatic corps in Budapest in the '30s discounted it as a phobia."[70] Horthy called on Hitler on August 22, 1936: "... it was rumored that they discussed Communism..." "Of course they did! Could you imagine the Regent overlooking a good opportunity like that?" — Baron Apor, permanent deputy of the foreign minister remarked.[71] After World War II, both Nicholas Roosevelt and John F. Montgomery felt that the anxieties of the aged admiral had been confirmed. In the eyes of these Americans, not only Hitler's Germany but also Stalin's Soviet Union was a threat compared to which Horthy's Hungary looked like paradise lost — especially with hindsight, seen from Washington, D.C., after the war.[72] At first Horthy seemed preferable to the Habsburgs, then to the Nazis, and finally to Bolshevism. Looked at from that angle, one can understand why an American envoy, a member of the Democratic party, found himself ever closer to the regent of Hungary, so that, in letters they exchanged in the early fifties, they — a retired American businessman and an admiral in exile — mutually addressed each other as "Dear friend!"[73]

March 15, 1939, was very likely a turning point in this relationship. A gala took place in the Royal Hungarian Opera House on the occasion of Hungary's national holiday, which was interrupted by shouts of "Justice for Szálasi!" (the recently imprisoned leader of the extreme right Arrowcross party). Horthy himself rushed to the nearby box and personally chastened the young rowdies. Montgomery, driven by curiosity, rushed there, too, and Horthy took this as a desire to come to his aid. "A few days later, the Regent asked me to call, thanked me for having come to his aid and presented me with his picture. I was a little surprised at his deduction, but did not see any reason to contradict him."[74] Montgomery placed photographs of the gala performance in his personal photo album and cherished them as long as he lived. He felt this incident at the Opera to have been a sort of epiphany illu-

---

70 Nicholas Roosevelt, "Introduction," in Horthy, *Memoirs*, 9–10.

71 Montgomery, Conversations, Apor, November 3, 1936. Cf. *The Confidential Papers of Admiral Horthy.* Eds. Miklós Szinai and László Szűcs (Budapest: Corvina, 1965), 82–93; *A Wilhelmstrasse és Magyarország. Német diplomáciai iratok Magyarországról 1933-1944.* Eds. György Ránki, Ervin Pamlényi, Loránt Tilkovszky, and Gyula Juhász (Budapest: Kossuth, 1968), 138-39; Pál Pritz, *Magyarország külpolitikája Gömbös Gyula miniszterelnöksége idején 1932-1936* (Budapest: Akadémiai Kiadó, 1982), 266–69.

72 Nicholas Roosevelt, "Introduction," in Horthy, *Memoirs*, 9-10; Montgomery, *Hungary, the Unwilling Satellite,* 11–12.

73 Montgomery to Miklós Horthy, September 4, October 8, 1951. Miklós Horthy to Montgomery, October 16, 1951; March 16, 1952; June 26, 1954. Hungarian National Museum.

74 Montgomery, *Hungary, the Unwilling Satellite,* 33–35.

Celebrating the national holiday in the Royal Hungarian Opera House
Budapest, March 15, 1939
The regent and his wife stand in the royal box; the Arrowcross demonstration
took place in the second box to the right upstairs

minating Horthy's politics and the chasm between the regent's attitude and
that of the Arrowcross, or Hungarists, or whatever the Hungarian National
Socialists called themselves at any particular time.

Admiral Canaris, chief of the *Abwehr* (the German counter-intelligence
service), relatively frequently traveled through Hungary. On such occasions
he would call on Horthy, and he invited him to a battue at Gödöllő. There in
the woods, at nightfall, the two Great War naval officers may well have
exchanged opinions about Hitler and Germany's prospects in a war. Canaris, who was to be executed as one of the participants in the July 20, 1944,
plot to kill Hitler, spoke frankly to the former Austro-Hungarian admiral.[75]

Mario D. Fenyo established in his book on Horthy and Hitler that
"American diplomats in Hungary, John F. Montgomery, Herbert Pell, and
Howard Travers (first secretary of the legation), were at pains to point out

75 J. F. Montgomery, Conversations, Horthy, November 8, 1940; J. F. Montgomery,
Hungary, the Unwilling Satellite, 46–7; Horthy, *Memoirs,* 157-58; Sakmyster, *Hun-
gary's Admiral on Horseback: Miklós Horthy, 1918–1944,* 155, 214, 221; Rudolf
Andorka, *A madridi követségtől Mauthausenig. Andorka Rudolf naplója* (Budapest:
Kossuth, 1978), 72; *Ciano's Diary 1939–1943,* ed. Malcolm Muggeridge (London-
Toronto: William Heinemann, 1947), 449.

July 4 celebration at the Washington monument in the City Park,
Budapest, July 4, 1938, U.S. Chargé Howard K. Travers speaking

to the Department of State that, despite appearances, Hungarians in general and Horthy in particular were not pro-German but rather pro-British and pro-American."[76] U.S. diplomats were prone to forgive Horthy for what he did in 1919 and 1920, for the White Terror and the rabid anti-Semitism associated with it, since they thought highly of his ability to maintain law and order and they remembered Hungarian consolidation in the twenties. It pleased them in particular that Horthy was enthusiastic about American

---

76 Mario D. Fenyo, *Hitler, Horthy, and Hungary. German-Hungarian Relations, 1941–1944* (New Haven and London: Yale University Press, 1972), 47. — Herbert Claiborne Pell (1884–1961), Montgomery's successor as U.S. minister to Budapest in 1941.

engineering, and that his son István spent a year in Detroit in the Ford factory. Horthy also proved receptive to American economic advice and
American loans.[77]

Montgomery was convinced by his conversations with Horthy that the
latter's opposition to the Nazis had grown steadily starting with the mid-
thirties, concurrently with an undiminished hostility to Bolshevism. But he
was also appreciative of Horthy's political successes at home and abroad.
Although Montgomery regularly met Horthy from his arrival in 1933, he
only started to record their conversations relatively late, in 1937, when,
most interestingly, Horthy offered a *tour d'horizon* of the European situation, also discussing the dictatorships.

> The conversation switched to Italy, and he spoke of the great work
> that Mussolini had done. He said that a dictator had a great advantage
> over a democratic form of government so long as the dictator didn't go
> too far.
>
> He mentioned Hitler's work in Germany, how he regenerated the
> German people who were in the depths of despair as a result of the Treaty
> of Versailles. He said that had France shown any moderation the situation
> today would have been different, but they were only anxious to do every-
> thing to destroy their foes, and now look at France. She is no longer the
> dictator of Europe.
>
> I mentioned England, and he said that he was very fond of the
> English people, had been around the world and everywhere the English
> were in charge things were well run, but he thought that England was
> now a decadent nation and was on the downgrade.
>
> He expressed the opinion that the greatest danger today was sub-
> versive activities of the Bolshevists. He said you could fight a foe you
> could see and meet, but all this undercover business was difficult to deal
> with that the nations should get together and go in and simply whip
> the Bolshevists. He was in hearty sympathy with Hitler's ideas on this
> subject.[78]

In time Horthy's tone changed. In January 1939, at a diplomatic luncheon, speaking at length in the presence of the British and the American minister, he declared that he had no intention of supporting anti-Jewish legislation then in preparation. He considered the bill to be inhuman, and he stressed
that it also put a disadvantage to "the patriotic Jews long resident in the
country who had helped to make it prosperous and who were as much Hun-

---

77 Sakmyster, *Hungary's Admiral on Horseback: Miklós Horthy, 1918–1944*, 154.
78 Montgomery, Conversations, Horthy, February 2, 1937.

garian as he was," a formulation that surprised the diplomats who heard him.[79]

With the outbreak of war Horthy's situation reports grew longer and his hostility to the Nazis more outspoken. Speaking of the Nazi-Soviet Pact, on November 16, 1939, he appeared in accord with general opinion in expressing doubts concerning the duration of German-Russian friendship. He spoke cautiously about the Germans but stressed toward the end that he wished to be rid of Nazi sympathisers in the Hungarian government, noting that he had already succeeded as regards Antal Kunder.[80] Horthy's low opinion of Imrédy was obvious, he explicitly stated that Imrédy "went crazy." Horthy also implied that he had personally tried to blunt the edge of the Jew Bill. He was obviously well aware of what Montgomery wished to hear.[81]

Less than three months later, on February 7, 1940, Horthy was more explicit in attacking Hitler himself. In Montgomery's words: "He thought Mr. Hitler was not the man to quit voluntarily. He said most people who had a love for their country, if they saw they were in the way, they would retire but he did not think Hitler in that category. He thought he wouldn't quit until he had to."[82] Then, on May 7 the same year: "He spoke of Hitler in terms of contempt and said everybody hated him. He told me again in detail how the Poles, the Czechs, and everybody else in this country had despised him, and said that if somebody came to him and said that Hungary would be better off if he would quit he would do so in a minute; however, no matter how much his country might suffer, Hitler would never quit."[83]

A few weeks later, on the twenty-fifth, when Montgomery handed over President Roosevelt's photograph, Horthy, as it were, compared Hitler to Genghis Khan, "who spent years preparing for attacks on other nations while they did nothing to defend themselves." Horthy added, continued Montgomery,

---

79 Quoted by Sakmyster, *Hungary's Admiral on Horseback: Miklós Horthy, 1918–1944*, 229. As Sakmyster notes, this exclamation was meant not only to win over the British and American diplomats: the regent (with a few changes in accent and style) also voiced his reservations to the German minister to Budapest. — This argumentation was not Horthy's alone: even the official representatives of Hungarian Jewry tragically distinguished between „good" Jews (i.e., assimilated, Hungarian-minded people with a long history in Hungary) and "bad" Jews. See, e.g., the address of Lajos Láng in the Upper House of Hungarian Parliament during the reading of the second Jew Bill on April 17, 1939. Records of the Upper House of Parliament of April 27, 1935 (Budapest: Athenaeum, 1939), IV:153–158.

80 Antal Kunder (1900–1968), engineer, government commissioner (1935), later president (1936–38), of the Office of Foreign Trade, minister of commerce and communication, as well as of industry 1938–39, and again 1944.

81 Montgomery, Conversations, Horthy, November 16, 1939.

82 Montgomery, Conversations, Horthy, February 7, 1940.

83 Montgomery, Conversations, Horthy, May 7, 1940.

...that Hitler had no idea of war at all, that all this was being done by the General Staff, but that Hitler was getting all the credit so that he might be built up into some sort of a god. He said that the Germans tried out their tactics and implements of war in Spain and that they found many things to correct; when these were corrected they decided to try them out on Poland. Hitler didn't think the Allies would go to war but they felt it necessary to try out their plans. After the Polish campaign they improved their technique again. In the meanwhile, the Allies did nothing, made no changes, and paid no attention to the lessons that should have been learned, and the Socialist Governments in Great Britain and France actually were cutting down and undermining the morale of the country while the Germans were working furiously in preparing to annihilate them.

Shunning responsibility, the regent acknowledged: "He said Hungary's position was one where her fate had gone out of her hands and there was nothing to do but wait and try to make the best of whatever happened."[84]

Very likely at that time already, Horthy, as was to be observed in 1944 by his daughter-in-law and reported in her memoirs, would not allow interlocutors to "get a word in edgeways," sometimes metaphorically covering his ears.[85] He spoke at length to all visitors, but he carefully chose his subjects and adjusted them to his listener. At the end of the year, in his penultimate conversation with the U.S. minister, Horthy forcefully stressed his friendly feelings for President Roosevelt, his admiration for the Royal Navy, and his hostility to the Nazis. "I am going to kick the Nazis out of Parliament," he said. Montgomery seemed surprised: "I said, "What will Germany say to that?" He said, "I don't care, I am going to do it now or later. In fact, I wouldn't have them in Parliament at all because that would be the simplest solution. In times like this Parliament is dangerous, but I don't want to ape the dictators. I am going to have a Parliament, but am going to kick the Nazis out." The regent added, "that he had issued a new order to the Army that no one was to engage in politics in any form, upon penalty of immediate dismissal, that every officer had to sign a statement acknowledging the receipt of this order, and he felt that this would have a decided effect,

---

84 Montgomery, Conversations, Horthy, May 25, 1940. Cf. Mária Ormos, *Hitler* (Budapest: T-Twins, 1993), citing data contradicting the above.

85 Countess Ilona Edelsheim Gyulai, *Becsület és kötelesség, 1918–1944* (Budapest: Európa, 2000), 1:246. This observation of Countess Edelsheim Gyulai comes from and refers to 1944. It is interesting to note that Minister Montgomery attributed the same tactics to President Roosevelt.

particularly as he had dismissed a lot of officers who had engaged in politics."[86] Montgomery must have known that, although Horthy had, in fact, lost control over the armed forces, he was there speaking the truth. A number of high-raking officers, of extreme right-wing allegiance, had been dismissed.

In late November 1940, when Horthy last spoke to Montgomery, he endeavored to suggest that Hungary's adhesion to the Triple Alliance had been effected in a manner which minimized the dangers that the move implied. He then repeated for a third time: "The Regent told me that in two weeks they expected to kick the Nazi Party out, that they were now in a better position to do so than before."[87]

In his 1947 book, Montgomery praised the "old sea dog," adding: "I myself have gone to him when I thought his government was doing things that it should not do, and he was always one hundred percent to my way of thinking, even when his foreign minister and prime minister were the ones of whom I complained."[88] What Montgomery perhaps did not wish to note was that Horthy's opinions were not always manifest in the events of current politics, although he insisted on his rights which changes in the constitution further supported. The foreign ministry and Horthy's private office knew why they limited the access of foreigners, particularly journalists, to the regent. They were afraid of his notorious outspokenness and of possible international diplomatic complications.

Estoril

Montgomery's support for Horthy went well beyond words. After the war he was one of a company of four he set up to provide regular financial assistance for the practically penniless Horthy family.[89] Between 1949 and the deaths of the ex-regent and his wife in 1957 and 1959, the former minister (or his daughter) provided a regular monthly remittance. It was he, too, who made arrangements by which Ferenc Chorin, Ernő and Sándor Páthy (who had belonged to Horthy's circle of acquaintances), and Countess Madeleine Apponyi, who was American, shared in this responsibility.[90] Horthy's

---

86 Montgomery, Conversations, Horthy, November 8, 1940.

87 Montgomery, Conversations, Horthy, November 22, 1940.

88 Montgomery, *Hungary, the Unwilling Satellite*, 42-43.

89 Edelsheim Gyulai, *Becsület és kötelesség 1945–1998*, 2:111, 150.

90 Montgomery to Mme Ilona Horthy, September 22, 1950; Ilona Bowden to Mrs. Jean Riddell[-Montgomery], June 10, 1957. Hungarian National Museum. Cf. Edelsheim Gyulai, *Becsület és kötelesség*, 1:251; 2:111, 150.

daughter-in-law, Countess Ilona Edelsheim Gyulai, noted in her recently published memoirs: "After the War, in exile, Hungarian Jews made a major contribution to the support of my parents-in-law, covering their living expenses."[91] Right up to his death in 1954, Montgomery offered assistance to the Horthy family, chiefly in financial matters. In a number of statements, and by offering financial and moral support, Montgomery as it were bore witness for Horthy in the court of history. Acting through Homer Cummings, Montgomery helped at a crucial point in Horthy's life, contributing to Horthy's release at Nuremberg, that is, to Horthy not being prosecuted as a war criminal.[92]

In 1947 Montgomery published *Hungary, the Unwilling Satellite,* an apologia for Hungarian politics in general and specifically for Horthy in person. He sent copies to former Budapest colleagues. Gaston Maugras, who had represented France, replied:

> I liked it very much. I thought it gave a remarkably accurate and lively account of what happened and passed a fair judgement on the actors. Now, having received the copy you were good enough to send me, I re-read it from the first page to the last and I do share your opinion that in those years when fear and greed combined made so many heads of State creep at the feet of the horrible war lords, Hungary shone among the nations by her courage and decency.[93]

In a letter to Horthy, Montgomery quoted this in full, emphasizing, "I thought you would be interested in the above comments coming from a French diplomat."[94] The old admiral expressed his gratitude, speaking of the tragedy of Hungarians "today abandoned by all nations," using somewhat odd and not exactly appropriate language. "Our neighbours resent our claim for what was ours for a 1000 years and which they got in spite of Hungarian majority. The Soviet tries shamelessly to exterminate our race as we are in the way of the unification of the North and South-Slavs. Germany resents the fact that we were not delighted or did not at least quietly accept their shameful occupation of our country. And finally the West looks upon us as exenemies although we only fought the Soviets and had a foresight and knowledge of things that proved to be better than theirs."[95]

Montgomery's support was appreciated by the Horthy family, and not

---

91 Edelsheim Gyulai, *Becsület és kötelesség,* 1:248.
92 Ibid., 2:199.
93 Montgomery to Miklós Horthy, October 8, 1951. Hungarian National Museum.
94 Ibid.
95 Miklós Horthy to Montgomery, October 16, 1951. Hungarian National Museum.

just because of the money. He helped with the sale of the *Hungaria*, a yacht that had been Hitler's gift;[96] he remembered the Horthys' golden wedding anniversary (1951) and Ilona Horthy's remarriage (1954).[97] Montgomery had no desire to take part in the politics of Hungarian exiles. He looked on the support he gave Horthy as his own private business. They exchanged letters only, that was all: they never met again after the war ended. Upon the ex-minister's death his daughter Ms. Montgomery Riddell continued the financial support of the Horthys right up to the end of their lives.

From Information to Intelligence

In the thirties Nazi Germany was increasingly identified by the Americans as the major threat to world peace, a view shared by Montgomery. It was only after the war, confronted with Stalinist expansion, that he showed understanding for the Hungarians, who, according to him "were always aware of being between the two fires of German and Russian imperialism. During those years," Montgomery continued in 1947, "most of us saw only one fire, the German one. Hungary's vision was far ahead of ours. Had we listened to Hungarian statesmen, we should perhaps have been able to limit Stalin's triumph in the hour of Hitler's fall."[98]

A conservative by nature, Montgomery had a proper respect for authority and felt most comfortable in the company of the like-minded of interwar Hungary. This defined the narrowly circumscribed circle of those who were his sources of information. He was fondest of the always well-informed Tibor Eckhardt and treated him as a confidant;[99] he looked up to Kálmán Kánya and appreciated his diplomatic cunning;[100] he liked Baron Apor, who had a flair for packaging everything unpleasant. He respected the apparent wisdom of Counts Bethlen and Teleki. He was overjoyed every time he

---

96 Edelsheim Gyulai, *Becsület és kötelesség,* 2:167, cf. the correspondence between the Montgomery and the Horthy families, Hungarian National Museum.

97 Mrs. István Horthy to Montgomery, June 25, 1954; Miklós Horthy to J. F. Montgomery, June 26, 1954. Hungarian National Museum. Cf. Edelsheim Gyulai, *Becsület és kötelesség,* 2:217–8.

98 Montgomery, *Hungary, the Unwilling Satellite,* 11. Cf. Antal Ullein-Reviczky, *Guerre allemande, paix russe: Le drame hongrois* (Neuchâtel: Editions de la Baconnière, 1947).

99 Montgomery, Diary, December 29, 1933.

100 Montgomery, „Footnotes" to a series on „Personalities," n.d. Miscellaneous articles, J. F. Montgomery Collection.

came across open hostility to Hitler amongst Horthy's intimates. He paid close attention to Count István Bethlen's alarm-raising speeches in Parliament, thus to his words on February 9, 1938: "... in foreign policy I used to be the spokesman of a pro-German line, but there is one thing that is obvious to me: if a *Gleichschaltung* of political life takes place in Hungary in terms of the ideas of the extreme right, then we shall end up as the servants of Germany and not her friends. That will be the end of an independent Hungarian foreign policy."[101] Montgomery was keenly aware of the growing hostility of these circles to the Nazis after the outbreak of the war, as confirmed by discussions he had with other diplomats, for example Jan Spisiak, the Slovak minister in Budapest, whom he reports as saying, "the relations between the Hungarian and German Governments were not so good as they might be since the Germans knew that both the Regent and Count Teleki were very anti-German. In fact, he said that practically Csaky was the only pro-German left. He said it may be true that one or two Cabinet Ministers had German sympathies, but they were in positions where they made very little difference and he thought that Csaky was not so pro-German as he had been and that in any case his influence was not as great as it might be."[102]

His official sources of information presented Montgomery with a blue-eyed image of Hungary. Whatever the subject, be it Hungarian intentions concerning the revision of the frontiers, German-Hungarian relations, or anti-Semitic legislation, most of what he was told in the Foreign Ministry on Dísz tér, in the prime minister's office in the Sándor Palace or by the regent in the Royal Palace, was sweetened and prettified.

To Montgomery's surprise, Count Teleki, who had seemed withdrawn and a man of few words, or else non-committal, after war broke out, openly sought opportunities for a meeting, meetings that peculiarly took place not in the prime minister's office, but in his home on József nádor tér. Officially calling on Teleki had seemed useless. He never said anything, but it was noted that, when Countess Teleki was "at home," her husband happened to be there, by chance as it were, and at times like that he spoke freely and honestly.

---

101 Parliamentary Committees, Hungarian National Archives, XIX:341–342. Quoted in György Ránki: *Emlékiratok és valóság Magyarország második világháborús szerepéről* (Budapest: Kossuth, 1964), 46.

102 Montgomery, Conversations, Spisiak, November 27, 1939.

103 Sir Owen St. Clair O'Malley (1887–1974), British minister to Budapest, "became an ardent admirer of Horthy", according to Sakmyster, *Hungary's Admiral on Horseback: Miklós Horthy, 1918–1944*, 244.

Owen O'Malley,[103] the British minister, made the same observation.

> He explained Count Teleki's conversation with me by saying exactly the same thing had been done to him. The last time I saw him he told me Count Teleki had told him that he didn't want him to call because every time he did so it got in the papers and the Germans made a face about it, saying that he was not calling on him any more because he never got any information anyhow. However, not long ago countess Teleki invited him to tea and he went up and found no one there but the Prime Minister who had proceeded to talk quite freely and fully contrary to any previous experience. In other words, paralleling both the circumstances and volubility of the Prime Minister in my case. He thought that both visits were the result of a growing conviction on the part of Hungarians that the war was going against the Germans and that it was better to be more friendly and more open with the Allied Powers, and also America since that country might have much to say about the events of the future whether she entered the war or not. He said it was true no such experience had happened to the French Minister but that this was natural because the Hungarians didn't trust the French but they did the British and Americans.[104]

Teleki's anxieties, however, were not concentrated on the French, but extended *a fortiori* to the British. As he spoke of England to Montgomery: "She had permitted the Germans to take Austria, the Sudetenland, Czechoslovakia and Memel, and Italy to take Albania and never did anything about it except make weak protests. Therefore, small countries couldn't be convinced that she ever intended to do anything but protest."[105]

In conclusion, Montgomery reveals himself as a good psychologist, trying to understand the prime minister's mind. "He seemed to have something on his mind, but couldn't get around to it. I think he wanted to apologize for Csaky and his idea was to give the impression that he had without actually doing so."[106]

What Montgomery recorded is bound to surprise those who know little about Kálmán Kánya, the foreign minister. This old man and experienced diplomat, a survivor of the Habsburg monarchy, moved about on the stage of European diplomacy as if he were playing with his sons. "de Kánya did not like it at all," his deputy, Baron Apor, commented in 1936, "because he had to go to Vienna for a conference with two other foreign ministers, both of whom were so young that their united ages were exactly the same as de

---

104 Montgomery, Conversations, O'Malley, November 15, 1939.
105 Montgomery, Conversations, Teleki, April 26, 1939.
106 Ibid.
107 Montgomery, Conversations, Apor, November 3, 1936.

Kánya's — 67. He felt as though he was compelled to talk to a couple of school-boys."[107] Years before the war, Kánya never left it in doubt what he thought about the Nazis and Hitler. As Baron Guy von Hahn, a Nazi agent in Budapest, tellingly put it: "Kánya was a friend of former Germany but hates the present-day Germany."[108] As early as 1935, Montgomery had doubts concerning Hitler's policies and reported with considerable forethought:

> If Hitler were an intelligent man, de Kánya said, he would at this moment make a public announcement that he would give up Austria and thus allay the fears of Italy and reassure the world as to his intentions. He felt sure, however, that he would not do this, and he feared he might even make more dramatic moves in the future.
>
> I mentioned that Napoleon was an Italian and always felt that he didn't belong in France which feeling was back of his desire to conquer the world. I suggested that Hitler being an Austrian might in the end be as great a disturber to peace as Napoleon for the same reason.[109]

Kánya understood the devil's kitchen of German foreign policy far better than the average well-trained diplomat. "He said 'You know, they have five foreign offices in Germany; one day von Neurath is in control, then the next day it is Goebbels, the next day Goering, then Rosenberg, and then Hess. Therefore, you could never control it absolutely.'"[110] There was good reason why the Italian and German ministers were dissatisfied with the Hungarian foreign minister.

> The Italian and German Ministers in Budapest, Vinci and Erdmannsdorff, according to Eckhardt, are very dissatisfied with de Kanya because he has not been more active in taking the part of Italy and Germany at London, and on other occasions.[111]

As time passed, and after he resigned his office, Kánya became ever more outspoken. "Mr Hitler was not a normal person," he told the U.S. minister on March 18, 1939.[112] He also predicted that the alliance between Hitler and Stalin would not last.

---

108 Montgomery, Conversations, von Hahn, November 12, 1935.
109 Montgomery, Conversations, Kánya, March 28, 1935.
110 Montgomery, Conversations, Kánya, December 1, 1937. Cf. Pál Pritz, *Magyarország külpolitikája Gömbös Gyula miniszterelnöksége idején 1932–1936,* 203–19.
111 Montgomery, Conversations, Eckhardt, November 6, 1937.
112 Montgomery, Conversations, Kánya, March 18, 1939.

de Kanya said that he had yesterday read a portion of MEIN KAMPF which somebody told him bore on the question of an alliance between Russia and Germany, and he found it very amusing because Mr. Hitler proved definitely that Germany never could be an ally of Russia, that it was absolutely impossible. He felt that a month would tell the story. Germany and Russia had made threats as to what action they will take in case peace proposals are refused. As they have been definitely refused it is now up to them to make good their threats. If they don't make them good in a month it will then prove that the German-Russian alliance is nothing except what can be seen on its face — that there is no understanding which would involve further cooperation between Germany and Russia — and the way was left open for a clash of interests which might bring Germany and Russia into antagonism: at least that is what he hoped.[113]

By way of a *bon mot*, Kánya added something important with which the Hungarian political class of the time agreed in practice. "He said there was no difference between Nazism and Bolshevism; in fact, he said, the only difference between Germany today and Russia was that it was colder in Russia."[114] Montgomery considered this the guiding idea of a Hungary drifting into war. He thought it so important that, in the preface to his *Hungary, the Unwilling Satellite,* published in 1947, he told off his fellow Americans for leaving this out of account. Horthy himself said much the same thing in the memoirs he wrote in Germany and Portugal, paradoxically in criticism of the basic idea of Montgomery's book, which he did not mention by name, but the reference is beyond doubt. "Hungary, for her participation in Hitler's war, had been called an unwilling satellite. It would have been truer to say that Hungary tried, with the relatively small means at her disposal, to defend herself against two encroaching forces: against the Soviets with all her available arms; against the Nazi ideology with all her diplomatic powers."[115]

An obvious endeavor on the part of the old ex-regent to prettify his own role and that of his country. You might call it a flight into selective amnesia.

Montgomery sometimes misunderstood his sources of information. It would appear that, on occasion, he wanted to misunderstand them. In this respect he was criticized even by some of those whom he wished to justify in the eyes of posterity.

András Hory was one of the leading diplomats of the Horthy era. In the twenties and early thirties he was the Hungarian minister first in Belgrade,

---

113 Montgomery, Conversations, Kánya, October 4, 1939.
114 Montgomery, Conversations, Kánya, March 18, 1939.
115 Montgomery, *Hungary, the Unwilling Satellite,* 11; Horthy, *Memoirs,* 255.

then in Rome, in 1934–35 the permanent deputy of the foreign minister serving under Kánya, and later minister in Warsaw. He wrote his memoirs between the mid-fifties and 1961. In them he charges Montgomery with misinterpreting an important observation by Kánya, which he quotes:

> In a book Hungary The Unwilling Satellite written with the best of intentions in the defense of Hungary, Montgomery, formerly the American minister, claims that the Hungarian government stressed the revision of the peace treaty of Trianon in our favor purely for reasons of domestic policy. He supports his view by citing a declaration, which Kánya made in his presence.
>
> In the above-mentioned work, reporting a conversation between Kánya and himself, he writes as follows. "..."
>
> Montgomery was no doubt guided by the best of intentions ... but ... for the sake of historical truth I am bound to contradict him. Neither the Hungarian nation nor the governments which represented it ever forgot, nor could they forget, the serious offences which afflicted us without justification ... I am convinced that Montgomery must surely have misunderstood something that Kánya meant to formulate diplomatically, the meaning of which may have been that the revision of the peace treaties had to be stressed also for reasons of domestic policy. That he should have used the word 'insanity' to characterize the endeavor to mend by peaceful means the cruel provisions of a treaty forced on us is purely and simply an absurdity.
>
> Perhaps I am guilty of ingratitude shown a friend of Hungary who tends to exaggerate out of sheer good will felt towards us, but I must note for the sake of completing the picture that Kánya, who treated the other ministers accredited in Budapest very much de haut en bas [condescendingly], did not take seriously an American minister who lacked diplomatic training and experience. One more reason why he could not seriously talk politics to him was because — as he told me himself — he spoke English with a dreadful American accent, and he could not understand half of what he said.
>
> After I read Montgomery's book I tried to reconstruct things that Kánya had said about revisionism in my presence, but I cannot recall anything that may have resembled the statement cited by the American diplomat.[116]

Hory was very likely mistaken. It can be presumed that Montgomery understood Kánya's words. It is certainly possible that Kánya was more open talking to him than when talking to his own staff.

---

116 András Hory, *Bukaresttől Varsóig*, 402–403. Hory might have been motivated by Montgomery's negative personal comment in *Hungary...*, 68.

Tibor Eckhardt, with Count István Bethlen, Count György Apponyi,
Jenő Rápolti Nagy, Zoltán Horváth and Károly Rassay

There is a surprising amount of information about Tibor Eckhardt in this volume. Montgomery and Eckhardt became such good friends that Montgomery addressed the Smallholder leader by his first name and referred to him as such (something infinitely more unusual at that time than it would be today). Eckhardt's photograph was on the wall of Montgomery's study.[117] Eckhardt was also a regular and frequent guest, and there is every indication that Montgomery facilitated Eckhardt's journey into exile both politically and financially. Already on December 29, 1933, barely six months after his arrival in Budapest, Montgomery noted in his diary: "Had Dr. Eckhardt up for lunch and had a very interesting talk with him. I find him an unusually intelligent man, and one whom I like very much. I believe my wife and I like the Eckhardts better than any couple we have met so far."[118] Reading the accounts of many hours of conversation with Eckhardt, one nevertheless wonders whether the Hungarian party leader knew that what he said about politics at home and abroad would be recorded, ending up,

117 Montgomery, Conversations, Kánya, December 1, 1937.
118 Montgomery, Diary, December 29, 1933

through various channels, as reports on Washington, D.C. desks. Was anyone aware that these conversations were in fact the building blocks out of which secret reports were constructed?[119] Why was it precisely Eckhardt who was — very likely — given a code number (79 — admittedly, only on one occasion), out of all of Montgomery's partners in conversation? Let us ask frankly: did Montgomery think of his conversations as intelligence work, and might we perhaps identify this or that one of his partners in conversation as agents? Paid agents, perhaps, at least in some cases?

Home again, years later, very likely after the war, Montgomery once again showed psychological acumen when he allowed doubts to surface in a biographical note on his friend.

> The stormy petrel of Hungarian politics. ... A brilliant man, more like an American politician than a Hungarian. Generally considered an opportunist, but actually is more of an idealist. While I was in Hungary, every time he had a chance to go in the Government or make some progress, he did something to make it impossible. He seems to be a great patriot and since he is now in America and the head of the movement for Free Hungary, he may do his country considerable service unless he does something to spoil it. Incidentally, he was the greatest duellist in Hungary during my time.[120]

That Montgomery preferred the company of the anti-Nazis was true not only for Hungarian politicians but also for fellow diplomats accredited in Budapest. Their conversations centered largely on the feasibility of Hungarian revisionism. In fact, the revision of frontiers was at the focus of diplomatic life throughout Montgomery's tenure, something that could only be achieved with German backing and support. As a result, the varied attempts by Hungarian diplomats to sail against the wind appeared in a peculiar light in the eyes of the U.S. minister. To give just one example, here is the description of the visit to Budapest of the Italian propaganda minister based on the account of Baron Apor, Kánya's then permanent deputy in the Foreign Min-

---

119 Eckhardt also had regular conversations with members of the U.S. legation other than the minister; several of those were quoted in the official reports to the State Department. Cf. NA, USSD, 864.00/868 and NAM, M1206/1/646–53. Quoted by Sakmyster, *Hungary's Admiral on Horseback: Miklós Horthy, 1918–1944*, 195 and 200 (notes #80, 96 on 428). Many of Montgomery's reports were based on Eckhardt's information not recorded in the Minister's conversations, NA, USSD, 864.00/1000, quoted by Sakmyster, 249 (note #40 on 435).

120 J. F. Montgomery, „Footnotes" to a series on „Personalities", n. d. Miscellaneous articles, J. F. Montgomery Collection.

istry, who was ever ready to explain away or prettify what was unpleasant. It is a brief cautionary tale that tells us much about what grieved Hungarian politics in 1936.

While the social events, gala at the Opera, etc. which the Hungarian Government had scheduled for the visit of Signor Dino Alfieri, [121] the Italian State Secretary for the Press and Propaganda, were cancelled on account of the death of King George,[122] the opening of the Italian art exhibition — which was the purpose of his visit — took place, although it was not the big event which had been anticipated.

The only member of the Diplomatic Corps that attended the opening of the exhibition was Mr. Grigorcea, the Rumanian Minister, who was also the Dean. Mr. Grigorcea had been very busy at the time on account of his king passing through Budapest the next day, but felt inasmuch as he was Dean that he should attend as he suspected that practically no one else would.

Signor Alfieri made a speech of a violent revisionist character, saying among other things that Mussolini was a determined friend of Hungary and Hungarians would see that when "something happens" the friendship of Italy would be material and not just a gesture. Mussolini did not consider the Treaty of Versailles or the Treaty of Trianon as binding, and Hungarians could count on Italy's help at the proper time.

Prince Colonna, the Italian Minister, and others of the Italian Legation seemed much agitated, and although the Hungarians present violently applauded, none of the members of the Legation joined in the demonstration. Mr. Grigorcea said that it was his original intention to stay only a short time and that he had seated himself where he could retire without attracting attention, but that he remained because he felt that if he got up and someone did notice him it might be felt that he left on account of the speech. He understood every word that was said but was not offended as he understood that it was merely an Italian gesture to keep Hungary in line. Nevertheless, the Italian Legation was much disturbed, as was State Secretary Alfieri, when they learned of Grigorcea's presence. Signor Alfieri wanted to know how he happened to be invited, and Colonna told him that he couldn't account for it.

Baron Apor, when I talked to him yesterday, laughed heartily about the incident. He indicated that he thought Alfieri was a fool, and said it

---

121 Dino Edoardo Alfieri (1886-1966), Italian lawyer, minister of press and propaganda 1936–39, Italian envoy to the Holy See 1939-40, ambassador to Berlin 1940–43. He was sentenced to death in the Ciano trial but escaped to Switzerland.
122 George V, king of England, died on January 20, 1936.

was a good thing that it was not the Yugoslav Minister instead of the
Rumanian Minister as the former would have gone up and made a scene,
and it might have been very embarrassing for Italy because Yugoslavia
and Italy were becoming more friendly all the time. He also said that
Colonna should have told Grigorcea about it in advance and given him an
opportunity to stay away if he wanted to. He said that when Eckhardt
came to Vienna while he, Apor, was Minister there and made a violent
revisionist speech, he had told the Rumanian Minister in advance that he
had better stay away. However, the Rumanian Minister said he didn't
mind and came, but afterwards told a number of people that he greatly
appreciated Apor's having told him as it showed his good-will.[123]

This is also a good example of the tact and skill (of what they would
have called the *Fingerspitzengefühl*) of the Hungarian diplomats who served
their apprenticeship in the Ballhausplatz.

Similar tact, this time on Montgomery's part, was needed when he made
up his mind in the spring of 1936 to seek an official excuse to absent himself from the unveiling of a statue of General H. H. Bandholtz in Szabadság

Dedicating the statue of Gen. Bandholtz on Szabadság tér, Budapest,
August 23, 1936, Chargé James B. Stewart speaking

---

123 Montgomery, Conversations, no heading, February 10, 1936.

tér that summer, on August 23 (the unveiling had originally been scheduled for the Fourth of July).[124] General Bandholtz had, on October 5, 1919, personally stopped the Romanian troops, part of the army of occupation in Hungary, who wished to break into the National Museum in order to remove objects of Transylvanian provenance, obviously in an effort to take over that part of Hungary not only in the physical but also in the historical sense.[125] First "… I have accepted to make a speech. This monument is the result of efforts by Americans of Hungarian descent and has been largely paid for by them. Many of them are coming over especially for the celebration. After they hear me speak they will regret it, but I cannot convince them in advance that this is so, and I don't know what would happen if I left the country before the event."[126] Montgomery soon made up his mind to make use of the good offices of his influential friend George Creel whom he approached asking "… you better arrange with the President and the State Department to instruct me to be home so that I can have something to show for my absence."[127]

In other words, Montgomery had no desire to take part in a Hungarian-American celebration that served the cause of Hungarian revisionism. He did not agree with revisionism. While *en poste* in Budapest it became clear to him that

> [t]he revisionism I found in Hungary was a curious myth rather than a clear program. National disasters are just as conducive to psychological derangements as national triumphs. The main symptom, in both cases, is the growth of legends. In Hungary, people spoke with religious fervor of the restoration of the thousand-year-old realm, quite oblivious of the fact that in King Stephen's time, Hungary did not have the frontier which she lost in 1919….
>
> As time went on and I gained the confidence of my Magyar friends, I discovered that many responsible Magyars were by no means in favor of a revisionist policy. On the contrary, they considered it a series handicap, because it had become a national obsession. … They also knew that revisionism was a dangerous toy and that Hungary was utterly unprepared for war."[128]

---

124 Montgomery to George S. Messersmith, March 24, 1936, Montgomery to George S. Messersmith, March 26, 1936, George S. Messersmith to Montgomery, March 28, 1936, M. C. Schallenberger to Montgomery, April 28, 1936 (cf. Statement of Military Service, War Department, Washington, D.C., March 31, 1936); Garret G. Ackerson to Montgomery, August 24, 1936. J. F. Montgomery Papers, MGN 353, Vol. III.

125 Bandholtz, *An Undiplomatic Diary,* 136–40.

126 Montgomery to George Creel, March 16, 1936. Strictly Personal Correspondence 1933–1937, J. F. Montgomery Collection.

127 Ibid.

128 Montgomery, *Hungary, the Unwilling Satellite,* 52–54.

There was much truth in this, but it is also, like much else in his 1947 book, evidence of superficial oversimplification and of intent to produce propaganda.

George Creel's intervention was not needed, the State Department acted on its own. Montgomery was given confidential advice from the Department "that they do not wish me to be here for that event."[129] Lt. Col. M. C. Schallenberger, the U.S. military attaché in Vienna, received similar instructions.[130] Montgomery expressed his regrets for not being able to give his speech or to attend the ceremony, and sailed home to attend the Democratic convention, due to nominate a candidate for the presidential election. He carefully chose the embarkation date to avoid giving offence. (He was well informed concerning the expected date of completion of the statue because the sculptor Miklós Ligeti — also the sculptor of the "Anonymous Notary" in the Budapest City Park — had modeled Montgomery's bust.)[131] An interesting point is that, for unknown reasons, General Bandholtz's widow also failed to attend the unveiling ceremony, coming to Hungary only a year later.[132] Hungarians in America commissioned the statue. *Szabadság*, the paper of Cleveland Hungarians, initiated a petition to be signed by a million demanding a just revision for "our unjustly truncated country."[133] The widow Bandholtz signed the petition and a headline declared: "If my husband were alive he would joyfully add his signature."[134]

Montgomery only quoted Little Entente colleagues in Budapest with approval if they spoke about the peaceful nature of revisionist demands. This started early in 1937 when Kánya, seeing that an Axis orientation led nowhere, made approaches to the Little Entente. "Mr. Bossy said that it was to the Hungarians' credit that they had never publicly said anything but that they were for peaceful revision and therefore they could not be accused of aggressiveness in a military sense."[135] Montgomery was happy to hear from Miloš Kobr, the Czechoslovak minister, that, according to him, "he felt that de Kanya knew that the Rome-Berlin axis was a bad thing for Hungary and that their friendship with Germany and Italy was now a liability rather than an asset and that he was anxious to strengthen his ties with the neighboring countries and to put Hungary in a more independent position."[136]

---

129 Montgomery to George Creel, March 24, 1936. Strictly Personal Correspondence 1933–1937, J. F. Montgomery Collection.
130 Montgomery to Martin C. Schallenberger, December 2, 1936. J. F. Montgomery Papers, MGN 353, Vol. IV.
131 Montgomery, Diary, June 26–27, 1934.
132 „Plans to Visit Hungary," *The Commercial*, June 8, 1937.
133 *Szabadság* (Cleveland), September 30, 1936.
134 Ibid.
135 Montgomery, Conversations, Bossy, February 5, 1937.
136 Montgomery, Conversations, Kobr, November 9, 1937.

Montgomery thought of Leon Orłowski, the Polish minister, as a personal friend, and they stayed in touch at the time of the latter's years of exile in the United States. Orłowski passionately hated Hitler. He was also pessimistic about the future of Hungary. Like many others, he was well aware that the hope of a revision of the frontiers would embroil Hungary in the war as Germany's ally.

> Mr. Orlowsky was very anti-German. He said that Hungary had become so much involved with Germany that there was no question she would have to come into a future war on Germany's side. He said the strange thing about it was that practically all the Hungarians believed that Germany would lose the next war, yet their craze to get their former territory back is so great that they throw all caution to the wind when that is dangled in front of them. He was certain that after the next war there would be no Hungary and the Hungarian people would be an island of some other nation.[137]

At other times Orłowski's words were even more unambiguous, although it was somewhat superficial on his part to blame Imrédy alone for Hungary's pro-Nazi foreign policy.

> As Orlowski sees the situation, Hungary, through the insanity of Imredy, became involved with Germany and she cannot get out of it. Actually no one from the Regent down wants to go to war with Germany and are anxious to find some way to get out of their present position into a more independent one, but they don't know how to do it. He believes that they like the Poles far better than the Germans and if left to their own free choice they would stick with the Poles, and as they are now they are afraid to do anything for fear of bringing German wrath upon them. [138]

Influencing the Press

In the mid-thirties Montgomery did his best to further the Hungarian cause in the American press, and thus to make sure that the image of Hungary held by Americans was as favorable as possible. He fully exploited the influence of George Creel, his best friend. He persuaded Creel, who had

---

137 Montgomery, Conversations, Orłowski, March 28, 1939.
138 Montgomery, Conversations, Orłowski, April 4, 1939.

been President Wilson's publicity chief, head of the Committee on Public Information in 1917–19, to visit Hungary, and this eventuated in 1936. The Society of the *Hungarian Quarterly,* including Count Pál Teleki, Béla Imrédy, Gyula Kornis, Count Antal Sigray, Baron Lajos Villani, Count Zsigmond Széchenyi, and author Zsolt Harsányi entertained him in the Hotel Dunapalota. József Balogh, the editor, thought it important that ex-Prime Minister Count István Bethlen should preside over the luncheon. "It would appear that Mr. Montgomery, the Minister, sets such great store by this guest, who is close to the President of the Republic, that he would be particularly grateful for Your Excellency's presence."[139]

Bethlen was happy to accept, all the more so since he was the power behind the *Hungarian Quarterly,* a semi-official publication he founded and controlled, and he knew that Creel was a member of the paper's American Advisory Board. The Budapest reception soon bore fruit: Creel sent an article titled "America's 'Detached and Distant' Fathers" and the *Hungarian Quarterly* promptly published it in the spring of 1937.[140] Now that Creel was with Hungary, Montgomery thought the moment opportune to somewhat mend Horthy's image in the U.S., and to use his influence to counter Archduke Otto's efforts in the interests of a Habsburg restoration. Montgomery was unaware that the mere notion of a Habsburg restoration was illusory; if U.S. foreign policy occasionally toyed with the idea, it was by then always with an anti-Nazi edge. As mentioned, U.S. foreign policy and also subsequent American heads of mission in Budapest had always supported Horthy against the Habsburgs. Both General H. H. Bandholtz in 1919–20 and Nicholas Roosevelt, the minister to Hungary in the early thirties and a distant cousin of the future president, thought the Habsburg archdukes ridiculous, and made straight the way for Horthy. Montgomery fitted into this policy line. He therefore kept Creel fully informed on the disadvantages that would ensue from Archduke Otto's return, and also of the advantages of Horthy's regency.

> As the Regent is the principal obstacle in his way an article on him should be of interest. When I say he is an obstacle in his way I don't mean that he is trying to prevent Otto's return, but that he fills the bill so

139 József Balogh to István Bethlen, November 28, 1936. Hungarian National Széchényi Library, Fond 1/322/3199.

140 George Creel, "America's 'Detached and Distant' Fathers", *The Hungarian Quarterly,* III (Spring 1937): 21–31. The title of the article is a reference to George Washington's famous presidential farewell address (1796), in which he called for American abstention from European affairs. Creel, however, appreciated President Roosevelt's foreign policy of active cooperation in an „interlocked and interdependent" world (Creel, 31).

well nobody seems to want to exchange him for Otto. There is hardly anyone here who will say that as long as the Regent is alive there is any probability of restoration. Further, it is interesting that while he is strictly constitutional, in that he does not interfere of the government any more than the King of England does, yet his prestige is so great that his influence is tremendous. It is doubtful if anything could be done which he opposed, although such opposition would have to be privately expressed as he has never taken any public position on any question.[141]

This letter to Creel, which exaggerated the regent's influence (and said nothing to explain the political or historical causes of this influence), accompanied photos, which the journalist György Ottlik had assembled for publication in *Collier's Magazine*.[142] Ottlik himself was a member of the circle close to Bethlen that had gathered around the *Hungarian Quarterly*. Montgomery later, under the influence of Antal Ullein-Reviczky's somewhat biased influence, took a poor view of Ottlik, characterizing him as a turncoat.[143] *Collier's*, however, did not want to publish anything by Creel and commissioned Walter Duranty instead. Montgomery, on the other hand, was determined to do without Duranty and dropped the whole project.

> I am terribly sorry that they are not going to let you write the article on Horthy. I am very much worried about Walter Duranty taking over the job. I am very much afraid that what he writes will not be acceptable here, and I should personally prefer that the article not be written at all with the material supplied you unless it is written by you. Walter Duranty is considered here and a good many other places as a propagandist for Soviet Russia, and I doubt very much if he could write a sympathetic article on the Regent. It is strange how American papers and magazines never seem to want anything but the old hooey that is ground out by the yard. If it is possible for you to kill the article I wish you would please do so because I will be put in a very embarrassing position if Duranty writes it and if it is not sympathetic, particularly as they furnished the material to you. Therefore if you can kill, or if you can save it and write it for some other magazine I should be very happy.[144]

141 Montgomery to George Creel, March 16, 1937. Strictly Personal Correspondence, 1933–1937, J. F. Montgomery Collection.

142 Cf. Creel's delighted answer to Ottlik concerning the background material for his intended article on Horthy, Washington, D.C., March 24, 1937. Strictly Personal Correspondence, 1933-1937, J. F. Montgomery Collection.

143 Antal Ullein-Reviczky to Montgomery, November 28, 1949. Miscellaneous letters and notes, J. F. Montgomery Collection.

144 Montgomery to George Creel, May 14, 1937. Strictly Personal Correspondence 1933–1937, J. F. Montgomery Collection.

In a letter to Creel dated February 1, 1938, Montgomery once again, and not for the last time, compared the constitutional position of the regent and the king of England. Here, however, reality appears through undiluted rose-tinted spectacles. This represents a summing up of all his illusions about Hungary, all his errors of judgement, and his blind loyalty to Horthy.

> ... as the Regent is the controlling factor in Hungary his importance politically is very great. You probably know that the Nazis had a meeting here and passed a resolution declaring him King. This made the Regent very angry and he made a speech in which he referred to a speech fifteen years ago in which he stated he would never become King, and he said that his position today is the same. He was very angry at even the suggestion that he was a candidate for the throne. Although the Regent is in no sense a dictator, since his position is constitutional — the same as that of the King of England — yet he has an enormous influence. He has never used this influence except in a proper and constitutional manner."[145]

The naive American, in his rapture, invested his hero with quasi-mythological strength.

---

145 Montgomery to George Creel, February 1, 1938. Strictly Personal Correspondence 1938–1939, J. F. Montgomery Collection. — The parallel between Horthy and the king of England remained a favorite of Montgomery's. It appears even in a late letter of the minister to *Time-Life* journalist Dana Munroe of April 6, 1951, an effort to defend Horthy, already in exile: „Admiral Horthy was no more a dictator of Hungary than the King is of England. You mention his use of the veto power. He never had that until the 1930s. I was in Hungary as American Minister when it was given to him and I don't remember his ever vetoing anything. He appointed Judges and all, but not on his own. Just like the King of England he appointed them on the recommendation of the government." (Hungarian National Museum) — References to a parallel with England arose even in Horthy's own thinking, and probably routinely. Speaking to the Polish journalist Konrad Wrzos in 1936, Horthy spoke of the priority of the Hungarian Golden Bull (1215) as compared to the Magna Carta (1222), boasting of the earlier beginnings of the Hungarian Parliament, at the birth of which, he added, "there were equal numbers of Hungarians and Englishmen alive, and while the English are a great nation today, the Hungarians diminished in terms of numbers in the course of the many battles they fought." Konrad Wrzos, *Wulkany Europy. Austrja — Węgry — Balkany* (Warszawa, 1936), 73. See István D. Molnár, *A magyarság a modern lengyel irodalomban 1919–1989* (Debrecen: Kossuth Egyetemi Kiadó, 1995), 41, 137. These arguments were often used by the Anglophile circles of contemporary Budapest, cf. István Gál, *Magyarország, Anglia és Amerika* (Budapest: Officina, 1944). For a brief version in English see Stephen Gál, *Hungary and the Anglo-Saxon World* (Budapest: Officina, 1st impr. 1943; 1944).

If he chose, however, he could make Hungary a dictatorship without any difficulty. On the other hand there could never be any other dictatorship in Hungary. This means that unless he radically changes his ideas there can never be any Nazi government in Hungary as long as he is alive, because neither the army nor the general public would ever go against the Regent. So as long as he stands for constitutional government there will be constitutional government. Despite all the assertions in the American papers that Hungary is like Germany, Italy, etc. under a dictator, Hungary has a democratic form of government which functions as it is supposed to. The Regent never interferes in political affairs and there is no other person who dictates in any way. While there is censorship over newspapers on foreign affairs, there is perfect freedom of speech and Opposition papers and candidates do not hesitate to say anything they please, although of course no one ever makes any remarks about the Regent. This is because he keeps out of politics and because he is so universally respected that any remarks about him would be greatly resented by everyone. While Hungary is a democratic country in that Parliament functions and is elected by the people, yet there has been in the past no secret ballot in the country districts and there are some restrictions on voting. So that from our point of view it couldn't be called a democratic government. However, while other governments are going towards dictatorship the Hungarian Parliament is now considering a bill for making the secret ballot universal, although it still restricts the electorate. Nevertheless it is a step towards democracy at a time when most other governments are going the other way.[146]

In maintaining good relations with the American press, Montgomery's primary purpose was to ensure that its view of Hungary and her head of state should be favorable. In 1934 John Gunther of the *Chicago Daily News* undertook a tour of Europe, which, in 1936, resulted in his *Inside Europe,* a best-seller and *succès d'estime* by an accepted authority on the politics of the pre-war era. Gunther spent quite a long time in Europe, interviewing numerous VIPs including the British author H. G. Wells and Czechoslovak statesman T. G. Masaryk. In May he also met Horthy, but the interview was not included in the book.[147] Gunther, however, pretty unfavorably commented on the White Terror and on Horthy's conversational style. He reported that his associates who knew his outspoken nature and his readiness to

---

146 Montgomery to George Creel, February 1, 1938. Strictly Personal Correspondence 1938–1939, J. F. Montgomery Collection.
147 Montgomery, Diary, April 18, May 29, 1934.

express what he had on his mind isolated the regent. Indeed, Gunther was quite stunned and bewildered to hear him speak about the Serbs, the Czechs, and the Germans, or in fact about anybody being mentioned to him.[148]

On other occasions, even journalists who enjoyed Montgomery's backing were not received in Buda Castle. Early in 1935 James A. Mills, the Associated Press Vienna correspondent, wished to interview Horthy, but the regent's private office almost aborted the project. It was only Montgomery's insistence — he called on András Hory, at the time the foreign minister's permanent deputy — that finally allowed the interview to take place. Montgomery's journal entry reads:

> The Press Department of the Foreign Office is very weak. Doctor Mengele[149] has not much conception of how to treat a correspondent and what is good publicity. They all complain bitterly if they have a bad press; they don't know what to do about it. It never seems to occur to them to treat the correspondents with courtesy whether they like them or not. The whole trouble seemed to be that Mr. Mills had gone to Captain Scholtz[150] before seeing Doctor Mengele and he was perfectly willing to have the whole Associated Press mad because he wanted to see the Regent without coming to him first.[151]

At Creel's request, Montgomery frequently facilitated the work of American journalists in Budapest. Sometimes their papers had reported unfavorably on Hungary or her leaders and that made things more difficult. At such times the Foreign Ministry, as it were, got its own back, as was to be expected, for instance, in the case of Lairds Goldsborough, the foreign editor of *Time* magazine.[152] Creel had backed Goldsborough's official request with a cable to his friend, but *Life*, published by the same stable,

148 John Gunther, *Inside Europe* (London: Hamish Hamilton, 1936), 8th printing (May 1936), 340; 15th printing (October 1936), 364–365.
149 Dr. Ferenc Marosy (Mengele) (1893–1986), head of the Press Department in the Foreign Ministry 1933–37.
150 Captain Endre Scholtz, aide-de-camp of the regent.
151 Montgomery, Diary, February 1, 1935.
152 József Balogh of *The Hungarian Quarterly,* however, sufficiently realized Goldsborough's importance and sent him, via the U. S. legation, a copy of "an exposé on Hungary's internal situation which we have been asked to treat as confidential matter not designed for printing." József Balogh to Garret G. Ackerson, May 7[?], 1937. József Balogh Papers, Fond 1/7/20, Hungarian National Széchényi Library.

published unfavorable comments on Horthy only a few weeks before Goldsborough's Budapest journey in the spring of 1937.[153] Montgomery promised his friend that he would do his best for Goldsborough, telling him, however, that *Time* had published more untruths about Hungary than any other news publication, and that they took a poor view of this in Hungary. Montgomery put his finger on something of importance.

> … Hungarians have a very foolish point of view about such things. They should make it a point to see people that give them unfavorable publicity with the idea of setting them right and making friends of them if possible. But they don't. They generally have nothing to do with any writer or newspaperman that gives them adverse publicity and only see those that they think are friendly. It is of course all wrong and only results in more misinformation about Hungary being spread around. But you cannot change that because the Hungarians have only friends or enemies, and the latter they don't want anything to do with at all. The Czechs know how to handle newspapermen, Dr. Benes in particular. The result is that they get good publicity, and Hungary doesn't.[154]

There was, of course, more to the success of Czechoslovak propaganda than Dr. Beneš's manners, but perhaps Montgomery did not know enough about history and politics to appreciate this. A later remark by Creel suggests that his aim in doing Goldsborough a favor was to secure a good press for Montgomery, given that "Time's boosts of Joe have helped him a lot," that is, their mutual friend, Ambassador Joseph Davies in Moscow.[155]

Montgomery's closest contacts in the Hungarian press were József Balogh, editor of the *Hungarian Quarterly* and of *La Nouvelle Revue de Hongrie,* and György Ottlik, editor of the semi-official *Pester Lloyd.* Both provided information, which Montgomery recorded in his "Conversations." Balogh spoke to Garret G. Ackerson, the second secretary at the legation, adding a string of domestic political news and rumors.[156] On another occasion Balogh, confirming what Orłowski, the Polish minister, had already told Montgomery, related that János Makkai, a government party back-

153 George Creel to Montgomery, April 21, 1937; Montgomery to George Creel, April 22, 1937. Strictly Personal Correspondence 1933–1937, J. F. Montgomery Collection. Cf. *Life*, March 29, 1937, 54.

154 Montgomery to George Creel, April 22, 1937. Strictly Personal Correspondence 1933–1937, J. F. Montgomery Collection.

155 George Creel to Montgomery, May 5, 1937. Strictly Personal Correspondence 1933–1937, J. F. Montgomery Collection.

156 Montgomery, Conversations, Memorandum, November 6, 1939.

bencher, author, and contributor to the right-wing *Magyarság* and *Új Magyarság*

> ... was going to America on behalf of Germany and said that so far as he knew Germany was paying his expenses either directly or indirectly. He said he had a very naive idea that he can make some speeches in America and that he had reviewed his speeches at the request of the F.O. They were very silly and as the man spoke very broken English the whole idea was fantastic. He didn't know what things of a secret nature he might have in his visit but as far as he knew the whole idea originated because Eckhardt was supposed to be having such a success and the Germans thought they should counteract it by sending another Hungarian to give the German side. He said that Teleki was aware of his mission and that he had approved, first, because pressure had been brought to bear upon him, and, second, because as he said he was a good man to get out of the country.[157]

There was a consensus among anti-Nazi members of the Hungarian political class that in a country drifting toward war close attention had to be paid to contacts with Britain and the U.S. Balogh primarily used his English-language paper when engaged in this particular battle. He paid with his life for what he achieved.[158] It should be stressed that Balogh enjoyed the backing and support of Horthy's closest circle, particularly Count István Bethlen, who pulled the strings at the *Hungarian Quarterly*. Horthy reminded Prime Minister Teleki that it was "a crime to forfeit the sympathies of the British and American peoples, we were able to call our own, as though it were unnecessary,"[159] around much the same time, late in 1940, that József Balogh reminded Count Bethlen that "we have known for years that we may perhaps have to cease to exist at a word of command from the government; it had, however, been Your Excellency's view that we must in no way further this process, at the most we may obey the order."[160]

---

157 Montgomery, Conversations, Orłowski, June 8, 1940. Cf. Ervin Csizmadia, *Ösztön és politika* (Budapest: Új Mandátum, 2002).

158 Tibor Frank, "Editing as Politics: József Balogh and *The Hungarian Quarterly*," *The Hungarian Quarterly*, 34 (Spring 1993): 5–13. For the complete text with notes see in Tibor Frank, *Ethnicity, Propaganda, Myth-Making: Studies on Hungarian Connections to Britain and America 1848–1945* (Budapest: Akadémiai Kiadó, 1999), 265–275.

159 Miklós Horthy to Count Pál Teleki, October 14, 1940. *The Confidential Papers of Admiral Horthy*, 151.

160 József Balogh to István Bethlen, December 19, 1940. József Balogh Papers, Fond 1/322/3248, Hungarian National Széchényi Library.

Press matters were only exceptionally Montgomery's business, mainly if the American press or journalists were involved, especially his good friend George Creel.[161] It was Garret G. Ackerson, the second secretary, who dealt with József Balogh and the *Hungarian Quarterly*. Ackerson and Balogh were friends even before the first issue appeared in 1936. They frequently met socially, facilitating their work, exchanging information.[162] The legation was an early subscriber and also provided Balogh with a list of potential readers.[163] Ackerson and Balogh collaborated in arranging the visits of famous American scholars such as Raymond Leslie Buell and John Boardman Whitton, compiling the lists of those invited to attend functions. On occasion Balogh published articles by visitors, sometimes subjecting them to heavy editing.[164] Balogh supplied the legation with occasional situation reports in English, compiled in the offices of the *Hungarian Quarterly* on Vilmos császár (today Bajcsy-Zsilinszky) út.[165] Ackerson was invited to *Hungarian Quarterly* at-homes presided over by Count Bethlen, and he was even given a copy of an article by Bethlen before publication.[166] Balogh, in turn, sought Ackerson's assistance when he hoped for a contribution from the likes of Walter Lippmann. Ackerson was unable to help and suggested that Balogh approach Nicholas Roosevelt, at that time on the staff of the *New York Herald Tribune,* or George Creel.

In the fast deteriorating atmosphere of 1940, after the collapse of France, Balogh wrote to Professor Gyula Kornis that he had "received instructions from the Foreign Ministry that it was desirable to give the HQ a more American orientation than hitherto. I do not know how that can be implemented, since we are now more isolated from the States than ever before."[167] In Ackerson's last month in Budapest, Balogh felt a real need to gather in the

---

161 Garret G. Ackerson to József Balogh, August 11, 1937. József Balogh Papers, Fond 1/7/25, Hungarian National Széchényi Library.

162 József Balogh to Garret G. Ackerson, December 18, 1935. József Balogh Papers, Fond 1/7/12, Hungarian National Széchényi Library.

163 Garret G. Ackerson to József Balogh, March 21, 1936; József Balogh to Garret G. Ackerson, March 23, 1936. József Balogh Papers, Fond 1/7/13–14, Hungarian National Széchényi Library.

164 Garret G. Ackerson to József Balogh, October 13, 1936; József Balogh to Garret G. Ackerson, April 24, 1937. József Balogh Papers, Fond 1/7/15; 1/7/18–19, Hungarian National Széchényi Library.

165 József Balogh to Garret G. Ackerson, May 7[?], 1937. József Balogh Papers, Fond 1/7/20, Hungarian National Széchényi Library.

166 Garret G. Ackerson to István Bethlen, May 10, 1937; József Balogh to Garret G. Ackerson, June 5, 1937. József Balogh Papers, Fond 1/59/307, 1/7/21, Hungarian National Széchényi Library.

167 József Balogh to Gyula Kornis, June 19, 1940. József Balogh Papers, Fond 1/1828, Hungarian National Széchényi Library.

The U.S. minister with first secretary Howard K. Travers

fruits of their friendship. "I should like to call at the Legation one day next week and ask your help in the matter of giving The Hungarian Quarterly a more American angle as requested by the Government. Their wish is that each number should contain two or three American articles, or ones dealing with Hungarian-American matters. I am at present not at all clear how we are to achieve this end."[168] Balogh asked Ackerson before he left to introduce him to his successor, "so that the connection with The Hungarian Quarterly may be maintained.[169]

After Ackerson and Montgomery left, Howard K. Travers, the first secretary, was Balogh's contact at the legation. They regularly lunched togeth-

---

168 József Balogh to Garret G. Ackerson, June 22, 1940. József Balogh Papers, Fond 1/7/39, Hungarian National Széchényi Library.
169 József Balogh to Garret G. Ackerson, September 17, 1940. József Balogh Papers, Fond 1/7/41, Hungarian National Széchényi Library.

er and otherwise met right up to Travers's departure in mid-December 1941. It was through Travers that Balogh invited Herbert Claiborne Pell, Montgomery's successor, to Count Bethlen's gathering, which was an opportunity where he, too, could meet the new minister. Pell in turn invited Bethlen on June 5, 1941, and Balogh suggested that Jenő Ghyczy, head of the Political Section in the Foreign Ministry, ex-Prime Minister Count Móric Esterházy, Count Jankovich-Bésán, and, "perhaps," Count Géza Pálffy, be fellow guests.[170] Together with the Minister Balogh urged that the United States facilitate the unhindered distribution if *The Hungarian Quarterly,* in view of its "non-political character."[171] An undated "Memorandum," drawn up probably for U.S. Minister Pell in 1941, vehemently opposed the idea that the "Quarterly should be taken to America:" Balogh and his patrons wanted it to represent Hungary — in Hungary.[172] Contacts between Balogh (and Bethlen) and the Legation were maintained just about to the day that war was declared.

Annus Horribilis: Farewell Calls

John Flournoy Montgomery, the envoy extraordinary and minister plenipotentiary of the United States of America, left Budapest for good in March 1941.

The precise reasons for his departure are not altogether clear. According to what Kálmán Kánya, the former foreign minister, told Montgomery, Béla Imrédy, the former prime minister, had called on Kánya on March 11, 1940, and he also visited the U.S. minister. According to Montgomery's much later account, Imrédy "came to see me one day in great excitement. He said that Csáky had told him that I had said in a recent conversation that Imrédy was intriguing against the Regent in various ways. Imrédy said this was not true, and he demanded an explanation."[173] What is odd about this story is that just before this conflict broke out Foreign Minister Csáky had informed the U.S. legation that "Mr. Montgomery enjoys the full confidence of the

---

170 József Balogh to Howard K. Travers, June 5, 1941. József Balogh Papers, Fond 1/59/313, Hungarian National Széchényi Library.

171 Herbert Claiborne Pell to István Bethlen, November 6, 1941. József Balogh Papers, Fond 1/59/327, Hungarian National Széchényi Library.

172 Memorandum, n. d. József Balogh Papers, Fond 1/324–5, Hungarian National Széchényi Library.

173 Montgomery, Conversations, Kánya, March 13, 1940; cf. Montgomery, *Hungary, the Unwilling Satellite,* 176

Hungarian government."[174] Nevertheless, it is true that, in spite of Montgomery's repeated efforts, the conflict was not settled before Csáky's death or Montgomery's resignation. Montgomery considered Csáky to be a determined supporter of the Berlin-Rome Axis, in other words a friend of Nazi Germany, and he had earlier informed the State Department accordingly.[175] Montgomery considered Imrédy's accusation to be unfounded. He wrote to Csáky asking for an explanation. How could anything said in their conversation have reached Imrédy's ears? The clumsy explanations by Csáky, who had a reputation for intrigue, put an end to personal contacts between the foreign minister and the U.S. envoy.[176]

Montgomery was very likely in the wrong. He had a poor view of Imrédy and made no secret of this in his conversations in 1938 and 1939 with Hungarian politicians close to him, such as Tibor Eckhardt, Baron Gábor Apor, Kálmán Kánya, Count István Bethlen, and the regent himself. He said much the same thing in his book on Hungary.[177] The incident could, however, have been part of a deliberate intrigue directed against Montgomery. On January 23, 1941, he made enquiries in the State Department asking if there was any truth in a rumor circulating in Washington, D.C. that the acceptance of his resignation was connected with the fact that, because of what had happened, he had called Count Csáky a liar (in confidence) and Prime Minister Teleki had declared him to be *persona non grata* as a result.[178] It is true that, as the documents show, Montgomery himself, after eight years *en poste,* initiated his resignation, and this was very likely connected with his wife's ill health rather than with politics. He suspected, nevertheless, right to the end that he was, as it were, recalled from Hungary, at the orders of the Hungarian foreign minister and with the approval of the prime minister. This is backed by his last conversations with László Bárdossy, Csáky's successor, and with Teleki himself, on February 13, 1941.[179] Teleki "told me emphatically that the story that he had made any request in connection with me was absolutely untrue, and he couldn't understand how such a thing could have originated, that he was terribly sorry to see me go as he consid-

---

174 Note by Foreign Minister Csáky to the U.S. legation in Budapest, February 20, 1940. DIMK IV:712.

175 Montgomery to Sumner Welles, April 4, 1939. Miscellaneous letters and notes, J. F. Montgomery Collection.

176 Montgomery, Conversations, Teleki, April 9, 1940; John V. MacMurray, September 28, 1940; Baron Heribert Thierry, October 11, 1940; Horthy, November 8, 1940.

177 Montgomery, *Hungary, the Unwilling Satellite,* 110–114.

178 Montgomery to the State Department, January 23, 1941, copy. Miscellaneous letters and notes, J. F. Montgomery Collection.

179 Official farewell visits to Foreign Minister László Bárdossy (foreign minister from February 4, 1941) and Prime Minister Pál Teleki, both on February 13, 1941.

ered me one of his oldest friends and a good friend of Hungary."[180] We can be sure, however, that Montgomery, "notoriously hostile to Germany"[181] (in the words of a permanent deputy of the Hungarian foreign minister), who carefully nursed his friendship with Horthy himself and those of his circle who kept clear of the Nazis, must, after the outbreak of war, have been a thorn in the flesh of the Nazis' friends in Budapest.

Foreign Minister Csáky died on January 22, 1941, and Prime Minister Teleki took his own life on April 3, 1941. On June 26, 1941, Hungary declared itself to be in a state of war with the Soviet Union, and on December 12, 1941, she declared war on the United States of America, after Great Britain had, on December 7, declared war on Hungary.

The days of grace of "the unwilling satellite" had run out. The war had started for Hungary, too. When Montgomery finally left Budapest in March 1941, the political import and message, the Q.E.D. as it were of his diplomatic career, must have been clear to him. In the last resort, the world as he knew it was divided between the Nazis and their enemies. That is what he stood for, and not only *ex officio:* it was his own deepest conviction. He despised the German Nazis and the Hungarians who did their bidding. He thwarted their plans in every possible way that was open to him. Whomever he identified as an enemy of National Socialist Germany could count on his support. Lacking the required diplomatic training and experience, and not possessed of a keen mind, he sometimes found himself at sea in an ever more complex world. A picturesque and remote country, a peaceful island seemingly calm and without a care in 1933, rushed towards the greatest catastrophe of her history in 1941. This deeply conservative, in many ways prejudiced American businessman accomplished much that was honest and important in the way of diplomacy in Budapest. His faith in Hungary could not be shaken; he was a friend who always took her part. John Flournoy Montgomery was not only a witness to Hungarian history: he belongs to it.

---

180 Montgomery, Conversations, Teleki, February 13, 1941.
181 Cipher telegram by János Vörnle, permanent deputy of the foreign minister to the Hungarian legation in Rome and Berlin, April 19, 1939. DIMK IV :178.

THE CONFIDENTIAL CONVERSATIONS
OF U.S. MINISTER JOHN F. MONTGOMERY
Budapest 1934–1941

CONVERSATIONS
1934

[1]

October 29, 1934[1]

The approach of the Parliamentary session, in which it is generally known that the much promised and much discussed secret ballot will be introduced,[2] has aroused considerable interest, and rumors of all kinds as to the character of the bill and its reception by Parliament are heard everywhere. Bethlen's supporters are sure that he will defeat the bill and overturn the present Government; and Dr. Imrédy, Count Paul Teleki, Keresztes-Fischer, and most often Bethlen himself are prominently mentioned as Gömbös' successor.

Dr. Tibor Eckhardt, who is to handle the bill in Parliament, is quite certain that it will pass and that the Gömbös Government will continue in power. In my despatch No. 118 of June 21, 1934, I outlined Dr. Eckhardt's plans based upon the full support of the Regent being given. Dr. Eckhardt now says that this support has been assured, that he personally had received the Regent's word that he, the Regent, would dissolve Parliament and call for a new election if the present Parliament refuses to pass the bill as now approved by the Regent. With this assurance, Dr. Eckhardt says there will be no question of the final passage of the bill, regardless of the opposition of Count Bethlen and the banking interests behind him. Premier Gömbös will make known at the proper time to the Party of National Union, and if necessary to Parliament, the extent of the Regent's support. At the present time the provisions of the bill, as well as the Regent's approval, are known only to a few, according to Dr. Eckhardt — and this includes only a few members of the Cabinet. The bill permitting the Regent to dissolve Parliament was passed.

---

1 Based on a conversation with Tibor Eckhardt.

2 The plan of the Independent Smallholders Party (in Montgomery's wording: Independent Farmers Party) to reform the suffrage was published at the end of August 1934, and discussion of the project dominated domestic politics for weeks. Eckhardt hoped that the secret ballot to be introduced would strengthen the Smallholders to such an extent that Gömbös would keep his power only through cooperating with Eckhardt.

In connection with the German commercial treaty, Dr. Eckhardt told me practically the same thing as Mr. Lucian Zell had told me previously: to wit, that the Germans had purchased a lot of Hungarian goods, turned the money into the Reichsbank which promptly blocked it. In the meantime, the Germans, instead of using the goods in Germany, sold them in foreign markets at reduced prices, greatly injuring Hungary's regular trade in these markets. Now Hungary finds herself with 30 million marks (according to Mr. Zell) or 15 millions (according to Dr. Eckhardt) frozen in the German Reichsbank. As a result, there is a great shortage of foreign exchange and the National Bank has refused practically every permit for the use of blocked pengő during the last week. In fact, at the present time there is practically nothing a blocked pengő can be used for.

Dr. Eckhardt, who is popularly picked as de Kánya's successor as Foreign Minister because of his great success last September at Geneva, denies emphatically that there is any possibility of going into any Government in the near future.[3] He does not deny that he is having an increasing influence in the direction of foreign policy; in fact, he says that he has a free hand in the settlement of any question that comes before the League, and that gradually he expects partly to direct Hungarian foreign policy.

de Kánya is a very sick man and not able actually to act as Foreign Minister. Under present conditions it is desirable for him to remain. Dr. Eckhardt assured me, however, that if there is a change the next man would be the one who took orders from him, Eckhardt.

Dr. Eckhardt's reason for not desiring to go into the Government at the present time is that he believes it is advisable to keep his own party intact until after the next election. If the secret ballot passes he is sure he will have the largest number of deputies in the next Parliament; then his position in the Government will be on quite a different basis than were he to enter now.

Dr. Eckhardt says he favors a more conciliatory policy towards the neighboring States and settling minor differences wherever possible. He favors continuing in the fight for revision but believes it should be done in such a way as not to make unnecessary friction.

Dr. Eckhardt told me that at the last session of the League he had brought up the question of the treatment of minorities in the Succession States and had proposed that a commission to investigate the matter be appointed. Dr. Benes significantly suggested that there were minorities in Hungary, whereupon Dr. Eckhardt immediately agreed to include Hungary in the investigation and pledged that Hungary would follow any recommendation made by the commission. Dr. Benes then said that the matter would

---

3 Kánya was foreign minister between February 4, 1933, and November 28, 1938.
  As to Eckhardt, see note #18.

have to be handled in the regular way and that nothing could be considered until Hungary went through the required procedure. This has disposed of the matter for the moment, but Dr. Eckhardt told me that it would be brought to the attention of the League at the next session in the orthodox manner. What Hungary really wants, according to Dr. Eckhardt, is to negotiate directly with the various States. At present she has no treaty with any of them regarding the treatment of minorities, the whole matter being a question between the League and the Succession States — something to which Hungary was not a party.

With reference to the Yugoslav-French accusations against Hungary in connection with the Marseille tragedy,[4] Dr. Tibor Eckhardt criticizes the Foreign Office severely for having contented itself with denials of the various accusations. He says that Hungary's hands are clean[5] and that he does not think in the long run Yugoslav-Hungarian relations will be impaired, but that after Hungary's complete innocence is shown they will improve. Dr. Eckhardt says the terrorist party that plotted the tragedy had never had any connection with any Hungarian officials, that this party was in opposition to the Hungarian Government before the war and the Hungarian Government never had dealings with it since. In fact, visas have been continually refused to the leaders of this party. The Hungarian Government is friendly with the Croatian Peasants Party, which is in opposition to the terrorists.

The so-called camp at Jankapuszta was a farm privately rented by a few Croatian refugees, and as other refugees crossed the line they came there to stay. All of them earned their living in the ordinary way: the Hungarian Government never had anything to do with them, although of course, was aware of their presence. Last spring when Dr. Eckhardt was at the League to discuss the border controversy the Yugoslav delegate objected to the fact that this camp was so near the Yugoslav border. This was the first complaint ever made about it, and Dr. Eckhardt at once assured the Yugoslav delegate that if Yugoslavia objected to it it would be closed. He immediately telephoned the Foreign Office and the camp was closed and some of the refugees deported from Hungary. Two of them have been mentioned in connection with the Marseille tragedy. Dr. Eckhardt thinks that if they could have stayed in Hungary and made a living they would not have been in a plot.

---

4 King Alexander of Yugoslavia and French foreign minister Louis Barthou were murdered in Marseille on October 9, 1934.

5 Actually, the assassination was prepared in Jankapuszta, Hungary, by émigré separatist Croatian *ustashi*. Though Hungary had limited responsibility for the murder, she was to face great international uproar, particularly in the League of Nations.

Dr. Eckhardt says that the plot was actually hatched in Belgium where there is a large number of Croats, where King Alexander was actually tried and sentenced to death and the sentence printed in a Belgian newspaper.

In connection with the Croatian terrorists, Dr. Eckhardt intimated that while Hungary had no connection with them, he was not so sure that Italy had not. This might account for the Italian Minister's nervousness as expressed to Mr. Riggs.[6]

---

6 Benjamin Reath Riggs was secretary at the U.S. legation in Budapest.

1935

[2] Conversation of Minister with Dr. Tibor Eckhardt

Budapest, January 7, 1935

Dr. Eckhardt said that Hungary's report to the League of Nations is ready. It will be submitted to Mr. Eden before it is printed. Mr. de Kánya is leaving Wednesday night for Geneva, but does not want the fact known that he is going. Dr. Eckhardt is leaving tomorrow for Vienna, where he will deliver a lecture tomorrow night and will join Mr. de Kánya on the train. They will arrive in Geneva on Thursday night.

The Hungarian report says that the Hungarian Government finds no responsibility, direct or indirect, on the part of any Hungarian official. It did find, however, the control of emigrants was not as effective as it should have been, and that passport matters had not been strictly handled. As a matter of fact, before the Marseille murders they had known that the passport situation was not satisfactory and had ordered new passports with the idea of completely reorganizing the passport department.

As a result of the investigations made, three gendarmes and one police official have been dismissed. The second chief of the passport department has been transferred from Budapest to the country. The gendarmes and police were dismissed because the control of foreigners was not effective; the passport official transferred because he did not report that his staff was not sufficiently efficient. In this connection he said that Hungary issued 300,000 passports a year, sometimes 300 in a single day; this is more than Germany issues. The reason for issuing so many is the necessity of Hungarians to go to other countries on account of the size of the country, property owned abroad, etc. Of the five passports complained about in the Yugoslav note, three are genuine. They are, however, Nansen passports issued under the authority of the League of Nations. Two are not genuine.

The report is mild and does not attack Yugoslavia or Czechoslovakia, nor go into the internal situation of Yugoslavia. Necessarily, as it goes into every detail of the Yugoslav accusations, it has to refute accusations made, and he thought possibly that some of the things said in this connection might be deleted by Eden. Essentially, the report would not be changed.

Changes in heads of National Bank and Ministry of Finance

Dr. Eckhardt said that Mr. Imrédy had resigned as Minister of Finance, and is being succeeded temporarily by Mr. Fabinyi,[7] who will also continue as Minister of Commerce. Mr. Jakob,[8] Imrédy's assistant, will actually conduct affairs. Imrédy will become President of the National Bank. The Bank of England was dissatisfied with Mr. Popovic[9] because of his sickness and asked that a change be made. Mr. Imrédy will not come back as Minister of Finance. This ought to be announced any moment, but Mr. Imrédy has actually taken over his new position and Mr. Fabinyi has taken over his new portfolio.

Secret Ballot

The Secret Ballot Bill is progressing and everything is satisfactory. Count Bethlen saw the Regent a week ago Saturday. The result of that conversation was that he called on Gömbös Sunday and told him he would not oppose the passage of the bill. Eckhardt admits that this does not mean that he might do so but indicates for the moment that he sees opposition as useless.

Rome Agreement[10]

Dr. Eckhardt said that there will be negotiated at Rome two agreements between Italy and France, one public and one secret. There will so be one public and one secret agreement for Central European States to sign. A part of the open agreement between France and Italy will concern Africa. The open agreement which the Central European States are to sign will concern political interference with other States, etc. The secret agreement will concern the guarantee of the independence of Austria.

The object of Mr. de Kánya's trip to Geneva is to consult in reference to whatever treaties Hungary is to sign and to have interpretations given with

7 Tihamér Fabinyi (1890–1953), minister of commerce 1932–35, minister of finance 1935–38.

8 Dr. Oszkár Jakabb (1888–?), employed by the Ministry of Finance from 1910, he became head of the Budget Department.

9 Dr. Sándor Popovics (1862–1935), secretary of state in the Ministry of Finance at the side of Sándor Wekerle, governor of the Austro-Hungarian Bank between 1909 and 1918, minister of finance in 1918, first president of the newly founded Hungarian National Bank from 1924 to 1935.

10 Franco-Italian agreement signed in Rome, January 7, 1935, later called the "Danubian Pact," unfavorable to the revisionist policies of Hungary.

regard to the necessary guarantees that will not involve Hungary in any agreement whereby she is compelled to use force of arms, regardless of the fact whether the other signatories are or are not.

Hungary will sign any pact which provides against changing frontiers by violence, but will not sign any pact which prohibits changing frontiers by peaceful means. Gömbös sent a letter to Mussolini in which he outlined Hungary's position.

Germany is familiar with Hungary's stand and knows what she will do and what she will not do. The German Foreign Office has advised the Hungarian Foreign Office that if any of these treaties are presented to her (Germany) she will sign them if they contain nothing offensive to Germany.

Gömbös Labor Program

The new cooperative labor program of Gömbös[11] is something similar to the NRA[12] and the Labor Board,[13] although it will not start at price-fixing or as rigid control as the NRA, but may work up to them.

[3] Conversation with Baron Bessenyey

January 15, 1935

Baron Bessenyey told me that it was quite true that Mr. Schussnigg was much more disposed to make some arrangement with Germany than Dollfuss; in fact, he was quite anxious to do so. He believed, therefore, the possibilities of some agreement were greater than they had been when Dollfuss was in power. At Geneva he said they did not know the exact text of the agreements negotiated at Rome, but that one of the reasons de Kánya had gone to Geneva was to insist upon a settlement of the Hungarian-Yugoslav controversy prior to any consideration of these agreements by Hungary. In other words, Hungary did not propose to sign or even negotiate any pacts

---

11 The principles of Gömbös for the "national organization of a lawful representation of interest" aimed at the establishment of chambers in the areas of labor and labor law, similar to Mussolini's system of Italian corporations.

12 Under the leadership of Hugh S. Johnson, the National Recovery Administration was one of the fundamental programs of the New Deal of President F. D. Roosevelt after June 1933, a political attempt to stop deflation.

13 Initiated by the early New Deal, the National Labor Policy Board was a new type of organization to represent the interests of U.S. employees.

until the Yugoslav business was settled. The Little Entente,[14] on the other hand, were trying to hold off the settlement of the Yugoslav controversy, to force Hungary into some agreement, but that Hungary would under no circumstances sign any pacts as long as the Yugoslav controversy was not closed.

Baron Bessenyey told me in confidence a very interesting thing in regard to Madam Gömbös. He said that she was an Austrian and lived in Vienna while he was there in the Legation. She was a very strong Nazi and participated in all the meetings of the Nazi party, and their great fear was that she would be arrested and, even though she was not at that time his wife, she bore his name, and it would be very embarrassing so they had arranged with the Austrian Government to prevent her arrest so as to save any embarrassment. In other words, if it hadn't been for their action she probably would have been arrested. I asked whether she was still a Nazi and he replied "No, now she is a good Hungarian." I said "Well, has this Nazi idea of hers any influence on Gömbös?" and he replied "No, it doesn't affect him. He only married her to make up for his children's sake, and he is not influenced by her in any way."

Baron Bessenyey told me that the Germans in one of their official papers were running a long series of attacks on Zita and Otto,[15] accusing them of being traitors, etc. The foundation of this attack was their acceptance of the Fascist doctrine in Austria and was directed more against Italy than anyone else. He characterized it bad taste.

[4] Conversation with Mr. de Kánya
Minister for Foreign Affairs

January, 30, 1935

Mr. de Kánya characterized the Rome Conference as a grand gesture that was necessary in view of Germany's attitude and might be useful. Whether it was useful or not depended upon the measures taken in the future. At the present moment nothing definite had happened, largely because the allies of France and of Italy — who were supposed to kiss and make up — were all taking occasion to think up everything they wanted and to put them forward

---

14 A primarily defensive alliance of Czechoslovakia and the Kingdom of Serbia, Croatia, and Slovenia (later Yugoslavia) (1920), Czechoslovakia and Romania (1921), as well as Yugoslavia and Romania (1921), directed essentially against Hungary.

15 Widow of the last Emperor of Austria and King of Hungary, Karl [I] IV, née Princess Bourbon-Parma (1892–1989), and her son, Otto von Habsburg.

as conditions to the signing of any agreement. He said that Hungary was perfectly willing to sign a treaty affirming the independence of Austria so long as she was not involved in a military way, and perfectly willing to make a treaty with any other country not to change frontiers by violence. The trouble was that the minute you started talking about a treaty with the Czechs they would begin to think of all the things they want to bind Hungary to and insist that they be in the treaty. Yugoslavia and Hungary could easily be friends and there would not be any trouble for them to negotiate a peace pact if Dr. Benes would only keep out of the picture. The trouble with the Little Entente was that the three countries had to act together, so it was hopeless to try to deal with Yugoslavia alone so long as Dr. Benes could think of conditions which would have to be fulfilled before Czechoslovakia would sign; and Yugoslavia couldn't sign under the Little Entente agreements until Czechoslovakia did. The whole thing seemed a hopeless mess. Nevertheless, it was better than it would have been had there been no Rome Conference. However, there might be a solution at any time if France and Italy are really determined to follow up the Rome Conference with some definite action.

Hitler, de Kánya said, could easily have prevented the Italian-French rapprochement if he had been disposed to give any real assurances to Austria and Italy regarding Austrian independence. Hitler, however, had more energy than brains, and the Rome meeting was the inevitable result of his failure to take proper action.

I mentioned the conditions the Prime Minister outlined in his Szolnok speech[16] — first, the settlement of the Yugoslav controversy; second, minority rights, and third, quality of armament. I told him it seemed to me they were thinking up new conditions that had not been mentioned before. He said they were only doing the same as everybody else. As things now stood, they were not prepared to accept anything else. He intimated that if the Little Entente were disposed to compromise they might, although Hungary would not compromise in such a way as to close the door on any of these questions.

I told de Kánya that I saw in the press that Sir John Simon[17] had said that Yugoslavia was going to take back some of the refugees. He said he had seen the same thing, but that is all he knows about it. The Yugoslav Minister, he said, had just left prior to his arrival and he had made no mention of the matter. de Kánya said, however, that unless Yugoslavia did some-

---

16 Prime Minister Gömbös declared the beginning of his reform program at a political rally in Szolnok organized by the government and attacked his conservative opposition (January 24, 1935).

17 British statesman (1873–1954), foreign secretary (1931–1935), a staunch supporter of the policy of appeasement of Prime Minister Neville Chamberlain.

thing soon Hungary would have to take the matter up with the League of Nations because it couldn't support these people indefinitely.

I asked de Kanya if it was true that Germany was backing Gömbös and France and Italy backing Bethlen. He thought this the most amazing idea. He said he never heard of it, and that there was nothing whatever to it.

[5] Conversation with Dr. Tibor Eckhardt

January 30, 1935

Dr. Eckhardt said that he had resigned as delegate to the League of Nations[18] and had cancelled his agreement with Gömbös — which agreement was to the effect that they were to work together. The reason for his action was as follows: Yesterday the National Union Party had a meeting, which meeting was distinctly unfriendly to Gömbös. He was accused of working with Eckhardt, who belonged to another party, and censured for having appointed him delegate to the League. Gömbös defended himself, and in the end Count Bethlen got up and proposed that his explanation be accepted, and that while his action not be approved a vote of confidence be given him. After the meeting Count Bethlen came to him and told him that he need not think because he had been given a vote of confidence the matter had been settled, that he wished to see him the next day (today) and take up with him the whole question of Eckhardt and his relations with him.[19] Immediately upon hearing of this, Eckhardt had a meeting of his own party, and as a result wrote a letter to the Prime Minister resigning his position and cancelling their agreement. The letter stated that this was done to avoid embarrassing the Prime Minister. According to Eckhardt, he was being used to confuse the issue in order that Bethlen might not openly oppose the secret ballot.

Therefore, when Bethlen called on the Prime Minister today the Prime Minister, who knew in advance what Bethlen was going to take up, pulled out Eckhardt's letter and explained to Count Bethlen that he need not discuss Eckhardt as he had resigned and the agreement had been cancelled;

---

18 Tibor Eckhardt was the Hungarian permanent delegate at the League of Nations in Geneva in 1934–35, where he ably and successfully represented the interests of the Hungarian government after the Marseille assassination.

19 A long political debate unfolded within the government party between Bethlen and Gömbös in 1934–35 on a number of issues such as the transformation of the party leadership, the domestic political methods of Gömbös, the suffrage bill, and the cooperation with Tibor Eckhardt and his party

therefore, they could discuss the question of the secret ballot without going into extraneous matter.

When Eckhardt left me he was supposed to go directly to Gömbös. I met Countess Bethlen[20] at the Archduke's about 6 o'clock, and I asked her if the Count was present. She told me that he was down at Mr. Gömbös' discussing the secret ballot with a lot of other men. I do not know whether Eckhardt was with this group, but I suppose not.

Eckhardt told me that while his resignation was a political manoeuvre, it was also due to his desire not to be involved in any defeat Mr. Gömbös might suffer in his own party. He felt that Gömbös' party, if put to a test, might defeat him as the meeting yesterday showed fully that Count Bethlen could control the party. Therefore, if his agreement with Gömbös stood, any defeat Gömbös suffered at the hands of the National Union Party would be considered as a defeat for him. He proposed to stand aside until Gömbös could find a way out.

The Regent and Gömbös were very close, and the Regent had promised him support. The question now is will the Regent make good. Gömbös' difficulty is to find means for bringing on a crisis that will put this to a test without having the crisis carry him out of office - that is, he must bring about a situation that convinces the Regent that the situation is covered by the promise he gave. In other words, that if he would go to the Regent now and ask him to fulfill his promise the Regent would simply say "Well, you haven't been voted out of office, they have given you a vote of confidence." The trouble is that the Regent's friends, the ones he plays bridge with,[21] etc., are all on the other side and are bringing pressure to bear. The Regent has promised that he would help Gömbös carry through his policies. Bethlen is guiding things along so as not to oppose these policies but bringing up other objections and trying to make it appear as though it was everything else but what it actually is. If Gömbös could get a secret ballot bill made an issue and stand or fall on that the Regent would fulfill his promise in Eckhardt's opinion. But they have injected the land reform and everything else, all of which affects friends of the Regent, making it uncertain what he will do. Eckhardt, however, believes in any case he will come through for Gömbös because he hates bankers, all of them, he hates the Jews, and he is politically tied up with Gömbös — because the Government of Gömbös was the Government in power and the Regent feels that the Government in power should be maintained. I mentioned to Eckhardt that the Regent had surprised me on New Year's Day by the way he commented on Roosevelt's great vic-

20 Countess Margit Bethlen was the wife of [ex-]Prime Minister Count István Bethlen.
21 Horthy's circle included Jewish businessmen and financiers such as Lipót Aschner, Ferenc Chorin, Jr., and Leó Budai Goldberger.

tory this fall.[22] I told him that if he had been a member of the Democratic Party he could not have been more enthusiastic, but I had figured out that the enthusiasm came from the fact that Roosevelt was in office and he considered it a Government victory. Eckhardt said this might be the case, but as a matter of fact, the Regent was a great admirer of Roosevelt and he had often discussed the matter, and the reason he admires Roosevelt is that he hates and loathes bankers and considered Roosevelt had given the latter a licking, which soothes him, and he was quite enthusiastic about it. Eckhardt said he didn't consider the Regent a very brilliant man, or even a great man, but that he always had the faculty of deciding the right way when necessary. He felt that the Regent would come through, although in view of the opposition brought to bear there was always a chance that he wouldn't.

Eckhardt said that Count Julius Karolyi[23] and Gömbös had had a meeting Sunday and that they had come to an agreement. He thought this might help lining up the Regent. Gömbös, he said, was determined not to compromise, and that if he was defeated Bethlen would not dare to go in as Prime Minister but would put in some dummy; just who, he didn't know. He didn't think that Keresztes-Fischer would come in because K-F was much interested at the present time in a gymnasium teacher and had only one idea, and that was to get out of office and marry the gymnasium teacher. He said he was anxious to resign as Minister of the Interior, wasn't taking any interest in anything but getting a divorce, so he was held in office with great difficulty.

Eckhardt thought that Fabinyi would remain as Minister of Finance and ultimately give up his other portfolio. Kallay,[24] he said, wanted to be Minister of Finance, and his resignation was due not only to his sympathy with Bethlen but to the fact that he was not appointed Minister of Finance. In other words, if he had been appointed Minister of Finance he would have remained, but not getting it he decided to go with Bethlen.

Eckhardt said that Archduke Albrecht, who is a member of his party, had talked to Bethlen and Bethlen had told him if there was a secret ballot put through he would be reduced to 20 seats in Parliament. Albrecht asked him how many he thought Eckhardt would have, and he replied 4 or 5 times as many. Eckhardt said his anxiety not to have the secret ballot is not because

---

22 The fall 1934 congressional elections in the U.S. resulted in 319 seats in the House (instead of the former 310), and 69 seats in the Senate (instead of the previous 60) for the Democrats. This was the second time in the 20th century that the party in power could increase its influence in Congress.

23 Count Gyula Károlyi, Hungarian prime minister in 1931–32.

24 Miklós Kállay (1887–1967), Hungarian statesman, minister of agriculture 1932–35, prime minister 1942–44.

of any fears for the country but fear of losing control. Eckhardt said that next Sunday he proposed staging demonstrations throughout the country. By demonstrations he apparently meant mass meetings because it openly developed that next Sunday there will be a students big mass meeting against Bethlen for the secret ballot down the river; following that, there would be such meetings throughout the country, all organized by his party. He said that the strength of his party was far greater than anybody imagined, and in many parts of the country, due to the local conditions, they were unable to organize openly and had secret organizations. This was due at the time to the opposition of the Government, and particularly local county officials. They had kept these secret organizations and in the meanwhile by growing the strength was far greater than anybody knew. He said there was an agricultural society with reading rooms in every little town, that this society was really an adjunct of the Independent Farmers, and they were in a position to bring out an immense number of people to demonstrations. He said that at the meeting they had Sunday, which was not much advertised, 8000 people turned out. I asked him what Gömbös would do if he were defeated. He said while Gömbös hadn't thought of it yet, he felt that he would undoubtedly take 30 or 40 members out of the National Union party and join the Independent Farmers Party — which would also be joined by the Christian Socialists. This would make a too large bloc to be comfortable for any Prime Minister. The result would be that they would have to have new elections, and if they were held they would be hot ones. He didn't think Gömbös would start anything like a Nazi party.

Speaking of his resignation as delegate, Eckhardt said the Regent would be much displeased with it, so he was going to ask for an audience immediately and explain to the Regent. He also felt that the country at large would be displeased but that he would blame it on the National Union Party and not on Gömbös.

[6] Conversation with Dr. Tibor Eckhardt

February 13, 1935

In today's conversation Dr. Eckhardt said that the so-called settlement between Gömbös and Bethlen is not really a settlement at all. Neither side won a victory, nothing is really settled at all, and nothing is going to happen right away. Insofar as Bethlen failed in his principal object, it is a defeat for him. His object was to stop the secret ballot, and he is now in a position where he will have to come out in the open with his opposition. The Regent has effectually taken away every other issue because he got Bethlen and

Gömbös together and announced that he wanted them to make up before
they left the room. Bethlen complained of everything he could think of, and
the Regent disposed of most of his complaints, leaving him in a position
where if he wants to stop the secret ballot bill he must come out and oppose
it as such.

On the other hand, it leaves Gömbös in a bad position because he will
have to try to make the best of the situation he is in, at least until the Regent
is certain that nothing else can be done. The Regent, it seems, wholly sup-
ports Gömbös and is in favor of everything Gömbös is for. However, he is
very conservative. He has looked up and found that never in the history of
the Austro-Hungarian Empire[25] had the King or Emperor dissolved Parliament so long before the close of Parliament or because of a disagreement in
the Government Party. Usually if the Premier could not hold his party in
line someone else was made Premier. If the Opposition got too strong then
the King or Emperor would dissolve Parliament at the request of the Prime
Minister, but never in order that he might put down trouble in his own party.

The secret ballot bill will be taken up this afternoon by the National
Union Party. Eckhardt does not know what is going to happen to it, but
Gömbös has not changed his mind, and he and Eckhardt are in agreement
on all essential points: Eckhardt says he and Gömbös are going to the same
place, and while travelling on different roads at the moment they are going
to meet somewhere along the line. He says that Gömbös thought of resigning but he, among others, urged him not to do so. He felt it much better for
him to stay in power under the present conditions than to sign and turn
everything over to Bethlen. He thinks that it is just a matter of time when
the Regent will back up Gömbös with a dissolution, but feels that the Regent
will have to try every other way first as he is very conservative and feels
that unless he follows precedents he will be taking an interest in politics
which he is not supposed to do.

Eckhardt said Antal[26] is going to be relieved of his present position (not
due to Bethlen opposition). He understands that the present Minister to Rumania, Bardossy, will take his place and that the press bureaus in the Prime
Minister's Office and Foreign Office will be combined.

Eckhardt said he has been having large meetings all over the country. He
held a meeting here somewhere across the railroad tracks. I said I saw nothing about it in the paper. He said it was a large and enthusiastic meeting.

---

25 Adm. Horthy modeled his political system, the way he governed the country, and his
"court" largely on the reign of Emperor-King Franz Joseph I.

26 István Antal (1896-1974) was head of the press department of the prime minister's
office after 1932, minister of propaganda between 1942 and 1944, and minister of
justice as well as minister of religion and education in 1944.

Eckhardt said the economic situation of the country is very bad and there is a great deal of feeling on the subject which is growing more bitter all the time, and that unless something is done the situation in time will become critical. If Bethlen were made Prime Minister he predicts there would be an outright revolution within 24 hours. He says the farmers cannot make a living off their land; it is getting harder and harder; there is no money in the provinces; the situation is very bad and there is a lot of resentment. He said Gömbös' speeches had held down the feeling to a certain extent, and added that Gömbös was going to make a speech Wednesday which will make everything lovely between him and Bethlen according to his promises to the Regent.

Eckhardt says he and his party as soon as Parliament adjourned are going to start a series of attacks on Bethlen, not personal attacks but attacks on his regime. I asked him if Gömbös had any objections to this; he replied no, saying he was in perfect accord. He said they were not just working together at the moment.

Eckhardt is going to jail for three days some time between now and June for dueling. He can take his own time about it and can pick his own jail. He will have his own food, and is looking forward to his "incarceration" and will have his picture painted while in jail.

Eckhardt reiterated that the Italians had supported Hungary, that he had been pleasantly surprised to see the extent of their support. I asked if there was any possibility of their having played a double game. He expressed himself very frankly. They couldn't he said. They were is constant touch with the situation through Aloisi[27] and of their conversations with the French. He said that there were no indications so far as he knew that Italy was less interested in Hungary than she had been. He never saw any evidence that Aloisi or anyone else was any less interested than Mussolini. He felt that the situation was unchanged.

Baron von Hahn,[28] Eckhardt said, was actually the Press Attaché of the German Legation, although not acknowledged as such. He thought he was quite a talker and fully informed on all his subjects. He didn't know how reliable he was; he had only met him once. He wanted to know if I had seen Goebel's speech. He said it was a very important speech because he said outright that from all he knew he felt very much worried about Austria, and mentioned that von Hahn had told him that the time is ripe for Germany to make up and annex Austria. He thought this was very important, and felt

---

27 Pompeo Aloisi (1875-1949), Italian diplomat, minister to Copenhagen, Bucharest, Tirana, ambassador to Tokyo and Ankara, Italian plenipotentiary to the League of Nations, chef de cabinet in the Italian ministry for foreign affairs.

28 Baron Wilhelm (Guy) von Hahn, Nazi agent in Budapest, nominally correspondent of the Deutsches Nachrichtenbüro (D.N.B.).

much disturbed about Italy getting mixed up with Abyssinia[29] because they
had lost several teeth over there already, and that Germany might take advantage of the opportunity to stir up trouble in Austria. He didn't like Italy mix-
ing up in Africa for fear she might lose prestige, and incidentally hurt Hungary.

With reference to de Kánya, Eckhardt said he was an old fox. He liked
him personally because he had always given him an answer. When he called
up from Geneva and talked with de Kánya the conversation never lasted
more than two or three minutes. No matter how important the subject de
Kánya always understood it and immediately gave the answer yes or no.
When he and de Kánya called up de Hóry from Geneva they couldn't get an
answer or any information. One day he talked three hours with de Hóry
without getting any results whatsoever. de Kánya, he said, was furious with
de Hóry and wouldn't talk to him from Geneva because he got so impatient,
so Eckhardt had to do the talking, and he never had a satisfactory conversation. He said he couldn't even get the figures on deportations without great
effort. de Hóry sent him hundreds of pages of junk, practically all of which
was worthless, nothing that he wanted. He also said de Hóry kept everyone
in the Foreign Office on the job all the time, and then never used them.
He said he was terribly afraid of responsibility and seemed to go to pieces
whenever direct questions were put to him. As Minister to Rome he did all
right because he had no responsibility. Eckhardt didn't seem to be enthusiastic about Khuen-Héderváry,[30] although he had nothing to say against him.
He was, however, quite enthusiastic about Apor,[31] whom he characterized
as a very able man.

Eckhardt wanted to know if de Kánya gave me information or whether
he dodged. I told him he never apparently dodged, but if there was something important that I wanted I never expected to get it out of de Kánya.
He said his idea was the Foreign Minister ought to give full and complete
information to everybody and not to deceive anyone. He had an idea that de
Kánya was old-fashioned in this respect because at Geneva he was terribly
nervous about Eckhardt talking with the press and wouldn't himself say
anything. He said, however, they got along fine and never had the lightest
difficulty.

He could not see the German bloc if it counted on Hungary because he
said under the present circumstances Hungary couldn't go to Germany; it

---

29 The Italian war against Ethiopia in 1935–36.

30 Count Sándor Khuen-Héderváry (1881–1947), permanent deputy of the minister for
foreign affairs 1925–34, Hungarian minister to Paris 1934–1940.

31 Baron Gábor Apor (1889–1969), diplomat, permanent deputy of the minister for foreign affairs 1935-38, Hungarian minister to the Holy See 1939–44.

was suicide. He said there was no one in Hungary who wanted to go to war with Germany, but realized that the Germans were of no particular use to Hungary except as a friend, as now. He felt the Germans had a curious psychology, and that the reaction on the Saar victory[32] had been bad. They had too great a victory and now were talking about doing something else. It would have been better if the victory had not been so great.

Eckhardt thought the position with France was much better and that she would have to do something for Hungary; that the Little Entente was now not very important to France and that they wouldn't have as much influence. The French wanted security, and now that security is more or less achieved by Italy and France, the Little Entente didn't mean so much to them as it did. Hungary's importance to France has increased; there is always the danger of Yugoslavia going with Germany because it had to be accepted as a danger when France made up with Italy, but if they kept Hungary independent Yugoslavia didn't mind. The importance of Hungary has increased by reason of the French-Italian rapprochement because Hungary is in the middle of the thing. If, for instance, Hungary should go to Germany they would have a solid pressure right on Austria and Czechoslovakia.

Eckhardt does not favor maintaining the pengő at its present level, but allowing it to sink to somewhere near its normal value and facing the situation and compromising with the creditors. They are paying on capital all the time, but if they paid it for the next hundred years they could never pay in full. His idea was that everybody ought to take their loss and put the pengő down where they can go ahead and face the future. The people are getting nothing with their sacrifices. It is getting worse all the time. He said the people are beginning to despair of getting anywhere. In other words, they are getting to where we in the States were a few years ago, only, of course, much worse and for different reasons.

[7] Conversation with Mr. de Kánya Foreign Minister on March 27, 1935

Budapest, March 28, 1935

Mr. de Kánya said that Germany's action in denouncing the Treaty of Versailles[33] was not in any way influencing Hungary's policy. Hungary had always claimed that she should be allowed to rearm in view of the fact that the neighboring countries were so heavily armed, but she had never in the

---

32 The Saar region was returned to Germany as a result of a plebiscite on January 13, 1935.
33 March 16, 1935.

past and did not expect in the future to do anything except through the regular channels and in the orthodox manner. Hungary could be counted on not to disturb the peace in any way, although she was anxious to have the privilege of rearming and a change of her frontiers to include some of her former territory. However, she expected to attain these aims by peaceful means and not by any dramatics.

In reply to my question as to just what Hungary intended to do at the present moment about disarmament, Mr. de Kánya said she intended to do nothing. Italy, however, was pushing the matter and would take it up at the coming Stresa conference[34] and at the meeting of the League of Nations.[35] It was evident from his remarks that he expected to leave the whole thing to Italy and that Hungary would make no move whatever.

Mr. de Kánya mentioned the anxiety of the Little Entente and seemed amused at Titulescu's antics, as he termed them. He could not understand why such heavily armed nations should be in such mortal fear of Hungary, even if she were rearmed proportionately, as Hungary with her present frontiers could not support an army that would be large enough to disturb the peace of mind of her neighbors.

Mr. de Kánya expressed himself as disturbed about conditions in Europe, which he said was largely the result of Hitler's Austrian policy and Mussolini's terrible hatred and fear of Hitler. He said that when he, de Kánya, talked to Hitler, the latter remarked that the fact that he was a great success in Germany and amounted to nothing in Austria was a source of great disappointment and shame to him. de Kánya thought that this was back of Hitler's Austrian policy. Mussolini talked to de Kánya about Hitler in such a way as to make him think the conversations at Venice[36] had so enraged Mussolini that he could not discuss Hitler in a calm manner. Hungary, de Kánya said, had tried to mediate and bring about a better understanding, without success. If Hitler were an intelligent man, de Kánya said, he would at this moment make a public announcement that he would give up Austria and thus allay the fears of Italy and reassure the world as to his intentions. He felt sure, however, that he would not do this, and he feared he might even make more dramatic moves in the future.

---

34 In response to Germany, the victorious Entente-powers (Great Britain, France, and Italy) declared their unity at the Stresa conference, April 11–14, 1935. The powers refrained from sanctions against Germany but emphasized the independence of Austria.

35 International organization initiated by President Woodrow Wilson and created by the Paris peace treaties of 1919–1920 for conflict resolution by political means. It was headquartered in Geneva.

36 Hitler and Mussolini first met in Venice on June 14–15, 1934; Mussolini was quite reserved on the occasion.

I mentioned that Napoleon was an Italian and always felt that he didn't belong in France which feeling was back of his desire to conquer the world. I suggested that Hitler being an Austrian might in the end be as great a disturber to peace as Napoleon for the same reason. Mr. de Kánya shook his head and said it might be possible. However, he hoped that Hitler did have peaceful intentions, and he was inclined to think that he had. The French Ambassador at Berlin[37] told the Hungarian Minister[38] that he had no doubt of Hitler's desire for peace, and Mr. de Kánya said he believed that this was true. He admitted, however, that his belief was based on hope, but that he couldn't explain how Hitler could keep up his Austrian campaign without disturbing the peace. With regard to Yugoslavia, Mr. de Kánya said that the feeling between the two countries had greatly improved, but no real rapprochement could occur until the charges before the League of Nations were disposed of. He did not understand why anyone should consider that Italy's friendly gestures towards Yugoslavia could be construed as indicating a cooling of Italian feeling for Hungary. The Yugoslavs and the Hungarians would have been friends long ago except for Hungary's friendship for Italy. It was the anti-Italian feeling that made Yugoslavia dislike Hungary. Any rapprochement between Italy and Yugoslavia would merely increase the prospect of Yugoslav-Hungarian rapprochement and would in no way affect Italian-Hungarian friendship.

[8] Conversation with Count Malagola Cappi

Budapest, March 29, 1935

Count Malagola told me that he had known King Alexander of Yugoslavia as a boy in Venice, that his father was a great friend of King Alexander's tutor, and that he had kept up the acquaintance with King Alexander until the time of his death.

Some years ago Count Malagola met Mussolini and told him that he was a great friend of Alexander and was going to Yugoslavia all the time, and if he could be of any service to Italy he would be glad to do what he could. Mussolini said that if there was anything he could do, he, Mussolini, would let him know.

A few weeks later he was asked by Mussolini to come to Rome. He went

---

37 André François-Poncet (1887–1978), French ambassador to Berlin 1931–38, to Rome 1938–40, and again to [the Federal Republic of] Germany (Bonn) 1953–55.
38 Szilárd Masirevich (1879–1944), Hungarian minister to Vienna 1921–25, Berlin 1933–36, and London 1936–38.

to Rome and Mussolini told him that he thought there were possibilities of doing something and asked him to take the matter up with Alexander, ascertain how he felt towards Italy, etc. etc. Count Malagola asked Mussolini if he could do so openly: i.e. tell Alexander he had a conversation with Mussolini, etc. Mussolini agreed that it was perfectly all right.

Count Malagola saw Alexander, and from then on acted as an intermediary between Alexander and Mussolini. In this way he conveyed the ideas of each to the other, and considerable progress towards a treaty was made. Just at the time, however, some Yugoslavs went to Trau[39] and smashed some Italian statues (lions) which caused a big incident and broke up the negotiations. However, they were taken up again, and then were broken off by other incidents. Finally, however, they came to almost complete agreement about three years ago, and Jeftic[40] came under an assumed name with Count Malagola to Rome. There, however, he met Balbo[41] and others who were opposed to the idea, and as a result thereof, all the work was lost. He said that while Mussolini all the time was anxious to be on friendly terms there were a large number in Italy who thought Yugoslavia would break up in a short time and kept urging Mussolini not to do anything but wait, etc. This always interfered with the actual conclusion of any pacts.

Count Malagola said that Italy had aided the Croats, had furnished them money and even bombs to go down and stir things up in Croatia, and that one time when he went to Yugoslavia, just as some bombing incident had occurred, Alexander was furious because the bombs came from Italy, this, that and the other, and that made a breach.

Shortly before Alexander's death they again got the thing straightened out, and Alexander told him that he was going to France to discuss with the French the whole proposition, and then he would probably go to Italy and see Mussolini. Alexander's assassination and subsequent developments threw everything in the air again. The feeling in Yugoslavia against Italy was terrible, but by reason of the French influence this was directed against Hungary.

Lately Mussolini became convinced that Yugoslavia was not going to break up, and he sent for Count Malagola and asked him to go and see Prince Paul and find out how he felt about the matter. Prince Paul told Count Malagola that he loved Italy, that he had always urged Alexander to make peace with Italy, and expressed himself as anxious to do something, but said that

---

39 Trogir, city in Dalmatia, Croatia.
40 Bogoljub D. Jeftić (1886–1960), Yugoslav statesman, diplomat, foreign minister 1932, prime minister 1934–35.
41 Italo Balbo (1896–1940), Italian Fascist statesman and aviator, air minister between 1929 and 1933, air marshal 1933, governor of Libya.

he would not make any proposition as long as Italy supported Hungary's revisionist plans against Yugoslavia; he wasn't in a position to agree to giving up any territory, and there was no use in discussing anything as he was tired of the revisionist activity.

Negotiations have continued through Count Malagola between Mussolini and Prince Paul, and they have arrived at a gentlemen's agreement that Italy would not support any claim Hungary might make for Yugoslav territory; Yugoslavia on the other hand would agree to give the Hungarian minority better treatment, not to deport any more people or close their schools, and to take back those who had been deported – and to conclude a treaty something on the line of the one of two years ago with additional variations to bring it up to date.

The speech that Count Viola de Campo Alto, the new Italian Minister at Belgrade, made was written by Mussolini himself after this gentlemen's agreement was concluded, and the only important word in the whole speech is the word "integrity" referring to territory. A copy of the speech was given to Jeftic, and it was to be delivered on a certain day. Jeftic, however, was taken sick and it had to be postponed until the next day. That afternoon came word from Italy that they must change the word "integrity" for "unity". It seems that the Yugoslavs had notified Rumania and Czechoslovakia about the speech, and the Hungarian Minister in Prague had found out about it. He telegraphed to Budapest and the Hungarians raised an awful rumpus in Rome. Count Viola de Campo Alto told him he had already given this speech to Jeftic and he couldn't change the word without seeing Jeftic; he knew it would not be satisfactory and that he would refuse to make the change without instructions from Mussolini himself, inasmuch as Mussolini had personally written the draft. They waited all afternoon for something; later in the day came a telephone message from Rome to go ahead with it as it was with the word "integrity".

Count Malagola has a rough draft of the things agreed upon three years ago. He is going to wire it out this afternoon and give it to me tomorrow morning. He doesn't know anything about Austria or any subsequent happenings.

Count Malagola is going to Belgrade and he will find out particularly what is going on. When he comes back he will tell in Italian to Mr. Riggs the whole story. He said that in his conversations with Alexander, the latter had gone so far as to suggest that a customs union between Italy, Hungary and Yugoslavia might be possible. Malagola said while it might be a good thing, the time for it had not yet come. It is his understanding that the present arrangement would be a treaty of amity and non-aggression and that Mussolini's idea was that it would be followed by military pacts.

Count Malagola said he is the poorest politician in the world and knows nothing about the subject. While he had heard discussions about Germany, they did not mean much to him. However, what he knows is three years old because the present discussions only prepared the way for what they were going thorough now.

Malagola claims the Hungarian Government knows nothing about this, so far as he knows, and he has never discussed anything with them. He also said that Prince Paul said that Rumania and Czechoslovakia could also be brought in line if desired with some sort of treaty. I asked Count Malagola what he thought there was for Hungary giving up revision, and he said he didn't know.

He said that part of the gentlemen's agreement included Italy's relation with the Croats, that Italy agreed to stop all her propaganda and activity in Croatia for good; that after the French had finished trying the suspected murderers of Alexander, Italy would try the two Croats now held in Italy, Pavelic[42] and [name missing], and that they would be punished.

[9] Re German, Italian and French influence in Hungary

Budapest, April 12, 1935

There is no question in my mind but that the present time is a very propitious one for such a settlement. Hungary, while still clinging to revision, realized that her immediate chances are slim. If proper provision was made for Hungary's minorities in neighboring countries to insure them equitable treatment I am of the opinion that the whole matter could be settled without any territorial readjustment — provided, of course, that they still permit Hungary to advocate peaceful revision. This latter will amount to nothing as Hungary would be willing to discontinue her annoying propaganda and it would tend to disappear in a short while. People, however, would never stand for any settlement that gave up all idea of revision, but the leading men of the country are well aware that it is a very foolish policy; that the past revisionist activities have done the country a lot of harm; further, that it is very important for Hungary to be at peace with her neighbors. I know this opinion is shared by such men as Count Paul Teleki, Eckhardt, de Kanya, Baron Apor and others.

One of the reasons that these men are of the opinion that further activity is

---

42 Ante Pavelić (1889–1959), Croatian émigré politician, leader of the Ustasha movement, considered to be the mastermind behind the murder in Marseille and sentenced to death; head of the "independent," pro-Nazi republic of Croatia 1941–45, escaped after the war and died in exile.

useless at the present time is because they know that if there was a plebiscite held Hungary could not carry any of the former territory. They know this because the Hungarian Government has taken a census in Czechoslovakia in densely populated Hungarian sections and discovered that a minority only would vote to come back to Hungary. I have this information definitely from an official of the Foreign Office who has charge of such work. The reasons that Hungary could not get a favorable vote are principally that the former subjects can get much higher prices for their product outside of Hungary; that they have a much higher scale of living; they are afraid that Hungarian landlords would take back the land that formerly belonged to them; and the lack of secret ballot voting in Hungary. In view of this, it seems hardly worthwhile to carry on revisionist activities. It is much more important to try to remedy the situation and hope conditions will be more favorable sometime in the future. It would, therefore, not surprise me at all if some solution of the Danubian situation was worked out before very many months.

[10] Conversation with Count Malagola
Budapest, April 27, 1935

Count Malagola returned from Belgrade yesterday and told me that the pact between Italy and Yugoslavia was coming nearer to completion and that he expected to go to Rome in May and see Mussolini; he hoped that shortly thereafter some definite action would be taken.

Italy's backing of the rearmament of Hungary and Bulgaria greatly disturbed the Yugoslavs, causing a temporary halt in the negotiations. The Italians were, however, able to convince the Yugoslavs that the rearmament of Hungary really meant nothing more than public acknowledgment of what the Hungarians had already done, and also that Italy's support of Hungarian rearmament put her in a position to control Hungarian action and avoid any menace to Yugoslavia.

I asked Count Malagola to find out what Yugoslavia would do with regard to Austria. Count Malagola said that Count Viola[43] told him that they were in perfect accord with the Italian policy as they did not want the Germans on the Adriatic. When Count Malagola had lunch with Prince Paul he mentioned this matter, and Prince Paul assured him that the Yugoslavs were perfectly willing to back the Italian policy so long as they were friendly with

---

43 Count Viola de Campo Alto, Italian minister to Belgrade.

Italy, as they were equally interested in keeping the Germans out of Austria. Their only interest in Germany was when they were unfriendly with Italy, and they did not want the Italian army in Austria as they felt it constituted a menace to Yugoslavia. Count Malagola also told me that the Italians had requested the Yugoslav Minister in Rome to be changed, and that this would be shortly. No successor has definitely been chosen, but he expected that the present Minister of the Royal Household would be.

[11] Conversation with Dr. Tibor Eckhardt

Budapest, April 27, 1935

In a conversation with Dr. Eckhardt last night he advised me that Hungary was negotiating very quietly a treaty of amity and non-aggression with Austria and that he expected this treaty to be signed prior to the Rome meeting.

The object of negotiating such a treaty at this time is to put Hungary in a position where she has already concluded her pact and can, therefore, resist pressure to induce her to sign any other pacts in connection with Austria, should she so desire.

Dr. Eckhardt also told me that the Italo–Yugoslav rapprochement was coming to a head and that it was not impossible that Hungary might join in if some agreement is concluded.

[12] Conversation with Baron Apor of F. O.

Budapest, May 9, 1935

Baron Apor stated that Minister de Kánya advised the Italians and the Austrians in Venice that while Hungary would attend the proposed meeting in June she would not sign anything unless, first, a settlement was reached on the Yugoslav complaint to the League of Nations; second, that the limitations on armaments were removed, so far as Hungary is concerned; third, that Hungary' rights under Article 19 of the Covenant[44] of the League are in no

---

44 According to Article 19 of the Covenant of the League of Nations "the Assembly may from time to time advise the reconsideration by Members of the League of treaties which have become inapplicable, and the consideration of international conditions whose continuance might endanger the peace of the world." Raymond Phineas Stearns, ed., *Pageant of Europe. Sources and Selections from the Renaissance to the Present Day.* Rev. ed. (Burlingame, N.Y.: Harcourt, Brace and World, 1961), 748.

way impaired. Neither would she sign any agreement binding her to the use of arms in defense in connection with any other nation. In other words, she would not commit herself to any guarantees that would involve force of arms.

I asked Baron Apor if there was any German pressure to keep Hungary from going to Rome. He said there was not; Germany apparently did not seem to object. In fact, they had got little or nothing out of the Germans in connection with the matter, so could tell very little about their attitude.

Baron Apor said that Italy intended to take these matters up with the Little Entente to see if some agreement could not be reached. Mr. Jeftic is expected to meet Suvich[45] in Venice sometime between now and the 20th of this month, and this will be followed by conferences with other members of the Little Entente.

[13] Conversation with Sir Patrick Ramsay British Minister

Budapest, May 10, 1935

The British Minister informed me yesterday that he, on instructions from his Government, delivered to Foreign Minister de Kánya the comments of the Yugoslav Government on the Hungarian reply to the Yugoslav complaint to the League of Nations. This reply was very long and detailed, and was evidently designed to keep the controversy alive.

The British Minister, however, informed Mr. de Kánya that Mr. Eden had induced the Yugoslavs to agree to accept the Hungarian reply, provided Hungary would make a declaration that she would not in future allow any terrorist activities. Mr. de Kánya thought there would be no objection on the part of the Hungarian Government, although they might like a statement from Yugoslavia in return. He promised to take it up with the Prime Minister and would advise the British Minister what could be done.

[14] Conversation with Baron Apor of F.O.

Budapest, May 24, 1935

Baron Apor said that they had had the Yugoslav matter settled. The Yugoslav delegate at Geneva had made a proposition that was acceptable to Hungary and that Wednesday night they considered the matter as closed. How-

---

45 Fulvio Suvich (1887–1980), Italian secretary of state for foreign affairs 1932–36, ambassador to Washington 1936–38.

ever, the next day they received word that the Yugoslav Government had repudiated the proposition put forward by its own representative, so that now negotiations had to be started over again.

Baron Apor's impression was that the Turkish Minister for Foreign Affairs, Tewfik Rusti,[46] was responsible for the Yugoslav action. He said that before Jeftic went to Bucharest he was quite agreeable to settling the matter and had promised to meet Suvich in Venice, but afterwards found it impossible to go either to Venice or Geneva. He knew that Tewfik Rusti was doing everything possible to prevent an Italian-Yugoslav rapprochement and to prevent the Rome conference. He thought possibly he was trying by this method to obtain permission to fortify the Dardanelles. At the present time the outlook for the Rome conference is not very good; he didn't think it would take place for some time.

Baron Apor said he had listened to Hitler's speech[47] and thought it was very well written in that it would have a public appeal. However, he could not see that it would change the situation in any way as nothing in the speech gave any actual assurances that he would act differently than he had before on the Austrian question or in general. He thought that Hitler's concession on naval matters had had a temporary good effect in England, but he could not see that it was of any great importance as the British were going ahead with their plans just the same, although apparently more friendly disposed towards Hitler. He thought Hitler had an idea of separating England and France. In his opinion this would be impossible as England is compelled to back French policy, due to her position in Europe.

Baron Apor said that Goring and his bride were expected today for a second honeymoon. They are going from here to Sofia, Sofia to Dubrovnik (Ragusa) and from there to Belgrade — covering exactly the same ground that they covered two years ago before they were married. At that time the Hungarians refused to receive the present Madame Goring, and he did not like it. The Yugoslavs, however, treated her as one of the party, which gave him considerable satisfaction. I asked him if Goring was going to make some more speeches in Yugoslavia. He laughed and said he didn't know, but no matter what he said, he was no good and no one should take him seriously.

---

46 Dr. Tevfik Rüstü Aras (1884–?), Turkish foreign minister 1925–38, ambassador to London 1939–42; a confidant of President Kemal Atatürk.

47 Hitler announced his 13-point peace plan on May 21, 1935, in the Reichstag. In contrast to the French plans aiming at collective security, he emphasized the importance of bilateral agreements.

[15]
Budapest, May 24, 1935

The Hungarian Government is quite pessimistic about the possibility of the Rome conference being held. Baron Apor is of the opinion that Italy's Abyssinian venture has so involved her that she cannot force through a Rome conference as she might be able to do otherwise. As a matter of fact, the Prime Minister and Baron Apor both told me within the last few days that they felt Italy's Abyssinian venture[48] was a great mistake and that they were much disturbed. The Prime Minister said "I wish the Duce[49] well, but I am afraid." Baron Apor feels that Italy is sacrificing her European position, and incidentally Hungary, in that she is compelled to agree to a great many things now that she would have never agreed to if she did not wish the sanction of the Powers on her Abyssinian venture.

[16] Conversation with Baron von Hahn
Budapest, November 12, 1935

Baron von Hahn was in this morning and I had a very interesting talk with him. He said that the appointment of General Stojakovics[50] to Berlin had no particular significance. However, it was dictated by Gömbös, who wanted a soldier there because he admired German military methods and believed Hungary could benefit considerably by having a Minister in Berlin who is an army man. de Kánya opposed the appointment but finally agreed to it.

According to Baron von Hahn, the object of Gömbös' trip to Berlin was to try to reconcile Italy and Germany, and that after his return he intended to make a trip to Rome, but received word from Rome not to come. The Italians advised both Austria and Hungary that they preferred that they should not be so open in their friendship as it would be much more useful to Italy if they could be friendly with Great Britain, not to antagonize that country, and thus preclude the possibility of retaliation. Great Britain is very much provoked with both Austria and Hungary, especially with the former.

Baron von Hahn was very critical of de Kánya and his whole policy. He

---

48 Italy's attack on Ethiopia.
49 Mussolini's title as Italy's dictator.
50 Döme Stojákovits, Hungarianized as Sztójay (1883–1946), lieutenant general, Hungarian minister to Berlin 1935–44, prime minister and foreign minister in 1944. Executed as a war criminal.

said that de Kánya has gotten Hungary into a pretty bad fix, and blames him for the sanctions speech of the Hungarian delegate at Geneva and for the one delivered later on by Gömbös. With the turn of events between Great Britain and Italy, and the latter's predicament, the Hungarian Government has become scared and does not know just what to do.

The Baron said that Mr. de Winchkler,[51] now Minister of Commerce, is favored by a great many people to succeed de Kánya as Minister for Foreign Affairs, and followed with the remark that de Winchkler is going to Berlin soon. I suggested that the trip might be for the purpose of receiving instructions as to how to act when he becomes Foreign Minister. He protested that this was not true, but that he was just going on certain affairs connected with commerce. I remembered that it looked to me as though the seat of the Government is moving to Berlin, and that I assumed I would have to move there soon in order to keep up with the Government. He laughed heartily but denied that there was any more to it than a friendly feeling between Hungary and Germany. At the same time he kept repeating what a mistake the Hungarians had made in tying up with Italy, and added that if they had listened to German advice they would not be in their present uncomfortable situation.

While the Government party is pro-German — with the exception of de Kánya who, he said, was a friend of former Germany but hates the present-day Germany — on the other hand, he believes the majority of the people of Hungary are anti-German. He lists first the Jews, second the Socialists and Liberals, and third the Monarchists. He said that Germany is in a position of being the secret love of Hungary which likes to feel close to Germany but does not want to acknowledge it.

Great Britain is trying to induce Germany to return to the League of Nations, but in Baron von Hahn's opinion, Germany will not do this. However, if forced to choose between Great Britain and Italy, he thought Germany would certainly choose Great Britain. At the present moment it has not been necessary to make a choice, but if sanctions are applied and pressure put on Italy, Germany will have to make a decision.

Unlike a year ago, Italy is now making very many friendly gestures to Germany. He cited the fact that the Italian Ambassador went to Munich recently for the dedication of the monument to those killed in Hitler's "putsch". He had not intended to place a wreath on the monument, but at the last moment he received an instruction from Rome ordering him to do so.

---

51 István Winchkler (1890–1940), government commissioner and president of the Office of Foreign Trade 1933–35, minister of commerce and communications 1935–36.

I told Baron von Hahn that I presumed that as soon as Great Britain and Italy became more seriously involved, I would wake up some morning to find that Germany had taken possession of Austria and Bohemia. "Certainly not Austria for the moment," he replied. I told him he was just spoofing me. He said, "No. For three reasons Germany does not want Austria just now. First, Communists. Austria is full of Communists and Germany does not want any more at present. Second, the Catholic Church. Germany has enough trouble with the Catholics now without having more of them brought into the country. Third, the taking of Austria would involve difficulties which might not exist at a later date." He didn't deny that they might take Bohemia. He said that Hitler told Gömbös when the latter was in Berlin that Germany had given up the idea of Austria for the present.

[17] Conversation with Baron Apor

Budapest, December 19, 1935

Baron Apor is under the impression that sanctions[52] are now to all intents and purposes finished. He has no idea that they will be immediately called off, and does not think that there will be additional sanctions imposed; his idea is that there will be a lot of talk and that sanctions will die of their own accord.

Baron Apor is also of the opinion that in the meanwhile both the Italians and Abyssinians may decide to make peace and then in the end some way out will be found, which while satisfying nobody will at least ensure peace. He thinks it is very naive of the British Cabinet that they have just discovered that the imposition of sanctions was apt to bring war. Everybody else seemed to understand that sanctions in the end meant war, and it was supposed that the British Government knew that they were facing a war and intended to go through with it. The Italians have been fully convinced of this and their great anxiety has been to keep France neutral as they feel that they are not helpless against Great Britain. They believe they are sufficiently equipped to do great damage to the British fleet in the Mediterranean. They hoped that after they were faced with the realities of war, British public opinion would not support the idea and then they would be able to conclude a satisfactory peace without a prolonged war.

---

52 After Italy invaded Ethiopia without a declaration of war on October 3, 1935, the Council of the League of Nations declared Italy an aggressor on October 7 and suggested financial and economic sanctions against her. Hungary opposed the sanctions in the League of Nations.

Baron Apor thought it was a strange state of affairs that the pacifists throughout the world were the most insistent on war, and now the Tories were most anxious to avoid it. He thought that the events of the last few days would make Hungary's position considerably easier, for although he said they had not been adversely affected by their refusal to vote sanctions they feared that if the issue was prolonged they might be. He thought that British prestige had been considerably injured by the Cabinet's squabble and lack of support of home for their peace program, but he added that as Great Britain is a big nation, it would not make a lot of difference in the long run.

1936

[18] Conversation with Baron Apor

Budapest, January 16, 1936

Baron Apor said that Benes had a very difficult time being elected President of Czechoslovakia and was practically compelled to buy his election. One of his friends or supporters approached the leader of the Hungarian minority and asked what was demanded in return for their vote; after consulting with his party, Benes' supporter was advised that they would want the constitution guaranteed, the peace treaty lived up to, and certain other material things such as school houses, etc. This was agreed to, and later the leader of the Hungarian minority was advised that although Benes as it turned out, didn't need the Hungarian votes, he would keep the promise made to him. The Hungarian leader learned that the votes of the Hungarian minority were the only ones which did not have to be paid for by positions or money.

[19] Conversation with Count Malagola

Budapest, January 23, 1936

Count Malagola told me that the French Legation is very much incensed because of the failure of the Italian Legation to attend a tea recently given by the French. Baron Beauverger[53] before extending the invitations called up Lepri of the Italian Legation and asked him whether they would attend, suggesting that in case they did not want to do so the French Legation would not embarrass them by sending invitations. Mr. Lepri replied that they would be glad to attend, that all the talk about not going out was nonsense. As a result of this conversation invitations were sent to everybody connected with the Italian Legation. Not one, however, either appeared or made any excuses.

Count Malagola saw Count de Senneville[54] last night and the latter was

---

53 Baron Edmond de Beauverger, secretary of the French legation in Budapest and chargé.
54 Aymar de Senneville, French major on the general staff, military attaché of the French legation in Budapest.

very angry, stating that if they did not want to come after the invitations were extended, common courtesy would demand under the circumstances they at least send some excuse.

Count Malagola blames this and all the actions of the Italian Legation here on Prince Pignatelli,[55] who is the Secretary of the Fascist Party. Prince Pignatelli is very bitter, and Colonna being a very timid person seems to be afraid of him. The result is that while on one hand he says that he has no objection to going out, when the concrete invitation is put to him he becomes panicky and doesn't know what to do. Count Malagola said that Viola, the Italian Minister in Belgrade, goes everywhere, and that as far as he knows from his conversations with both Viola and Colonna they have no instructions not to visit sanctionist homes.

[20] Conversation with Count Malagola

Budapest, January 23, 1936

Count Malagola has just returned from Belgrade where he has been for the last few days in response to a message from Prince Paul. Prince Paul told him that he had been very much embarrassed by the receipt of information that the British fleet would like to come to the Adriatic and visit the port of Split. Prince Paul said that this was an unsolicited visit and one that he did not appreciate, as he felt that British warships should keep out of the Adriatic at this particular time. He asked the British not to send a fleet, calling their attention to the fact that they paid a visit last year, and he wished Signor Mussolini to know that if the British send a fleet despite his message he had done the best he could to stop the visit, but if they came there was nothing he could do about it.

He expressed to Count Malagola the greatest friendliness for Italy and said that despite the fact that he was very friendly toward Great Britain he had not lost his feelings of friendliness for Italy and that he wished Signor Mussolini's attention called to the fact that Yugoslavia was blind in one eye and did not notice therefore the trade that was still going on between the two countries.

Prince Paul felt that the sanctions were not having any effect, and that Italy would win out in her Abyssinian venture. He hoped that when it was all over, Italy and Yugoslavia would then be very close and that some coop-

---

55 Prince Ricardo di Montecalvo Pignatelli, representative of the Italian Fascist party in Hungary.

eration along the lines suggested by his brother[56] would become effective. He suggested to Count Malagola that at the proper time Italy establish a permanent exhibition in Belgrade for Italian goods, etc.

[21] Conversation with Tibor Eckhardt

Budapest, February 8, 1936

Dr. Eckhardt did not take a great deal of stock in the idea of any Danubian economic settlement. He thought the whole thing was started again by Titulesco because he wanted to impress the French Foreign Minister and increase his own importance and that of his country in order to keep the French gold flowing. He did not think that the Little Entente could agree among themselves on any Danubian economic policy. Czechoslovakia was very anxious to propitiate Hungary and be friendly with Austria at the present moment, and he thought they would be willing ultimately to go into the Rome pact, although they would undoubtedly try to get the Hungarians to give up revision but would be unsuccessful; he still thought they would go in when the opportunity is offered. This would not be of course until after the present Italian-Abyssinian affair was settled, so he didn't see that anything could be done for the moment.

Titulesco was very anxious to bring Soviet Russia into the Danubian area, but his king didn't agree with him. Neither one, however, wanted to go into the Rome pact. Yugoslavia didn't want to join any pact. When talking to the Minister of Agriculture from Yugoslavia last week, Eckhardt was told by him that the Yugoslavs would not sacrifice their trade with Germany for any advantages they could secure through a Danubian pact as their German trade was more important. Eckhardt, therefore, thought the idea of a Danubian pact was merely a delusion and that nothing actually would ever develop from it.

Dr. Eckhardt told me that King Edward the 8th[57] received Mr. de Kánya very warmly, and that Mr. de Kánya said that afterwards he received enough invitations in London to keep him there for another six months. The king also told de Kánya in confidence that after he was crowned he expected to come to Budapest again, but he didn't want that talked about for the moment.

Dr. Eckhardt said that he had recently been in touch with one high in the councils of the Nazi party (whose name he said he couldn't mention) and that he had remarked to this person that he was glad to see that Hitler final-

56 Reference to King Alexander of Yugoslavia?
57 King of England, January 20–December 10, 1936.

ly had come to his senses with regard to Austria and had changed to a sane foreign policy. The Nazi replied that Eckhardt was quite mistaken: Hitler hadn't changed his mind about these questions or anything else, that he was just as determined as ever. The only difference was that while in the past he got his advice on foreign affairs from Rosenberg, Von Neurath, Von Blomberg, and Göring, he now took advice only from General von Blomberg, and the latter's advice was to the effect that Germany could not put its army into proper shape for any offensive or defensive measures within three years, and that therefore Hitler must give up all ideas of doing anything during that period of time. The result is that they are making no moves whatever now.

[22]

Budapest, February 10, 1936

While the social events, gala at the Opera, etc. which the Hungarian Government had scheduled for the visit of Signor Dino Alfieri,[58] the Italian State Secretary for the Press and Propaganda, were cancelled on account of the death of King George,[59] the opening of the Italian art exhibition – which was the purpose of his visit – took place, although it was not the big event which had been anticipated.

The only member of the Diplomatic Corps that attended the opening of the exhibition was Mr. Grigorcea, the Rumanian Minister, who was also the Dean. Mr. Grigorcea had been very busy at the time on account of his king passing through Budapest the next day, but felt inasmuch as he was Dean that he should attend as he suspected that practically no one else would.

Signor Alfieri made a speech of a violent revisionist character, saying among other things that Mussolini was a determined friend of Hungary and Hungarians would see that when "something happens" the friendship of Italy would be material and not just a gesture. Mussolini did not consider the Treaty of Versailles or the Treaty of Trianon as binding, and Hungarians could count on Italy's help at the proper time.

Prince Colonna, the Italian Minister, and others of the Italian Legation seemed much agitated, and although the Hungarians present violently applauded, none of the members of the Legation joined in the demonstration. Mr. Gri-

58 Dino Alfieri (1886–1966), see note #121 on p. 54.
59 George V, king of England, died on January 20, 1936.

gorcea said that it was his original intention to stay only a short time and that he had seated himself where he could retire without attracting attention, but that he remained because he felt that if he got up and someone did notice him it might be felt that he left on account of the speech. He understood every word that was said but was not offended as he understood that it was merely an Italian gesture to keep Hungary in line. Nevertheless, the Italian Legation was much disturbed, as was State Secretary Alfieri, when they learned of Grigorcea's presence. Signor Alfieri wanted to know how he happened to be invited, and Colonna told him that he couldn't account for it.

Baron Apor, when I talked to him yesterday, laughed heartily about the incident. He indicated that he thought Alfieri was a fool, and said it was a good thing that it was not the Yugoslav Minister instead of the Rumanian Minister as the former would have gone up and made a scene, and it might have been very embarrassing for Italy because Yugoslavia and Italy were becoming more friendly all the time. He also said that Colonna should have told Grigorcea about it in advance and given him an opportunity to stay away if he wanted to. He said that when Eckhardt came to Vienna while he, Apor, was Minister there and made a violent revisionist speech, he had told the Rumanian Minister in advance that he had better stay away. However, the Rumanian Minister said he didn't mind and came, but afterwards told a number of people that he greatly appreciated Apor's having told him as it showed his good-will.

Baron Apor went on to say that despite sanctions there was any amount of traffic between Italy and Yugoslavia, which he said nobody seemed to notice, and also added that he had learned through their Minister at Angora [= Ankara] that the Turkish Prime Minister had been endeavoring to form a Mediterranean pact but that Prince Paul refused to go into it unless Italy did, and this killed the project.

[23] Conversation with Foreign Minister de Kánya

Budapest, February 11, 1936

Foreign Minister de Kánya said, in reference to the proposed Danubian pact, that there could not be any Danubian agreement without Italy and Germany; nor could there be any agreement directed against any Power. In other words, any movement directed against Germany or against Italy would not be successful as these two Powers are more important economically to the Danubian States than any others. He said that no real effort had been ever made to make an agreement with all Powers concerned — which is the only way one can be made. Any offensive or defensive plan masked as an economic plan cannot succeed.

Hungary is ready at all times to join any plan made by the Powers concerned — which must include Italy and Germany — which has no political object. The position of the Little Entente is the same. Neither Czechoslovakia nor Yugoslavia could or would have any plan that did not include the major Powers interested, Italy and Germany. Czechoslovakia is more dependent on Germany than Hungary, and there is nothing that can be offered to any Danubian State that can replace Italian or German trade.

He said that he knew from a confidential source that Hodza did not make his proposals seriously, but only to project himself into the limelight, as he felt he must follow in Mr. Benes' footsteps. Hodza felt safe in advancing such ideas because he knew they would never succeed, and they can always blame Hungary. As a matter of fact, Hungary has always been willing to enter into any non-political economic pact: it was Czechoslovakia that denounced the treaty between Hungary and Czechoslovakia, and not Hungary. It is true that Hungary had refused offers with economic advantages in exchange for giving up her rights under Article 19, but she has never refused to enter into any trade treaty non-political in character unless it was not to her advantage economically.

In London he had a long interview with King Edward, who was most friendly and spoke very highly of his visits to Hungary, saying confidentially that as soon as he was crowned and felt that he had established himself he would make another trip to Budapest, the first place he intended to visit. de Kánya said that after his audience he was deluged with invitations of all kinds and was certain that it had a very beneficial effect all around.

He talked with Baldwin,[60] Eden, Chamberlain, and Vansittart,[61] and all were extremely friendly, and none mentioned sanctions. He, however, brought the subject up when talking with Vansittart, and explained Hungary's position. Vansittart said that it was all forgotten so far as they were concerned and would not hold it against Hungary. Both Eden and Vansittart told him that they were anxious to settle the Italo-Ethiopian matter, but that they intended to do nothing more but would wait for some Italian move. de Kánya then said, "If we could only keep Mussolini from talking. He talks too much; it does much harm and no good."

de Kánya was not worried by Schussnigg's visit to Czechoslovakia or

---

60 Stanley Baldwin, 1st Earl Baldwin (1867–1947), British prime minister 1923–24, 1924–29, 1935–37.

61 Robert Gilbert Vansittart, Baron Vansittart (1881–1957), British diplomat and statesman, permanent undersecretary of state in the British Foreign Office 1930–38, an advocate of an anti-German British foreign policy

anything that had been done. He is in close touch with Schussnigg and is advised of every move the Austrians make and is in full accord. Austria will do nothing against Hungary or Hitler. Confidentially, he told me that Schussnigg would make a visit to Hungary in March to let the whole world know how things stand between Austria and Hungary. He dismissed the return of an Emperor to the Austrian throne with a shrug, and then said that it was in Hungary's interest that Austria had no Emperor as Yugoslavia had said it would be a causus [=casus] belli.[62] He knew that if Austria had an Emperor Yugoslavia would not hesitate to enter Austria via Hungary. However, he saw no chance of an Emperor being enthroned in the near future.

de Kánya said that when he was in Paris he had intended to make a protocol call on Flandin,[63] but when he saw what was in the papers and what was on he simply sent cards and left Paris. He knew that if he called on Flandin it would be heralded as a visit of great importance and would have to spend the next six months explaining to Italy and Germany.

He said that the King of Rumania was his neighbor at the Ritz Hotel in London and was the only member of royalty that was not invited to visit some member of the British royalty. He also said that Litvinoff had been so pleased with his audience with King Edward that he would hardly speak to anyone, and afterwards referred to Titulescu as "that little gypsy".

[24] Conversation with Madame Grigorcea
wife of the Rumanian Minister

February 15, 1936

Madame Grigorcea told me last night about the same story as Count Malagola had told me with reference to her husband having attended the opening of the Italian art exhibition.

She also told me that on December 6 (the Regent's name-day) the Turkish Minister, Bebec,[64] the Austrian Minister, and the Italian Minister were the only members of the Diplomatic Corps that attended the gala performance at the Opera. The Turkish Minister said so long as he was going he wanted to get a box where he would be seen by the Regent and others, so he took a very

---

62 Cause for war.
63 Pierre-Étienne Flandin (1889–1958), French statesman, several times minister, prime
    minister 1934–35. As foreign minister he was unsuccessful in suggesting the use of
    French military forces during the German occupation of the Rhineland in 1936. He
    was a member of the Vichy government and was sentenced as a result after the war.
64 Correctly Erkin Behic [Behidj].

prominent box on the upper tier. In the address which was made, a good deal was said about Hungary, her wrongs, and it started with the Turkish invasion, and the speaker told of the horrors that had occurred, how towns were plundered and everything stolen, how Christian children were taken off to serve in harems, and young men taken along to serve with a special division of soldiers, etc., etc. The audience applauded enthusiastically, and the Turkish Minister, not understanding what was being said, joined in the applause.

The Turkish Minister had no idea what was said that evening until some time in January when he received a sharp note from his Foreign Office saying that they had heard the speech on the radio and had noticed with great displeasure that the only three Ministers present were the Austrian, Italian and Turkish; they couldn't understand his presence when the Diplomatic Corps was not there as a body, nor could they understand why he had not made a full report on the speech. An explanation was demanded because of his presence, as well as a copy of the speech. The Turkish Minister in great excitement rushed around town secure a copy but found that no one seemed to have a copy, and hasn't been able to secure one.

[25] Notes on Hungarian opinion regarding German action

March 12, 1936

1 *Archduke Albrecht*
  Dr. Tibor Eckhardt
  George Ottlik[65]

Disturbed at Germany and believe the steps that have been taken are wrong. Are of the opinion that France should have been told of intention to denounce the treaty in view of Soviet-French and Czechoslovak pacts, and that Germany would have been justified in denouncing it if after such warning pact was concluded.

Believe, however, that Germans should not have sent troops into the Rhineland, but rather negotiate for that privilege; and that even if they did send troops they should have been only a few. They do not think that 50,000 troops which are now in the Rhine bear out Hitler's statement in reference to "symbolical" occupation.

---

65 György Ottlik (1889–1966), journalist, diplomat, editor of the *Annuaire* of the League of Nations (1927–1934), *La Nouvelle Revue de Hongrie* (1935–39), and *Pester Lloyd* (1937–44).

View with grave concern the entrance of the Soviets into Central Europe, particularly the fact that the Soviets are establishing an air base capable of holding 1000 airplanes on the Hungarian frontier, and are of the opinion that Hungary cannot view this with equanimity. Are afraid that Soviet menace may compel Hungary to move closer to Germany, provided Germany is willing to guarantee assistance in case of attack.

2 *Prime Minister Gömbös*

Not disturbed by German action denouncing the Locarno Pact[66] and going into the Rhineland. In fact, seemed pleased. Only comment was that the British were smart and that they had adopted the right course. When I told him that Great Britain was considering backing up France he said, "Oh, no, Great Britain is too smart to do that." When I then remarked "So you think nothing will come of it", he said, "No, no," smiling broadly, "No, they will do nothing, Great Britain is too smart."

3 *Baron Apor*

Believes that in view of the Soviet Russian treaty, France might have expected some action by Germany. However, he doesn't approve of the steps taken, nor does he believe that they will profit Germany in the long run. He seems to think it will arouse distrust and retaliation on the part of other Powers which are not expressed in sanctions or direct action, but will nevertheless injure Germany. He also believes that Germany's future intentions are unmasked and Europe will have less illusions concerning her ideas of peace.

[26] Conversation with Mr. de Kánya, F. O.

Budapest, April 1, 1936

In the conversation which I had last night with Mr. de Kánya, he told me that the Rome Protocols just signed[67] had not changed the situation that existed previously and that there was nothing new whatever. The activity of

---

66 The Locarno treaties (October 16, 1925) were signed to provide international guarantee for the security of the French borders, as well as of the Rhineland, and ensure the admission of Germany to the League of Nations.

67 On March 23, 1936 Gömbös, Mussolini, and Schuschnigg signed, in Rome, the implementation of the Rome protocols of March 17, 1934, referring to the cooperation of Austria, Hungary, and Italy.

France and Czechoslovakia have compelled them to meet and to reaffirm the Rome Pact of 1934, but there was no secret agreements of any kind and nothing that changed the situation. It was merely, to use his own words, a demonstration.

Mr. de Kánya told me that the thought the present tension in Europe was all due to Mussolini, that he kept things stirred up; starting with his Abyssinian venture and continuing it until now. He said he told Mussolini this but got no reply. Mussolini merely smiled. He said Mussolini was quite good-natured.

On general lines, Mr. de Kánya asked me if I knew what impression the British Minister[68] had of Hungary. He said that he was considered to be a friend of the Little Entente. He mentioned the Rumanian Minister[69] as one whom he never sees except when he meets him socially, adding that since he has been in the F. O. for more than three years, the Rumanian Minister had just entered the door only three times and never had called on him. I expressed surprise. He said he assumed it was due to orders from Titulesco whom he considered Hungary's greatest enemy. He presumed that he didn't want Grigorcea to be contaminated by the F. O.

[27] Conversation with Baron Apor

Budapest, April 2, 1936

Baron Apor said the Rome pact does not change the situation in the slightest degree. It is merely a demonstration to show that Austria, Hungary and Italy are still working together and was necessitated by the Hodza attempt to pull Austria into the Little Entente. Further, it was noticed that Italy has not given up her interest in European affairs and will have to be reckoned with in anything concerning Central Europe. The French seem to like it and the Germans voice no objection.

Both de Kánya and Gömbös saw the German Ambassador in Rome and he was kept in touch with everything that was done. Hungary had assumed no guarantees of any kind.

General Gömbös' position has not changed. As a matter of fact, Baron Apor said he was not really pro-German: he is just entranced by flag waving and dramatics, and that the trip to Rome hadn't changed him in this respect. However, he did not direct foreign affairs — which is completely

---

68 Sir Geoffrey Knox.
69 Basile Grigorcea.

under the control of de Kánya — and, therefore, what Gömbös thought was not so important.

I asked Baron Apor if they had discussed in Rome the Soviet menace — as exemplified by the airports in Czechoslovakia. He said that they had not because the Hungarian General Staff did not want advice or assistance from anybody: they wished to be completely independent. They felt that no one knew what would happen in the future, and if they got tied up with any one Power, they might find themselves in a war in which they had no interest or thought of entering. That is what happened to them in the last war, and they didn't want to repeat it.

de Kánya said Mussolini is directly responsible for the nervousness now existing in Europe and that he had told him so at Rome; if Mussolini had used ordinary diplomatic means he could have accomplished everything that he had accomplished up to now without upsetting the whole world. He deplored his haste and ill-considered speeches and moves, which he thought unnecessary. He said Mussolini looked well and was very confident. He didn't seem to be the least worried nor to care how nervous the rest of the world was. de Kánya feels that but for the action of Germany, Italy would be in a terrible position, but that Hitler has saved Italy.

[28] Conversation with Baron Apor
Budapest, May 15, 1936

In my conversation yesterday with Baron Apor, I mentioned my trip to Berlin, and particularly the fact that according to information I received there the Germans were anxious to have a strong Hungary and seemed to have no other thought than that it should be independent. Baron Apor said that while the Germans might feel that way, anyone who knew German character could well understand that any favors they extended would be dearly bought. Further, as the Germans become successful their egotism grows and they become different people. Therefore, it might be highly favorable to be tied up with the Germany of today and disastrous with the Germany of tomorrow. Hungary has had one experience along this line and most Hungarians do not care to repeat it. Hungary desires to regain her former territory and prestige, but would prefer to remain in her present state rather than be a vassal of Germany. Nevertheless, it might be that there is nothing else for Hungary to do. She would not voluntarily choose that role.

[29] Conversation with Baron Apor

Budapest, November 3, 1936

Baron Apor told me that Hungary was perfectly willing to do anything in connection with the recognition of Italian sovereignty over Ethiopia that Italy wanted them to do. They had written Count Ciano and asked him if he wanted Hungary to do anything, and had also discussed it with Schmidt,[70] the Austrian Foreign Minister. They have just heard from Ciano, that he wanted Hungary to recognize the situation in Ethiopia, but that he preferred to have them wait until after the meeting in Vienna when probably both Austria and Hungary will act together.

Baron Apor said that Count Ciano looked like a gigolo.[71] He did not seem to think much of his ability. He said that Oxenstierna[72] who was Gustavus Adolphus's[73] great chancellor had once delegated his son to represent Sweden at an important meeting with representatives of other powers, and that when the son demurred and said, "Father, I don't know anything about foreign affairs," his father said, "Never mind, the world is run by fools, anyhow, so go ahead." Baron Apor thought that Ciano's delegation by Mussolini was based upon the same idea. He said that de Kánya did not like it at all, because he had to go to Vienna for a conference with two other foreign ministers, both of whom were so young that their united ages were exactly the same as de Kánya's — 67. He felt as though he was compelled to talk to a couple of school boys.

Apor said that the Regent's meeting with Hitler was merely formal. The Regent had been wanting to go to the mountains in Germany to hunt for years, and finally made up his mind to do so. Etiquette demanded that he call upon Hitler who was in the neighborhood.[74] The Regent had refused an invitation to dinner, because he felt that it would be taken too seriously, so he only went for tea and the conversation had no significance whatever. No one from the Foreign Office accompanied him, and the Regent did not refuse to take anybody along at all. No one had suggested that he do so, as everybody knew that the Regent was not conversant with foreign affairs and had no particular aptitude in that respect, and they preferred to let him say anything he wanted to, or talk about anything he wanted to, as he always

---

70 Guido Schmidt (1901–1957), Austrian secretary of state for foreign affairs, minister from February 1938. After the war he was accused of participating in the secret preparation of the *Anschluß*.

71 A man living off the earnings or gifts of a woman (Italian).

72 Count Axel Oxenstierna (1583–1654), chancellor of Sweden 1612–54.

73 Gustav II Adolph (1594–1632), king of Sweden 1611–32.

74 Regent Horthy visited Hitler in Berchtesgaden, Bavaria, on August 22, 1936.

Kálmán Kánya and Italian foreign minister Count Ciano, 1938

does, knowing that it would have no significance due to the very fact that he was unaccompanied by anyone from the Foreign Office. In other words, they did not want anybody to go along with him, because that would then look to the Germans as if the meeting had more significance than a mere social call.

He said that the Regent had not refused to tell de Kánya what they talked about. On the contrary, de Kánya had never asked him. I said that it was rumored that they discussed Communism. He said, "Of course, they did! Could you imagine the Regent overlooking a good opportunity like that?" But he said that they had never asked him about it because they did not want to know. The Regent's visit had no significance whatever, beyond that of a social meeting, it was entirely friendly so far as he knew, and no incident occurred which was displeasing to the Regent, or if it had, the Regent had never mentioned it.

I asked Baron Apor about Spain, and he said they would follow Germany and Italy and recognize Spain if Germany or Italy wanted them to, and he understood they did. He could not see, however, that Hungary's recognizing either Ethiopia or the insurgents in Spain[75] had any significance whatever, and as far as they were concerned, it was merely a matter of pleasing two big powers with whom they were on friendly terms.

---

75 Gen. Franco's forces.

He mentioned Gömbös' death,[76] and I told him that de Kánya told me that the Regent seemed to be relieved when he heard that he had died, and Baron Apor said, "Yes, he did." In fact, he said that was the best solution. I asked him what the Regent meant by that, and he said that Gömbös was clinging to his job like a woman to her lover, and that it had gotten very embarrassing. When he asked for his leave to go to Bavaria, the Regent was all for refusing it, so as to force him to resign, but they told him that he was in such bad shape that if he were refused the leave it might kill him, and the Regent had to give him six weeks leave, but told him he would not give him any more. They felt sure, however, that at the end of the six weeks he would come back and try to hold his job still, and therefore, his death solved the problem.

He said that Daranyi was terribly bored with his position and did not want to be Prime Minister, but the Regent had insisted upon it, because he wanted the situation to develop and felt that Daranyi could smooth things out. I asked him if this meant that Daranyi would not be there very long. He said, "Not necessarily, because it might take some time before there would be any other person who could be appointed without starting a furor." Daranyi was acceptable because he was a mild person and everybody felt that he was temporary, so were much more disposed to accept him than they would somebody who they felt was a more permanent appointee. He thought, however, that Daranyi would have to stay until everything had been ironed out and some one man came more to the fore than now, and this might take some time. Daranyi, however, was perfectly willing to give up the position, which he did not like, and go back to agriculture, which he liked very much.

[30] Conversation with Baron Bessenyey

[no date][77]

This conversation was very
limited and the only thing he said
which interested me was that
Count Ciano was bringing his wife[78]
and that since she was supposed to

---

76 Prime Minister Gyula Gömbös died on October 6, 1936.
77 Accompanied by his wife, Italian foreign minister Count Ciano visited Budapest on November 13–16, 1936. This conversation with Baron Bessenyey most likely immediately preceded the visit. (Misplaced by Minister Montgomery in his MS.)
78 Mussolini's daughter Edda

look like her father, he was quite
interested in seeing her, as her
father certainly would not take any
prize in a beauty show, an he could
not imagine what a woman looked like
who resembled Mussolini.

I told him that I heard
that Count Ciano looked like a gigolo
and he said he thought that he was
too fat to look like a gigolo.

[31] Conversation with Baron Apor

Budapest, November 16, 1936

Baron Apor told me last night that the only thing important that happened at the Vienna conference[79] was that Mr. de Kánya had so worded the declaration on rearmament that it annoyed the Little Entente without giving them any place to come back. Both he and Mr. de Kánya assured me that the Hungarian policy regarding armaments would not change and they had no intention of making any announcements. Mr. de Kánya gave the same assurance to the Yugoslav Minister.[80] The Yugoslav Minister told me that Count Ciano had told him that Mussolini's reference to revision was only made to please Hungary in return for Hungary's stand on the matter of sanctions. He assured the Yugoslav Minister that it was entirely authentical that no reference should be made to revision during the Regent's visit to Rome.[81]

---

79 The Vienna meeting of the Austrian, Hungarian, and Italian foreign ministers on November 11, 1936.
80 Alexander Vukčević.
81 November 23, 1936.

[32] Conversation with Mr. Ruedemann General Manager of the European Gas & Electric Company

Budapest, November 18, 1936

Mr. Ruedemann told me that a number of Hungarians, including various people in the Ministry of Finance, had told him that he or the President of his company, Mr. Bolton, should know the Regent; that in view of the immense concessions they had and the importance of their development, the matter should be gone over with the Regent.

The President of his company was now in Rumania but would come back when such an interview was arranged. He said the British Legation told him that if it was a British company they would arrange an interview.

Mr. Ruedemann complained of the trouble which they have in connection with getting in their equipment. He said that practically none of it could be secured in Hungary and had to be imported. Before, however, they could import anything they had to make application to the Ministry of Industry, who in turn had to inquire of the Chamber of Industry whether the article desired could be made in Hungary. After this information was secured, the matter was referred to the Department of Commerce and to the Department of Finance, who had the final say. Their application was treated in each Ministry just like anybody else's. They got no priority over an application for a box of golf balls. The result was that even though they worked strenuously, they were unable to get permission to import anything in less time than six or seven months.

He told me that last summer they lost a bit in a hole, in which they had invested $100,000, and before they could get any equipment necessary to remove the bit they lost the hole. He said that if they should strike oil or gas now they would be in an awful fix. He said the company employed about two hundred people, but oftentimes a large majority of them are laid off waiting for supplies, and his company's investment is now about $1,000,000. As their first contract with the Hungarian Government runs only five years, it is important, both for the Government and for his company not to waste any time. If it keeps on as at present they will waste about two and one-half years in the five, and it will make a lot of difference as to whether his company wants to keep on or not; and it may also mean a great deal to the Hungarian Government because every day that they are hindered in their work is a day lost when they might be finding oil. It is possible that at the expiration of their contract they will not have found oil in sufficient quantities to justify their continuing. On the other hand, if they could have devoted their whole time to the work they might find a great deal of oil.

In other words, while they were losing only money, the Hungarian Government might lose the prospect of getting oil, and if their company once gives up it is not probable that any other company is going to come in here and hunt for oil. Therefore, some way of facilitating the securing of supplies and of helping their company is very important for the Hungarian Government; in fact, more important than practically anything else.

[33] Conservation with Baron von Hahn
Budapest, November 27, 1936

Baron von Hahn is very pessimistic about the situation in Europe. He thought that at any moment fighting may break out on three fronts: Spain, Czechoslovakia, and Siberia. He said that the Russians were sending enormous quantities of ammunition, guns and men to Spain; there were 35 ships on the way there now, and that was the reason Franco hadn't been able to take Madrid. It was evident that Franco could not win out unless he had help, and he thought Italy would have to supply that help.

Baron von Hahn wanted to know what I thought about England, what attitude she would take if Germany and Russia went to war. I told him I didn't know, but I didn't believe that England would do anything unless the fighting was on the western front. He, however, brought up the Japanese question and said that the English were very much worried about the Japanese, and it was their customary policy to let someone else do their fighting for them; he thought they would be interested in seeing the Soviets fight the Japanese and would encourage it in the hope of eliminating the Japanese as a factor in the Far East.

Baron von Hahn also told me that there had been a number of protocols signed at Vienna, and among them was one that provided in case one of the three Powers being engaged in war, the other two Powers would observe an attitude of benevolent neutrality. He said that his Minister had asked Ciano what they meant by this, and Ciano illustrated this by saying the same attitude Italy had observed with regard to Spain.

[34] Conversation with Baron Apor
Budapest, December 1, 1936

Baron Apor considers the German-Japanese pact[82] on Bolshevism as silly and of no importance, except that, in his opinion, it lessens the danger of German aggression. He does not think, however, that the Germans have

---

82 Germany and Japan signed the Anti-Comintern Pact on November 25, 1936, in Berlin, which served as a basis for German-Japanese cooperation and aggressive expansionism far beyond its name.

any idea of going to war with anyone at the present time; he believes that their armament is entirely defensive. He is certain of one thing: i.e. whatever ideas the Germans may have they are certainly not in a position at the present time to carry on war because their economic position is so bad that they could not begin to support one. He feels that the economic position of Germany is much worse than generally supposed, and he is certain that it is a matter of great concern to the heads of the German Government. He says that he told de Kánya when he read in the paper that Hitler had had several conferences with Cardinal Faulhaber[83] this was an indication of how bad the situation is because Hitler would never begin to compromise with the Catholic Church unless he needed help.

Baron Apor explained his statement that the German-Japanese pact had lessened the danger of German aggression by saying that the last war had proved that no one could wage a successful war in Europe unless they were allied to either Russia or Great Britain; Great Britain, because she had the navy to assure her of supplies; Russia, because she had the supplies. Germany by her Japanese pact had alienated both Russia and Great Britain, and, therefore, had put herself in a position where she could not wage a successful war. Therefore, instead of increasing the danger of war, in his opinion, it lessened it, although he didn't think there was any particular danger so far as Germany was concerned for the reasons mentioned above.

Baron Apor went on to say that Germany was so afraid of war that at times it is very ludicrous. The articles that have appeared in the German press on revision which created much resentment here were due to the great fear the Germans have that Hungary through revision might drag them into a war. One had to understand the German fear of war to interpret not only their attitude toward revision but everything else they were doing such as the concluding of the German-Japanese pact.

Baron Apor felt that the situation in Spain was very bad, but he didn't think it would lead to any war. In his opinion, whoever finally got control of the country would not get much and would have to have a foreign loan and foreign help to even reorganize the country. So in the last analysis he couldn't see anything but a White victory — either by arms or by control afterwards — because he didn't believe that Great Britain or Italy would stand for a Red government in Spain, because with a Red government there Portugal would go red; and certainly France would, so Great Britain would be deprived of her army. Baron Apor said that Great Britain had the navy but France had the army, and Great Britain counted on the French army for defense.

---

83 Michael von Faulhaber (1869–1952), cardinal archbishop of Munich, a critic and opponent of Nazism.

[35] Conversation with Mr. Baranyai of F. O.[84]

Budapest, December 3, 1936

Mr. Baranyai told me that they had been quite embarrassed when Arcos[85] first made his declaration that he no longer represented the Madrid Government and had gone over to the Burgos[86] side, and for a while they didn't know what to do. Now, however, they were gradually beginning to deal with him as before. In other words, all Spanish matters are handled through him just the same as if he was the Chargé[87] of the Spanish Government. He thought that the Hungarian Government would soon recognize Franco, but in any case they had in effect because they were dealing with Arcos who had declared himself under Franco.

[36] Conversation with Baron Apor

Budapest, December 16, 1936

Baron Apor told me that the article of Herr Rosenberg on revision[88] did not indicate any deterioration in German-Hungarian relations. He said that Germany had always told Hungary that it would not back Hungarian revisionist moves so far as Yugoslavia and Rumania were concerned and that anything Germany did in that connection was no violation of any agreement or anything the Hungarian Government had already been told. He said there were two reasons for the article in question: 1, that Germany was desperate for food supplies which she hoped Rumania would supply; 2, the other was that Herr Rosenberg himself was very much peeved because a lot of girls who had been sent to Hungarian villages last summer for the purpose of spreading Nazi propaganda were expelled by the Hungarian authorities. He added that Herr Rosenberg had no official position[89] and that the propaganda he conducted did not always have the sympathy of the German Government. The girls mentioned above were expelled after they had discussed the

---

84 Dr. Zoltán Baranyai, ministerial councilor in the Hungarian foreign ministry.

85 Carlos Arcos y Cuadra, Spanish chargé in Budapest.

86 Conservative Spanish city, center of the government of Gen. Franco from July 1936. It became the symbol of Franco's politics.

87 Temporary chief of diplomatic mission.

88 Alfred Rosenberg published his article in the *Völkischer Beobachter* on November 15, 1936, on "The Oppression of Peoples and the Revision of Treaties."

89 Rosenberg was then the head of the foreign department of the Nazi Party, i.e., not a government official.

matter with von Neurath, who advised them to expel the girls at once — and they followed his advice.

Baron Apor said that there was Nazi propaganda and that there had been complaints made to the German authorities about it, but that while the propaganda was very annoying it was not so widespread as to cause concern. It took money to conduct propaganda and the Hungarian Government was watching the situation carefully and knew that Germany couldn't spend any great amount of money here without their knowledge. They felt reasonably certain that such money as they were spending was not a large amount.

I told Baron Apor that I knew von Mackensen had been called down a number of times because of German propaganda. He admitted this was true but he said that von Mackensen was about as bad, as his own Government didn't approve of the propaganda but they couldn't always control the Nazi party.

Baron Apor mentioned German propaganda in Austria and said that while in his opinion three-fourths of Austria was Nazi, there was no particular trouble, and that Germany had stopped spending money there. He felt that whatever Germany did here was no menace to Hungary in view of the fact that there was practically no German Nazi sentiment in Hungary as there was in Austria. He said the Hungarian Government was annoyed at the things that had been done but were not particularly disturbed.

Baron Apor said that nothing had happened to change the situation and that Hungary was well contented not to have too close affiliations with Germany, that if Germany would announce she was backing Hungary's revision claims against all three countries they would be more nervous than they are now because it would indicate that Germany was getting too friendly for company.

[37] Conversation with Baron Apor

Budapest, December 16, 1936

Baron Apor told me that the economic situation in Germany was getting very bad, particularly a great shortage of food. He said that in recent years Germany had been making trade agreements with Danubian countries by which they exchanged their various products in return for food products. They had now owed Hungary and Yugoslavia quite a lot of money for goods which these countries were unable to absorb, and in view of the rise in the world's food products in the world markets and the fact that Hungary and Yugoslavia could not obtain gold for their food products, the possibility of Germany continuing to get her food from the Danubian States was not very good unless she was prepared to put up gold — which was the last thing she wanted to do or could do.

Baron Apor attributed the German gestures towards Yugoslavia as evidenced by Rosenberg's article — which caused so much furor here — to the fact that Germany was so desperate for food products she hoped to induce Rumania to give her some supplies.

1937

[38] Conversation with Foreign Minister de Kánya

Budapest, January 25, 1937

In a recent conversation with Mr. de Kánya the Minister for Foreign Affairs, he told me that the Regent would make a state visit to Warsaw in the near future. He said that this was at the suggestion of the Polish Government, although it was very pleasing to the Hungarian Government to have the Regent make the visit. As both he and Madame Horthy made an excellent impression in Italy, and inasmuch as there is a certain amount of such visiting to be done, the Regent, although no politician, had shown that both he and Madame Horthy made splendid representatives for their country.

[39] Conversation with Dr. Tibor Eckhardt

Budapest, January 25, 1937

In a conversation yesterday, Dr. Eckhardt told me that he had given the Prime Minister, Mr. Daranyi, a list of the reasons why he considered Minister of Interior Kozma should not be retained in office.[90] These cover the fact that he is a large stockholder in the radio-broadcasting and picture producing companies, and that this was incompatible with his position as Minister. Eckhardt spoke particularly of all the decrees which have been issued in favor of the picture producing companies since Mr. Kozma took office.

Eckhardt said he expected Kozma to resign within a week or two. If he did not, he would present in Parliament the same list furnished Mr. Daranyi, which would then have to make an investigation. If Kozma resigns he believes that Prime Minister Daranyi would take over the Ministry of Interior,[91] or if he did not, Mikes, now Secretary of State, would become Minister. If Kozma refuses to resign so that it would be necessary to take the matter up in

---

90 Minister of the Interior Miklós Kozma resigned on January 29, 1937.
91 Prime Minister Kálmán Darányi was commanded on February 3, 1937, to act as a temporary head of the Ministry of the Interior.

Parliament he predicted a coalition Government including his own and the Christian Socialists[92] headed by Prime Minister Daranyi.

[40] Conversation with Baron Apor

Budapest, January 29, 1937

Baron Apor told me quite confidentially that Poland and Rumania had an arrangement whereby Rumania agreed not to let Russian troops through their territory. I asked if this was a formal agreement, or how it was done. He said that Poland and Rumania had simply made a new treaty, or come to a new understanding, and Poland had said that they would consider by this arrangement any passage of Russian troops through Rumania without Poland's consent would be a violation, and that Rumania had agreed to this construction of the agreement.

Baron Apor is not so optimistic as Mr. de Kánya as to the possibilities. He felt that France would not want the Little Entente to become too friendly

Baron Gábor Apor upon his arrival as Hungarian minister to Vienna, 1934

---

92 A reference probably to the Christian Economic and Social Party.

with Hungary and that she would put pressure on at the proper time to prevent it. He said that France was much opposed to the Yugoslav-Bulgarian treaty[93] and had made protests both at Belgrade and Sofia. However, he confirmed de Kánya's statement that the various Ministers had called and he thought there might be a possibility of an era of better feeling for the time being. However, he said Rumania could not be depended on. While they had an anti-Russian policy now they might call Titulesco back tomorrow and be pro-Russian again.

Baron Apor confirmed the fact that Poland is making every effort to line up all the various countries against both Germany and Russia, and that Poland had requested Hungary to become more friendly with Rumania.

Baron Apor also told me that he had heard from their Minister in Paris[94] that the French were bringing pressure on the Russians to get them to change their attitude on Spain. He said that the Franco-Russian pact had only been agreed to in principle. The details had never been drawn up and Russia was very anxious to have this done. The French have now told the Russians that if they would give up their Spanish policy and conform to the Franco-British policy they would proceed with the construction of the treaty. However, he said this did not come from official sources but was information picked up by their Minister in Paris from newspapermen, but people who were well-informed and reliable. He thought there might be something to it.

[41] Conversation with the Regent

Budapest, February 2, 1937

The Regent asked me about the floods in the United States and told me about the floods they used to have in Hungary. He expressed great sympathy and said "Isn't it too bad, President Roosevelt has done everything just right and now this terrible thing has to happen."

The conversation switched to Italy, and he spoke of the great work that Mussolini had done. He said that a dictator had a great advantage over a democratic form of government so long as the dictator didn't go too far.

He mentioned Hitler's work in Germany, how he regenerated the German people who were in the depths of despair as a result of the Treaty of Versailles. He said that had France shown any moderation the situation today would have been different, but they were only anxious to do every-

---

93 The Yugoslav-Bulgarian treaty of friendship was signed on January 24, 1937.
94 Count Sándor Khuen-Héderváry (1881–1947).

thing to destroy their foes, and now look at France. She is no longer the dictator of Europe.

I mentioned England, and he said that he was very fond of the English people, had been around the world and everywhere the English were in charge things were well run, but he thought that England was now a decadent nation and was on the downgrade.

He expressed the opinion that the greatest danger today was subversive activities of the Bolshevists. He said you could fight a foe you could see and meet, but all this undercover business was difficult to deal with that the nations should get together and go in and simply whip the Bolshevists. He was in hearty sympathy with Hitler's ideas on this subject.

[42] Conversation with Mr. Bossy Rumanian Minister[95]

Budapest, February 5, 1937

Mr. Bossy confirmed the statement that Rumania was anxious to be on more friendly relations with Hungary and that she had asked the good offices of the Polish Government to that end. He told me that he had a number of conversations with Mr. de Kánya but that so far there had been no indication of what Mr. de Kánya's ideas were, nor had he made any suggestions as to how it could come about except that Rumania must first recognize the equality of Hungary and give better treatment to the Hungarian minorities. He said Rumania was perfectly willing to recognize the equality of Hungary, but first there must be some gesture on Hungary's part, no matter what it was. For example, he said Hungary had signed the Kellogg Pact[96] and if Daranyi or de Kánya would publicly state that they have no idea of aggression against Rumania that the Prime Minister could well arise in Parliament and recognize the equality of Hungary; and also better treatment of minorities would naturally follow. He denied that there was any real complaint in respect to the treatment of minorities and said the Hungarian Government had never given them any specific incidents and had only made general statements.

---

95 Raoul Bossy, Romanian minister to Budapest 1936–39.

96 Initiated by French foreign minister and Nobel laureate (1926) Aristide Briand and U.S. Secretary of State and Nobel laureate (1929) Frank Billings Kellogg, the Briand-Kellogg [or Paris] Pact was signed in Paris on August 27, 1928. Hungary joined the Pact in Budapest, on February 14, 1929. "The Pact for the Renunciation of War" meant to unite "the civilized nations of the world in a common renunciation of war as an instrument of their national policy." Raymond Phineas Stearns, ed., *op. cit.,* 902–3.

I asked whether in their desire for friendship with Hungary, Rumania was joined by the other members of the Little Entente, and he said "Yes, very much, all three governments are willing and anxious to be friendly but they think the first move should come from Hungary, or at least some suggestion that could be used for a conference." I asked whether Rumania and Yugoslavia would make separate treaties of friendship, or whether they would insist upon being made with the Little Entente. He said "Of course, this is a matter for conference, but I think it should be made with all three countries."

Mr. Bossy said that it was to the Hungarians' credit that they had never publicly said anything but that they were for peaceful revision and therefore they could not be accused of aggressiveness in a military sense. He thought now it would be a good time to reiterate these statements. Anything, no matter how small, that could be used as a gesture form Hungary would be welcome.

I asked Mr. Bossy if he was optimistic in reference to something actually being accomplished, and he replied he was very much so, although his colleagues, Mr. Kobr[97] and Mr. Vouktchevitch,[98] were very pessimistic and didn't think anything could be accomplished. He has had two or three conference with de Kánya in fact, had dinner with him last night, but so far de Kánya has never given him any idea that his advances were welcomed. On the other hand, he had not indicated that they were unwelcome. In fact, he didn't know what was going on in de Kánya's mind.

He mentioned Hitler's speech and its lack of reference to Czechoslovakia as one of the friendly countries, and said he thought that it was high time for the Danubian countries to get together, or at least be more friendly. Otherwise, their position later in reference to Germany might not be so happy. He thought this particularly applied to Hungary as well as Czechoslovakia.

Mr. Bossy said that recognition by Hungary of the existing boundaries was not necessary. The Succession States held the territory and therefore will not require Hungary to make this recognition.

---

97 Miloš Kobr, Czechoslovak minister to Budapest 1933–38.
98 Alexander Vukčević, Yugoslav minister to Budapest 1934–38.

[43] Conversations

Budapest, February 9, 1937

with
Mr. Vouktchévitch, the Yugoslav Minister,
Mr. de Kánya, the Hungarian Foreign Minister
Mr. Bossy, the Rumanian Minister

The Yugoslav Minister, Mr. Vouktchévitch, greatly astonished me at the Nuncio's[99] tea last Saturday (February 6th) by saying that he had information that I had sent a telegram to the Department of State saying that the Little Entente had gone to Mr. de Kánya with an offer to compose their differences. He was very positive in his statement and reiterated several times with the additional statement that there could be no mistake. He denied categorically that the Little Entente had made any such offer or that he himself had made any offer or suggestion to Mr. de Kánya. He admitted that he had called on Mr. de Kánya several times and when the subject of better relations with his country had come up and a non-aggression pact had been suggested, said that these suggestions had come entirely from Mr. de Kánya and not from him.

When I saw Mr. de Kánya yesterday (February 8th) and told him that the Yugoslav Minister had made this statement, Mr. de Kánya said that the truth of the matter was that Mr. Kobr, the Czechoslovak Minister, had come to see him shortly after the Rumanian Prime Minister had talked to the Hungarian Minister in Bucharest, that Mr. Kobr made definite suggestions of a non-aggression pact, that Mr. Vouktchévitch indicated a knowledge of the object of Mr. Kobr's visit and had said that he personally had initiated the Bulgarian-Yugoslav pact when he was Minister in Sofia and that he asked Mr. de Kánya what he thought of such a pact with Hungary. Mr. de Kánya told me that he understood that Hodza had denied the Czechoslovak offer, and that neither this denial nor what the Yugoslav Minister had to say made the slightest difference to him. He was interested only in the settlement of the difficulties, and any move in that direction was welcome. The important thing was that there was a disposition towards peace and better relations, and he was willing to meet his neighbors more than half-way to that end.

Mr. de Kánya said that he fully realized all the difficulties and that he did not think he would ever live to see it accomplished. He expected no miracles and knew that it was a long road ahead to the actual settlement of their difficulties.

---

99 Mgr. Angelo Rotta, apostolic nuncio [envoy of the Holy See] in Budapest.

Mr. de Kánya said that the Rumanian Minister had suddenly quit calling on him and he thought that this was the cause of the bad reception of the Rumanian Prime Minister's statement that relations with Hungary were improving. He also thought that the Rumanian Government was weak and that it might be succeeded by the Manui [= Maniu] party, and that Titulescu would return.

Mr. de Kánya said, however, that the rapprochement between Yugoslavia and Italy would make for certain improved relations with Hungary, and he felt that Poland was giving Rumania good advice. He thought that although there were many uncertainties the situation was not as hopeless as it has been before.

Mr. Bossy, the Rumanian Minister, in a conversation which I had with him about a week ago was very enthusiastic over the idea of a Hungarian-Rumanian or Little Entente rapprochement. He confirmed Mr. de Kánya's statement that Poland was making an effort to better relations between the two countries and said that he had had a number of conversations with Mr. de Kánya to that end, but that Mr. de Kánya had not made any suggestions as to how it could come about, except that Rumania must first recognize the equality of Hungary and give better treatment to Hungarian minorities. He said Rumania was perfectly willing to recognize the equality of Hungary but first there must be some gesture on Hungary's part, no matter how small. For example, he said that Hungary had signed the Kellogg Pact and that if Daranyi and de Kánya would publicly state that they had no idea of aggression against Rumania then the Rumanian Prime Minister could well arise in Parliament and recognize the equality of Hungary and better treatment of minorities would naturally follow. He denied, however, that there was any real complaint with respect to the treatment of minorities and said that the Hungarian Government had never given them any specific instances and had made only general statements. I asked him whether in their desire for friendship with Hungary, Rumania was joined by the other members of the Little Entente. He said, "Yes, very much, all three governments are willing and anxious to be friendly but they think the first move should come from Hungary, or at least some suggestion that could be used for a conference." I asked whether Rumania and Yugoslavia would make separate treaties of friendship, or whether they would insist on these being made with the Little Entente. He said, "Of course, this is a matter for conference, but I think it should be made with all three countries."

Mr. Bossy said that it was to the Hungarians' credit that they had never publicly said anything but that they were for peaceful revision and therefore they could not be accused of aggressiveness. He thought it would be a good time to reiterate these statements. Anything, no matter how small, could be used as a gesture would be welcome. He told me that he had had a number of conferences with Mr. Kánya but that they had never gotten any further. On the other hand he had not indicated that the conversations were unwelcomed.

In a second conversation which I had with Mr. Bossy directly after I was accused by the Yugoslav Minister last Saturday, Mr. Bossy was disposed to hedge very materially. I told him what Mr. Vouktchévitch has said, but I couldn't get him to commit himself. He still expressed the idea that Rumania was anxious for peace with Hungary. In fact, he said that Rumania was in the position of a girl in love with a man but he would not speak and she could do nothing but wait.

Mr. Kobr, the Czechoslovak Minister, has been making repeated and sudden visits to Prague during the last two weeks. He was to be at the diplomatic mass on Sunday[100] but his place was vacant. Mr. de Kánya told me that he had asked to see him today, and he assumed it was something in connection with their previous conversations. Mr. de Kánya said that he knew unofficial negotiations were going on between Czechoslovakia and Germany. He personally couldn't see how anything could come of these as long as the Czechs had their treaty with Russia. However, if such a treaty did come about the Czechs would be much less interested in making peace with Hungary.

[44] Conversation with Mr. Kobr, Czechoslovak Minister

Budapest, February 11, 1937

Mr. Kobr told me that he had called on Mr. de Kánya and suggested to him that Hungary ought to make some sort of peace with her neighbors and have them recognize her rights to equality. He told Mr. de Kánya that he knew that Italy, Germany and Austria were all ready to recognize Hungary's equality but that this was not enough and it would be a very simple matter to have the Little Entente also recognize this equality without in any way touching on the question of revision. He suggested to Mr. de Kánya that Czechoslovakia was willing to make the same sort of a 10-year non-aggression pact that Germany had made with Poland,[101] and if Hungary was will-

---

100 On the anniversary of the coronation of Pope Pius XI (February 6, 1922), the papal nuncio, Mgr. Angelo Rotta, celebrated a mass in the Mátyás church in Buda Castle every year. The diplomatic corps were invited by Jusztinián Cardinal Serédi, prince archbishop of Esztergom, and a confidant of the pope.

101 On January 26, 1934, the Berlin declaration on the political relations between Germany and Poland stated "they would seek the solution of contentious questions through peaceful means."

ing to do this and also to define an aggressor Czechoslovakia was ready to give them in turn recognition of rights to equality.

Mr. Kobr said that he felt that Mr. de Kánya was shrewd enough that this offer had considerable advantage to Hungary, but he said that he (de Kánya) was very anxious and so far had not given them any reply. Mr. Kobr also thought that it was possible Italy was not in favor of Hungary doing anything and that this might be the reason Mr. de Kánya hadn't done any more. He thought also that Mr. de Kánya was too old and not energetic enough.

Mr. Kobr mentioned Eckhardt and said that he was a friend of Hodza, the Czech Prime Minister, and that he was a more intelligent man, that they were very much pleased to see him coming into power. He felt that opportunities for better relations, or at least discussions, were more favorable with Eckhardt than with de Kánya.

Mr. Kobr confirmed Mr. de Kánya's statement that unofficial negotiations were going on between Germany and Czechoslovakia, but said that Czechoslovakia couldn't make any agreement with Germany without the consent of the Little Entente.

Mr. Kobr told me that he had a wire from their Minister in Washington who told him that he had been to the State Department where they told him they had information that the Little Entente had offered Hungary a nonaggression pact. When I first saw Mr. Kobr he seemed to be terribly nervous and talked so much and so loud that I couldn't even ask him a question. He kept this up for about fifteen minutes. Everything I said was lost in his flights of oratory, mostly directed against everybody who was spreading rumors — presumably the Hungarians, but also some Rumanian news agency that had printed a report about a change in the Little Entente. Finally, however, he ran down and I got a chance to talk to him.

[45] Conversation of February 13th with Baron Apor of F.O.

Budapest, February 15, 1937

Baron Apor told me that there was no truth in the statement that the Hungarian Government had made a démarche at Vienna with regard to the intentions of the Austrian Government so far as Otto is concerned. He said that it would be very embarrassing to the Hungarian Government to have Otto restored in Austria but that the Hungarian Government took the position that this was entirely an internal question and was for Austria alone to decide. Inasmuch as the Hungarian Government took the same position with regard to its own affairs it would be very odd for it to take any other position with regard to Austria.

Baron Apor said that in his opinion 1/3 of Austria was royalist, 1/3 Nazi, and 1/3 Socialist. The French and the Czechs are now very much worried about Germany and therefore both are in favor of restoring the monarchy in Austria. The Czechs have for years subsidized the Socialists and therefore had considerable control over them, and it is highly probable that the Socialists would agree to return to the monarchy, not only because of the Czechs but also because they realize it would help to prevent Austria going Nazi. Nevertheless, there were many countries that are violently opposed to the restoration, and no one knows what would happen if it were done. He said that Germany and Yugoslavia both had tried to induce the Hungarian Government to protest, and both of these Powers were very determined to prevent a Hapsburg being named Emperor.

In connection with the Nazi movement in Hungary, Baron Apor mentioned von Mackensen. He said he (von Mackensen) was a very difficult man to deal with and was not cut out to be a diplomat; he was a soldier and that made it much more difficult to control him. He said that von Mackensen believed in associating with those in power, particularly military people, and lately he refused to meet Count Bethlen because he was in opposition to the Government. He said that when he talked with him once lately, von Mackensen mentioned Gömbös as one of the greatest men of Europe. Apor laughed at this and said that he told von Mackensen that while he was sorry to see Gömbös die, if he hadn't died he would have been out of office by September.[102] Von Mackensen was astonished and was disposed to dispute this, saying it could not be possible. Apor laughed again and said that he apparently knew very little of what was going on in the country.

Baron Apor didn't think the Nazi movement was growing as much as Baron von Hahn thought.

[46] Conversation with Mr. de Kánya

February 22, 1937

The Little Entente. He said that there had been no further conversations since I last called upon him. He said, however, that the Foreign Minister of Rumania had discussed the matter with the Prime Minister of Yugoslavia during the recent Balkan Conference at Athens,[103] and that he understood

---

102 Regent Horthy refrained from forcing the prime minister to resign with a view to his serious state of health; Gömbös died on October 6, 1936, near Munich.
103 The Balkan Conferences were organized annually starting October 1930.

that they were to discuss it with the Czech Prime Minister, after which he thought he would hear more from them.

He considered the situation was improved, that the feeling between Yugoslavia and Hungary was getting better all the time, and that he still felt they were on the way to a better understanding with the Little Entente, which would bear fruit in time. He said that all four countries were toning down their press, and that he felt the situation was very satisfactory. This was something, he said, that could not be done in a hurry, as it wasn't a question of just offering a peace pact and immediately accepting it.[104] It was a question of making a better understanding all around, and gradually working up to something definite at the proper time. He said that the people of Hungary and all the Little Entente countries had been so worked up against one another that you couldn't change them in a few days, and no country could do anything without the support of their own people.

The Hungarian people are most interested in seeing that their fellow-Hungarians in other countries are properly treated, and in order to accomplish this they would go a long way. He said that they had to be convinced that they were accomplishing something, otherwise they would not want to do anything. If the better feeling that now exists bore fruit in the better treatment of Hungarian minorities, than a whole lot of things could be done. In Yugoslavia, he felt that it had, but as far as Czechoslovakia and Rumania were concerned, there had not been anything to indicate that they had changed their policy toward the minorities, although at present, there were no particular evidences of any new oppression, in fact, everything was very quiet.

[47] Conversation with Mr. de Kánya

February 22, 1937

Restoration.[105] Mr. de Kánya does not think that restoration will take place in the near future. He said that Mr. Schussnigg was a very well-balanced man and would not do anything rash. He knew very well how strong the opposition of Germany and Yugoslavia and the Hungarian Government would be, and he told me confidentially that he had discussed the matter with Mussolini, and that Mussolini did not think that anything should be done at the present time. He said that Mr. Kobr had told him that Czechoslovakia was now in favor of restoration as an antidote for the Anschluss.

---

104 Foreign Minister Kánya immediately rejected the Czechoslovak and Romanian proposals of January 22, 1937.

105 Comments here refer to the restoration of the rights of the Habsburg house to reign.

Mr. de Kánya did not know whether Rumania was still opposed or not, but he did know the opposition of Yugoslavia and Germany was very great. He did not know what would happen if restoration did take place, but he said that inasmuch as he did not consider it a possibility in the immediate future, he had not given much time to considerations of what the Germans and Yugoslavs would do, except that he knew it would be a very bad situation. As far as Hungary is concerned, while restoration in Austria might make it more difficult for the present Hungarian Government, he did not believe that there was any thought of restoration nor any possibility of it. The Hungarian Government is introducing a bill to fix the succession, and they would hardly do this if there was any idea of there being a king on the throne very soon.

I asked him if he thought it was possible for a man to be king of two countries in these days, and he said he did not unless two countries were going to join together. The difficulties of restoration in Austria were great, but the difficulties in Hungary were greater, and particularly so if it were the same king, because that is what the Yugoslavs feared most. Their opposition to a king in Austria is based on the idea that it meant the return of the Austro-Hungarian Empire. If there were separate kings it would be easier, but any Hapsburg on the throne of either country would be opposed violently by Yugoslavia. If a Hapsburg returned to the throne in Austria, the Yugoslavs would concentrate on Hungary and make it practically a cause of war if Hungary followed suit. He did not believe, however, that there was any use in speculating at present, as restoration wasn't imminent in either country, and conditions might change by the time there was a possibility of restoration.

[48] Conversation with Tibor Eckhardt

March 6, 1937

Bethlen Negotiations. Mr. Eckhardt said that the Prime Minister and Mr. de Kánya had asked Count Bethlen to conduct negotiations with the Rumanian Government on the subject of the treatment of minorities, taking advantage of the opening given by the Rumanian Government in having expressed the desire for better relations with Hungary. Count Bethlen was asked to do this because he is a Transylvanian, and his brother is the leader of the Hungarian Minority in Rumania and it was thought that through the Rumanian Minister here and his brother in Rumania, he might make more progress than the Foreign Office could. In view of the fact that the Foreign Office did not desire to commit themselves as they believe that the Rumanian Government is not strong enough at the present time to live up to any promises they might make, Count Bethlen is supposed to deal with the Gov-

ernment unofficially through the Rumanian Minister and with various people in Rumania through his brother;[106] the idea being that if by this method
the question of minorities can be settled, the Hungarian Government is ready
to enter into some negotiations for a treaty of friendship or something similar.

Count Bethlen has had several conversations with the Rumanian Minister and during at least one of these conversations, the Yugoslav Minister
was present. The basis on which Count Bethlen is working is that they forget every other subject and discuss how the provisions of the Treaty of Trianon could be carried out in a manner satisfactory to the Rumanian Government and to the Hungarian minority.

Mr. Eckhardt said that it was too soon to report any progress, particularly
in view of the Iron Guard[107] trouble in Rumania. The Government at the present time is on the defensive, and any movement toward better relations with
the Hungarian minority might weaken them, unless they could get support
from the opposition or at least be sure that it would not be used against the
Government.

Mr. Eckhardt said that the Yugoslav Minister's participation in the conference was merely a gesture and that relations with Yugoslavia were improving every day. He had been invited because it was felt that in view of the
improved relations, the Yugoslav Government might like to know what was
going on with their ally, and might even be inclined to assist. (In this connection, it is interesting that Kobr told me of these conferences. When I mentioned that I had seen the Yugoslav Minister the night before and he had not
said a word to me about them, he said that the Yugoslav Minister had not
mentioned it to him either. He had learned of it from the Rumanian Minister,
and he asked me not to tell the Yugoslav Minister that he, Kobr, had told me
about it.)

[49] Conversation with Mr. Tibor Eckhardt

March 6, 1937

Nazi Propaganda. Mr. Eckhardt said that during the last six weeks the
German Government had greatly increased the amount of money which
they were spending in Hungary for Nazi propaganda. It had been known for

---

106 Count István Bethlen had no brothers; this must be a misunderstanding or a mistake.
    His cousin Count György Bethlen was vice-president (1924) and, subsequently, (1926),
    president of the National Hungarian Party in Transylvania.
107 *Garda de Fier,* Romanian Fascist organization, founded by Corneliu Zelea Codreanu
    in 1927. Known and feared for its mystical nationalism, anti-Semitism and brutality,
    the *Garda* was active between 1930 and 1941 under different names.

some time that some of the men prominent during the Gömbös administrations had been acting as go-between for the German Government and the Hungarian Nazi Party, but there had never been any direct evidence, and while the Government had repeatedly warned von Mackensen, they had done nothing further.

The great increase in the amount of money spent during the last six weeks had given impetus to the Nazi movement, and the Government therefore had determined to make an investigation and to take some action. Mr. Eckhardt and Prime Minister Daranyi had discussed the matter a few days ago, and yesterday the Prime Minister discussed it with the Regent.

Although the investigation has only been under way for about a week, they have discovered evidence that certain German firms were engaged in transferring money for Nazi activity. No action will be taken until the investigation is completed, but Mr. Eckhardt thought that the matter would have to be taken up seriously with the German Government, and that some drastic steps would have to be taken to remedy the situation and prevent further interference in local politics by the German Government.

The group Mr. Eckhardt said has charge of acting in Hungary on behalf of the German Government is composed of Andrew Mecser,[108] leader, Bela Marton,[109] former secretary of the National Union Party under Gömbös, is acting as administrative officer; Colonel George Biro,[110] formerly connected with the Hungarian secret service, is acting in a similar capacity with this group; and these, with Andrew Toth,[111] John Szeder[112] and Francis Ra[j]niss,[113] make up the group. They have been keeping in close touch with Mackensen and von Hahn and had been furnishing money and directing secretly the Hungarian Nazi Party. The German Government itself had no direct connection with the Hungarian Nazis.

Francis Ra[j]niss is the editor of Uj Magyarsag, a Government newspa-

---

108 András Mecsér, *vitéz* (1883–?), extreme right wing, pro-Nazi politician, MP, follower of Gömbös, later minister to Berlin during the Szálasi regime.
109 Béla Marton, *vitéz* (1896–1960), executive director of MOVE during the presidency of Gyula Gömbös. MP from 1931, follower of Gömbös, an organizer, subsequently national executive secretary general of the National Union Party [NEP].
110 György Biró, *vitéz* (1882–?), retired colonel working for the secret service, MP of the National Union Party [NEP] from 1935.
111 Dr. András Tóth, *vitéz* (1892–?), lawyer, right-wing politician, organizer of the Alliance of Veterans. MP of the National Union Party [NEP] from 1935.
112 János Szeder (1896–?), racist politician ("defender of the race"), executive vice-president of MOVE, MP of the National Union Party [NEP] from 1935.
113 Ferenc Rajnis (Rajniss) (1893–1946), extreme right-wing journalist and politician, MP from 1935, minister of religion and education in the Szálasi government of 1944–45.

per, which is violently pro-German; and all the men mentioned are former followers of Gömbös and are still members of the National Union Party.[114] Mr. Eckhardt said that the policy of Uj Magyarsag was disapproved by the Hungarian Foreign Office, but that Prime Minister Daranyi had hesitated to remove Ra[j]niss and change their policy on account of German pressure, particularly in view of the fact that there had not hitherto been anything definite to connect him directly with the German Nazi movement in Hungary.

Mr. Eckhardt was sure that disciplinary measures would have to be taken against all the men named above, and he thought that protests would probably be made to Berlin; but he said that nothing could be determined until the results of the investigation were known. He is working with Mr. Daranyi in this matter and has delayed his trip to Italy for the purpose of keeping in touch with the investigation.

Mr. Eckhardt said that the Jews were very much excited by the apparent increase in Nazi sentiment, and had exaggerated the results obtained by Nazi propaganda out of all proportion to the actual facts. As a matter of fact, he said, that the Nazi movement was made up entirely of unemployed and dissatisfied people who were receiving some sort of compensation for being Nazis. He estimated that the whole movement was not supported by more than 10% of the population and 5% of the electorate and that even that following could not have been obtained except by the spending of considerable money.

Mr. Eckhardt said that there were some curious disappearances which looked as though they might have been caused by the investigation being made. First, von Mackensen suddenly decided to take a vacation in Athens. Von Hahn became enamored of skiing in Austria and had gone there. The Chief of Police of Budapest, who has been peculiarly derelict in many matters in connection with Nazi activity, had to go away suddenly for his health. He did not know whether all these vacations were actually caused by the investigation, but it was generally supposed that these individuals thought it a good time to be somewhere else. The Chief of Police is Tibor Ferenczi.

Mr. Eckhardt said that as a result of this group having gone so far without the Government suspecting it, Mr. Tahy,[115] Under-secretary in the Prime

---

114 Eckhardt speaks here of the MOVE coup, an attempt of the extreme right to remove Prime Minister Darányi [MOVE = Magyar Országos Véderő Egylet, Hungarian National Defense Association]. The affair compromised Hans Georg von Mackensen, German minister to Budapest, a patron of the so-called "Gömbös-orphans" (Mecsér, Marton) who was recalled by Berlin.

115 Dr. László Tahy (1881–1940), diplomat, politician. Hungarian minister to Ankara, Turkey, between 1914 and 1933, minister to Bern, Switzerland and the League of Nations in 1934, secretary of state in the prime minister's office from January 1935, MP from 1935, secretary of state in the Ministry of the Interior after 1938.

Ministry who is directly in charge of political affairs will be retired. Mr. Mikecz,[116] who is one of Mr. Eckhardt's followers, and is now Under-secretary in the Ministry of the Interior, will succeed Mr. Tahy. Mr. Mikecz was until a few months ago in charge of the Press Bureau in the Prime Ministry and is considered quite an able politician. When the Minister of Interior, Kozma, resigned, the Prime Minister assumed his portfolio, because Mr. Eckhardt wished Mr. Mikecz to be the real head of the Ministry of Interior until the secret ballot bill was drawn up.

In view of the necessity of transferring Mr. Mikecz to the Prime Ministry, it has now been arranged that Mr. Lazar,[117] the Minister of Justice, will be charged with drawing up the secret ballot bill, and Justice Scell,[118] now Vice-President of the Supreme Court Administration will probably be appointed Minister of the Interior.

[50] Conversation with Mr. Tibor Eckhardt
March 6, 1937

Tisza Irrigation Project. Mr. Eckhardt said that conditions in the eastern part of Hungary had been bad ever since the war, because the control of the upper Tisza had passed into the hands of the Little Entente, and that all the elaborate storage dams which Hungary had built had been destroyed.

Therefore, there had been a constant shortage of water on the great plains, and most of eastern Hungary. The Hungarian Government is now considering a plan to build a canal from Csepel Island near Budapest to the Tisza river,[119] for the purpose of diverting water from the Danube to the Tisza. They would then build a dam on the Tisza river for the purpose of storing this water, which could be used for irrigation as needed. He said that the Tisza is ten meters lower than the Danube, and therefore, the water would run by gravity, and the only expense would be the cost of the project. He

---

116 Dr. Ödön Mikecz (1894–1965), lawyer, lord lieutenant 1932–35, minister of justice in the governments of Darányi and Imrédy.

117 Dr. Andor Lázár (1882–1971), lawyer, minister of justice 1932–38.

118 József Széll (1880–1956) lord lieutenant 1908–17 and 1925–32, second president of the Court of Public Administration 1933–37, member of the Upper House of Parliament, minister of the interior 1937–38.

119 By this time the project of a canal connecting the Danube and the Tisza rivers had a long history. It was seriously considered in 1839, 1868, and 1907, but subsequent governments were all deterred by the estimated costs. The Tiszalök dam was started in 1942, and another power station was also being built at Kesznyéten, Zemplén County, on a canal starting at the Hernád River.

said that the Danube had more water than it needed, and the International Danubian Committee had agreed to this diversion of the Danubian water.

The total cost of the project would be Pengő 300,000,000; Pengő 200,000,000 for the canal itself and 100,000,000 for the dam and restoration of irrigation systems. The Regent is very much interested in the matter, and Nicholas Kallay, former Minister of Agriculture, had been appointed to take charge of the project. The only question now is to get the money, but he felt that they would find ways and means to get it as it is a very necessary project.

[51] Conversation with Tibor Eckhardt

March 6, 1937

Crops

Mr. Eckhardt told me that he feared that next year the crops would not be good on account of the very bad winter we had. He suggested to the Prime Minister that provisions be made to retain the balance of last year's wheat crop, so that there would be no shortage of food. He said that if the crop was bad, the situation of the peasants who receive no pay but only a portion of the crop would be terrible, and there would be a corresponding unrest; and if no wheat was retained there might be even famine.

[52] Conversation with Tibor Eckhardt

March 6, 1937

Communist Propaganda

Mr. Eckhardt told me there was a curious kind of Communist propaganda coming into both Hungary and Rumania from Czechoslovakia. It consisted of Bibles with interpretations justifying and approving communism. Mr. Eckhardt said that these were not being distributed in Czechoslovakia, but that a number of them had been found in Hungary and at one spot on the border, they had confiscated several hundred copies.

[53] Conversation with Mr. Milos Kobr Czechoslovak Minister, on March 10

March 11, 1937

Mr. Kobr is getting so worked up over Mr. de Kánya that it is almost impossible to talk to him any place where Mr. de Kánya is present. Last night at the Turkish Legation at a dinner given for de Kánya, Mr. Kobr got so excited and so loud in his denunciation of de Kánya — calling him almost every name he could think of — I had to move away from him several times. One time he took me clear into another room and began to talk about the Nazi business, and apparently he knew everything we knew. He then said in a loud voice: "Why don't the damned fools do what we want them to, come in and stop Germany?" I asked him who the "we" were, and he replied the Little Entente. I asked "Is the Little Entente endeavoring to make peace with Hungary?" and he replied "Yes, but that old devil, etc., etc.,", so that I had to suggest that we better go and talk to someone else. People could hear him shouting even from the other room, for several persons asked me what was going on.

Countess Csáky, sister of Istvan Csáky (Secretary of State in the F.O.) mentioned in the early part of the evening something about the Nazi trouble and said there was nothing to it at all. I asked where she heard that, and she said that Mr. de Kánya told her. I said that perhaps de Kánya didn't tell her everything. She said "Yes he did, he tells me everything." I then said "You had better ask him again for you must have misunderstood him." She said she would. Later in the evening I saw her take de Kánya out in the hall and have a long conversation with him. She came right back to me in a very triumphant manner, and I got up and listened to what she had to say. She said that de Kánya was very angry because she brought the matter up again. He said that politics was nothing for a woman; they couldn't understand why she thought there was anything to the Nazi story and why everybody was trying to quarrel with Germany and everyone else. Besides, he said that Germany was an enemy of Czechoslovakia and that was enough. I asked her "Do you believe this?" She said, "Of course, Mr. de Kánya always tells the truth." I said, "Well, I think you must have not heard him well," but she was very indignant in her denial.

In the early part of the evening, Countess Raphael Zichy[120] and Mr. de Kánya had a long talk. I asked Countess Zichy to go home with me, and on the way home the Nazi business came up and she told me that de Kánya

---

120 Marchioness Edina Zichy-Pallavicini.

had told her substantially what we know about the Marton group, etc., but that Mr. Daranyi did not want to make any fuss or do anything until after the secret ballot and other bills had passed. He then proposed to have a house cleaning. Countess Zichy thought it a mistake, that he ought to take drastic action now. However, she said he is nobody's fool with that Chinese face of his. I said "What do you mean?" She replied, "Didn't you ever notice his face, it is just like a Chinese or Mongolian face." This conversation ties up pretty well with what Eckhardt has told us.

[54] Conversation with Tibor Eckhardt
Budapest, April 15, 1937

Dr. Eckhardt said that Prime Minister Daranyi was fully informed concerning his recent speech; he did not approve it, but he did not object.

Eckhardt's reference to people in the army, the Regent's household, and the gendarmerie referred to individuals who had been electioneering for the benefit of the Marton group and in the interest of the Nazis. He did give the names of the individuals and the information about their conduct to Daranyi, but the latter felt that to try them now would displease Germany, and he did not want to take any action at the present time that would do that; that was the reason he gave for not proceeding against the Marton group.

The Regent was also informed about the Major of the Guard who was engaging in Nazi activity, but he likewise had done nothing.

Eckhardt told me that as soon as he left me he was going to see Szell, the new Minister of the Interior, about the gendarmes and immediately after that would see Rőder, Minister of Defense,[121] about the soldiers who were mixed up in Nazi activities. Eckhardt said he had the full support of Bethlen and the Christian Socialist party, and that he was determined that something must be done to prevent the Nazis from spreading propaganda and putting Hungary in the same position as Austria now was. He said if the Government takes no action he will. He proposed within six weeks to form a force of 50,000 men who would be prepared to act against Nazi activity wherever it occurred. I asked him if this would be a uniform force. He replied not uniform but at least they would have caps or some distinguishing mark.

I told Eckhardt that Mr. Zell[122] had told me lately that some prominent Jew had talked to him and told him that the Jews were willing to put up

---

121 Gen. Vilmos Rőder (1881–1969), colonel general from 1941, minister of defense 1936–38.
122 Julian Zell.

considerable money to back Eckhardt's campaign against the Nazis. I said that I told Mr. Zell I didn't want to know the name of the Jew as I didn't take part in local politics and, therefore, I didn't know who it was, but I thought he might be interested in the fact that the Jews were ready to put up money. I told him this because I wanted to get his reaction. He thought a minute and then said: "Well, I don't need any money now, but if we have to start to fight then I will." Then the conversation went on to the Jews. He said he had not changed his attitude towards them. He said he thought as he always had: he was against the cartels and everything they represented, but he was not against the Jews as such. What he was most against was the interference of other countries in Hungarian affairs. He said that several Jews had come to him and told him that if he or Bethlen became Prime Minister and they could feel a little secure, the Jews of Hungary are willing to raise 300 million pengő for farm relief. Mr. Philip Weiss[123] was one of this group. I had heard this already from Aschner[124] who was here to see me last week, but I said nothing to Eckhardt.

I asked Eckhardt about the duel which I heard he has refused, and told him I couldn't understand why he did because I thought he never refused a duel. He said he was a man of peace now and that a man had no right to challenge him for a duel because he hadn't mentioned his name. He said that if had made some remarks about diplomats in Hungary there would be no reason for my challenging him to a duel unless I admitted that I was guilty of the things he condemned. That is exactly what he told the man who challenged him. He said that he hadn't mentioned his name, but the fact that he took it upon himself indicated his guilt and therefore he was forwarding his name to his superior so that he could be tried for his offense.

Eckhardt claimed that the reaction of the newspapers to his speech[125] was favorable, that the only unfavorable reaction came from the Government press which, he said, was terrible. He said in Parliament that he was generally supported and that he had no criticism of any kind from anyone made to him personally since he made his speech.

I asked him why he didn't become Prime Minister and he said he hadn't any majority. I said "Well, can't you get a majority of the Government party, etc.?" He replied "Not the majority to do the things I want to do, and don't want to be Prime Minister until I am in a position to put my policies through.

---

123 Fülöp Weiss (1859–1942), banker, president of Pesti Magyar Kereskedelmi Bank (Hungarian Commercial Bank of Pest) 1921–1938, member of the upper house of parliament.

124 Lipót Aschner (1872–1952), general manager of Egyesült Izzólámpa és Villamossági Rt. (United Lightbulb and Electric Co.) after 1921.

125 A reference to Eckhardt's speech of (probably) April 5.

The present Parliament has no interest in farm relief or anything in which I am interested, and I couldn't control it. It would be more susceptible to the cash provided by Mr. Chorin[126] than to me, and until I have a majority of my own, I will never be Prime Minister."

[55] Conversation with Mr. de Kanya
Minister for Foreign Affairs

Budapest, April 16, 1937

Mr. de Kanya said that while the Nazis have been making propaganda in Hungary for some time it was not any more intensive at the present time than before. He thought that Mr. Eckhardt might be right in a good many things he said, but he felt that like all politicians he talked too much. These questions could be much better handled privately and in due time so as not to give offense. The Nazis, he said, were like the Communists: unable to restrain themselves from making propaganda wherever they went. It was the essence of their faith, and if there were only two Germans in the country they would try to make Nazis out of them and parade them around. He said that when he was a young man in the Foreign Office in Vienna[127] the then Foreign Minister, Arenthal,[128] had told him that when he was dealing with the Germans he should always remember one thing: that all of them, including Bismarck,[129] were subjective. Mr. de Kanya said he had always remembered that and his experience had confirmed it. They were utterly unable to understand anyone opposing them and not wanting to do what they wanted done. He said that when von Mackensen had called upon him to propose certain things he had told him that he couldn't do them and wouldn't do them. von Mackensen got so upset that he was unable to continue the conversation.

Mr. de Kanya commented on the fact that von Mackensen was so unhap-

---

126 Dr. Ferenc Chorin, Jr. (1879–1964), general manager, subsequently president of Salgótarjáni Kőszénbánya Rt. (Salgótarján Coal Mines Co.), president of GyOSz (Gyáriparosok Országos Szövetsége = National Association of Industrialists) 1928–42, member of the Upper House of Parliament.

127 Kánya worked for the joint Austro-Hungarian ministry for foreign affairs in Vienna between 1905 and 1913, where he became consul and subsequently envoy extraordinary and minister plenipotentiary.

128 Count Aloys Lexa von Aerenthal (1854–1912), Austro-Hungarian foreign minister 1906–12.

129 Prince Otto Eduard Leopold von Bismarck (1815–1898), chancellor of Germany 1871–90.

py here and so anxious to get away. He said he couldn't understand it. I told de Kanya it was because he gave him (von Mackensen) hell all the time. He laughed and said "Yes, he told me he was between two fires, the Germans thought he had gone Hungarian and the Hungarians were blaming him for being too German." de Kanya said, however, this was nonsense, he realized that his position was uncomfortable, but a diplomat should be used to such things and the situation was in no wise disagreeable. The German Minister had a fine position here and von Mackensen, particularly on account of his father.[130] He said the trouble was that von Mackensen was no diplomat, he was a soldier and should never be any diplomat.

Regarding the neighboring countries, de Kanya said that while nothing definite had been accomplished all countries were agreed that the strange situation of the past should not exist, and he felt that the matter was progressing as well as could be expected. Mr. Antonescu[131] had told the Hungarian Minister in Bucharest only recently that they were anxious to better the feeling between Hungary. He said, however, he couldn't hurry as there were many things which handicapped him to bring them about. The principal one was the fact that these three countries had a treaty directed against Hungary. They told him it was a defensive treaty and would never think of attacking Hungary, but he said that was nonsense: it was a treaty antagonistic to Hungary and it was difficult to make treaties of friendship with three countries which had among themselves a treaty directed against Hungary. However, he felt things were moving along and were better than they had been before.

Mr. de Kanya told me that Minister of Defense General Roder was going to Berlin next week on an official visit,[132] and they didn't want it known. I asked him if this was to be a discussion of military plans prior to the German trip to Rome. He said "No, just an official visit." I then said "Well, they might accidentally discuss it?" He laughed very heartily and said "Well, they might." Mr. de Kanya referred to the present friendship between Italy and Germany and said it surprised him and he didn't know how long it would last; in fact, he was inclined to think that it couldn't last. Nevertheless, at the present moment, it was functioning 100%.

---

130 Field Marshal August von Mackensen (1849–1945), one of the most successful generals of World War I.

131 Marshal Ion Antonescu 1882–1946), Romanian minister of war, prime minister 1940–44.

132 Minister of Defense Vilmos Rőder visited Berlin on April 20, 1937.

[56] Conversation of the Minister[133] with Baron Apor on May 25, at which Mr. Travers[134] was also present

Budapest, June 1, 1937

The following points appear to have been discussed at the conversation in the Foreign Office which took place last Tuesday:

1. Foreign Minister de Kanya had told the Minister some months ago that the Regent and Madam Horthy would probably go to Warsaw. Baron Apor said that this visit would not take place at the present time.[135]

2. Baron Apor said that Mr. de Kanya had been impressed with the friendly spirit in which the Hungarian delegation to the Coronation[136] was received in London. Both Mr. Eden and Mr. Vansittart went out of their way to be friendly toward Mr. de Kanya and they showed a considerable interest in affairs of this part of Europe. The essential points from the conversations in London were sent to the Department in telegram (no. 22 of May 25th.)

3. The points raised in the conversations with Count Ciano[137] were covered also in telegram no. 22.

4. Baron Apor intimated that Hungary still expected Italy to give military aid to Hungary in case of a crisis.

5. In reply to the Minister's[138] question regarding rearmament, Baron Apor said that the Hungarian Government had no intention of doing anything at the present time. Mr. Travers gained the impression that special emphasis was laid on the phrase "at the present time." The Minister, however, seemed to think that although conversations have undoubtedly taken place, nothing new need be expected in the near future.

6. Regarding Colonel Beck's[139] recent visit to Bucharest, Apor said that Warsaw seemed highly pleased and that, so far as the Hungarian Foreign Office could see, nothing tangible had been accomplished.

7. Apor saw no reason for Mr. de Kanya to retire from the Foreign Office. He thought it very unlikely that Count Bethlen would wish to assume the

---

133 John F. Montgomery.

134 Howard K. Travers was second, subsequently first secretary at the U.S. legation in Budapest.

135 Accompanied by Prime Minister Darányi and Foreign Minister Kánya, Regent Miklós Horthy paid a visit to Poland on February 4–10, 1938.

136 George VI (1895–1952) was crowned king of England on May 12, 1937.

137 Count Ciano visited Budapest on May 19–22, 1937, to accompany the king and queen of Italy.

138 John F. Montgomery

139 Józef Beck (1894–1944), Polish officer, foreign minister 1932–39; visited Bucharest in April 1937.

position of Foreign Minister. (Dr. Eckhardt told the Minister a few days ago that Daranyi and de Kanya were not getting along particularly well together. Eckhardt heard this first from Homan[140] and then gathered the same impression from certain remarks made by Daranyi. However, Eckhardt was unable to explain the root of the trouble and did not know how serious it was.)

8. Apor said that Blomberg's visit would be merely a return of the recent visit made by Roder to Berlin.

[57] Conversation with Mr. de Kanya

Budapest, October 29, 1937

Mr. de Kanya told me today that he was definitely certain that there would be no war in Europe in the immediate future. Great Britain and France do not desire war. He knew Germany did not wish a war, and he hoped that Mussolini didn't, although he was not certain about that. He said, however, that Mussolini could not fight a war by himself. He, therefore, was absolutely convinced that there would be peace for at least the time being regardless of the Spanish situation and any other questions that might come up, because he said that when people desire peace they can always find a way out.

Mr. de Kanya said that negotiations with the neighboring countries were at a standstill. The Yugoslavs and the Czechs were willing to do something but the Rumanians were not. The present Government in Rumania does not feel secure and fears the effect of any agreement with Hungary on the coming elections.[141] After the elections something might be done, but for the moment at least things were at a standstill. In the meanwhile, the feeling between all the various countries is much better, although Mr. de Kanya said of course they were not embracing one another yet. As a matter of fact, any agreement concluded would only be a stepping stone for what he hoped to accomplish, as due to the feeling between all these countries every move forward had to be made gradually.

De Kanya said that Maugras, the French Minister, called upon him about a week or more ago and assured him that the French Government had no objection to any arrangement with the Little Entente and denied that they

---

140 Bálint Hóman (1885–1951), historian, director of the Hungarian National Museum, professor of history at Pázmány Péter University in Budapest, minister of religion and education 1932–38, 1939–42.

141 The unpopular Tatarescu government was unable to get 40% of the votes in the Romanian elections of late 1937, the minimum requirement to form a new government. This started a continuous shift to the right in Romanian politics.

had ever opposed it. Mr. de Kanya said he didn't know whether they had or not. It seemed dubious.

Mr. de Kanya told me that Mussolini was strong for a rapprochement with the Little Entente, but that Germany was not so keen about them making up with Hungary. However, they were anxious to be on better terms with Yugoslavia and Rumania, but inasmuch as the Little Entente States refuse to deal separately they had convinced the Germans it would be necessary to deal with Czechoslovakia and had stopped their opposition. As matters stood now they were in favor of peace with the Little Entente, even though Czechoslovakia had to be included.

Mr. de Kanya said that the visit of himself and Prime Minister Daranyi to Schussnigg [= Schuschnigg][142] meant nothing and was only a matter of courtesy. The feeling between the two countries is entirely amicable, there was no disputes to settle and it could have no particular importance.

Mr. de Kanya spoke of the visit of himself and Daranyi to Berlin, which he said he thought would be on November 20.[143] I asked him if the Regent was going and he said that so far as he knew he was not. He said there was a story in yesterday afternoon's papers to the effect that the Regent was going, and he indicated it might be true. He promised to let me know if plans were changed should the Regent go.

[58] Conversation with Tibor Eckhardt
Budapest, November 6, 1937

Mr. Montgomery saw Dr. Eckhardt last evening, and in the course of their conversation obtained the following information.

Baron Apor will go to the Royal Palace to take the place of Mr. Vertesy as Chief of the Regent's Cabinet.

Mr. Bardossy, at present Hungarian Minister in Bucharest, will come to take Apor's place as Under Secretary of State in the Foreign Office.[144] Eckhardt said that Apor had already refused the position at the palace but that he will be forced to take it in about six months time. It is felt that there

---

142 Kálmán Darányi and Kálmán Kánya met Austrian chancellor Kurt von Schuschnigg in St. Gilgen on August 21, 1937.

143 Darányi and Kánya did indeed pay an official visit to Germany between November 20 and 29; the regent, however, did not join them.

144 Prospective prime minister László Bárdossy (1941–42) returned from his ministerial post in Bucharest only in 1941 when he became foreign minister.

should be someone near the Regent who is well informed on foreign affairs, and therefore Apor will have to be sacrificed to do this job.

Eckhardt said that Germany and Italy are pressing the Hungarians very hard for a full alliance with Rome and Berlin. Kanya is dead against it and will refuse to sign any such alliance. Apor is also against it. The Regent is inclined to be for it, and so is the Army, except General Roder, the Minister of Defense. Eckhardt said that Roder is already being attacked for his opposition. The Italian and German Ministers in Budapest, Vinci and Erdsmanndorff, according to Eckhardt, are very dissatisfied with de Kanya because he has not been more active in taking the part of Italy and Germany at London, and on other occasions.

Eckhardt said that the position of Hungary is very bad from an international point of view. The Regent, he said, is not necessarily pro-German or pro-Italian, but he is susceptible to pressure and no counter-pressure is being exercised from the other side by the English or the French.

Eckhardt said that it would be virtually impossible for Hungary to remain neutral in the event of a war, for the Hungarians would probably side immediately with Germany if a German army came here and promised the return of the former territories for an alliance between Hungary and Germany.

Eckhardt believes that his speech at Kormend kept the Regent from going to Germany.

Eckhardt said that he is still on good terms with Daranyi, and that the Kormend speech[145] was helpful to the Prime Minister.

Keresztes-Fischer,[146] according to Eckhardt, will soon be forced to leave the Palace.

[59] Conversation with Mr. Kobr[147]

Budapest, November 9, 1937

I asked Mr. Kobr in reference to the negotiations between Hungary and the Little Entente, and he told me that Yugoslavia and Czechoslovakia were ready to go ahead and that he felt that so far as they were concerned there would be no difficulty in coming to an understanding with Hungary. Rumania was not yet ready to make an agreement as the minority question was too difficult for the present government to handle. He said, however, that

---

145 Eckhardt spoke at an anti-German, anti-Nazi legitimist meeting of the opposition forces at Körmend on October 10, 1937.

146 Lt. General Lajos Keresztes-Fischer (1884–1948), military aide-de-camp of the regent and head of his military office 1935–42.

147 Miloš Kobr was Czechoslovak minister to Budapest.

King Carol was in favor of an agreement with Hungary and that his Government was doing everything possible to induce Rumania to make such an agreement; King Carol is now in Czechoslovakia and that the Czechs were making a special effort to influence him to take some definite action.

I told Mr. Kobr that Mr. Maugras, the French Minister, had told me that in his opinion Hungary, while anxious to make a treaty with the Little Entente, had no intention of ever carrying it out so far as Czechoslovakia is concerned; they were willing to include Czechoslovakia because they had to in order to settle affairs with Rumania and Yugoslavia. Mr. Kobr said that he thought there might be some truth in it as Italy was anxious to have Hungary more friendly with Rumania because they themselves wanted to make some acquaintance with that country, but couldn't do it as long as Hungary was unfriendly. He said that the Italians needed oil and were, therefore, anxious to be friendly with Rumania. He said that both Germany and Italy were anxious that Hungary settle its differences with Yugoslavia and, therefore, that Czechoslovakia was the only country whose friendship was not sought by either Germany or Italy at the present time, and therefore there was no pressure on Hungary to be friendly, nor would there be to keep any agreement they make. Nevertheless, he felt that more intelligent Hungarians, particularly de Kanya, were sick of revision and that as any agreement made would not mean any change except restore what you might call normal relations, it would be more advantageous to Hungary than to Czechoslovakia economically, and therefore could not be so lightly disregarded — particularly in view of Italy's action denouncing all preferences and the state of trade between Germany and Hungary with the difficulty of getting any real money.

Mr. Kobr told me that Mr. de Kanya and he had discussed this matter frankly from every point of view, and that in any case present conditions could not and should not last, and that they never could get anywhere if you assumed somebody was going to break the treaty before it was consummated. Czechoslovakia was anxious for political reasons to have more friendly relations and would do everything possible to bring them about and see that they were maintained. He felt that Mr. de Kanya was honest in his intentions and so far as he was concerned he trusted him. He said that the French consider de Kanya pro-German, but he did not think he was at all. On the contrary, he felt that de Kanya knew that the Rome-Berlin axis was a bad thing for Hungary and that their friendship with Germany and Italy was now a liability rather than an asset and that he was anxious to strengthen his ties with the neighboring countries and to put Hungary in a more independent position. He told me that de Kanya told him that the Germans and Italians were pushing him for an alliance but that he did not intend to go into it. I asked him if he believed Mr. de Kanya was telling the truth all the time, and he replied that he did. (The French Minister told me that he distrusted de Kanya thoroughly and said that he did not believe he ever told the truth. Mr. Maugras also said he considered Kobr an incurable optimist.)

Concerning local politics, Mr. Kobr is under the impression that the Nazis have made great headway. He believed that the local situation had changed very materially during the last six months. The younger element in Hungary seemed to be more attracted to the Nazis than ever and he felt that the farm laborers, due to their economic condition, had been converted to Nazism in great numbers. The Regent, he felt was inclining in the same direction. He mentioned the fact that the Regent had always been pro-English, and it ought to be a good idea if the British were to pay more attention to him, i.e. send some of their bigger men here to see him. I asked if he didn't think it a good idea if the Regent were invited to England sometime. To my surprise he thought it would be a fine idea.

Mr. Kobr told me that de Kanya was making an expose on foreign policy in the committee at Parliament today, and he promised to send me as soon as he got it a complete report of what de Kanya said, for he stated that what appears in the papers will not be all that is said.

Kobr told me that the Czechs had no idea that Hitler meant to try to take any portion of their territory forcibly. Hitler's object was to divorce Czechoslovakia from France and Soviet Russia and that he had made numerous offers of friendship if Czechoslovakia would do this. He said that at the height of the Goebels' propaganda against Czechoslovakia, Hitler sent secret emissaries to Prague with offers along this line. Czechoslovakia had no intention of doing anything of the kind because if it did it would be left to the mercy of Germany. He didn't feel that their situation was dangerous so far as Germany is concerned because he said they were well armed and that the risk involved is too great for Germany to take.

I asked Mr. Kobr about the confiscation of Baron Perenyi's estate.[148] He said that this had been settled. He told me that they were embarrassed by these confiscations, which were made just at the time of the Sinaia conference.[149] It seems that the military authorities wanted to fortify the forest near Baron Perenyi's estate and near the estates of some other Hungarians, and without the knowledge of the Foreign Office had taken steps to expropriate them. As soon as Krofta found out about it, he stopped it. It had come at a particularly unfortunate time, but it had in the end done no harm.

Mr. Kobr also told me that they hoped to settle all the claims of Hungarians in connection with the confiscation of estates, expropriation he called

148 The Hungarian government repeatedly signaled its concern about the expropriation of Hungarian estates in Czechoslovakia. Cf. DIMK II:252 (September 24, 1937).
149 The conference of the Little Entente countries was held in Sinaia (Romania) on August 31 – September 1, 1937.

it. He particularly mentioned Archduke Joseph, saying that he was very hard up for money and he felt sure that for 10 million crowns or something of the kind he would give up all claim to his Czechoslovak estates and that he had recommended that this be settled, and felt certain it would be soon.

[60] Conversation with Tibor Eckhardt

Budapest, November 13, 1937

Dr. Eckhardt told me that when Mussolini and Hitler met[150] it was arranged in advance that they were not to discuss Austria. Mussolini, however, did have a conversation with Goring. Mussolini admitted that German interests in Austria were in preponderance, but said that he wished the independence of Austria. The independence of Austria, Mr. Eckhardt said, was of vital importance to Hungary. As a matter of fact, de Kanya was now in constant touch with the Austrian Government, and they were acting together on all subjects. The meetings of Daranyi, de Kanya and Schussnigg were merely for that purpose.[151]

Dr. Eckhardt said that he did not feel Hungary had been sold down the river at all. In fact, he said that Ciano had written a special letter to de Kanya in which he emphasized that Italian interests in Hungary were just as great as ever and they had no intention of lessening their interest. Economically, Dr. Eckhardt said, Italy was not in a position to help Hungary as she had in the past. There was a will to do so but that Italy was bankrupt and simply could not do it. While he believed that Italy must maintain her interest in Austria and Hungary it was strange that di Vinci, the Italian Minister, was very pro-German and very openly so. He didn't believe that the Italian-German rapprochement had lessened Hungary's independence. In fact, he thought Hungary was getting more independent all the time. The more they were pushed the less they were disposed to act. In fact, he said it was Hungarian nature not to act but to react, and the reaction against pressure of any kind was to resist.

Regarding relations with Spain Dr. Eckhardt told me very confidentially that last September both Hungary and Austria had secretly given de facto recognition[152] to the Franco Government but not de jure.[153] This means that

---

150 Mussolini paid an official visit to Hitler on September 25–29 being received with quite exceptional magnificence and splendor.

151 Schuschnigg officially visited Budapest on October 23, 1937; previously, Darányi went to see him at St. Gilgen, Austria, on August 21.

152 Hungary recognized the Franco government on September 14, 1937.

153 *De facto:* in fact, in reality; *de jure:* by right, according to law (Latin).

they recognize Bailen as the agent of the Franco Government and deal with him but they have no representative to the Franco Government whatever. The only representative they have is with the Republic Government at Valencia. He said this was equivalent to what the British were doing and was only to protect trade interests.

In regard to the internal situation he was certain that the electoral reform bill would come up in December. He said that it had been agreed upon in principle but the actual bill itself had not been agreed upon. He denied that there was any cooling between himself and Bethlen, and said they were working entirely together. He said it was a curious fact that one part of the Government Party was against Daranyi and doing everything they could to get him out and put Bornemisza[154] in, while the Opposition was solidly back of Daranyi. Therefore, the actual opposition was within the Government party and not outside it; he said that he hoped and expected in about three months to force the resignation of Bornemisza as he had Kozma.

Next week he said he expected to make an expose in Parliament of the Nazi activity. He said there were lots of army officers affected but he didn't intend to touch that subject at present. His present drive would be in connection with the activity of the Nazi group and that he had evidence which he expected to place before Parliament which he thought would be sensational and would result in some drastic action being taken. Later he expected to bring up the army officers involved, but he would not touch that now. (When I called upon Dr. Eckhardt, there was an army officer, a General, there talking with him.)

Dr. Eckhardt said that his speech on the subject of restoration did not mean that he was backing restoration at all. He said his whole idea was to settle the question so that the Legitimist group and the rest of Hungary that was opposed to the Nazis could work together. He said that when he saw Otto he advised him to cease propaganda and await results. He told him he certainly would not be king unless it was by the unanimous will of the people and that as long as they made propaganda there would be resistance to it and they would not accomplish it. Otto, however, did not agree with him and said they must make propaganda to keep the subject alive. Dr. Eckhardt said that his speech was in line with the advice he gave Otto, that there should be no restoration without the consent of the constitutional factors and that when it was constitutionally possible then it should be done. He thought if Otto and the rest of them would accept this principle and announce it the whole difficulty that now exists would be eliminated because the subject

---

154 Géza Bornemisza (1895–1983), minister of commerce and communication, and also of industry 1935–38, 1943–44.

would be dropped for the moment and any thought of restoration by a "putsch" or any other means would be dismissed. He thought Otto made a mistake not to follow his advice because he didn't believe the way he was going now he was accomplishing anything, whereas if he followed his suggestion and the Legitimists take their place with the others as they should, if the Regent died or something else happened they might well have a restoration with the consent of everybody. Now there was a large part of the people who thought restoration meant reprisals and would continue to oppose it for that reason.

In regard to the Little Entente he said that relations could be summed up as follows: there was no difficulty with Yugoslavia at all, both Prince Paul and Stoyadinovitch[155] were in favor of an agreement with Hungary. As a matter of fact, they had actually taken steps to give better treatment to the Hungarian minority, and Stoyadinovitch had even threatened that if the Rumanians didn't make some agreement that he might do it independently regardless of the Little Entente. Therefore, so far as Yugoslavia was concerned, there is a perfect understanding as long as Prince Paul and Stoyadinovitch are in control. He said, however, that both the Church and the Army were opposed to Stoyadinovitch and he didn't know how long the Government would last or what would happen if the new government came in. He said the Serbs as a whole didn't like the idea of making peace with Hungary.

Czechoslovakia was also perfectly willing to do anything they could to bring about better relations with Hungary. He said that he had personally conducted negotiations this summer on behalf of de Kanya with Krofta[156] and that both he and Hodza were perfectly reasonable and willing to come to an agreement along the Hungarian lines. Both Yugoslavia and Czechoslovakia had been bringing pressure on Rumania to come into line, and Krofta told him that the position of the Hungarian minority in Rumania was intolerable. He said, however, that while the Czechs were now willing to make an agreement one of the difficulties was that their laws were such that minorities have no rights whatever and that if an agreement was made any time they might legally expropriate property all over again. Therefore, the Hungarians wanted the law changed so as to put their minority on the same basis as the rest of the population and not be treated as enemies. Krofta was willing to do something along this line but Benes didn't want to go this far for reasons of pride. Therefore, he felt that the situation would never be

---

155 Milan Stojadinović (1888–1961), Yugoslav minister of finance 1922–26, prime minister and foreign minister 1935–39.
156 Kamil Krofta (1876–1945), Czech historian, Czechoslovak minister to Vienna, minister for foreign affairs after the election of Beneš as president 1936–38.

right until they could change the laws in such a way as to make Hungarian property safe.

In Rumania he said the present Government was weak and that they didn't dare to make an agreement in regard to minorities. He said that Titulescu had so worked up the population that no party was willing to sponsor the idea of treating the Hungarians better. The King was willing and was using his influence, but even he couldn't go very far. He said that Chamberlain last spring at the Coronation[157] had told King Carol that for reasons of the dynasty he should come to some agreement with Hungary, and the King would like to do so. He didn't see much prospect of anything being done so far as Rumania is concerned, although he knew both the Government and the King would like to do it. He told of a friend of his who had a plant in Transylvania and who had recently been instructed to dismiss a certain number of Hungarians and to employ Rumanians, but he was told what Rumanians to employ. As the Hungarians were skilled workmen it would be very difficult to take their place. But the Rumanians he was supposed to employ know nothing about the business and are mostly friends of officials who want jobs. He says he is faced with the possibility of having to quit the business because he couldn't employ the people he wanted to employ and keep in business. He says that the Liberal Party in Rumania is the one to be most likely to do something if it is possible to do anything, but he is very pessimistic about it.

Regarding Nazi activities he said that while there was a number of different parties and leaders they all differed on a great many subjects, but they all seem to be united on the idea of winning German influence to predominate. He felt sure that German money was being spent and that Mr. von Hahn was in touch with various people who were engaged in propaganda. He said that Mr. von Mackensen didn't trust anybody, so the result was he went around in the villages and saw the Nazi agents, himself, which resulted in lots of difficulties with the Foreign Office. The present Minister[158] so far as he knew hadn't become involved openly.

Mr. Eckhardt didn't think the British were doing anything here whatever. He said that as far as their activity was concerned, they might as well not have a Legation here. Mr. Knox[159] didn't concern himself with anything so far as he knew and he was satisfied that no one else was making any attempt to influence the Regent or anyone else in the Government. In fact,

---

157 The coronation of King George VI.
158 Otto von Erdmannsdorff.
159 Sir Geoffrey Knox, British minister to Budapest.

no one ever saw him, or had any contact with any Britisher any more except on rare occasions when Mr. Knox went to the Foreign Office.

Regarding Mr. Daranyi. He said that he was a man of no ideas whatever. Gombos was full of ideas, but Mr. Daranyi merely consulted everybody and tried to reconcile all opinions. The result was that the one who made the biggest fuss generally got his way.

Regarding Germany. He said that the General Staff in Germany would never start a war as long as they would have to defend two frontiers. If something happened in France so that that country was no longer a danger he thought they would start a war tomorrow. Or if things worked around so they had an alliance with Russia they would be in a position to go to war. As things were at present, they were not at all anxious to go to war or even stir up any trouble because they were negotiating with Britain on the colonies and they proposed to lie low for the present.

Mr. Eckhardt said that he received a copy of the orders to the Austrian Nazis. These were to the effect that they were not to create any trouble for the present. He thought that they should lie low for the same reason. He believed Hitler was a factor for peace, to the extent that he follows the advice of the General Staff which he seems to be doing, according to Mr. Eckhardt. If he died and Goring and Goebels took his place, then it would be quite a different situation.

Mr. Eckhardt said that Czechoslovakia realized it cannot defend itself, but Mr. Benes had told him that the defense of Czechoslovakia was up to the rest of Europe.

[61] Conversation with Baron Apor at F. O.

Budapest, November 17, 1937

Baron Apor feels that Nazis haven't made any gains whatever during the last six months. He says there is more talk about it, that is has become a political issue, and that a lot of people are trying to ride into prominence or power by either favoring it or opposing it. Actually it is, however, of no more menace now than it was six months before, and he doubted if they could have actually as many supporters as they had then. He said there is a lot of talk of people in high places who are Nazis but he didn't believe it was true.

Baron Apor said that they had given de facto recognition to Spain in September at the request of Austria. He said that Austria and Hungary had agreed to act together in this matter; in fact, on most questions concerning foreign affairs, and that Austria desired representatives in the territory held by Franco for trade reasons. At the same time, they wanted the matter kept quiet because there was some difficulties at Valencia[160] which they wished to straighten out before the announcement was made. As far as Hungary is concerned, they had no representatives in Franco territory and they were perfectly indifferent as to whether the Government gave recognition or not. He said the matter would be announced today, that it would have been kept secret longer except that fool Festetics[161] had asked about it in Parliament and de Kanya had to give a reply. They felt that they had to consult Austria and to decide to make it public because they knew it would not be kept quiet long.

He said that there are no signs of Britain doing any counter Nazi activity in Hungary, although the Germans are conducting a witch hunt for it. He said they were terribly nervous about it, going around attacking everyone in the hopes of finding it under a sofa or some place.

Baron Apor said the Rumanian Cabinet changes make absolutely no difference so far as Hungary is concerned. Nothing could be done until after the elections. No Cabinet would face an election after having granted favors to the Hungarian minority.

Baron Apor volunteered the information that in connection with Britain, Leith-Ross'[162] visit was in connection with trade barriers; he said following von Zeeland's[163] ideas. Leith-Ross saw de Kanya, Daranyi, the Finance Minister and everyone, but nothing came of it as it is impossible to let down the barriers here at the present time. He said that there was no political significance in the visit whatever, and he was more or less on a fishing expedition.

I told Baron Apor that Countess Zichy[164] was going to open a bazaar and wanted each country to turn in articles of their own manufacture. I told him I couldn't see how we could donate many things unless we gave articles brought in duty-free. He said this could not be done under any circumstances. I told him that Countess Zichy has seen de Kanya, and de Kanya had said it was perfectly all right, that it made no difference whatever, and that he didn't object to us giving away a box of cigarettes but to put it up for sale at a bazaar would make an awful mess.

---

160 Seat of the Spanish Republican government after November 6, 1936.

161 Count Sándor Festetics (1882–1956), Hungarian National Socialist MP.

162 Sir Frederick William Leith-Ross (1887–1968), chief economic advisor of the British government 1932–39, director general of the ministry of economic warfare 1939–42, deputy director general of UNRRA for Europe 1945–46.

163 Paul van Zeeland (1893–1973), Belgian statesman, prime minister 1935–37; his government aimed at financial reconstruction *(Sanierung)* and social reforms in his country.

164 Probably the Marchioness Edina Zichy-Pallavicini.

Baron Apor thought the visit of Lord Halifax[165] to Berlin might have considerable importance. He said the Germans were crazy with anxiety to make up with the British and that something might come of such unofficial negotiations, but if they don't Britain was in no wise bound. He thought Italy was also dying to come to good terms with Britain. The fact that Halifax went to Germany and that no one was going to Italy might make quite an impression on the Italians. He said that the present British Ambassador to Berlin[166] was to all intents and purposes a Nazi, while his predecessor, Sir Eric Phipps,[167] was violently anti-Nazi. I told him I couldn't believe this as I talked with Sir Eric quite a few times and he never expressed any such opinion. He said anyhow the Germans thought he was and that was his reputation. He didn't know whether the British knew Henderson was Nazi before they sent him there or not.

[62] Conversation with Baron Apor at F. O.

Budapest, November 30, 1937

Baron Apor said that he had only seen Mr. de Kanya for a few minutes and therefore he did not know the whole story.[168] However, he did know, first, that the commercial relations had been satisfactorily settled. They were going to ship wheat and flour to Germany, but hereafter the shipments to Germany would not exceed the imports from Germany. He said that these imports would consist in part of armaments, which had already been contracted for and were in connection with the rearmament policy of Hungary. Second, that the Germans had given them a definite and unequivocal promise on the subject of propaganda in Hungary. They said that they would not make any propaganda and that if the Hungarians found that propaganda was being made by any of their agents and would notify them they would recall them. Third, he said that on the subject of revision that Hungary did not ask Germany to back the revisionist policy and would not expect them to do so. However, they did ask that no articles again appear in the German

---

165 Edward Frederick Lindley Wood, 1st Earl of Halifax (1881–1959), viceroy of India 1925–29, lord privy seal 1935–37, lord president of the council 1937–38, secretary of state for foreign affairs 1938–40.

166 Sir Nevile Meyrick Henderson (1882-1942), British diplomat, ambassador to Berlin 1937–39, enthusiastic supporter of Prime Minister Chamberlain's policy of appeasement.

167 Sir Eric Phipps (1875–1945), British minister to Vienna 1928-33, ambassador to Berlin 1933-37, and to Paris 1937-39.

168 Kánya had returned from Germany the previous day.

papers such as the Rosenberg article of last spring since it made bad feeling here. Fourth, he had not discussed with Mr. de Kanya the Halifax visit and knew nothing about it. He knew nothing about the Delbos[169] visit here, but if he was coming the Hungarian Government hadn't yet been notified. He didn't think that he would. The reports of a Ciano visit which appeared in the papers Monday were untrue. He said, however, that it was certain that Ciano would come to Budapest or de Kanya would go to Rome sometime in the near future, but not this year.

In regard to the Szalasi meeting at Debrecent [sic], he said that this meeting had not been prohibited for the reasons given in the papers. The meeting was held but it was stopped because shortly after the meeting began one of the speakers arose and said that what Hungary needed was a king, that he therefore proposed and proclaimed on behalf of the party that Nicholas Horthy be made king, and he hailed him as King Nicholas the First. This was greeted with tumultuous applause, and the gendarmes immediately closed the meeting. He said that when General Roder informed the Regent of this that the Regent was furious, and the General thought he was going to have a stroke. The Regent said that his worst enemy could not have said anything worse for him and that he considered that any Hungarian who tried to be king or permitted himself to be made king was a traitor to his country because it immediately made a bad situation and that Hungary had enough troubles without that.

The papers were then asked to say nothing about it and therefore, it gave the reason it did because there had to be some reason for closing the meeting.

[63] Conversation with Foreign Minister de Kanya

Budapest, December 1, 1937

Mr. de Kanya told me that the visit to Berlin was a return visit of von Neurath's.[170] However, they naturally discussed all the problems that existed between the two countries, but had not discussed any alliance, or anything of that nature. Hungary expected to maintain its independent policy as before. It was still willing and anxious to come to an agreement and make non-aggression pacts with the Little Entente States, and nothing that happened in Berlin had changed their mind in this respect.

It was true that Germany didn't like Czechoslovakia, but he was quite certain that they had no idea of going to war or taking any direct action in

---

169 Yvon Delbos (1885–1956), French radical-socialist politician, several times minister.
170 Baron von Neurath visited Budapest on September 20, 1936.

connection therewith. In fact, he said he was quite certain that Germany had no intention whatever of going to war at the present time. The thing that Germany was most anxious about was an understanding with Britain. Lord Halifax's visit was a little of a disappointment, but they still had hopes that it would be the beginning of negotiations which would ultimately end satisfactorily. He said that one thing was certain: as long as there was any hope of Germany coming to an understanding with Britain she would take no action of any kind that would upset the peace of the world. He said that Germany had no alliance with Italy, only an understanding, and that one of the reasons she had made no alliance was because it might handicap her in making up with Britain.

He said Hungary's position, if you could compare a small thing to a big thing, was that as long as there was hope of making up with the Little Entente she would never make any agreement with Germany, but the more the delay in coming to an agreement the more Hungary would from necessity go towards Germany. He said that the understanding and policy of making up with the Little Entente was largely his personal policy, and he didn't know what would happen if he were no longer Foreign Minister, and for that reason he was anxious to conclude some agreement as soon as possible but not at the sacrifice of Hungarian interests and principles.

de Kanya told me that the Germans were particularly distrustful of Schussnigg. He said that he had spent a lot of time trying to explain to them that he was not an enemy of Germany but that he was a very reliable man and otherwise trying to sell Germans that idea. However, he was unable to convince them. They still consider Schussnigg an enemy. However, he was positive they would take no action in Austria for the present on account of the negotiations with Britain and that they hoped ultimately Austria would sign the Anschluss of its own accord. I asked what Germany wanted of Czechoslovakia and he replied they wanted autonomy for the Sudetenland. I said "Maybe something like they have in Danzig!" He laughed and shrugged his shoulders, indicating that was the idea.

de Kanya told me that they had come to an understanding with von Neurath with regard to German propaganda in Hungary. The latter had promised to stop it and to see that anybody who offended in that respect was recalled. I asked him if this included Baron von Hahn, and he replied "Von Hahn is a stupid fellow. We have thought of having him recalled, but we might get somebody worse." He said "You know, they have five foreign offices in Germany; one day von Neurath is in control, then the next day it is Goebels, the next day Goering, then Rosenberg, and then Hess. Therefore, you could never control it absolutely." von Neurath had promised that he would see that it was controlled and they felt they could not at least do better than they have been. de Kanya said that they have never been asked

Kálmán Kánya, 1942

to sign the anti-Communist pact. Nobody had mentioned it, and that they would do it if they were asked.[171]

I asked if Germany agreed to support Hungary's military equality, and he replied "Yes, they did that six years ago."

I asked what the next move was, and he said "Well, just watching and waiting." I asked him if he was going to make any announcements or do anything spectacular. He replied "No, just keep them guessing."

In regard to commercial concessions, he said there were no concessions at all. They had merely come to an understanding in principle that will be worked out by the next commission. However, there would be no increase of Hungarian exports to Germany. I told him I understood that part of the

---

171 The Anti-Comintern Pact was signed on February 24, 1939.

imports from Germany were to be rearmament. He looked terribly astonished and asked who told me that. I didn't want to put Apor in bad, so I said
everybody up there knows about it and that our Military Attache says everywhere he goes he stumbles over a Hungarian officer. He laughed, shrugged
his shoulder, but wouldn't commit himself.

In regard to the meeting at Debrecen, he said that Balog[172] was the man
who got up and made the speech in favor of making the Regent king of
Hungary, and that Szalasi was not in favor of it. Balog, he said, was a little
dippy. He said he had talked to the Regent about it and that the Admiral was
terribly upset. I asked what effect the thought it would have on the Nazi
party and he said he didn't know anything about local politics but thought it
had never amounted to much anyhow. I asked him if he had a nice place to
live when the Nazis might run things here and he said no, that he thought he
would be out in the cemetery long before that.

I said "I suppose you have already explained all your action satisfactorily to Mr. Knox."[173] He said, "No, Mr. Knox is not coming before Friday."
I said, "Yes, you want time to think up a good story" and he said "I know
my story."

I also told him that some Hungarian who had been to my office commented on the fact that I had a picture of Tibor Eckhardt and none of the
Foreign Minister, and that I told the person in question that Tibor offered
me one but the Foreign Minister had never offered one. He said he would
correct that and would give me one.

[64] Conversation with Regent Horthy

Budapest, December 16, 1937

In a conversation with the Regent yesterday he expressed great satisfaction with Italy's action in reference to the League of Nations.[174] He said it
pleased him very much because he considered the League merely an adjunct
of the French Foreign Office. He went over at great length Hungary's experiences with the League and seemed quite bitter at the accusations made
against Hungary at the time of King Alexander's death, and also because of
the fact that the League had never paid any attention either to the treatment

---

172 This reference by Kánya was probably made to the Debrecen MP (1935–39) István
    Balogh, Jr., who was expelled by Szálasi from his party in December 1937.
173 The British minister to Budapest.
174 Italy left the League of Nations on December 11, 1937.

of the minorities. He thought that the whole idea of the League was wrong anyhow: "There should be one for Europe, one for the two Americas, and one for Asia." He couldn't understand Haiti helping to settle the affairs of Central Europe.

I told the Regent that I thought Mussolini's action came at an unfortunate time following the anti-Bolshevik pact,[175] and just in the midst of the Japanese-Chinese war[176] it was apt to strengthen the idea of an alliance between Germany, Japan and Italy. He thought this was true. He then said that of course, one could not blame Japan for being afraid of Russia and taking some action to defend itself because Russia was in a position to make an airplane attack on Japan and that they lived in constant fear that she would do so. He said, however, as a sort of after-thought, "But I don't know why the Japanese should attack China." I said maybe they have in mind ultimately aiming at the British and Dutch possessions in the Far East. He looked quite astonished and said "Do you think so?" I told him I didn't know anything about it but that on reading the London Times I had gotten the idea that the British seemed to think so. This thought seemed to disturb him, and then he said, "Well, I was there once and they are only little monkeys anyhow."

He made no mention of any of the attacks on American and British boats by the Japanese; nor did I. Nor was anything said about the possibility of any difficulty between these nations. I told him that when I saw the President,[177] the President inquired about him and had expressed appreciation of the Regent's interest in him. He again expressed his admiration for the President and told me that I should write the President that he sends his love. He said we were very lucky to have a sailor for a President, that he had seen a movie lately of our fleet and it was wonderful and that this was the result of having someone for President who knew something about ships.

I told the Regent that I had heard sometime back he wanted to send the President a message but was not allowed to do so,[178] and that I had told the President of this; that the President had told me to tell him not to bother with the Foreign Office the next time. The Regent laughed and said "Well, I will send him a message two or three years from now. Or is it three?" It did not occur to me until afterwards that he referred to the next elections.[179]

---

175 Italy joined the Anti-Comintern Pact on November 6, 1937.
176 July 7, 1937, is usually considered the beginning of the Japanese war on China. The Japanese did not actually declare war on China until 1941.
177 President Franklin D. Roosevelt.
178 The Hungarian ministry for foreign affairs often tried to contain the "private" initiatives of Regent Horthy.
179 The subsequent U.S. presidential elections were scheduled for fall 1940.

1938

[65] Memorandum[180]

Budapest, January 22, 1938

I find that in Rumania there are two schools of thought in regard to Madame Lupescu.[181] Everybody with whom I discussed the matter, with the exception of the Minister (Mr. Gunther),[182] felt that she is a very important factor in the situation. One American newspaperman representing REUTER'S, Stevens by name,[183] who has been there twenty-two years, told me that there wasn't the slightest question in anyone's mind that she was the one who received money on behalf of the King, and that anyone who wanted any favors was compelled to go to her and make their arrangements. He told me that on the previous Friday one concern that he knew had paid her money at her house for the privilege of doing something that was entirely legitimate and not in any way in violation of any law. He said that he personally had been an intermediary in making the arrangements but that he had not been present when she received the money, although he knew the money that was paid to her and all about it. He said this was quite well understood. Her influence on the King, according to Mr. Stevens, is based not so much on her sexual attraction but upon her usefulness as an intermediary.

Mr. Hibbard,[184] Secretary at the Legation, told me that there was no question about the King taking money out of the country for a long while, and that it was his opinion that Madame Lupescu's frequent trips abroad were for this purpose.

The Hungarian Minister, Mr. Bardossy, told me the same thing. He said her influence was enormous and that practically nobody was appointed to

---

180 The Memorandum recounts a visit of Minister Montgomery to Romania in January 1938.
181 Magda Lupescu (Magda Wolff) (1896?–1977), the lover of Romania's King Carol II, exerted significant influence on interwar Romanian politics and social life. Their liaison forced the king into exile in 1925 but he returned again in 1930. The king married her in his later exile following World War II and presented her with the title Princess Elena.
182 Franklin Mott Gunther (1885–1941), U.S. minister to Bucharest 1937–41.
183 Francis B. Stevens, U.S. correspondent for Reuter's.
184 Frederick P. Hibbard, secretary at the U.S. legation in Bucharest.

any position if she objected. Also, this was not because of her physical attraction but because she was the one person whom the King did trust and that he couldn't afford to offend her.

The American Minister, Mr. Gunther, does not think she has any influence at all with the King. He said that she merely was a friend who had given the King courage to do the things he ought to do; in other words, she made a man of him and she did not have any influence otherwise; and of the stories concerning her taking money, etc. were merely lies put out by unfriendly people, Hungarians, for example.

As to the effect of the Jewish drive. I did not discuss this with the Minister, but everybody, including the Hungarian Minister, were of one opinion. That is that the Jews who had been there a long while and who belong to the Union of Rumanian Jews will not be so much affected as the Zionists, who are the class of Jews that came in since the war. Further, those who belong to this latter class who can pay properly will not be disturbed in the end. Further, many Jews belonging to the first class will have some difficulties since they are out in the villages and will naturally be affected by anti-Semitic ideas of the Government. The richer Jews of that class can retire and keep to themselves whereas the poor ones who are in business will be subject to all sorts of indignities, although they may not be compelled to leave the country. The Hungarian Minister and others consider the Jewish drive merely a red herring to distract the attention of the people from the King and his activities. They think that it will be temporarily effective, although in the end it might compel the Government to take action against other Jews; in other words, to extend the Jewish drive. However, all were sure that the wealthy Jews will not be disturbed as far as the Government is concerned, if they come through properly.

The King is a large owner in all the factories and industries in Rumania. Most of these are run by Jews. These Jews are the old-timers and they are pretty safe because the King cannot afford to lose them as they are the only ones who can run the businesses from which he gets a large income.

Politics. Every party in Rumania has in the past had two branches. They have always split on one question: those who are in favor of being independent and those who are willing to be subservient to the King. As regards the Liberals, a large part of the party are with the King, and while I was in Rumania it was announced that a minority branch had again joined with the majority so that this party is now united. This is the party of big business run by the Bratiano brothers,[185] and the party which lost the last election.

---

185 Ion Constantin (Dinu) Brătianu (1866–1850), Romanian politician, leader of the Romanian Liberal party, several times minister between 1933 and 1945; and probably also Gheorghe Brătianu.

Mr. Goga[186] belongs to the minority group of the Iron Guard. The head, Coindreau [=Codreanu], remained independent, and Goga preferred to be with the King. For that reason, although his party received only 9% of the vote, the King put him in power. The last election was lost, according to the Hungarian Minister, because the Minister of Interior was not strong enough. He said that the ordinary way of running an election in Rumania was to have the proper number of ballots put in and to use the gendarmes to see that it was properly done. This last election, the Iron Guard intimidated all the Jews by telling them they would kill them if they didn't count the votes properly, and the Minister of Interior didn't take proper counter action. He seemed to be bluffing himself. The result was that the Government lost.

The Minister of Interior in the present Cabinet[187] is supposed to be a strong man capable of holding his own. However, the Government apparently doesn't want to take any more chances than necessary so they are making a series of decrees with the apparent object of creating utter confusion. For example, one of the first decrees they issued does away with all party symbols which have been used in the past. A vast majority of Rumanian voters are illiterate, therefore, it has been necessary to have symbols. The peasants of Maniu's party had a circle and the Iron Guard had a square with two dots in it, etc. It has taken years to teach the peasants these symbols. Now the Government has abolished them, and more than that they say that symbols hereafter will be a square not any bigger than a centimeter in which there will be dots to indicate the party. The number of dots each party will have will depend upon the order in which their candidates are filed. Almost immediately it was announced that the Government party and the Liberal party had filed their candidates, the Government party first, the Liberal party second. This means the Government party will have one dot and the Liberal Party two dots. This gives the Liberal party the old Iron Guard insignia. As there are some 35 parties and all the dots will have to be in a square no bigger than a centimeter square it will take a magnifying glass to be able to count them, and as the average peasant cannot count over three or four it will be almost impossible for him to determine his party.

The Hungarian Minister[188] says that he often doubts they will have an election. He thinks that the reason they do not declare a dictatorship now is because they haven't the guts, but he also thinks that if they find as they approach the election — despite everything they intend to do — there

---

186 Octavian Goga (1881–1938), Romanian poet and translator, politician, prime minister 1937–38.

187 Armand Călinescu (1893–1939), Romanian minister of the interior 1937–39, prime minister 1939, murdered by the Iron Guard.

188 László Bárdossy, later to become Hungary's prime minister.

is any opportunity to lose it they may call it off and establish a dictatorship.[189]

It is pretty well understood that the Liberal party has an understanding with the King and they hope that the Goga government will in any case last no longer than six months and that the Liberal party will return. They also think that having the Iron Guard insignia they may poll a big vote and that it is possible that if the Government finds that with everything they have done they are losing they may throw everything over to the Liberals; or if they lose the election the King will call upon the Liberal party again because they are bound to make a big showing.

The Hungarian Minister thinks that the Hungarians are going to be more affected by the measures taken against the Jews than the Jews themselves. In the first place, he said many Hungarians are Jews and they will get short shrift. In the second place, they said all the rich Jews who run their factories will be compelled to dismiss Hunarians as they have become alarmed and will want to put themselves right. In the past they resisted government pressure because the Hungarian workmen were employed a long while and knew their work, so they didn't like to make changes. Now he said many of them feel that if they don't follow of their own accord they will be in bad, and also that the Government may later come to them and demand that they dismiss the Hungarians and at the same time tell them who they must employ: which means they will have to employ people who have no experience and are unfit for the work. Therefore, he thinks the Hungarians will in any case be the chief losers. Already he said this has happened. He says that the Government, however, claimed that as soon as the election is over they want to negotiate with Hungary an understanding and that he is waiting ready to begin discussions whenever they can. He thinks that in the meanwhile, Hungary is in a difficult position because her minorities will be persecuted and there is nothing much she can do about it because of her anxiety to conclude a treaty which will in the long run protect the Hungarian minority. He expressed the opinion there might not be much left to gain if it kept on.

As to where Rumania is going, everybody seems to think she is going ultimately to Germany. For the present, nowhere. She is going to keep her present relations but lean very much towards Italy. She will make no open break with Czechoslovakia and France and will appear to be more friendly to Italy than to Germany, for two reasons: 1. that this will offend France less; 2. that it will disturb the influential Jews in Rumania less. Neverthe-

---

189 King Carol II actually dismissed the government of Octavian Goga on February 12, 1938, and introduced his own dictatorship.

less, the Hungarian Minister and everybody I talked to thinks that in the long run Rumania is going towards Germany and that regardless of what she does in the meantime that is what will happen.

[66] Conversation with Mr. de Kanya, Foreign Minister
Budapest, January 25, 1938

Mr. de Kanya said that he had very little information from Rumania except what came from the Hungarian Minister there. The Minister had written that Mr. Goga assured him every time he saw him that after the election things would be much better and Rumania would become one of Hungary's best friends, etc. Mr. de Kanya, however, expressed the opinion that he was not so certain of this, although he hoped it were true.

Mr. de Kanya also said that from what the Minister had written he didn't see how Goga could win the election. However, he hadn't paid much attention to this as his policy was to wait and see what happened. Therefore, domestic political developments didn't interest him a great deal. He agreed that the present Government is the King's personal government. He thought that Rumania's foreign policy in fact would be similar to that of Yugoslavia and Poland. It would neither go pro-Italian or pro-German, but that it would be as friendly as possible with both, and that ties which bound it to France would be loosened. Mr. de Kanya felt that for many reasons, Rumania would not dare to give up completely its French alliance. One, because it has Soviet Russia for a neighbor, and second, because its army has been supplied by France and Czechoslovakia and it would be in a difficult position if the possibility of getting ammunition, etc. from these sources were cut off. He thought it a perfectly natural development, and from a Rumanian point of view sound policy since it made its position more secure in that it no longer definitely takes sides.

Mr. de Kanya said that Mr. Kobr had been in to see him with all sorts of suggestions in regard to Czechoslovakia's intentions with regard to Hungary, and expressed its willingness to make almost any sort of an agreement. de Kanya had told him there was no use to discuss it until they were in a position to make an agreement. Since they couldn't do so without Rumania and Yugoslavia, and Rumania wasn't in a position to do anything, it was futile to have conversations.

Mr. de Kanya doesn't think that the Little Entente is weaker so far as Hungary is concerned. So far as France is concerned, yes. He mentioned that it was rather ironic that Czechoslovakia was now worrying so and was so desirous of making up with Hungary but could not do so because of the Little Entente — the very organization that was designed to protect Czechoslovakia.

Mr. de Kanya said that Mr. Kobr had told him of the negotiations between Czechoslovakia and Germany, apparently trying to impress him with the idea that they were important. He knew, however, they concerned only minor matters and did not in any sense mean that there would be any abandonment of Germany's antagonism toward Czechoslovakia.

Mr. de Kanya thought that as the situation now stood there had been an improvement so far as this part of the world is concerned because the relations of Hungary with the Little Entente and the relations of Italy with Yugoslavia had greatly improved, and that therefore there was little or no tension, and the dangers of any incidents which might cause war was negligible. He also thought the European situation as a whole was better. He didn't think Germany was disposed to do anything since there was a possibility of making some agreement with England, and he knew that Italy was very desirous of coming to an agreement with England. Count Bethlen had just returned from Italy where he had a long talk with Mussolini, and his impression was that Mussolini was very anxious to conclude some arrangement with England. Since both Germany and Italy have hopes of an understanding with England nothing much could happen.

Mr. de Kanya said he heard the idea that Germany did not desire colonies, only a free hand in Central Europe which, of course, particularly meant Austria. When he was in Germany he talked with Hitler[190] and he knew that Hitler would never give up his idea of absorbing Austria. Hitler told him that Lord Halifax had offered to arrange for some colonies conditional on peace in Europe and particularly conditional on giving up his ideas regarding Austria and Czechoslovakia. Hitler had told Lord Halifax,[191] and repeated again to Mr. de Kanya that he did not consider the two questions related at all and that he would never make any agreement on one question which would involve abandoning the other. Mr. de Kanya felt that even if he were to make an agreement it would be kept for only a short time; if he got Austria in return or on condition that he give up demanding colonies, or vice versa, it would not be long until he would be making the same demands that he had given up.

Mr. de Kanya said there was no attempt on the part of Italy to get Yugoslavia to join the Rome Protocols[192] because there wasn't a possibility of getting her to do it. This would mean a real break with France and the Little

---

190 Kánya negotiated with Hitler between November 20 and 29, 1937.
191 Lord Halifax, lord privy seal, visited Germany on November 17, 1937, not long before he became British secretary of state for foreign affairs on February 25, 1938. Hitler received Halifax on November 17.
192 The Rome Protocols were signed by Austria, Hungary, and Italy on March 17, 1934, and they came into effect on July 12, 1934. The supplementary protocols were signed on March 23, 1936.

Entente, and Yugoslavia's idea — like Poland's — must be to keep in independent position and she would do nothing that would mean a definite alliance in favor of any power. The same thing he felt was true of Rumania.

In regard to why Mr. de Kanya so many times denied that Hungary had been asked to join the anti-Communist pact, he said he had only denied it as many times as he had been asked the question, and if people keep on asking him he would have to keep on denying.[193] Mr. de Kanya said that Austria's position naturally wasn't happy and as far as that is concerned Hungary was not happy about Austria's predicament. If Germany absorbed Austria, either directly or indirectly, it would be very unpleasant to say the least for Hungary. The Hungarian people didn't relish the idea of having a nation of 80 million people, no matter who they were, for an immediate neighbor.

As to Mussolini's policy with regard to Austria. Mussolini had expressed the idea that he was no longer depending on his army to save Austria, he was depending on his friendship with Germany to save her. In other words, as long as he could keep on friendly terms he was in a position to induce the Germans to do nothing. Mr. de Kanya, however, agreed that a good army would be much better and without that Mussolini's success in keeping the Germans out of Austria was not so much due to his friendship with Germany as to Germany's desire to be friends with England.

Mr. de Kanya said that his Polish visit[194] didn't mean anything. He was going along to discuss affairs in this part of the world. He said relation with Poland were very close and that possibly in five or ten years they might be a definite ally of Poland. I asked him why not in six months, and he replied "Well, that is too soon." He didn't say so but gave me the impression that the main object of his visit is in connection with this idea. Possibly they feel that Hungary's position is not so happy as it was and they would like to strengthen the ties with Poland if possible.

With regard to Boehle's[195] [= Bohle's] visit, he referred me to his announcement that he had nothing to do with anybody except German citizens. He said this announcement was correct and that he had no complaint in regard to German activity at the present time. Since they have been to Germany, he said, all the Nazi activity that had been going on had ceased, and as far as he could see the Hungarian Government knew they were keeping their word.

---

193 Hungary actually joined the Anti-Comintern Pact only after the resignation (November 28, 1938) of Foreign Minister Kánya, on February 24, 1939.

194 Kánya visited Poland accompanying Regent Horthy and Prime Minister Darányi between February 4 and 10, 1938.

195 Ernst Wilhelm Bohle (1903–1960), leader of the *Volksbund für das Deutschtum im Ausland* (VDA), the foreign organization of the National Socialist German Workers' Party *(Nationalsozialistische Deutsche Arbeiterpartei,* NSDAP) 1933–45, German secretary of state for foreign affairs 1937–41.

[67] Conversation with Baron von Hahn
Budapest, January 27, 1938

Baron von Hahn told me today that Germany and England had reached a perfect understanding in that both knew what the other wanted and what each was prepared to concede. While they were far from an agreement, Germany was encouraged to believe that some understanding was possible and, therefore, as regards England, Germany was wholly friendly.

von Hahn confirmed de Kanya's statement that Hitler had told Lord Halifax that Germany could not make any agreement conditional on it not disturbing the peace of Europe because he said Germany had no idea of disturbing the peace, and to make such a pledge would bind her in such a way that no nation could be bound. I asked him how far they had gone on an understanding. "Well, they had agreed about Austria and that as a result of that understanding Germany had no idea of making an Anschluss or any attempt to combine Austria and Germany," he said. However, he added, she did expect to force a Government in Austria which would be very friendly, and that the British had agreed to this solution of the problem. He said England had stated that they could not object to Germany being friendly with any neighboring government and that short of an absolute Anschluss or absorption they would be entirely satisfied.

He reiterated that Germany was entirely a peaceful nation, and while he thought Italy might start trouble if the British became involved in Japan, Germany would not do a thing. He thought Italy was anxious to make up with England, but England was not interested. He said England was preparing to send her boats around the Horn and that eventually she was disposed to do this rather than to concede anything to Mussolini in the Mediterranean.

As regards Czechoslovakia. I asked him how he could reconcile his statement that Germany was going to keep the peace and cause no trouble with his statement about Czechoslovakia. His only answer was the situation changes quickly. "Who would think that Yugoslavia a few years ago would be so friendly towards Italy today, and things may change in Czechoslovakia," he said. I took that to be an idea that they either will dictate to the Czechs or start something over there, something like on the order in Spain.

[68] Conversation with Baron Apor
Budapest, February 9, 1938

Baron Apor said that the Foreign Office knew nothing of Rustu Aras'
visit to Budapest until the day he arrived, and it was impossible for him to
go down to meet him because it was the same time that the Regent was
leaving for Poland.

Rustu Arras called up and wanted to see the Prime Minister after his
arrival, and Apor went there with him. He said that Rustu made a long high-
sounding speech to the Prime Minister which the latter didn't understand,
and when Apor translated it to him the Prime Minister kept a straight face,
but his eye twinkled and he said "Tell him the same thing for me." Apor
said he almost burst out laughing.

The object of the Rustu Arras visit was that Turkey desires to become a
friend of Hungary, and Rustu Arras was full of ideas as to what he could do
for Hungary; among them to help Hungary's rapprochement with Rumania.
Apor said that he seemed to be quite worried for fear that Yugoslavia and
Bulgaria were becoming too friendly and that they together might menace
the Greeks, who are his allies. Therefore, apparently he decided to cultivate
Hungary. He proposed that when he got home he would arrange with his
Prime Minister to make a visit to Hungary sometime this spring.

Apor said that he had heard nothing from Germany that gave any definite clue as to what has taken place.[196] It was all a surprise and it was too
soon definitely to form an opinion as to what had happened. He thought,
however, that is was a victory for the Party and that they were taking over
the army. He said the German army had been loyal to whatever government
was in charge and they were trained to obey. He didn't think they would
ever make any "putsch" against the government.

He said that in his opinion Ribbentrop was an incredibly stupid person
and knew nothing about foreign policy, and he couldn't imagine him at the

---

196 Preparing partly for the *Anschluß*, Hitler dismissed Foreign Minister von Neurath,
an opponent of his war policy, on February 4, 1938, and placed Joachim von Ribbentrop in his stead. At the same time, he used fabricated excuses to get rid of
adversaries of his plans such as Field Marshal von Blomberg, minister of war and
commander-in-chief of the armed forces, and General Werner Freiherr von Fritsch,
commander-in-chief of the army, and established the *Oberkommando der Wehrmacht*
(OKW, the high command of the armed forces) under General Wilhelm Keitel.
Within days, sixteen generals were dismissed and 44 downgraded [William L.
Shirer, *The Rise and Fall of the Third Reich: A History of Nazi Germany* (New
York: Simon and Schuster, 1960), 311–321]. All this contributed to the growth of
the immediate influence of the NSDAP and of Hitler in person on German foreign
policy and the control of the Wehrmacht.

head of the Foreign Office. He didn't see that von Neurath would have much influence as the Privy Councillor and is faced with people who hate one another and wouldn't work together. Besides, whatever information they got would have to be through von Ribbentrop, so he regarded it merely as a useless body. He said he had no indication of what the effect of the change regarding foreign policy would be. He knew the Austrians were very much worked up and that possibly the Czechs were too. Anybody's guess was as good as another's at the present time.

Baron Apor said that the Hungarian Government had made no protest concerning the treatment of Daranyi in Berlin as compared with Stoyadino-vitch.[197] He did admit, however, that Goring had made a big to-do about Stoyadinovitch and that it caused comment. He said that the Germans had spoken to the Hungarians about it by way of explanation, but the Hungarians themselves had not made any protest. Even Stoyadinovitch had mentioned to their Minister that he didn't like it.

Apor said there were no political implications of the Regent's visit to Poland.[198] Hungary had always been close to Poland and wanted to keep close. He had heard nothing from de Kanya and knew nothing about what had been going on, but he didn't assume there was any more than consultations about affairs in general such as would take place when two Foreign Ministers of friendly countries met.

In regard to Germany's refusal to permit visitors to come to the Eucharistic Congress,[199] Apor said that the Hungarians didn't regard this as aimed at them, although naturally they didn't like it. They knew it was because of Germany's quarrel with the Catholic Church.

Apor said he didn't know anything about the commercial discussions.[200] It wasn't in his section and he never paid any attention to it.

---

197 As to the ceremonies, the Berlin reception of Darányi in November 1937 lagged far behind that of both Mussolini (September 25–29, 1937) and Yugoslav prime minister Stojadinović (January 15, 1938), for which Baron Neurath offered apologies to Darányi (DIMK I: 509–10). Nazi Germany paid particularly great attention to the symbolism of diplomatic formalities, which was also clearly understood by the Hungarian premier.

198 February 4–10, 1938.

199 Hitler did not allow German Catholics to participate at the 34th Eucharistic World Congress in Budapest, between May 26 and 29, 1938. This decision arose partly from the anti-religious policies in Germany and the sour relationship between Nazism and the Roman Catholic Church, partly from the episcopal letter of the Hungarian prince primate issued to the Congress and read in all Hungarian churches on December 31, 1937. This letter mentioned the "devotees of race- and blood-worship" as well as "the pretentiousness of unreliably pushy dwarf leaders."

200 This is a vague reference to the preparations for the armaments program declared a little later by Darányi in Győr on March 5.

I asked Apor regarding Major Szalasi and the internal situation.[201] He
said I probably knew more about that than he did. All he knew about it was
that he had asked friends of his who lived out in the country and they told
him that as far as they knew the only people interested in the Nazi movement in Hungary were the unemployed and people who had something to
gain out of it, most of whom are former Communists. He didn't think there
was any widespread interest in Szalasi or his movement.

The electoral reform bill[202] he had paid no attention to. He assumed it
would pass. He knew there was some discussion going on but didn't know
anything more than what was in the papers. No one had mentioned anything
to him about it, it not being in his section.

[69] Conversation with Foreign Minister de Kanya

Budapest, February 23, 1938

Mr. de Kanya told me today that while he was much upset over Hitler's
move in Austria[203] it was not so much because of that had been done but the
way it was done and the possibilities that it offered. He said that Hitler and

---

201 The era saw the rise of political forces on the extreme right. In October 1937 the
Hungarian National Socialist Party was formed out of several extremist parties and
groups. Szálasi was repeatedly brought to court and sentenced to ten months in
prison on November 29, without, however, legal validity. Well known for his extremist
views, László Endre, the chief constable of Gödöllő, became deputy lord lieutenant
of the county of Pest, on January 11, 1938. Shifting to the right also continued inside
the government party, signaled by the presidency of András Tasnádi Nagy and the
vice-presidency of Dániel Mocsáry. When Szálasi's party was dissolved by the minister of the interior on February 21, placing the party leader and his 72 "movement
activists" under police control, forces of the government party exerted considerable
influence, partly publicly, for the benefit of the Arrowcross leaders.
202 As a safeguard of the electoral reform, Act XXVII of 1937 prohibited the Hungarian
House of Representatives from sending the bills it accepted directly to the regent for
approval. In case of disagreement the joint session of the two houses made a decision, without debate, by secret vote. The debate on the electoral bill started in the
House of Representatives on March 23, 1938.
203 On February 12, 1938, Hitler ordered Austrian chancellor Kurt von Schuschnigg to
Berchtesgaden and demanded, as if in an ultimatum, that the chancellor permit the
functioning of the Austrian National Socialist movement, the extension of the domestic rights of the Austrian Nazis, amnesty for the locked-up Austrian Nazis, and the
appointment of Nazi sympathizer Dr. Arthur Seyß-Inquart (1892–1946) as minister
of the interior, Edmund Glaise-Horstenau (1882–1946) as minister of war, and Dr.
Hans Fischboeck as minister of finance. After somewhat toning down the original
instructions, Hitler made Schuschnigg sign the German demands, the fulfillment of
which practically meant the end of Austrian sovereignty.

Schussnigg had had quite a lively discussion and had come to no understanding until Hitler called in four Generals[204] who told Schuschnigg that they had the army ready to go into Austria and that the soldiers were anxious to go, and told him of the plans they had. As Schuschnigg had no support from anywhere there was nothing that he could do but submit, although he stood his ground very well and did not give everything they wanted. Actually, de Kanya thought they had got very little. Seyss-Inquart was Schuschnigg's best friend and he had every confidence in him, and although Mr. Hitler also liked him his appointment was not necessarily an indication of Nazi control. The most important thing was what is going to happen next, whether the Germans would be content for a while and, if so, for how long, and more particularly what the other Great Powers did in the meantime. He thought that if Schuschnigg could retain Austrian independence for a few years he might acquire enough support to survive. I asked Mr. de Kanya what he would have done under similar circumstances. He didn't want to reply to this question and kept saying that Germany would never touch Hungary, that he had personal assurances from Hitler that he didn't want a single town in Hungary. I finally insisted that he pretend he was in that position anyhow. When I finally got him so he had to answer he said, "Well, we would not do it." He added that Hitler knew Schuschnigg would. Also, Mr. de Kanya at this point said that besides Hungary would have help. I asked from whom. He shrugged his shoulders and wouldn't answer. So he said he couldn't see any reason why Hungarians were nervous because Hungary's position was quite secure as compared to Austria, Czechoslovakia, Poland, and Rumania. They had no enemy at their frontier as all these countries had, and Poland had two. Therefore, any apprehension at the moment was unjustified. He blamed everything on the failure of France and England to take any positive action, so that everything went back to the failure of the Hoare-Laval formula[205] and the sanctions which forced Italy and Germany together. He didn't think it could be so easy to make up with Italy now as there are many complications.

I asked Mr. de Kanya about Szalasi. He said he didn't know a great deal about it except that they had gone too far and had to be stopped. He said it

---

204 German generals such as Wilhelm Keitel, Walter von Reichenau, and Roman Sperrle were present at the arrival of the Austrian chancellor at the entrance of the Berghof, Hitler's "eagle's nest" in Berchtesgaden.

205 Commissioned by the Council of the League of Nations, British foreign secretary Sir Samuel Hoare and French prime minister Pierre Laval submitted a secret plan on the partition of Ethiopia on December 9, 1935, which would have enabled Italy to keep the territories already taken over. The plan became public and was considered a betrayal of the League of Nations; it led to the immediate fall of Hoare.

was more as a warning to army officers than anything else. As Eckhardt had told me that the Regent would soon issue special orders to the army prohibiting it from engaging in politics I said to him "Why doesn't the Regent issue orders to the army forbidding it from going into politics?" He looked at me, smiled and said nothing. Then I said, "When is he going to do it?" He still shrugged his shoulders and refused to answer, so apparently this is going to be done very shortly.[206] He indicated, but didn't say, that the Regent was back of the Szalasi arrests and that it came from his resentment at the time he was proclaimed King. In other words, he indicated that that was the turning point so far as the Regent was concerned and since then the Nazi agitation had annoyed him. He didn't think it would affect relations with Germany. I told him I heard there was a courier coming from Germany. He said, "Yes, couriers always have been coming to Szalasi but it didn't necessarily mean they were Government couriers." He said there are lots of couriers in Germany, and smiled.

Mr. de Kanya told me about Poland the same as before. They wanted to get as close to Poland as they could. I asked if he wanted a military alliance with Poland, and he replied no, because when you look into it, Hungary has nothing to gain from a military alliance with anyone if it means that they have to go to their aid. What Hungary wants is someone to guarantee its independence. Poland is in a more dangerous position than Hungary, and Hungary could not be bound to go to her aid. Besides, Hungary would have to go through Czechoslovakia; further, Hungary has nothing to aid her with. In regard to Poland, he said the situation as far as Hungary is concerned was the same as with everybody as it had been with regard to Austria. When he made his first speech five years ago in Parliament he said that Hungary could not guarantee the independence of Austria because that could not be guaranteed by any small Power. It would have to be done by the big Powers. The situation was the same in regard to Hungary today: it was not in a position to guarantee anything, or even to be tied up in any alliance with any country that might draw it into a war. He agreed with me that the only winner of a war in Europe would be the Bolsheviks, and there wouldn't be much left for anyone else. However, he said that Germany really didn't want war. When he was there the last time he talked to a number of Generals and others and they all said they didn't want war. The trouble with the whole thing was that Hitler's success had been based upon sensations, and the German public expects something new and sensational to develop now and then. He said those damn silly speeches and this idea of producing sensa-

---

206 In a radio broadcast on April 3, 1938, the regent proclaimed that "he would contain political agitation in the army."

tions is what makes it dangerous. Actually they don't want war, but said at the same time this made the Austrian situation better, because he didn't think Hitler had gone as far as he might have gone if he didn't want to save future moves for the right time. He hoped this might be several years, but it would be necessary to make another move.

With regard to Mr. Eden,[207] he said he liked Eden personally but thought him a terrible Foreign Minister and thought everything wrong with Europe was due to him. He also said that the situation was better now because there was at least one foreign policy. For some time back there were two foreign policies, Eden's and Chamberlain's. He had heard also that Lord Halifax had agreed to Hitler's taking over Austria, provided he didn't do it by force, but added he had no positive information to that effect.

I asked about the Eucharistic Congress, that is, as regards the Germans, and he said that naturally the Catholics didn't like it, but it was more due to Germany's quarrels with the Church than any feeling towards Hungary. As a matter of fact it was a good thing because they didn't have room enough for the delegates anyhow, and those who came from other countries would spend more actual money, and those from Germany would only increase their debt.

I asked de Kanya what is going to happen in April. He asked what I meant. I said the British are saying that April is going to be the critical month, indicating that something important is going to happen, and added that is it. He replied he didn't know why it should be in April any more than in March.

As I left he expressed his opinion of war and indicated that anybody was crazy who contemplated war, that another war would be the end of everything. He said that Hungary's whole foreign policy was directed toward peace and because he fully realized nobody could gain by a war. In fact, everybody would lose. He referred to Spain, the killing of women and children, and said the horrors of the next war would be something better not to think of.

[70] Conversation with Baron Apor

Budapest, March 7, 1938

Baron Apor stated with regard to Daranyi's speech that it was made for home consumption and that there was a great deal of feeling that there should be some action on all these different questions; that the plan of capital tax

---

207 To protest the policy of appeasement, Anthony Eden resigned as foreign secretary on February 20, 1938.

was figured up by Imredy and Teleszky,[208] and that it doesn't contemplate as far as he knows any 25% tax; he thought it was about 8% and that it would go so much a year for ten years on fortunes and overtax in addition to income tax. He thought Parliament would pass it.

He said that they didn't consider Daranyi's speech[209] as a unilateral action, although he admitted it might be considered as such; that they had discussed armaments with all the Little Entente States and he said that the General Staff of Yugoslavia told them lately they could do as they pleased so far as Yugoslavia in concerned. They all knew they were doing it, and the reason Daranyi mentioned it was because people in the country were clamoring for some action, and he thought it was for them to let the people know they were doing so. He said the rearmament program did not contemplate raising a large army; it only contemplated rearming the one they had. He said the guns they had were pre-war material[210] and that they had no modern equipment whatever, and the whole idea was to make the present army up-to-date and effective.

Apor said that the Foreign Office considered the most important international development was the British-Italian conversations[211] which they hoped would be successful. They had heard from Ciano that he is very optimistic. He said that they understood that all negotiations had been going through the widow of Austen Chamberlain[212] and that it was she who convinced Chamberlain that the Italians were sincere. As to the question as to whether Mussolini acquiesced in the Berchtesgaden meeting, Apor said they didn't know but they couldn't see whether it made any difference. Mussolini was in no position to object or do anything about it if he had known. They had no knowledge as to how soon he was advised. The Hungarian Government was advised only the day before. He thought if the Italian-British agreement were made then Mussolini's position would change in regard to Austria and he would again be in a position to do something. The Hungarian Foreign Office hoped very much that this would come true.

Apor did not think that the party had taken over the German army. His

---

208 A tax on private wealth was planned to be introduced in connection with the armaments program of the government. János Teleszky (1868–1939) was finance minister in 1912–17.

209 A reference to Prime Minister Darányi's speech in Győr on March 5, 1938.

210 Meaning: pre-World War I.

211 The Chamberlain government negotiated with Mussolini on the Mediterranean area and Central Europe, which led to the British-Italian agreement of April 16, 1938. Italy received a free hand in Ethiopia and Spain and strengthened her power in the Mediterranean region

212 Sir Austen Chamberlain (1863–1937), British foreign secretary 1924–29. Chamberlain was the half brother of Prime Minister Neville Chamberlain.

opinion was that Hitler had no idea of putting the party in charge and that was the reason he had taken over the army himself. If he put the party in charge he would have had to put Goring at the head of the army, and this would have put him in too dangerous a position to suit Hitler. Further, Hitler, Goring, Hess, and all the rest of them hated one another and Hitler would not go too far in elevating one over the other — particularly in the case of Goring who already has received considerable preferment. He believed Hitler's idea was to keep the army as it was for no other reason than to protect himself against the party, because if in time the party turned against Hitler, he would have the army at his back.

Apor said that while there have been negotiations supposed to have been going on in Rumania, actually there had been none as Tatarescu had to go to Ankara and all kinds of places and, therefore, never had any actual work been done. They hoped for something but up to this moment nothing had been accomplished.

Mr. de Kanya found Schuschnigg very confident that he would be able to maintain the independence of Austria. The happenings at Berchtesgaden and his subsequent speech had brought support from a great many quarters that were indifferent before. Schuschnigg felt that if they were to hold a plebiscite they would not win, and that they now are toying with the idea of having one.

[71] Conversation with Mr. Remenyi-Schneller, Minister of Finance

Budapest, March 18, 1938

Mr. Remenyi-Schneller said that everything had changed since ten days ago[213] and it was impossible to tell what their plans would be, or how effected. He admitted things were paralyzed and something would have to be done, but that at the moment they were entirely at sea. They couldn't make any plans until things calmed down or until they knew whether they would calm down. He thought they had and that after a week they would be able to make new plans. They had originally intended to make the loan next month.[214] Now they didn't know what to do.

---

213 Germany conquered Austria on March 12–13, 1938 ("the *Anschluß*").

214 This was an internal loan in connection with the armaments program declared in Győr.

[72] Conversation with Mr. de Kanya, Foreign Minister

Budapest, March 22, 1938

Replies to questions attached hereto:[215]

Political 1. Mr. de Kanya said that Hungary's attitude towards Germany would be the same as it always has been. They had a traditional friendship between the two countries, they agreed in general on all problems, and there was no reason why their attitude should change in any way. There was every reason why it should not. Hungary would naturally stand for independence. What Germany would demand of them he didn't know. So far nothing. They were naturally nervous at having so big a neighbor, but he said when he was in Mexico[216] the Mexicans were always nervous about having the United States for a neighbor. He said that was true everywhere, little nations always are nervous when a big neighbor is at their door, and of course, in the present situation that was intensified because when any nation had an active policy, as Germany has at the present moment, no small nation could be completely happy that they were neighbors.

2. He didn't attach any importance to this.

3. Hungary will not pursue any course different from what she has in the past, except that she will make greater effort if possible to obtain new friends and new support, although he didn't know where that would come from, but intended to stay close to Italy and to Poland, and they were continuing negotiations with the Little Entente and were hoping that the Great Powers might show some interest in them, but from what had taken place in Austria he didn't have much hope that this interest would be anything substantial.

4. Hungary and Italy would continue to be friends on the lines of the Rome Protocols, although of course, the Rome Protocols actually would not exist. This would have to be adjusted to suit the present situation.

5. He didn't know what the Government would do about the Nazis locally as he didn't concern himself with local affairs. He realized that they would have considerable trouble along this line. He thought the Austrian Nazis were more radical, and of course, for the moment, much more zealous than the German Nazis, and it was unbelievable that they wouldn't start trouble down here, but he thought this could be taken care of.

6. He didn't believe that Germany wanted physically to annex Hungary because he said in the first place Hitler's policy had always been concerned

---

215 The questions are not attached to the document.

216 Kánya was the last minister of the Austro-Hungarian Monarchy to Mexico between 1914 and 1919.

with Germans abroad. To take over a friendly country that was not German would make a terrific impression, and besides, he didn't believe that they would dare to Germanize the Hungarians because history had shown that this was impossible and would make them lots of trouble which he didn't believe they wanted to undertake.

7. He said Hungary had no advantage that he could see in allying itself with Germany or any other Power and they had no intention of doing so. Hungary's policy would be to try propitiate everyone and align itself with no one. He admitted they might have to do lots of things they wouldn't do if they had their own choice, but he wouldn't admit that they would ever become completely subservient to Germany or any other Power.

8. He said they naturally didn't like the purge in Austria; strictly speaking, however, it wasn't the concern of the Hungarian Government. Personal friends were concerned and it was not nice to contemplate it, but officially it was the affair of the German Government, and in his position he didn't feel that he ought to comment.

9. The Polish-Lithuanian question[217] he considered as settled, and he thought that Beck had handled the matter well. He was sure that Germany wanted Memel; in fact, he said that Stresemann had told him (when de Kanya was Hungarian Minister in Berlin) that they would never give up the idea of having Memel, so he had no doubt that Germany wanted just as much today, and probably more.

10. The Hungarians in Czechoslovakia were demanding self-government,[218] but the Hungarian Government would not make any demands on the Czechoslovak Government. They took the position that this was an internal affair, and they wouldn't complicate matters by any demands of that nature. All they were asking for was decent treatment of the Hungarian minority; if they obtained that then they would be satisfied.

---

217 The Polish-Lithuanian conflict of March 16–19, 1938, resulted in the recognition of the border of Wilno (Vilnius) and the success of the Polish ultimatum.

218 The various parties of the Hungarian minority in Czechoslovakia merged in 1936 as the United Hungarian Party, and, in an effort to join the ever more militant revisionist claims of Hungary as well as the Sudeten German Party of Konrad Henlein, they became increasingly vocal in their demands for political autonomy.

[73] Conversation with Mr. de Kanya, Foreign Minister
Budapest, March 22, 1938

I asked Mr. de Kanya regarding the Little Entente. He said that the Rumanian Government had answered the Hungarian proposal made last year at Sinaia.[219] He didn't know what the answer was, whether it was satisfactory or not. It had been given to the Hungarian Minister at Bucharest and he was bringing it up here next Monday or Tuesday. The delay was occasioned by the necessity of clearing up some points that were not quite clear.

Mr. de Kanya told me that within the week, Mr. Erdmannsdorf, the German Minister, had been in and told him that the assurances made by Mr. Hitler which were given to Italy, Switzerland and France also applied to Hungary, and that he was calling officially to give such assurance.

[74] Conversation with Dr. Tibor Eckhardt
Budapest, March 22, 1938

Dr. Eckhardt told me that on last Monday the Regent had called Daranyi and told him he must do something to clear up the Nazis. The Regent expressed concern, and Daranyi promised him to do something. Eckhardt said, however, he had done nothing so far as the Cabinet was scared to death. Eckhardt said that he would wait until Easter and if the Government didn't take proper steps against the Nazis he would break his alliance with Daranyi and attack him.

Eckhardt expects the secret ballot bill to pass by Easter.[220] I asked Eckhardt about the break in his party.[221] He said three of the men had been asked to leave, but three of them were a surprise. He didn't seem particularly disturbed because he said he would rather have two people that he could depend upon than 100 that he couldn't, and said he didn't care how many left he would make no effort to hold them. As to the future of his party he

---

219 This is a reference to the draft of a protocol prepared by László Bárdossy, then Hungarian minister to Bucharest, on the occasion of the Little Entente conference in Sinaia, early September 1937. The document was handed over to all three participating powers.

220 The discussion of the bill started on March 23 in the House of Representatives, and it became an act on June 3, 1938. Act XIX:1938 made secret ballot nationally accepted.

221 Six members of the Smallholders left their party on March 21; they moved later toward the extreme right-wing Hungarist Movement.

Tibor Eckhardt speaks at a meeting of the Smallholders Party, 1930s

was not very optimistic. He told me that at the election on Sunday the Nazis spent more money than he ever spent in any election in Hungary. He said that they had opened up barrels of wine every place and had conveyances out to take people to the polls and had done everything possible. As a result they polled about one-third of the vote, and while there would have to be a run-off he expected to see the Nazi elected if they spent as much money at the next election as they did at the last. He said that if they kept up this expenditure of money on that scale he thought nobody could compete with them. He saw his position and that of his party as precarious, that there would be a lot of people run to the Nazis, that is where his ex-members were going, and that in view of the plight of agricultural labor and the economic condition of the country he couldn't see how his party could do anything more than survive. He didn't think very highly of the prospects. He said however, he would not join the Government in any case.

Incidentally, in talking to the caddy yesterday afternoon, they all had stories of money being spent by the Nazis and presents which were given to very prominent people with the compliments of Adolph Hitler. These included all kinds of things, in one instance a cow. One caddy from Budaors said that one of the prominent Svab farmers was presented with a cow and told that it was from his friend Adolph Hitler. These stories may be exaggerated, but on the other hand, they may not be so much.

[75] Conversation with Mr. de Kanya

Budapest, March 23, 1938

Mr. de Kanya said that Schuschnigg was badly fooled by Seyss-Inquart. He had told de Kanya when he was last up there about a week before the blow-up that he had every confidence in Seyss-Inquart and that the latter would certainly never do anything against him personally or against the interests of Austria.

[76] Conversation with Philip Weiss and Victor Bator[222] of the Commercial Bank

Budapest, April 7, l938

In a conversation this morning with Messrs. Weiss and Bator I learned that the bill which is to be presented to Parliament this morning against the Jews[223] has been prepared with their knowledge and consent and they completely approve of it.

Mr. Weiss said although the bill made him a Christian, until it was passed he was a Jew and, therefore, he spoke as a Jew in saying that they could be well satisfied with the bill.

Mr. Bator said that Mr. Imredy was behind the bill and that he had spent yesterday afternoon with Mr. Imredy going over all the provisions. Mr. Imredy and Mr. Daranyi had explained that it was necessary to do something to stop the spread of anti-Semitism and give some satisfaction to those who were clamoring for action against Jews, and it was hoped that this bill would do that. I asked him if he thought it actually would, and he replied, "Well, even Mecser has expressed satisfaction, and he is a most violent Nazi."

The provisions of the bill in general differentiate between Jews and Gentiles for the first time. In other words, heretofore there has been no difference legally but hereafter there will be. However, any Jew who became a Christian before August 1, 1919 is treated as a Christian; everybody who fought in the war is treated as a Christian. Therefore, this makes a good proportion of the Jewish population Christian.

The main provision of the bill itself provides that 80% of all people

---

222 Viktor Bátor (1891–1967), lawyer, chief attorney of the Hungarian Commercial Bank of Pest, emigrated to New York before Word War II.
223 Act XV:1938, the so-called Jew Bill I of May 29, 1938.

employed by any business must be Christian. However, in the case of banks, etc. five years are given to put this provision into effect. In the case of technical industries, ten years. As far as the Commercial Bank is concerned, it will make no marked difference. They put about ten employees a year on pension, and that is all that will be necessary to change during the five years.

The provisions of the bill are that during the time when the change is made 95% of all employed will be Gentiles. After the proportion 80:20 is reached, then they can be employed in that proportion. The same thing applies to doctors, lawyers, and it will be accomplished by the medical association and the bar associations admitting people on the 95:5 proportion until the 80:20 proportion is reached.

Mr. Weiss said that the bill was in a sense drastic but it was not humiliating to the Jews, and, therefore, they could well be content.

I asked Mr. Weiss before Mr. Bator came in how soon Imredy would be Prime Minister,[224] and he replied he hoped soon. I said, "Do you figure it will be soon?" and he replied "I wouldn't be surprised, we are all pulling for him." I asked if Imredy is a Nazi or an anti-Nazi; he replied Nazi. I then said "Why do you want him?" and he replied "We have to have someone who is a little Nazi, and we have confidence in his ability and confidence in him that he would not to anything radical. We think the situation needs a strong hand, and, therefore, we prefer Imredy to Daranyi."

When Bator came in — and after Weiss had left — I asked him the same questions and got practically the same replies. Both of them said that the conception of this plan was Imredy and intimated that he was practically the master mind in the Government now. They seem quite content with him.

[77] Conversation with Dr. Imredy, President of the National Bank

Budapest, April 9, 1938

Dr. Imredy called today in connection with the New York World's Fair.[225] The Hungarian Government expected to participate in the fair and had hoped to spend about 1.6 million pengo on the Exhibition. Dr. Imredy told me that due to the change in the international situation which had mate-

---

224 Béla Imrédy became prime minister of Hungary as of May 14, 1938.
225 The New York World's Fair of 1939–40 was opened on April 30, 1939. Its Hungarian pavilion was an extremely modest achievement, reflecting upon the reserved approach of the Hungarian government. For political reasons Germany did not participate in the fair at all.

rially affected their possibilities of obtaining foreign exchange, the Hungarian Government didn't see how it could possibly go through with their project in connection with the New York Fair.

Dr. Imredy was very anxious that this be understood and that it not be considered unfriendly on the part of the Hungarian Government. Since 45% to 50% of their business was now with Germany and brought them no foreign exchange, and the proportion of their other business also produced no foreign exchange, they would now probably have to buy many products which they formerly got from Austria and might also be compelled to make other exports. Also, he intimated that they were not in a position now to be as arbitrary with Germany as they had been in the past. Therefore, they might have to sell the many products that had produced exchange before, thereby lessening the possibilities of getting exchange. Under such circumstances, the Government was loathe to do anything that required foreign exchange that they could possibly avoid. He said it wasn't that the situation had changed so much for the moment but they didn't know what the possibilities were and therefore, the question of foreign exchange had to be more carefully considered than ever.

I asked Mr. Imredy about the Rockefeller Foundation pengo,[226] and he asked that I write a memorandum for him as he didn't know anything about it. He would see what he could do.

I asked him about the bill that was introduced yesterday, and he said it was very necessary on account of the young people who were being attracted by anti-Semitic propaganda. He felt that while the bill would not satisfy everybody, particularly the Extremists, it did satisfy the more moderate element and that this would divide the extreme element.

Dr. Imredy didn't expect Daranyi to fall very quickly. He does expect a demonstration, probably tomorrow, but does not think this important. He said although Daranyi has a reputation of being inactive and hesitant, he has actually accomplished more in a year and a half than Gombos accomplished all the time he was Prime Minister. Gombos, however, had a way of appealing to popular imagination and seemed more firm and active. Daranyi lacked the ability to put himself over to the public or make known what he had done. To that extent he had suffered.

As for his being Prime Minister, Dr. Imredy didn't think much of the possibility, intimating that he couldn't afford it. Also, without saying so, he

---

226 The Rockefeller Foundation seriously supported Hungarian research and public health at this time. The money allotted to Hungary was probably handled by the Hungarian National Bank in a separate *pengő* account. Because of the steadily changing exchange rates, payments were at times difficult to make; this may have been the problem in this case as well.

conveyed that he was running things as it was and that he was quite well satisfied to have it remain that way. Nevertheless, he didn't bar the possibility of his becoming Prime Minister by saying that he would not under any situation. In fact, he listened with interest to what I told him when I said that Tibor Eckhardt and a whole lot of other people had thought that he was the only one for the moment. My general impression is that he would give anything to be Prime Minister but he cannot bear to give up the 150,000 or more pengo a year that he is receiving because he has no money and I think he is anxious to accumulate a little. When I told him that Philip Weiss was strong for him he let out a hearty laugh.

[78] Conversation with Countess di Vinci, wife of Italian Minister

Budapest, April 14, 1938

Countess di Vinci told me yesterday that she wondered what kind of a reception Hitler would get when he went to Italy. Of course, the official reception would be wonderful, but what the other people would think of it she didn't know. I asked her if they didn't like Hitler, and she replied "No, no, they didn't like him." She thought the majority of the people would be pretty sour about his being there.

I mentioned Eden and she at once blamed him for everything that happened and said that if the present British Government had been in power Austria would not be German now. She mentioned that now the French were getting very friendly with the Italians, saying all kinds of nice things about them, which amused her. I said to her "Well, both the Italians and French amuse me because they are the same people and they like one another very much, just like the Americans, and the English." She agreed quite readily that this was so. I said that I couldn't imagine the Italians fighting the French, no matter what happened. She said, "No, no, we are the same people, after all."

[79] Conversation with Finance Minister Remenyi-Schneller[227]

Budapest, April 14, 1938

Mr. Remenyi-Schneller said that the situation looked quite good to him politically. He felt that the Regent's speech and the introduction of the Jew Bill, etc. had changed the situation and that now there was no opposition except from a few people who were hoping to capitalize the Austrian situation for their own benefit. He said that economically business was very bad as the Jews seemed scared to death. He said he hoped they would calm down before long and that business would get back to normal.

Mr. Remenyi-Schneller said that the Jew Bill had to be written so as to give some satisfaction to the anti-Semites and at the same time not to destroy the opportunity to raise the money for the 5-year plan. He said that any sincere person should be satisfied because the bill was a commencement and if public sentiment demanded more drastic measures the principle has been laid down and it was now easier to do it. Further, anyone that knew anything about Hungary knew that the idea of pushing the Jews out overnight was ridiculous as the Gentiles were not sufficiently versed in business to take their places. He said there would have to be a big change in sentiment toward business before they ever would begin to run the industries.

Mr. Remenyi-Schneller told me that when he first started working in a bank, he was almost considered a traitor to his class, all kinds of people came to him and told him that no gentleman would go in at the bottom like he did and work up. He said he only received 60 pengos a month and he had to do work that was considered beneath any gentleman or any member of the family. While sentiment had changed there was still a good deal of that idea that a gentleman should go in at the top, but he thought things were improving and that sentiment might change rapidly in the future. However, it would have to change quite a bit before Hungarians could really be considered as adept in business.

---

227 Lajos Reményi-Schneller (1892–1946), lawyer, general manager of the National Credit Institute after 1927, and of the National Institute for Land Credit after 1936. He was minister of finance all through 1938–45, generally considered a prop of the Germans in the Hungarian government.

[80] Conversation with Baron Apor

Budapest, April 21, 1938

In reply to the question

> Is it true Germany will not permit
> the export of lumber to Hungary?"

Baron Apor said "No, it is not true", and went on to say that German imports would not be affected by more than 10% if they took all the Austrian lumber as it is so far away from where they need it most that it is better to sell it to Hungary and take wheat, etc. in its place and get their lumber on their clearing arrangements with northern countries. Hungary expects to get the same amount of lumber as before from Austria.

In reply to the question

> Is it true that Germany will not grant exchange to
> permit tourists to visit Hungary?,"

Baron Apor said "Not entirely," and added that it is true there will not be so many German tourists here, but that is not because Germany will not grant exchange. This has been on a reciprocal basis and thousands of Hungarians visited Austria every year. Most of them, however, were Jews, and since they will not be permitted to go to Austria, or wouldn't want to go if they could, they have cut down the number of Hungarians who will go there, and correspondingly the number of Germans who will come to Hungary.

In reply to the question

> "Are there any new developments in
> Hungarian foreign trade, especially
> with regard to England?"

Apor said there are none he knows of, although says he knows very little about the subject.

Passports Hungary does not expect to limit the issuance of passports. They will, however, take more care to whom they are issued. They have discovered not only carelessness but fraud in their passport department and that many people who are not Hungarian citizens have secured passports. Therefore, they are going to be more careful in the future.

Rumania Baron Apor thinks the Rumanian situation is not so bad as they make out. He believes that the so-called Iron Guard scare is largely engineered for the purposes of the King and that he might get rid of some of his enemies, particularly those who have been opposed to Madame Lupescu.

The reply which the Rumanians gave to the Hungarian offer for rapprochement[228] was not satisfactory since it not only gave no commitments on the subject of minorities but didn't even mention minorities. They expected to continue negotiations but they were not very hopeful of ever doing anything.

Rome-Berlin Axis Baron Apor doesn't believe that the Rome-Berlin axis is as strong as previously. In fact, he says to all intents and purposes the axis is finished. The minute Italy made up with England the situation was altered. If they make up with France it will be altered still further. There can be a Rome-Berlin axis only as long as the two parties are not committed to anyone else. The minute a third party makes an arrangement with either of the parties to the axis, then the question is, in case of difficulty, which commitment is the stronger. In other words, if the Italians had to chose now between Germany and England, what reason is there to think that the Rome-Berlin axis is any stronger than the commitments to England. In view of the fact that the Italian people are terribly worked up by the German occupation of Austria, it is quite probable that the Rome-Berlin axis at the present moment is not as strong as the commitments to England, although the latter have just been made. Tomorrow the situation may change; nevertheless, the Rome-Berlin axis is no longer what it was.

Czechoslovakia Baron Apor says that he hasn't the slightest idea what Hungary will do if the Germans should go into Czechoslovakia. Everything would depend upon circumstances and conditions. Certainly they are not going to rush headlong into anything that would get them into difficulties if the Government can help it, but he said quite frankly that if Germany went into Czechoslovakia it would be difficult to hold the Hungarian people back. He thought, however, that people in Slovakia were so frightened now that if the Germans came in they might come over to Hungary at once. The Slovaks preferred the Hungarians to the Germans. He stated there was no agreement with Germany of any kind.

Baron Apor said Benes had asked Stoyadinovitch to agree to help them in case of invasion, but Stoyadinovitch said that it would be impossible because they would have to cross Hungary, and by the time they whipped the Hungarian army there would not be any more Czechoslovakia.

Apor said that one of the great mysteries was why Benes didn't mobilize the Czechoslovak army when Hitler was threatening to go into Austria. He knows positively that if they had, Hitler would never have gone in, and even

---

228 The Romanian counterproposal of late March 1938 did not provide an acceptable, substantial reply to the Hungarian propositions.

when they first went in they would have withdrawn. He said the Czechs had a good army and the Germans were particularly fearful of starting a war. Benes for some reason no one can understand did nothing, and now Czechoslovakia is in an entirely different position than she was before Germany absorbed Austria.

Italo-British Rapprochement[229] The Hungarian reaction to the Italo-British rapprochement and the Italo-French moves was that it was very pleasing inasmuch as it was a move towards peace. He thought that if France settled her internal troubles and again had taken the position she had before, the situation so far as peace is concerned would be excellent. But everything at the moment depended on France since Russia had practically become non-existent so far as European politics are concerned.

Hungarian Army Baron Apor said there wasn't any question in the world that the Hungarian army would fight if anybody invaded the country. He didn't like the question as to whether the Germans would and kept saying "Why should they?" When I insisted on an answer he said they would fight even if they didn't have a gun, they would fight anybody. I told him I had heard that army officers say that resistance would be useless; he said that didn't make any difference, if any foreign army touched Hungarian soil they would feel different about it. Not only that, one of the reasons the Germans would never take Hungary was because of this Hungarian characteristic, that they would never cease to fight anybody who took them over.

[81] Conversation with Mr. de Kanya
Budapest, May 3, 1938

Mr. de Kánya is of the opinion that Germany is not more active in Hungary than previously. He thinks various Hungarians, hoping to profit by the Nazi movement, are very active and that this will not stop, but he doesn't think it is going to be of importance. He knows nothing about any special prices given to people who are Nazis, nor does he know anything about the purchase of arms in exchange for grain. In effect, he says, this may be the case but there is no proposition that involves any such exchange. He has no doubt they will sell grain to Germany and buy arms from Germany and that

---

229 The British-Italian agreement of April 16, 1938, was brought about by Italian fears of the *Anschluß* as well as British endeavors to ease the tension in the Mediterranean. Britain acknowledged the Italian conquest in Ethiopia, and Italy promised to withdraw her volunteers from Spain.

one may offset the other, but there is no agreement of any kind that he knows of to that effect or that makes it compulsory.

Mr. de Kanya doesn't know what Hungary will do if Germany has trouble with Czechoslovakia. As far as he is concerned, it will do nothing. However, the temper of the Hungarian people is such that the matter might be taken out of the hands of the Government and anything might happen. He believes that the best policy in fact, the only policy for Hungary, is to do nothing. Action of any kind could involve one hundred complications, all of which would be disastrous. He is very positive that Germany does not want Slovakia. He says, however, that any solution that brings Slovakia back to Hungary, or brings any portion of Czech territory to Hungary, which is obtained by violent means or by agreement only with Germany will be a mistake. He hopes that events will shape themselves so that everybody will want to find a solution and he thinks this is the only way that it is safe so far as Hungary is concerned. To accept favors at the hands of any Government over the protest of other Governments would make Hungary a partner of the Power that did them the favor. As the next war will be fought largely in this part of the world, it is important for Hungary to be neutral if possible. Otherwise, she will be the theater in which the war is fought. de Kanya thinks the Italo-British agreement is a step towards the settlement of European difficulties and that a Fanco-Italian agreement when finished is also a necessary step. He said there were difficulties in the way but he hoped that they would be overcome.

Mr. de Kanya said that Mr. Hitler was not popular in Italy now and that there was a great deal of feeling about the occupation of Austria. However, so far as he knew, Mussolini still intended to stick to the Rome-Berlin axis, and at the present time, it is only Mussolini who counts.

There is nothing new on the Hungarian minority question.

He doesn't know what to think of the local political situation. He only threw up his hands when I asked him.

I asked about the revisionist meeting[230] and his alleged apology to Czechoslovakia. He said that he had called in Mr. Kobr and told him that the revisionist meeting was not sponsored by the Government and that they disapproved of the meeting at such a time and of the violence and manner of the speeches. He made no apology, nor did he disavow revision. This appeared correctly in the Czech papers, but on the radio they had it that he had gone down to the Czech Legation and made a humble apology. This, of course, annoyed him very much. He said that the Government felt that during such

---

230 This is a reference probably to the political meeting of the National Front in Budapest, on April 16.

troubled times it was a mistake to hold such a meeting and make such violent speeches. It put Hungary in a very bad position and that was the reason he had taken the trouble to advise Mr. Kobr of his opinion. He had no objection to publication as it appeared in the Czech papers.

In regard to the general European situation, Mr. de Kanya says he doesn't expect any war in the immediate future, and he doesn't expect any solution of the Czech problem very soon. He is quite of the opinion that Mr. Hitler doesn't desire war and that, therefore, he will risk no violent action which may involve him in war. If he invaded Czechoslovakia at the present time and the Czechs resist there is war, even though only with Czechoslovakia. Therefore, he does think that things will be stirred up in Czechoslovakia for a long while before any definite solution is reached. In any case, he thinks Mr. Hitler will risk nothing unless he is sure he can get away with it without going to war. Of course, Mr. de Kanya said, everybody had a right to their own opinion and his might change tomorrow, but that is the way he saw things at the moment.

[82] Conversation with Dr. Tibor Eckhardt

Budapest, May 5, 1938

Dr. Eckhardt said that the German Minister[231] had not mentioned the subject of Nazis or anything else of a political nature to him. While he, the German Minister, was extremely friendly — in violent contrast to his predecessor — Eckhardt said that he did not know whether it had any significance, or why it was. At least so far he has not revealed any ulterior motive; and in any case it would have no effect on him, Eckhardt.

Dr. Eckhardt said the Germans were undoubtedly spending lots of money here but that the Minister himself was not involved in any way. However, he said he had evidence of things that von Hahn was doing which was perfectly incredible. Eckhardt said that about 50% of the Government party were pro-Nazi.

Dr. Eckhardt thought that Daranyi was very weak, in fact incredibly so (to use his own words), and that there would have to be a change of government. He expects Imredy to succeed Daranyi and said he (Eckhardt) desired to be a member of the Cabinet himself. Previously he felt he had more influence outside the Cabinet, but under the present circumstances he felt the situation was the reverse and he wished to be in the Cabinet.

---

231 Otto von Erdmannsdorff.

Dr. Eckhardt said that the Nazis had sent 60 men to Germany to learn the technique of becoming terrorists and that on May 9 they expect to begin their Hungarian campaign. He himself, Bethlen, Szell and the Chief of Police were on the proscribed list. This campaign, he thought, would take the form of bombs and other methods used in Austria. He said he was informed that at the meeting which he expected to address at Bekes on June 15 the Nazis would begin their campaign against him. I asked where he got all this information and he replied that he had members of his party who belonged to the Nazi party and kept in touch with everything they did. He told me that they had secretly organized a military division of his own party consisting of young men who didn't mind fighting. He would have 400 of these at the meeting at Bekes on the 15th of June and they had now in every city a group of this kind.

As far as Czechoslovakia was concerned, he felt everything depended upon England. He said that the Germans would not be in Austria if it hadn't been for the Halifax visit, and he felt certain that the Germans would not go into Czechoslovakia unless England indicated that they would do nothing or as long as he felt there was a possibility of England taking some action. In any case, he didn't believe it would develop rapidly, although the end might come suddenly as it did in Austria.

Dr. Eckhardt said that the Regent was now fully aware of the dangers of the Nazi activity, although a little late, and that last week every officer in the army had had to sign a statement promising to attend no meeting and to take no part in any political activity, etc. General Ratz[232] personally read this statement and discussed it with the General Staff and informed them that extreme measures would be taken to eliminate all political activity from the army. Dr. Eckhardt said that a number of younger officers have already been dropped and a close watch was being kept.

I asked Eckhardt about General Ratz, whether he was pro-Nazi, etc., and he said while he might be the action of the Regent had considerably intimidated him and that for the moment he was engaged in eradicating politics from the army.

---

232 General Jenő Rátz (1882–1952), chief of the Honvéd general staff 1936–38, minister of defense 1938, minister without portfolio 1944.

[83] Conversation with Mr. Kobr

Budapest, May 24, 1938

Mr. Kobr said that the trouble in Czechoslovakia was a deliberate plot on the part of Germans to ruin the "Dolezite pokyny."[233] They expected 20,000 people to come to that and the Germans were trying to create a war scare to prevent people from coming. Also, it was part of their settled policy to stir up the Sudeten Germans and he thought they would keep it up until after the elections on June 12th. He didn't think, however, anything would come of it or that there would be any war. He said his Government has had to call out the army to stop the riots and to preserve order.[234] It had no other purpose.

I told him I had been up to the Czech border and described to him everything I saw. He agreed that there is no evidence of any military activity on the Hungarian side along the border and that the Hungarians were being especially careful not to provoke incidents. However, he said he heard that the Hungarians were mobilizing their army further back and named different regiments that had been called out, and said also that they were commandeering automobiles, etc. I asked him if he believed it and he said no he didn't, but he wasn't sure it wasn't true. He thought that the Hungarians were being especially careful not because they minded having incidents in order to stir up trouble, but because of the Eucharistic Congress they didn't want any unpleasant incidents to happen while that was in session.

[84] Conversation with Baron von Hahn

Budapest, May 24, 1938

Baron von Hahn told me all German diplomats and he himself had strict instructions not to discuss Czechoslovakia with anyone. He said that I would find no diplomat would enter into discussions which concerned Czechoslovakia. He then proceeded to say that he thought the Czechs were trying to provoke the Germans into war, that they realized they couldn't last and were anxious to start a war when it was least advantageous for Germany. The Germans knew that France would fight if they got into a war with Czecho-

---

233 Dôležité pokyny: "important orders" concerning the mobilization of the Czechoslovak army.

234 In response to the German and Sudeten German provocations, the Czechoslovak government ordered a partial mobilization on May 20, 1938. This was followed by the so-called May Crisis of Czechoslovakia.

slovakia. They were definitely sure of that inasmuch as the French line was almost impregnable[235] and it was difficult for the Germans to invade France. The German line was practically as good and he didn't think the French could invade Germany. If war were declared now the first thing that France would do would be to pour troops into Spain. Therefore, the first battle-ground would be Spain. This would put the Germans and the Italians at a disadvantage and would spoil everything there. Germany was doing her utmost to keep from having a war and he was astonished at the calmness and the repression of the German people in the newspapers at this difficult time. I told him I thought in any case Czechoslovakia wasn't quite right. A year from now if the Germans and the Poles and the Hungarians worked on the populace properly it would be much easier. He agreed quite heartily. I told him that if Germany didn't want war they could probably accomplish what they wanted in Czechoslovakia without war. He thought so too.

Baron von Hahn commented on the amount of information the Hungarians had of what was going on in Czechoslovakia. From what he said he thought it was amazing, and I gathered the idea that this information is being passed onto Germany. When he left he said he agreed with me that nothing will happen in Czechoslovakia for at least a year unless, of course, the Czechs succeed in provoking Germany to the point where they can no longer stand it. "We certainly cannot see them killing our Germans and doing nothing about it."

[85] Conversation with Dr. Tibor Eckhardt

Budapest, May 25, 1938

Dr. Eckhardt told me that a few days ago Dr. Imredy called on him and they had a long conversation and had come to a perfect understanding. Eckhardt is to go in as Minister of Commerce in August or September.[236] A new election under the secret ballot bill is to be held next spring. Before the election Imredy and Eckhardt will form a new party which will include a portion of the National Union Party, and Independent Farmers, and Christian Socialists. In fact, it will unite the conservative elements of these parties, that is, those who do not belong to the extreme Right.[237]

---

235 The French Maginot Line was a superb defense system established in the 1930s in the event of a possible German attack on France. It was dedicated to French minister of war André Maginot (1877–1932).

236 Tibor Eckhardt in fact never became a member of any government.

237 The plan was never to become reality.

[86] Conversation with Baron Apor – October 19
Budapest, October 20, 1938

Baron Apor said that Imredy's statement published yesterday (October 18th)[238] represented no change in Hungarian foreign policy, but it had been considered necessary because of rumors that de Kanya was trying to organize a bloc consisting of Poland, Italy and Hungary to combat Germany, and Imredy's statement was supposed to deny this rumor and to reaffirm Hungary's friendship for all three Powers.[239] Incidentally, Apor said that the rumor of Hungary's intention to desert Italy and join Germany was false. Beck's Chief of Cabinet, he said, was here to acquaint the Hungarians with Beck's intentions in connection with his visit to Rumania. Beck, he added, long had the idea of reconciliating Hungary and Rumania — an objective not possible before but which now seemed able of accomplishment.

Apor had not heard that Rumania wanted any part of Ruthenia,[240] although it had consistently claimed a small part which Benes had prevented them from receiving. However, he said this was not regarded as important. Nor would Hungary object to Rumania getting territory it desired, provided Hungary got what it wanted.

The Hungarian-Slovak conversations, Apor went on to say, had not been resumed, but discussions were now going on concerning them at Prague between the Czechs, Germans and Italians, and it was hoped that as a result thereof Czechoslovakia might have a new satisfactory offer to make Hungary who, however, would not resume conversations unless some satisfactory proposal had been made.

Apor does not expect an actual customs union to be made between Czechoslovakia and Germany, but both of these countries, he said, had informed Hungary that they were working out a plan which approached that envisaged by a customs union without actually including one. Apor thought that Czechoslovakia economically could do nothing else. He does not like the idea of a customs union between Germany and Hungary, finding that the idea is unpopular in Hungary and that it would be resisted officially.

---

238 Prime Minister Béla Imrédy gave a statement to the Hungarian News Agency on October 18, 1938, arguing for a program of strengthening the relationship with the Axis powers.

239 Kánya himself told German secretary of state for foreign affairs von Weizsäcker on October 12, 1938, "that the tendentious rumors as to the Hungarian government's willingness to enter into a new kind of bloc policy be considered exclusively the evil brainchild of our enemies." DIMK II:781.

240 Sub-Carpathian Ukraine.

Apor denied the rumor that Antal's resignation had anything to do with Imredy's statement of yesterday. Antal, he said, had resigned a week ago and he thought there would be no reaction thereto as the former Chief of the Propaganda Bureau generally is unpopular.

Germany, said Apor, had not made an offer of economic help to Hungary, and he did not bar the possibility of her doing so.

MAGYARSAG of Sunday was suppressed, he said, because it contained articles on Hungarian foreign policy of which the Government disapproved. He did not know whether the Nazi movement in Hungary had increased or not as he said he was not familiar with the local political situation, but his impression was that this movement had increased.

Anti-Jewish feeling he thought was growing in the country, but this feeling was of long-standing and at times it had been more violent then it has been in the past few years or is even now. However, it had not been as dangerous for the Jews in the past as it is now because formerly it was a purely domestic problem.

[87] Conversation with Mr. Milos Kobr

Budapest, October 26, 1938

Mr. Kobr told me that the Hungarian Minister at Prague had been handed this morning at eleven o'clock the Czechoslovak reply to the recent Hungarian note offering to leave the fate of certain towns to arbitration by the Germans and Italians and other towns to arbitration by the Germans, Italians and Poles. Their reply had been an acceptance of German and Italian arbitration, but a rejection of Polish.[241]

I asked Mr. Kobr if they were going to permit the Hungarians to enter Thursday as requested, and he said No, that the whole thing would be done in three or four days and it would be no use going into certain portions of the territory in advance. He said that the Czechs had already made preparations for that part of the territory they knew they were going to lose, and that the whole matter would be concluded by the first of November.

---

241 Preparation of the so-called First Vienna Award.

[88] Conversation with Mr. Rasic, the new Yugoslav Minister

Budapest, October 27, 1938

Mr. Rasic said that Yugoslavia had a desire to have closer friendship with Hungary, that her Prime Minister's one desire was for peace in order to raise the standard of living for his people, and, therefore, he would do all possible to increase friendships of his country.

Mr. Rasic felt that his predecessor had somewhat changed the relations between Hungary and Yugoslavia and that he would do all possible and had during his brief stay here made statements to the press and to officials of the Government expressing the friendship of his country for Hungary. He said that a few years ago Yugoslavia had seven neighbors, of whom five were enemies and two friends; now they were all friends.

Poland, Mr. Rasic said, desired a common frontier with Hungary to thwart German territorial expansion, to keep Bolshevism at her back, and to provide an economic unity between Poland and Hungary, A common frontier would provide Poland with direct access to the Adriatic, Hungary direct access to Gydnia [=Gdynia].

Mr. Rasic said that Yugoslavia didn't want Germany down to her borders and that he was highly in favor of Hungarian friendship and an eternal pact, and begged my assistance to do what I could to bring about such a thing. He hoped to accomplish what Vuk[c]evic's successor accomplished in Bulgaria. He showed every evidence of being very anxious to be friends with Hungary and make some arrangement toward that end.

Mr. Rasic said Rumania would oppose a common frontier between Poland and Hungary because she wanted to keep a direct line of communication with Prague. He said Czechoslovakia was not the country it used to be and any agreement with Czechoslovakia could not be considered in the same light as in the past, indicating that his country would not be apt to go to its defense. (Later he said his country despised the Czechs and had contempt for the Rumanians.) He added that under the Little Entente Agreement they still were obliged to go to the assistance of Czechoslovakia in case Hungary attacked that country.

"We've got to make up with Hungary. I was sent here for that purpose, and we will have to get together and resist Germany," he said. He added several times that his country wanted to act officially in the Anglo-Saxon cadre as opposed to the German.

Mr. Rasic said that he felt the Hungarian-Czechoslovak problem would be solved within a day or two in Rome[242] because both Germany and Italy

---

242 German foreign minister von Ribbentrop negotiated with Mussolini and Count Ciano in Rome between October 27 and 30 on the fate of Czechoslovakia.

desired a speedy solution, as did the Czechs. He did not believe Czechoslovakia would give up possession of the border towns, nor grant plebiscites,
and while they were open to arbitration they would subscribe to no scheme
which deprived them of Ruthenia.

[89] Conversation with Dr. Tibor Eckhardt

Budapest, November 16, 1938

Dr. Eckhardt said that Mr. Imredy's position was very bad, and that he
would be out of office within two weeks or a month. He said that the meeting last night did not come to a vote because the opposition did not want to
put the Government out of office at this particular time.

After the meeting forty of the most prominent members[243] of the National Union Party met — among whom were Mikecz,[244] Bornemisza, Sztranyavszky,[245] Korniss [sic],[246] Zsitvay,[247] Marschall,[248] Bansaghy,[249] head of
the University student group, Lanyi,[250] Vice President of the [   ] House.
In another room there was a joint meeting between the Christian Socialists
and the Independent Farmers Party. The 40 members of the National Union
Party signed a declaration on withdrawing from the Party and gave the declaration to Mr. Sztranyavszky for use when necessary. The Independent
Farmers Party passed a resolution giving authority to Dr. Eckhardt to join
with this group and the formation of a new party, and the Christian Socialist
party passed a similar resolution.

According to Eckhardt, Mr. Daranyi while not present is conversant with
the details and will also join the party. Count Bethlen is sympathetic but
will remain independent. This group, according to Dr. Eckhardt, controls an

---

243 These were conservative "dissidents" from the NEP party, opponents to Imrédy.
244 Ödön Mikecz (1894–1965), lawyer, lord lieutenant, minister of justice 1938.
245 Sándor Sztranyavszky (1882–1942), lord lieutenant, secretary of state in the Min-
    istry of the Interior 1926–31, president of the NEP party, Speaker of the House
    1935–38, minister of agriculture 1938.
246 Gyula Kornis (1885–1958), Budapest University professor, member, and subse-
    quently president, of the Hungarian Academy of Sciences, MP for the NEP party,
    Speaker of the House.
247 Tibor Zsitvay (1884–1969), government commissioner/lord lieutenant 1919–20,
    Speaker of the House 1926–27, minister of justice 1929–32, MP for the NEP party.
248 Ferenc Marschall (1887–1970), secretary of state for agriculture 1934-38, minister
    1938, MP for the NEP party.
249 György Bánsághy, *vitéz* (1895–?), founder of the University Battalion, later of the
    Turul Alliance, MP for the NEP party.
250 Márton Lányi (1882–?), lawyer, former lord lieutenant, MP for the NEP party.

Tibor Eckhardt addressing a political meeting (1920s)

overwhelming majority of Parliament. While the Social Democratic party will not join they are so opposed to Imredy they would vote with them against the Government. He says that this is a very deep secret, that nobody knows about it — least of all Imredy — and he begged me to keep it very confidential.

Imredy's position and loss of prestige, according to Eckhardt, is due to the fact that at the time the international situation looked serious, the Regent, de Kanya, Imredy, Count Bethlen and himself held a consultation and all agreed that whatever might come Hungary would remain neutral. The army leaders were of the same opinion. This was held before the trip to Berlin, and they fully expected the Germans to sound them out, but it developed that the Germans felt that they should bring the matter up first, and as they were too happy not to say anything about it, not a word was said. This was not at all pleasing to the Germans. Therefore, Mr. Imredy's position so far as Germany was concerned, was not good after the Munich settlement. While his position up to this point was fine, he should have put on his hat — to use Mr. Eckhardt's expression — and walked out and let de Kanya handle foreign affairs so that de Kanya could say "Of course, Imredy would have done the right thing if he was doing it" which would have made negotiations with Germany much smoother. Imredy's presence made things much more difficult. When he discovered this, he turned and went back on everything he said and tried to be pro-German, even called in Nazis from the town and tried to get them to join his party, all of them refused, and did everything that he had hitherto been against, including an attempt to govern without Parliament, which, although he denied, there is no question about because the matter was discussed in the Cabinet and was opposed by the three Ministers who resigned, and also by Count Teleki and Keresztes-Fischer. The latter two incidentally, he claimed, were sympathetic with this party movement. In fact, he said he thought Keresztes-Fischer might resign almost any time.

[90] Conversation with Dr. Tibor Eckhardt

Budapest, November 22, 1938

At five this afternoon there is to be a party meeting. Just before going to Parliament, Mr. Brandt,[251] Member of the House, will present Dr. Imredy with a letter signed by 61 members of the Party announcing their withdrawal from the Party. These will unite with the Christian Socialists and Independent Farmers to form a United Hungarian Party.[252] Dr. Imredy will either have to resign immediately or face Parliament tomorrow. If he faces Parliament, as soon as he makes his speech, Mr. Sztranyavszky will rise and move a vote of no confidence, seconded by Dr. Eckhardt, which — according to Eckhardt — will result in the fall of the Government.

The Regent was informed this morning by Szell and obtained his consent to go ahead. No promises have been made with regard to the Cabinet, but inasmuch as the 61 include people, plus members of the Opposition, up to 80, the United Hungarian Party will in addition, as soon as it is known to be the dominant party, form a new Cabinet. The probable Cabinet as now talked of — subject to acceptances — will be:

Prime Minister	Sztranyavszky, or Korniss
Interior	Keresztes-Fischer
Education	Count Paul Teleki
Home Defense	Werth, present Chief of Staff
Agriculture	Daranyi (or Foreign Minister)
Finance	Fabinyi, although he has not yet been consulted
Foreign Affairs	Csaky insisted upon by de Kanya, who wants to retire
Mikecz	head of a new Ministry, Public Welfare, which will have to do with unemployment.
Eckhardt	Minister of Agriculture if Daranyi becomes Foreign Minister; if not, head of a new Ministry having a land reform program.

251 Vilmos Brandt (1888–?), retired lord lieutenant, MP.
252 The new party was not established despite the political regrouping within the government party.

Dr. Imredy when expected to fall last Thursday suggested to the Regent that in this event Ratz be asked to form a new Cabinet. The Regent refused. Imredy was the principal advocate of sending the Hungarian army into Ruthenia.[253] Eckhardt doesn't know whether they have gone in or not; as far as he knows they are still arguing. The Regent and de Kanya opposing.

As far as he knows there are actually no Hungarian soldiers in Ruthenia. He says that there are only 24,000 Czech soldiers in the whole of Ruthenia. He doesn't know whether the Ruthenians have actually made a protest for Hungarian protection. He has been so busy with Hungarian domestic politics he hasn't paid much attention to this. Nor does he know what Czech reaction would be. He thinks it would make no difference. The principal thing is what the German reaction would be. Incidentally, he said that America is doing Hungary a great favor because at the moment Germany is so occupied with the United States[254] it would be a good time to go into Ruthenia. He knows nothing about the Germans in Ruthenia or the Poles.

Germany is opposed to Hungarian aspirations in Ruthenia on principle, but he isn't certain whether they care very much except that they feel that they have Czechoslovakia and that Hungary has been conceded enough. He doesn't know anything about Hungarians in America requesting intervention. He hadn't heard of it. The same reason as above.

The invasion of Ruthenia might be a popular issue, and for that reason he thought even Imredy might order it despite the Regent in a last desperate effort to save himself, although he felt this to be suicide, but he didn't feel it impossible.

He thought the pengo would have to be devaluated. He said that since they have taken over the new territory the relations between the Crown and the Pengo was such that school teachers were getting 500 pengo a month whereas one in Hungary was getting 200. Also, other salaries were out of proportion. He couldn't say something had to be done; he couldn't see anything else but devaluation. At what figure he didn't know.

---

253 The military action in the sub-Carpathian area was decided at the extraordinary cabinet meeting of November 18, 1938; it was, however, stopped as a result of German and Italian government protests on the 21st. The actual occupation of the sub-Carpathian region was carried out as of March 15, 1939.

254 U.S. ambassador Hugh Wilson was recalled from Berlin for "consultations" on November 14, 1938, in the aftermath of the *Kristallnacht* pogrom. He never returned to his post. Hans Dieckhoff, the German ambassador in Washington, D.C., reported at the same time that "a hurricane is raging here;" he was also recalled on November 18 and was not to return to Washington, D.C. The German chargé d'affaires in Washington, D.C., suggested to his government on November 30 that "in view of the strained relations and the lack of security for secret material" in the embassy building, the "secret political files" should be removed to Berlin (William L. Shirer, *op. cit.*,433, note).

He said there was tremendous pressure put on Hungary by the Italians and the Germans to do something about the Jews. He said that even back in Daranyi's time Daranyi complained about the German Minister coming and demanding action against the Jews. He felt something would have to be done to satisfy those countries but he didn't believe, or at least he hoped, that nothing would be done in haste, or that it would be done in such a way as to lose the benefits of being the only country in which the Jews were treated decently. He was sure there would not be any violent persecutions, and he believed that they fell heir to a certain amount of business by being not anti-Jewish, and that he hoped and believed that they wouldn't lose that by falling into the German trap. There were other ways to satisfy Germany by putting pressure on them all the time, and not in such a way as to crucify them or earn the title of being a Nazi or anti-Jewish country. He feels that the Jews have to go, but he says there never was a time when all these things could be done like now. He says before the Jews opposed every step, but now are unopposed to anything so long as they can save their skins. He says the public landowners were of the same opinion; Bethlen was reconciled to the revision of large estates.

The Nazis will be furious about this and they would vote in Parliament for Imredy. Sztranyavszky is reputed to be one, but isn't. Eckhardt says Sztranyavszky will go after the Nazis. While not a man of great ability, like [   ], he can address a meeting and carry off things while making a good appearance.

Werth is cleaning up the Nazis now and is expected to, and that is what the Regent is determined to do.

[91] Conversation with Dr. Tibor Eckhardt

Budapest, November 30, 1938

According to Dr. Eckhardt, Imredy has been able to remain in office through German support, for which he was obliged to agree to the discard of de Kanya, hands off in Ruthenia, and giving the Germans in Hungary the right to organize. It is expected that through a new Press Bill to be passed next week all Opposition press will be suppressed. Also, all permission for the holding of political meetings will be denied. A new anti-Jewish bill is also expected to ensue.

The Regent knew nothing of Imredy's arrangements until they had all been completed, and then he was persuaded by Teleki and Keresztes-Fischer to agree to them, but he did demand that Imredy suppress Szalasi, Hubay and the Nazis in general. de Kanya was not pleased when he was dropped.

The second government of Béla Imrédy, November 15, 1938
(Seated in the front row are Kálmán Kánya, Béla Imrédy, and Count Pál Teleki)

He feels offended and has soon nobody since his resignation was accept-ed.[255] He was the brake on the Government and now that he is gone there would be nothing to retard it. In short, Eckhardt believed that Imredy will now become a dictator and the Regent will find himself in discard.

It was interesting that both the Italian and the German press had con-ducted a campaign in favor of Imredy, whereas in the beginning they were opposed to him. It was thought now that Nazi methods would be used in Hungary and that there would be no freedom of the press or the right to assemble. The Nazi movement in Hungary could be expected to abate and later increase in its activity.

Baron Vegh[256] is reputed to have been the principal assistant of Imredy in making these arrangements with the Germans.

As regards Ruthenia, the Germans on Monday last informed the Hunga-rian Government that they would consider it an unfriendly act if Hungary were to persevere in its efforts to acquire this region. Imredy had been obliged to recede from his position and the question of Hungarian acquisi-tion of Ruthenia is a dead issue.

---

255 Foreign Minister Kánya resigned on November 28, 1938.
256 Probably Dr. Miklós Végh, chief of protocol in the Foreign Ministry.

Conditions were bad in the Uplands because after twenty years absence from Hungary the situation there did not correspond with that in Hungary proper. Slovakia would be better off if it had been returned to Hungary than remain in the Czechoslovak State because the question of crops and markets would have been easier to work out. In the present situation the Uplands will suffer.

Eckhardt thought that Imredy's adoption of Nazi principles would be unpopular and thought that he would attempt to form a new Government party. The only way to combat him was to work for dissolution within his own party. Eckhardt thought that a coalition party might be formed against him (Imredy) which would include Bornemisza, Mikesz, and Count Bethlen. He also thought that Korniss would retire. He was the political person most dangerous to Imredy: while he had the manners of a priest he had the heart of a Jesuit. Imredy was, however, so mad for power that he might even go against the Church.

[92] Conversation with Prime Minister Imredy

Budapest, December 1, 1938

At the beginning of the conversation, Dr. Imredy was not disposed to discuss any of the questions put to him, and referred me merely to his public statement adding that he had nothing to add thereto. It was impossible to obtain an answer to questions regarding future policy. He took refuge in the statement that he was no Foreign Minister,[257] and he knew nothing about the Foreign Office and he would say nothing regarding it because he could not commit the new Foreign Minister in advance. Also, he did not know whom would be appointed as next Foreign Minister, but that there would be no change in Hungarian policy.

The Prime Minister commented on the interest shown in America in the Jewish question abroad, and he said he could not understand America's attitude since it had its own Negro problem. The Minister said he saw no comparison between the Negro problem and the Jewish problem because save in some minor instances in the South, the Negroes were not prejudiced against. During the course of the conversation the attitude of the Prime Minister was hostile to America but, probably in consideration of the personal friendship between the Minister and Dr. Imredy, his attitude was not more hostile than

---

257 This was technically incorrect as Imrédy acted also as foreign minister between November 28 and December 10, 1938.

it had been in the past with reference to American affairs, when Dr. Imredy had spoken in an official capacity.

Imredy would not discuss the past and present attitude of the German and Italian press towards him and his Government.

He would not express a view concerning Hungarian policy vis-a-vis Germany, and he simply did not bother to answer questions regarding future control of the press and political activities. He did say that the new Jew Bill would not be inhumane, and would not differ greatly from the one now in force, but he could not give me the details of the new Bill because they were still differences in detail which had to be worked out. For instance, the question of whether the terms of the bill would follow racial or religious lines. He voluntarily promised to provide me with details of the new Bill before it was presented to Parliament, but he refused to answer my question if the Bill would be parallel to the German Nuremberg law, he denied absolutely that Germany or Italy ever had urged Hungary to take more drastic action against the Jews. He was astonished and said that if such action had ever been taken he had never heard of it. The Minister expressed the regret that there was now nobody at the Foreign Office with whom he could have conversations, and therefore, he had come directly to the Prime Minister who was acting as Foreign Minister. Dr. Imredy said that he did not propose to remain on as Foreign Minister but would appoint somebody to this position within a few days but he had not decided who would be appointed.[258]

In brief, the Foreign Minister[259] adopted the attitude which he always had assumed in official conversations. He reproached the Minister for accusing him of moving his Government closer towards Germany. The Minister said he had not accused Dr. Imredy of anything, but he had only voiced a natural apprehension and had acted solely with the desire to obtain accurate information to transmit to his Government and so to avoid possible misconceptions.

[93] Conversation with Count Stephen Bethlen

Budapest, December 1, 1938

Count Bethlen said that the Regent was uncompromisingly against any German Nazi activity in Hungary. Imredy had promised to put an end to the Nazi activity when first he became Prime Minister. He had not done so, but had excused himself in saying that he had too many other preoccupations.

---

258 The regent appointed Count István Csáky foreign minister on December 10, 1938.
259 Meaning Imrédy.

After his recent resignation[260] he had given the Regent a definite promise to carry out an anti-Nazi program and on this basis he had been reappointed. The Regent really was opposed to Imredy, but on the advice of two prominent Statesmen[261] whom he had consulted and who had advised him that sentiment in the country had grown in favor of Imredy, he reappointed him. This was justified by the fact that there had been a reaction in favor of Imredy throughout the country.

Bethlen said that he had voted with the opposition against Imredy because he felt the latter was playing a dangerous game in that he was following a Nazi political thought. He also thought that Imredy was not competent nor trustworthy.

He did not feel that Imredy had made a definite deal with Germany, but nevertheless, he was playing a German game and encouraging Germany in the hope of perpetuating himself in office with German support. He did not think Imredy would or could keep his promise to the Regent to curb the Nazi activity in the country, and he hoped that public sentiment would turn against Imredy within a month or two.

The turn of events in Ruthenia was having a definite effect in the country, especially with the soldiers who were returning from the frontier and were bitter against Germany for not permitting Hungary to proceed in Ruthenia. In consequence, the feeling in the Army had become anti-German and he felt that this same feeling now permeated the nation. The country had not been properly informed of the real political situation and it knew little about Imredy and his politics. Soon the country would become better informed and as the Opposition was not impotent but strong, it might eventually be able to overthrow Imredy.

As regards the Jew question, Bethlen said that the Regent realized that something must be done to solve it, but he would never stand even an approach to the German treatment of this question, and would not support in office any Prime Minister who attempted to do so. He said that the Regent was determined in his stand on the Jewish question and on foreign policy. However, he was not as well informed as he should have been and in consequence Imredy had been reappointed on false pretenses.

He attributed no importance to the recently formed German Volksbund,[262]

---

260 Count Bethlen and his group voted against the government in the debate of the House on the agenda, whereupon Imrédy and his government tendered their resignation on November 23, 1938. The regent, however, told Imrédy on November 27 that he did not accept his resignation, though he warned him to thrust back the parties of the extreme right and to abstain from dictatorial methods threatening the constitution.
261 Count Pál Teleki and Ferenc Keresztes-Fischer.
262 On November 26, 1938, Imrédy permitted the foundation of the *Volksbund (Volksbund der Deutschen in Ungarn),* the organization of the Germans in Hungary.

Kálmán Kánya and Count István Bethlen at a garden party, May 1937

and refuted Eckhardt's statement that this would be a uniform organization.

In the Ruthenian question, de Kanya had sent a note to the Italian and German Governments informing them that the situation in Ruthenia is untenable and suggesting that Hungarian troops move in to restore order, following which a plebiscite would be held. A note was received in reply from Berlin indicating that the German Government was apathetical regarding events in Ruthenia, but warned of the strength of the Czech Army and expressed the fear that were Hungary to move into Ruthenia her army would be defeated by the Czechs. In any event, the note ended, Germany could not be of assistance to Hungary because she had acted as an arbitrator in the Czech-Hungarian boundary dispute.[263] The Hungarian Minister in Rome called on Mussolini and informed him of the contents of the German note, whereupon Mussolini agreed to the Hungarian proposal to go into Ruthenia and restore order and he called in the German Ambassador to inform him of this action. Thereupon, the German Ambassador said that Mussolini did not have a correct interpretation of the German note and on the contrary his country was unalterably opposed to Hungary marching to

---

263 Reference to the First Vienna Award.

Ruthenia. The German Government then addressed a new note to Budapest in which it was said that Germany having acted as an arbiter would be embarrassed by Hungary's taking action beyond the terms of the Vienna award, and, therefore, if Hungary advanced into Ruthenia Germany would consider it an unfriendly act. The German Government also asked Mussolini to address a similar note to Budapest.

In response to my question if Imredy would attempt to suppress the press and curb political activity, Bethlen said that Imredy would like to do so, but that he would not dare to because he would be opposed by the Regent, and, therefore, he did not believe he would do it. Imredy, he said, was trying to fight fire with fire, and in doing so was playing a dangerous game, which he was incapable of playing, and Bethlen was confident that the entire situation would change within two months.

de Kanya, Bethlen said, had resigned from the cabinet simply because he could not get along with Imredy, who had interfered in foreign affairs and so had handicapped the Foreign Minister by trying to overbid him. When de Kanya found that Imredy was to remain as Prime Minister he would not remain on even for a day.

Bethlen was of the opinion that Baron Apor had left the Foreign Ministry precipitately on a holiday because he felt that either Czaky or Bardossy would become the new Foreign Minister. Both of these men were junior to him, and he would not continue to serve as Under Secretary under either of them. In consequence, he went on leave immediately after de Kanya resigned and was not expected to return to the Foreign Office, but probably would get some post abroad.[264] Bethlen considered Apor to be the best man in the whole Foreign Service and regretted that circumstances had forced him out of his position.

[94] Conversation with Count Teleki, Minister of Education November 30

Budapest, December 7, 1938

Count Teleki obviously was embarrassed by the questions I put to him regarding Hungary's future foreign and domestic policy. He cast about for answers, obviously intent upon avoiding untruths. He appeared not to wish to admit that Imredy had placed his Government closer to Berlin, but he said that the country was anti-German. Military officers had reported the troops returning from the border to be bitter against Germany. A retired

---

264 Baron Apor became minister to the Holy See as of January 1939.

General, acting as a news reporter, in plain clothes, had been with the troops at the border, and had reported a distinct anti-German feeling amongst them. In addition, he said, Hungarian students had held a demonstration before the German Legation, in the course of which they serenaded it with scurrillous songs. The country, he said, was so anti-German as to represent a danger. He himself was both anti-German and anti-Nazi, and so it was difficult for him to discuss these matters.

[95] Conversation with Dr. von Erdmannsdorff German Minister

Budapest, December 17, 1938

Dr. von Erdmannsdorff said that the Prime Minister gave him the impression of a man who didn't know quite what he was doing. He seemed to have a lot of ideas but when it came to executing them he was at a complete loss.

von Erdmannsdorff said he didn't know anything about the Jew Bill,[265] but when I told him that I heard its provisions were very drastic he said these people cannot do without the Jews. "I have talked to the Regent several times and told them that they have to do it gradually. Otherwise, there would be chaos."

We discussed at length Hungarian characteristics and ability with regard to business, farming, etc., and we had the same opinion, that Hungarians have yet to learn to work, start at the bottom. Until they learn that they cannot do without the Jews, or someone else must take the Jew's place.

I spoke about land reform. von Erdmannsdorff said "How can they have any land reform when they have no money to buy the land?" I said to him that they were going to have a bill out soon. He said it was all nonsense to go into any radical land reform unless it had been well planned and everything prepared for its proper execution. I said that I thought the Jew Bill and Land Reform Bill are matters of political expediency. Imredy is trying to head off Hubay[266] and Szalasi, and he replied "Yes, yes," but he also said "He is a fanatic, he also wants to save the Church. He is not going to sell Church land, he is going to lease it, and in that way avoid their losing their property." I told him I heard that Imredy spent four or five hours in church every day, and he said he hadn't heard that but wouldn't be surprised.

---

265 Reference to the second Jew Bill then in the making.
266 Kálmán Hubay (1902–1946), right-wing journalist, Hungarist, subsequently Arrow-cross politician, MP.

Otto von Erdmannsdorff, German minister to Budapest,
November 20, 1940

I asked if he had heard that they were going to have a larger army. He had heard that but didn't know whether it was so. I said I am told they are, and I hope they know what to do with it when they have it. He laughed.

I asked what he thought about Csaky. He said, "He has changed a lot since he became Foreign Minister." I said, "More self-possessed." He said, "Yes, he is more self-possessed." I said he looked to me quite confident, and I added that I hoped it was justified. He laughed.

Mr. von Erdmannsdorff talked very freely. It is my first political conversation with him; I have never tried it before. His ideas on the Jew Bill rather astonished me. However, he is not a Nazi and I am told almost resigned at one time because he didn't want to cope with the Nazis. However, apparently he has talked with the Regent on the subject, and one could reasonably infer that the ideas he presents so far as the Jews are concerned are the ideas of his Government, that is, they would understand it if the Hungarians did not get rough with the Jews at once.

[96] Conversation with Prime Minister Imredy

Budapest, December 19, 1938

Jew Bill[267]

The Jews are actually going to be considered on a racial basis but the Bill is not written that way: it is entirely on a religious basis but in effect it is racial. In other words, they have not dared to face the wrath of the Catholic Church by making it entirely racial.

The Jews will be divided into three categories:

1. definition of a Jew: first, the Jews, that is, the Jews who belong to the Jewish Church; those belonging to the Jewish race are not considered being based on religion;

2. those whose father and mother are or were Jews. There is an exception to this. Those whose parents were converted at or on a certain date and if married before the Bill is introduced. The date the Prime Minister thought would be about the same as the last date. This means that all those who marry hereafter — their children, even of mixed marriages, will be held as Jews.

3. Those who have at least two real Christian grandparents. That does not mean converted Jews, it means born Christians. If their parents were Jews but were converted before, if their grandparents were Christian they qualify, but they must be born Christian.

The bill itself won't speak of Jews as a race, only as a religion. In business they can only employ 12%; it must be reduced to that ratio in four years. Jewish war veterans (with certain exceptions — that is those who have silver medals and certain other prerequisites) can be 3% above that figure.

Editors, lawyers, directors, engineers, newspapermen, actors, and theatrical people are reduced to 6%, but there are no dismissals. It simply means they cannot employ any new Jews until the percentage gets down to 6%.

The editor or leader cannot be manager except for Jewish newspapers. Any paper, however, can be Jewish if it says at the top it is Jewish. It can be daily and the Hungarian language, or anything else.

A theatrical manager cannot be a Jew.

Jews will have a right to vote, but they vote as a minority. They can elect M.P.'s and representatives to local municipal councils, but not more than at a ratio of 6%, that is, in their proportion; and that is the percentage of the editors, doctors, etc.

---

267 Act IV: 1939, the so-called second Jew Bill, was promulgated on May 5, 1939.

Business. Those who export one-third of their production will have three additional years to make the change.

There will be no restrictions extended to other professions not covered.

No new Jews in the diplomatic service, Foreign Office, or in any other Government department; but no dismissal of those there.

No new ownership of agricultural properties. Gradual liquidation of all Jewish agricultural property. Town property not covered, but there will probably be another bill introduced to cover that.

Jewish war veterans will be prevented from engaging in public service.

As I said, the Jews will vote as a minority, but only in a proportion of 6%. However, there are exceptions in cities where the Jews pay more than a certain amount of the taxes; they can have more deputies, but it is only temporary.

Jews who emigrate will probably be considered as expatriates, although this bill doesn't provide for that.

They are going to organize a committee composed of Gentiles and Jews to supervise emigration on a large scale. He is meeting with Hevesi[268] and other Jews tomorrow to discuss the provisions of the bill and to make arrangements to organize the emigration. He says at least twenty to twenty-five thousand must emigrate. Samuel Stern,[269] president of the Jewish Parish, told him that the Jews can arrange emigration for 50,000. This mixed commission will supervise emigration; they can take their property with them so far as foreign exchange permits. He claims, however, they are going to try out some foreign exchange scheme, probably with Jews in other countries, whereby they can get the transfer of property.

The Army Bill provides for expropriation of property only of concerns making war materials in peace times and in time of war if production cannot be assured.

Tradesmen. They are going to license all independent tradesmen. These must have a certificate from the administrative authorities but it must be reduced to 6%, but only by preventing new enterprises. In other words, only as they go out of business or change.

Conversion doesn't count. So far as parents are concerned, unless they were converted, if the parents are Jewish the children are Jewish. The only chance for them is so far as the grandparents are concerned.

Conversion doesn't count at all so far as people are concerned, or so far as parents are concerned unless the parents were converted on a certain

---

268 Most probably Simon Hevesi (1868–1943), leading chief rabbi.
269 Samu Stern (1874–1947), businessman, agricultural entrepreneur, president of the Israelite (Neolog) Congregation of Pest as well as of the Neolog National Office, chairman of the Jewish Council in 1944.

date. If the parents were converted on a certain date, probably the same date as before and the date hasn't been fixed, probably they can qualify. But they must have in addition to that at least two grandparents who are real Christians. Parents cannot be converted.

If after this bill they marry they are Jews if the person himself doesn't qualify as a Christian.

[97] Conversation with Mr. Bruce[270]

Budapest, December 29, 1938

Mr. Bruce called this morning and told me that the Hungarian Government had complained to the Germans about delays in shipments, both in and out of Germany. He said that poultry had been held up and that they were having all sorts of difficulties. Imredy told him that they had a reply and that the Germans said this was not intentional, but that it could not be helped. Bruce said that Quant[271] had a lot of information to the effect that the German railway system had broken down because either there was a lack of equipment or, according to another story, because they discharged all the Austrian railway men and the Germans haven't proven competent to handle the situation. He said that Mr. Ackerson[272] was lunching with Mr. Quant today and could no doubt get all the information from him on this line.

Mr. Bruce is principally concerned with the Jew Bill. He said that Imredy hadn't given him any idea that it was to be so severe. He thought it was going to affect Hungarian foreign trade and said that there had already been a bad reaction in England. A number of Jewish agents were being refused licenses here and the result was that they had again to cut down on the purchase of Hungarian goods.

Bruce said that from his conversation with Imredy he had come to the conclusion that he was a fanatic, that he felt he was the only man who could lead this movement through these difficult times, and that to maintain his position he must do certain things and that was the basis of all his actions.

---

270 Henry J. Bruce, British adviser to the National Bank of Hungary 1931-39.
271 Richárd Quandt (1899-?), general manager of the Hungarian National Bank 1939–44.
272 Garret G. Ackerson, third, subsequently second secretary of the U.S. legation in Budapest.

1939

[98] Conversation with Baron Apor of December 30

Budapest, January 3, 1939

Baron Apor said he knew nothing about Ciano's visit as he had been away, but he hadn't made any inquiry. All he did know was that he had been told at the Foreign Office that the Italians didn't expect to have any crisis with France, they were only trying to get some concessions. He said this was told him because he was going to Rome. Otherwise, he knew nothing. He assumed that Ciano was to help Hungarians at Berlin as Hungarian-German relations were very bad.

Apor told me that he had never been considered for Foreign Minister by de Kanya, first, because under no circumstances and conditions would he be Foreign Minister, either now or any time in the future. He said he didn't make speeches, and further, he wanted nothing to do with politicians. He insisted that there was no possibility of his ever being Foreign Minister as he would never have it. In the second place, Imredy would never appoint him for he quarrelled with him right along. He said he also quarreled with Gombos continually; he didn't like any of them, and he didn't want to have anything to do with them. He hoped he would never be in the Foreign Office again. He said he had resigned in writing on October third: that the reason he resigned was that he discovered Csaky who was in constant touch with Imredy was intriguing to become Foreign Minister, and Apor had no desire to stay in the Foreign Office under the circumstances. He agreed with de Kanya that he would remain as long as he did, but that the day he resigned his (Apor's) resignation was to take effect, and that was the reason he left at the same time as de Kanya.

Apor said that de Kanya had recommended both Bardossy and Csaky and that he had discussed these recommendations with Apor. The National Union Party did not put the veto on Csaky entirely, they merely insisted on Bardossy when the Prime Minister told them he intended to appoint Csaky. As a result of this Bardossy was actually appointed. He went to the Regent, kissed his hand, and everything was ready for the announcement when Imredy and Bardossy got into an argument over foreign policy and Bardossy refused to stay. The result was that there was no objection by the party under the circumstances to Csaky's appointment.

Apor said he considered Imredy a man in the wrong position. He is not

Baron Gábor Apor around 1934

competent for his job, although he possibly is quite competent for the work he used to be in. The result was that he was uncertain and vacillated all over the place.

Apor said he attended Bela Daranyi's[273] party for Ciano, not especially because he wanted to see Daranyi but because he knew there would be a lot of pretty girls there and it always amused him highly to see Ciano and the girls, he being such a terrible ass and always made a fool of himself. He said he was not at all disappointed and got a lot of amusement out of it.

Apor seems to be much more optimistic about conditions in Europe than he was the previous time I talked to him.

[99] Conversation with Mr. Vornle,[274] Permanent Assistant to Minister for Foreign Affairs

Budapest, February 7, 1939

In an interview granted to the Minister this morning, at which time he introduced Mr. Travers to Mr. Vornle, the Minister asked concerning Russia's object in closing its Legation in Budapest and suggesting Hungary do

---

273 Béla Darányi, general manager of Futura, the Hungarian Cooperative Centers Commercial Co., after 1938.

274 János Vörnle (1890–?), permanent deputy of the foreign minister 1938–42, Hungarian minister to Ankara 1942–44. As opposed to most Hungarian diplomats active in neutral countries, he did not renounce his obedience even to the Sztójay government of 1944.

likewise in Moscow. Mr. Vornle stated that the Hungarian Government does not consider that the act was necessarily against Hungary but was a warning to small nations not to become involved or sign the Anti-Comintern Pact.

Upon being asked when Hungary would sign the Anti-Comintern Pact, Mr. Vornle states that a commission in Japan is now studying the wording of the pact to be signed, that it will be forwarded here in a short time — possibly two or three weeks - when Hungary will actually sign the pact.[275] Another delay in the signing is because of the absence from Budapest at this time of the Italian and German Ministers. The Minister jokingly asked if when Hungary signed the pact if Hungary would also assist in the armament of the islands in the Pacific and stated that Hungary joining such a pact would be misunderstood in the United States. He said that people now thought that the Anti-Comintern Pact was also a military pact because Csaky had told the Minister that if our country became involved in a war with Germany that Japan would attack the United States. Mr. Vornle said that it had been rumored that there had been secret clauses to the pact but he had never seen them, and that the only thing that Hungary was doing was fighting Bolshevism, and as the Bolos had been in Hungary they were very much against them.

Asked about the Munkacs incident, Mr. Vornle stated that the incident of January 6th[276] had been settled by the Czechs paying exactly what they were asked by Hungary, i.e. for damages incurred. He stated, however, that there had been a further incident three days ago and that a protest has been made at Prague.

Asked concerning the delimitation of the Czechoslovak-Hungarian frontier, Mr. Vornle stated that a commission is now working upon the frontier and he hopes that a definite decision will be forthcoming in the near future.

Concerning anti-Hungarian activity in Slovakia and Ruthenia, Mr. Vornle stated that there had been some such activity but he believes that such anti-Hungarian activity had been discontinued.

Concerning the articles appearing in the UNIVERSAL of Bucharest and VREME of Belgrade, he does not believe that these articles will affect an improvement of relations between these States and Hungary. At the same time, he mentioned that a new Government has been formed in Yugoslavia and that he had every reason to believe that it would be friendly to Hungarian interests.

The Minister mentioned anti-Hungarian propaganda in Slovakian and Ruthenian languages being broadcast from Vienna. He said that he understood that such broadcasts have already ceased.

---

275 Hungary joined the Anti-Comintern Pact as of February 24, 1939.
276 Czechoslovak-Hungarian border incident at Munkács (Mukachevo) on January 6, 1939.

Concerning the Hungarian-French trade agreement he knew no details but stated that the Hungarian Minister at Paris[277] was very pleased and said that it would probably improve Hungarian exports to France.

Mr. Vornle confirmed the rumor that a Hungarian Legation has been opened in Cairo[278] and stated that commercial discussions were under way. He said that Count Semsey has already arrived there and that Egypt was always a good customer of Hungary, and he hoped that it would continue to be.

Concerning the establishment of a Legation at Tokyo, he said that it would be established in the very near future. The money has already been appropriated, but that no Minister has been appointed.[279] The money, however, he said was the most important point.

Concerning the rumor that the Vatican has attempted to influence the Hungarian Government to moderate its anti-Semitic program, Mr. Vornle said that the Vatican had done nothing about it through the Government but that the Bishops were especially active and indicated that they had probably orders.

With reference to the visit to Budapest of Arthur [sic] Henderson,[280] Mr. Vornle stated that Mr. Henderson's visit was not to mediate between Hungary and Rumania but merely to discuss the present political conditions in Central Europe. He stated, however, that Mr. Henderson did leave Budapest for Bucharest and indicated that was probably the reason why the German press had stressed the possibility of mediation.

Concerning the bomb outrage at the Budapest synagogue,[281] Mr. Vornle said that he should like to know how had perpetrated the outrage and so would the police. He said that the only thing that was known to the police was that there were three persons involved. The investigation is still going on. The Minister asked why it was that the synagogue had not been protected by police, and he replied that none of the churches in Budapest were protected, and that such an attack was unforeseen as there had not been a bomb outrage in Hungary for a thousand years. Mr. Montgomery stated it seemed strange that half an hour after the incident there were only four police there and that the firemen arrived a long time before any police, that in the meantime there were 5000 Nazis outside who attempted to cause trouble with the

---

277 Count Sándor Khuen-Héderváry.

278 Count Andor Semsey, Hungarian chargé in Cairo.

279 György Ghika was appointed consul general with the title of minister.

280 January 15–18, 1939: This is a mistake. The visitor was certainly the British ambassador to Germany, Sir Nevile Meyrick Henderson (1882–1942), who negotiated in Budapest, and not Arthur Henderson, who died in 1935.

281 February 3, 1939: Arrowcross bombing attack on the synagogue in Dohány utca.

police. Mr. Vornle appeared very much annoyed and said that he had never heard of such a thing, whereupon the Minister said that his own press office had given us that information.

[100] Conversations with Mr. Vornle and Dr. Eckhardt

Budapest, March 16, 1939

Mr. Vornle said he doesn't know where the troops are in Ruthenia[282] but that there will be an announcement at 8 p.m. tonight. Eckhardt said he understands that the Hungarian scouts have reached the Polish border. Ambassador Biddle[283] at Warsaw said that the Polish troops are lined up on the border waiting to greet their Hungarian brothers.

Vornle said the Germans are making no objection about Ruthenia. Eckhardt said that there is an informal article in the papers this morning from Germany which says that the Vienna Award is no longer valid and that the Ruthenian question is now purely Hungarian.

Eckhardt, however, said that he learned that German troops have gone into Slovakia and that they are now on the Ruthenian border; he doesn't know what this means. However, he doesn't believe that Germany would object because it is more of a Polish problem than it is a Hungarian one and that they have been making energetic complaints to Germany for some time about the Vienna Award. Therefore, he thinks Germany will not now do anything.

Vornle said that Rumania had acquiesced in the occupation of Ruthenia. However, they were asking for certain territorial adjustments where a railroad goes twice out of Rumania into Ruthenia. They want to get the whole line. This would involve about 15,000 population, and it would be discussed.

Eckhardt said that he understands six divisions of the Rumanian army are mobilized on the Hungarian frontier. He doesn't know what this means, but he thinks it is probably for fear that Hungary will make some sort of a move into Transylvania, not because they are going to object to Ruthenia.

Vornle said that the Italians haven't objected to the Ruthenian move. Eckhardt said they haven't heard a word of any kind from Italy.

Eckhardt said that the radio at Vienna hasn't sent out any anti-Hungarian

---

282 The sub-Carpathian area.

283 Anthony J. Drexel Biddle, Jr. (1896–1961), U.S. minister in Oslo 1935–37, ambassador to Warsaw 1937-39, subsequently attached to the Polish government-in-exile up to 1944.

propaganda for two days. Vornle said that he thought they weren't making propaganda.

Eckhardt told me that yesterday there was a Gauleiter from Vienna who made a speech here saying that Prague, Krakow and Budapest were all the beneficiaries of German culture and owed everything to Germany. He said the name of this man and a reference to his remarks is in the MAGYAR NEMZET of today.[284]

Eckhardt said that Slovakia is legally independent but occupied by German troops. Hungary has acknowledged this independence and will send a mission there. He said, however, that Slovakia won't last six weeks; they cannot exist economically as they are. They will have to become part of Germany.

Eckhardt said that the Bratislava Handelbank has been acquired by the Vienna Lehner Bank with the absorption of Austria and that now the Dresdenerbank and another German bank, the Lehnerbank and the Handelbank had formed a company to take over Slovakia and they would control all industries and everything else.

Eckhardt said that Bohemia had been officially proclaimed this morning as a part of Germany and not a separate province. All former Czechs will have to take out German citizenship.

Eckhardt said that the Hungarists had practically disappeared, so far as he is concerned, as he has heard nothing of them. The most active man was General Ratz. It was a movement that he is the president of called Honszeretet, which means "Love of Country." Ratz was just elected two weeks ago as president. It was some of his followers who were given the boxes last night[285] and occupied by the young men who hollered for Szalasi. The Hungarists, or what is left of them including Hubay, were very much upset about it and denounced it this morning very vigorously. He doesn't know why the Regent received Hubay, unless it was to give him hell. He was sure it wasn't to tell him he was a nice boy. The Foreign Office said they didn't know that the Regent had received him.

Eckhardt has heard the story about the retired General of the Army who

284 Alfred Eduard Frauenfeld (1898–1977), engineer, Nazi *Gauleiter* in Vienna. In a lecture in Bratislava (Pozsony, Preßburg) he declared that "in the course of history Europe reached as far as German influence did." He who "possesses the Ostmark, rules over Europe," he continued, and compared the role of Hitler in the German world to that of the pope among Catholics. *Magyar Nemzet,* March 16, 1939.

285 The regent personally disciplined some of the right-wing demonstrators in the Royal Hungarian Opera, where he participated at the celebrations of the national holiday of March 15, 1939. Minister Montgomery was present and rushed to the regent after hearing of the disturbances. Horthy interpreted this as a gesture of loyalty.

Béla Imrédy leaving the headquarters of the Party of
Hungarian Renewal, October-November 1940

resigned from the Order of the Heroes, etc. but only as gossip. He doesn't
know it is so and didn't attach any importance to it anyhow. He said the
Army was rapidly being deNazified and that every few days a lot of officers
were being left out and he felt that the Army at present was all right. This
last move of Hitler in particular had a big effect. He thought now they would
go after the Nazis and all kindred organizations harder than ever because of
the German occupation of Slovakia. They couldn't afford to have any such
organizations get a foothold.

He thought Parliament would be dissolved somewhere around the month
of May.

He said that Imredy still had hopes of returning. He wants to be the German leader. He said that he had an understanding with Teleki that the next
election would be more or less united. If the parties were not united the can-

didates would be so arranged that each party would get a return. The whole election would be directed against the Nazis and all their kindred spirits.

He couldn't see any change in the Cabinet until after the election.

He said that on Saturday at 5 p.m. there will be a conference of all former Prime Ministers and various party leaders. He had just been invited to attend. The object of this conference was to determine what they were going to do with Ruthenia. His impression is that it would be an autonomous province. He said the situation there is that the Ruthenians are Greek Catholics where Ukrainians were Russian Catholics. The Ruthenians inclined to western civilization; the Ukrainians to the east. The peasant class were all Ruthenians whereas the upper classes were Ukrainians. The Hungarian Government was working with the Ruthenian peasant class and would establish a Roman Catholic Church there, whereas the Germans had been trying to establish the eastern church there.

The next question was when Hitler will be here. He said that some people will resist until the last man. He doesn't think that Mr. Hitler will try it soon, but of course he doesn't put it beyond him. He says that Hitler's move in Czechoslovakia more or less tears the mask off his face since he has always claimed that he was taking territory because the Germans were mistreated. Now he is taking territory definitely non-German. His answer, of course, would be that the Czechs invited him in, but that wouldn't fool anybody. He said, however, that the taking of Czechoslovakia was worth more to Hitler than anything he did before because he acquired enormous resources which were worth more than Austria and the Sudetenland put together. He got the Skoda works.[286] Czechoslovakia was a very prosperous country, so he has gotten all that. While he loses face by being proven a hypocrite and liar, etc., yet he has gotten a big advantage and now has 90 million people and has increased his resources tremendously. He says that he doesn't know how much in the way of munitions, etc. the Germans have, but that the German General Staff had told members of the Hungarian General Staff that last September the German Army had ammunition to last them exactly three days. Therefore, he thinks from this point of view, the question of Czechoslovakia will be a big thing since it enables them greatly to accelerate their rearmament program and gives them an immense boost in that respect.

---

286 The biggest Czech industrial company founded by the German engineer and industrialist Emil von Škoda (1839–1900) in Plzeň (Pilsen). It became well known as an ammunition factory in both world wars. It was one of Europe's single largest factory complexes.

[101] Conversation with Mr. Vornle at the Foreign Office
Budapest, March 18, 1939

Mr. Vornle, when asked about the Prime Minister's speech in the upper House yesterday, in which Count Teleki said:

> "Thus our resolution and action was
> rendered possible also by Germany's
> quick resolution, by the close friend-
> ship which Germany and Italy, these
> two great and old friends of ours, had
> shown, and are showing us, as well as
> by the policy we pursue leaning on them,"[287]

reiterated that Hungary had absolutely no knowledge of Germany's intended move until after it had taken place in Slovakia and Bohemia, and that Hungary had an agreement whatever with Germany as to united action. There had been, however, discussions with Germany and pressure brought by both Poland and Italy, and the Germans had agreed that later on — time indefinite — they would not mind if Ruthenia was taken by the Hungarians. However, there was no agreement as to time, and therefore, their statement that they had no understanding with Germany was correct. They acted when they did because they knew that if they didn't take it Germany would take it, and unless they were in possession of it, Germany would not keep her promise. Therefore, they chose to construe the German promise as authorizing their action, and would continue to talk that way. Actually they never knew when they started whether Germany would approve or not, but felt that under the circumstances she could not do otherwise.

The Prime Minister's speech simply means that Hungary's position vis-à-vis Germany is such that nobody can even afford to lose an opportunity to pay compliments.

The mobilization is in effect for practice. He wouldn't advise any Americans to leave. He thought my grand-daughter would be perfectly safe. They had no idea of having a war with any power. They were, however, taking over Ruthenia, and the Army was mobilized, and the General Staff was going through the routine which they would go through in case of war.

He had read Mr. Chamberlain's speech but he didn't know of any reac-

---

287 Gróf Teleki Pál *Országgyűlési beszédei*, Vol. II, 1939–1941 (Budapest: Studium, 1941), 118. – Teleki originally thought that it was neither worthwhile nor necessary to pursue the involvement of the Germans excessively as the border changes obtained without them would meet the satisfaction of the Western powers more readily.

tion to it. He couldn't see any war this year; he thought there might not be any war at all.

He denied that Mr. Daranyi had gone to Berlin.

[102] Conversation with Mr. de Kanya Former Minister for Foreign Affairs

Budapest, March 18, 1939

Mr. de Kanya said that while the Vornle version about Germany's acquiescence in Hungary's action regarding Ruthenia was true, actually Germany had weeks ago told Hungary that she didn't care what she did in Ruthenia. His version is that ever since the Germans had stopped them from taking Ruthenia, the Poles, Hungarians and Italians had been bearing down on Germany and they said that later on they could go in, but two weeks ago in response to continued inquiries, etc., they said they didn't care what they would do. The Hungarians, however, didn't know what this meant. They didn't know whether they would have any German support if they did and, in fact, it was said in such a way they didn't know what to do. Therefore, when the German action took place they went in to keep Germany from taking it, and of course, now give the credit to Germany, which is the only thing they could do.

Mr. de Kanya said that Teleki's ideas in regard to Germany were perfectly sound. Imredy was scared to death of the Germans and had given them everything. He said he made one concession after another they didn't even ask for, even when he protested. The crowning absurdity was the signing of the Anti-Comintern Pact, which was totally unnecessary, and he wouldn't have done it. He left office because he got tired of Imredy's policy. He stated that first he thought he would better stay and save the situation as much as he could, but later he determined that he had better get out, as it might bring things tom a head sooner. He thought Imredy was crazy and couldn't account otherwise for his action. However, he said that Teleki and anybody else would have to say nice things about Germany and talk pro-German all the time, they couldn't do anything else.

He said that Mr. Hitler was not a normal person, that he was without honor and without shame; that he had told Mr. de Kanya last August voluntarily that Hungary should have her historic borders in Czechoslovak territory returned to her, and that when the time came he would see that Slovakia and Bratislava and the whole came back to Hungary. He said that while at the time he didn't attach too much importance to this, he didn't think that

Kálmán Kánya around 1940

within eight months, or whatever it is, Mr. Hitler himself would occupy Slovakia.

Mr. de Kanya said the Hungarian Government hadn't the slightest intimation of Hitler's move in Slovakia and Bohemia, and neither did the Italian Government. Neither one knew anything about it until it happened.

I asked him where Germany would go next, into Hungary, Poland, Yugoslavia or Italy. He said it will go into all of these unless they are stopped, but where they will go next nobody knows because Hitler dares not tell anybody anything. His Foreign Office never knew his plans, nor did his Generals. Even when they mobilized the Army, the Generals didn't know the objective until the last minute. He said he felt that he was a man of destiny and couldn't be stopped and unless England and France or somebody did something they would keep on going. He couldn't stay still, first, because it was against his character, and, second, he had to produce new victories all the time. He said there was no difference between Nazism and Bolshevism; in fact, he said, the only difference between Germany today and Russia was that it was colder in Russia.

Mr. de Kanya said he didn't think mobilization was anything more than an army manoeuvre. Of course, they did have in mind that Rumania might take some action and though it was well to show their strength. Hitler having taken Slovakia, he said was menacing the Poles because they were too close. He thought the Germans didn't like the Hungarians and Poles having a common border; however, they felt they could take care of that in time if they wanted to, so it made no difference.

[103] Conversation with Mr. Orlowski the Polish Minister
Budapest, March 22, 1939

The Polish Minister told me that they were doing everything possible both here and in Bucharest to calm the situation. The Hungarians were disturbed by Rumanian mobilization and the concentration of troops on the frontier; the Rumanians were alarmed by Hungarian mobilization and were starting general mobilization. It said it was all nonsense but it may mean a serious situation; almost anything could happen.

He did not know anything about German troops in Hungary and believed there was no basis for such a rumor. He said that while he was certain Hungary would resist if Germany wanted to come to Hungary, he was equally certain that if Germany wanted to go through Hungary to Rumania they would not have any difficulty making an agreement with the Hungarian Government by promising them Transylvania. In fact, he said no Government could hold the people back. He didn't think such an agreement had been negotiated, but it certainly wasn't beyond possibility. He was telling the Hungarian Government that they were very foolish to take any chances of precipitating a world war because if they did, this would be the theatre of a war. He said the Russians would be compelled to fight if German troops entered Rumania and that if Hungary permitted German troops to go through and join with them this would become the theater of war between the Russians and Germans.

In regard to Danzig,[288] he was vehement in stating that he was very positive that the Poles would never permit the Germans to take Danzig, even though it was a Free City, by ultimatum or by any other method except by

---

288 Today Gdańsk in Poland.

compensation. There was a possibility by compensating them there might be some arrangement made, but such an arrangement would not be anything as they shoved on the Czechs. The Poles would fight.

He said as far as he knew, the Poles would be neutral in a war as long as they could, but that they certainly would not be happy with the Russians and Germans fighting beneath them. He knew that ultimately they would have to join a war, but they would make every effort to stay neutral as long as possible.

He believed that Germany would concentrate on this part of the world for if a war was declared because it offered the least resistance and the supplies of Hungary and Rumania would enable to last very much longer than they could otherwise.

The position of the Italians he didn't know, but he hoped they were weakening. He felt that it would have a decided effect not only on the situation if Italy should leave the Axis.

[104] Conversation with Mr. Bossy the Rumanian Minister
Budapest, March 22, 1939

Mr. Bossy didn't think that Hungary was figuring on attacking Rumania at the present moment. He felt that whatever plans they had were in connection with the war; that he had no doubt they had an agreement with Germany whereby they would join with Germany in an invasion of Rumania as soon as a war was declared. He said nothing about any German troops in Hungary.

[105] Conversation with Mr. Orlowski the Polish Minister
Budapest, March 28, 1939

The Polish Minister said that the Foreign Office did nothing but lie to him. Csaky was entirely incompetent and he couldn't tell the truth if he tried. He said he knew positively that the Hungarian Minister to Germany[289] came here in an airplane on Sunday (March 19) with information that Germany would approve the Ruthenian venture and also further incursion into Slovakia on condition that Hungarian troops be placed on the Rumanian frontier. Thus Germany was able to frighten Rumania into a trade agreement

---

289 Gen. Döme Sztójay.

at the expense of Hungary:[290] Hungary paid for the mobilization, Germany got the trade treaty. Further, Hungary was encouraged to take Slovak soil which was used to frighten Slovakia into a treaty with Germany which gave them military possession of a large part of Slovakia. In fact, the best part.

Mr. Orlowski was quite certain that the eastern portion of Slovakia, that which is not occupied now by German troops, would probably be given to Hungary. He felt that Hungary would make further demands — with German support — and that Germany now having Slovakia by the throat would be quite happy to see it reduced to the area which they have possession of so that they could be incorporated into the Reich and an independent Slovakia forgotten.

Mr. Orlowsky was very anti-German. He said that Hungary had become so much involved with Germany that there was no question she would have to come into a future war on Germany's side. He said the strange thing about it was that practically all the Hungarians believed that Germany would lose the next war, yet their craze to get their former territory back is so great that they throw all caution to the wind when that is dangled in front of them. He was certain that after the next war there would be no Hungary and the Hungarian people would be an island of some other nation. He said Poland would fight to the last ditch before they would give up Danzig. He admitted the possibility of some deal, but said that if they tried anything on the lines of Memel[291] the Poles would absolutely refuse. I told him they might offer them Lithuania. He said they might offer them New York City too, but it would have to be something they had and wanted, something that the Germans had and the Poles wanted. He said that Lithuania was a gallant little country and the Poles were determined to defend it, and if the Germans tried to take over Lithuania, the Poles would go to war. He said the Poles were not Czechs — and neither English nor French — so they wouldn't give up their allies or leave their allies in the lurch, and Lithuania was their ally.

---

290 The German-Romanian commercial treaty was signed on March 23, 1939, for five years. It connected Romania to a new Central-European economic system in the making, led by Germany. "The plan means the complete reorganization of the Romanian economy. ... Upon the implementation of the reorganization Romania will produce, preeminently and probably overwhelmingly, raw materials and industrial products needed by the German economic life," reported Hungarian minister Bárdossy from Bucharest after the treaty was signed. DIMK III:671.

291 The Memel area *(Memelland)* along the Baltic seaside lies north of the lower course of the Memel (Neman) River around the city of Memel (today Klaipėda, Lithuania). It was detached from Germany by Article 99 of the Treaty of Versailles, came first under French control, then received autonomous status in 1924 and fell under Lithuanian rule. In an ultimatum of March 23, 1939, Germany demanded and succeeded in obtaining the *Memelland* from Lithuania, to which it was returned only as a Soviet member state of the Soviet Union after World War II.

[106] Conversation with Dr. Tibor Eckhardt

Budapest, March 28, 1939

Eckhardt told me that Csaky said absolutely nothing before the Foreign Affairs Committee of Parliament. To every question he was asked he replied that there would be another meeting next week and the answer then would be given. Eckhardt, therefore, is completely in the dark so far as real information is concerned with reference to Hungarian foreign policy.

Eckhardt told me, however, that someone had come down here in a plane on Sunday, March 19, and had given the German consent to Hungarian occupation of Ruthenia. He also felt that at that moment Germany had not actually consented and had not made up its mind what she was going to do. He based this belief on the fact that a number of German officers were killed or captured in Ruthenia, unaware that Germany had given her consent. He also said there was a General and a number of officers escaped. It was his impression that Germany had used Hungary's mobilization as a threat against Rumania and that this was part of some understanding with Germany by which Hungary was to get not only Ruthenia but some portion of Slovakia. His impression was that the Hungarians would now make further demands upon the Slovaks with German approval, and would take over considerably more Slovak territory than they now have. He was certain that the Hungarians had originally no idea of going anywhere but into Ruthenia and that they wouldn't have gone into Slovakia as they have without German consent. He said that at points they penetrated into Slovakia as far as 35 kilometers.

Eckhardt said that Csaky had told him very confidentially that Pelenyi had written him that Secretary Welles[292] had told him that Germany would dominate Europe for the next five years. This was in connection with Eckhardt's saying to Csaky that Germany's domination couldn't last over a year and Hungary should be careful. Csaky used Welles' supposed statement to defend Hungary leaning toward Germany since they could not do anything else, now that Germany was to dominate Europe for the next five years.

---

292 Sumner Welles (1892–1961), U.S. undersecretary of state 1937–43, expert on Latin America. — Montgomery found out that Count Csáky's statement was made at a secret meeting of the Committees for Foreign Affairs of the Hungarian Parliament. Cf. Montgomery's report No. 1536, dated May 4, 1939, to the Secretary of State, explaining in great detail his inquiries concerning Csáky's statement on Sumner Welles declaring "that Germany would dominate Europe for the next five years." Miscellaneous letters and notes, J. F. Montgomery Collection.

[107] Conversation with Mr. de Kanya

Budapest, March 30, 1939

Mr. de Kanya said he hadn't been consulted about foreign affairs for some time. He was taking things easily and hadn't bothered at all. Ha had, however, heard considerable complaints about the Foreign Office and a great many fears expressed as to Hungarian foreign policy involving them with Germany. I told him the things I had heard about a possible deal with Germany and he seemed very much interested. In fact, he said, "Ah, that accounts for some things." He thought it was all quite probable.

[108] Conversation with Mr. Orlowski

Budapest, April 4, 1939

The Polish Minister has calmed down quite a bit so far as the Foreign Office is concerned and Hungarians in general. He says that while Csaky is no longer the friend of old he does not talk to him in the same way that he did; he cannot definitely say that he has actually lied outright to him, although by inference and in effect he has.

As Orlowski sees the situation, Hungary, through the insanity of Imredy, became involved with Germany and she cannot get out of it. Actually no one from the Regent down wants to go to war with Germany and are anxious to find some way to get out of their present position into a more independent one, but they don't know how to do it. He believes that they like the Poles far better than the Germans and if left to their own free choice they would stick with the Poles, and as they are now they are afraid to do anything for fear of bringing German wrath upon them. He said that Csaky thought of making a trip to Poland but the Germans vetoed the idea.

Orlowski doesn't think that the Hungarian situation is impossible. His Government is doing everything possible to induce the Hungarians and the Rumanians to make up and come to some sort of an arrangement in the way of a non-aggression pact and if this can be put over he believes that given a little time, Hungary will gradually veer towards Poland and away from Germany. As things stand now, he cannot see how the Hungarians cannot help but go to war on Germany's side, if there is a war, particularly if it started in this part of the world. He thinks the Germans got complete control of them, not because they love the Germans but because they fear them.

Orlowski said he believed that another German move would have to be made within four months, otherwise there would be a complete collapse in Germany. In which direction this move would be made he says he doesn't have any idea. He has no doubt that Poland was supposed to be the next victim but he thought that Chamberlain's statement[293] had put an end to that, although nobody could be sure.

He didn't believe that Hitler would actually move into Hungary, but he did think they would be more and more overbearing and if neither avenue was open to them he didn't think it was impossible that Germany would decide to take over Hungary, not because they could get any more that way but for the moral effect and what they could get out of it. If they made a move in another direction there would be no point in coming here, but if Great Britain guarantees to close the doors in other directions he believes they will have to go somewhere.

I got the idea from my conversation that things are considerably improved between Hungary and Poland since my last conversation with him and that he is very hopeful that things will improve in that direction.

[109] Conversation with Count Teleki Prime Minister
Budapest, April 26, 1939

Henry J. Bruce, the British Adviser of the National Bank of Hungary, told me a few days ago of a conversation that he had with Count Teleki in which he told him that he could not do much in the way of creating good-will in England because of Count Teleki's interview regarding the President's message to Hitler and Mussolini and because of unfriendly articles which appeared in the semi-official PESTER LLOYD.[294]

---

293 British Prime Minister Neville Chamberlain declared in the House of Commons on March 31, 1939, that "in the event of any action which clearly threatens Polish independence ... His Majesty's Government will feel themselves bound at once to lend the Polish Government all support in their power. "

294 President Roosevelt turned to Hitler and Mussolini in a telegram on April 15, 1939, and called upon them to declare that they would not attack any of the 31 countries listed by him. The list included Poland, the Soviet Union, France, and Great Britain. In a Reichstag speech of April 28, Hitler responded to the president, trying to make him and his very effort seem ridiculous. The president's message was officially handed over to János Vörnle, permanent deputy of the Hungarian foreign minister, by Minister Montgomery on April 19. DIMK IV:177. — Count Csáky's Rome interview in the April 20, 1939, issue of *Magyar Nemzet*: "I am unable to consider the recent U.S. intervention into the affairs of Central Europe without a certain bias. We want to be left calmly working on the side of our proven friends..." (p. 4). Cf. the lead article of the *Pester Lloyd* of April 19, 1939 which pointed to "intimate and friendly relation with the Axis powers" as the safest of the guarantee of the peace demanded by the president.

Subsequently, I was advised by Count Csaky that the Prime Minister wished to see me, and an appointment being made, I was received by the Prime Minister. I had assumed that from what Mr. Bruce had told me, Teleki was very much upset by Csaky's interview and that the object of calling me was to make some sort of an apology. However, although he apologized more or less indirectly for Csaky's statement, he gave as his opinion that the President's message to Hitler and Mussolini did not show a proper understanding of the situation in Europe, that it put small countries on the spot. I pressed him to tell me in what way they had been injured, but he was very vague and just kept saying over and over that, of course, he was not a diplomat or anything of the kind, but from a common sense point of view, he thought it was hard on the little countries and did not do anyone any particular good.

Count Teleki said that the trouble with small countries was that they didn't know how much dependence to place upon England: She had permitted the Germans to take Austria, the Sudetenland, Czechoslovakia and Memel, and Italy to take Albania and never did anything about it except make weak protests. Therefore, small countries couldn't be convinced that she ever intended to do anything but protest.

I told him that I felt that the situation had now changed and that I didn't believe that it was safe to count on England's continuing to overlook everything that happened in Europe. He seemed very doubtful that they would do anything. He said that in Italy they didn't expect war immediately, and while he didn't know the German point of view, Italy didn't expect any war this year or for some time.

Count Teleki said that the Jew Bill would be taken care of by compromise and said that it would be much better for the elections if the Upper House refused to pass the bill, but he was thinking only of the good of the country rather than the election. He said the elections would be in a few weeks and thought that the Government would have a majority, but if they had a huge majority the difficulty was in getting them to work together, which took lots of time, effort, etc. In other words, the main tenor of his talk was concerning the difficulties of his position.

He was very pleasant, told stories and although I was there an hour, I could barely get away. He seemed to have something on his mind, but couldn't get around to it. I think he wanted to apologize for Csaky and his idea was to give the impression that he had without actually doing so.

Just before I left, I brought up the subject again and told him that I thought it rather odd that Count Csaky felt called upon to answer since the message did not concern Hungary and particularly so as no other country had taken the same position. He said, of course, the message did not show much understanding and that, while Hungary had not been mentioned, it was a small country and it made it very difficult for them.

I took advantage of the occasion to tell him of the unreliability of the Foreign Office. He asked for examples and I cited the fact that the Foreign Office had given me four versions as to whether or not the Hungarian Government had an understanding `with Germany when it occupied Ruthenia and that none of these versions had been correct. I told him all of them in reply to his query and went on to say that all were incorrect because I had information from an unimpeachable source that not only had Germany been consulted, but she had offered to take the territory for Hungary and the offer had been refused. The unimpeachable source, of course, was the Prime Minister himself since Mr. Bruce had told me that in his conversation with the Prime Minister, the latter had made this statement. I brought this up to get his reaction. He began to talk slowly and carefully and while he never once denied my statement, he continued his circumlocution and would not commit himself. For obvious reasons, I did not wish to confront him with the fact that I had quoted him because Mr. Bruce had given me the information in confidence and it would have put him in an embarrassing position if I had.

I began to wonder, and I still wonder, why he had called me since there didn't seem to be any object to it. I am also at a loss to explain why he denied, at least by implication, the very facts which he so ardently wished Mr. Bruce to make known in England.

When we left the realm of politics, he changed completely and became very friendly, regaled with stories long after I first attempted to take my leave.

Subsequent to the above conversation, I sent him a summary of Count Bethlen's Easter article[295] which is similar in idea and approach to President Roosevelt's message which Count Teleki said indicated a lack of knowledge of European conditions. I made no comment in transmitting this summary other than to say that the Prime Minister might find it interesting. I hoped, however, it would occur to him that President Roosevelt could be

---

295 Gróf Bethlen István [Count István Bethlen], „Az európai helyzet," *Pesti Napló,* April 9, 1939. — This conversation is a good example of how Montgomery's conversations served as the basis of his reports, in this case of No. 1534, dated May 4, 1939 to the Secretary of State, on his "Interview with the Hungarian Prime Minister." The official report quotes substantially from the text of the relevant conversation but puts it into a somewhat different context and has a lot to add on Teleki's behavior, which is not fully described in the conversation. Miscellaneous letters and notes, J. F. Montgomery Collection.

excused for his lack of information in view of the fact that the most distinguished international authority in Hungary, whom many consider one of the most astute men in Europe, likewise had been guilty of ignorance, and possibly suggest to Count Teleki that there was a lack of understanding on his part, not on that of the President. Actually, I do not believe that Count Teleki's remarks concerning the President's message represent any conviction on his part, but constitute rather an alibi to cover his embarrassment at Count Csaky's indiscreet statement.

[110] Conversation with Mr. Nicholas Kallay

Budapest, May 5, 1939

Mr. Kallay came up to me and said he knew about the letter Csaky had written me, and he seemed to believe that the questions asked by Csaky were true. I assured him that they were not, but he didn't seem convinced. He told me the third question concerning a high official that was supposed to be contributing to the Benes campaign fund was President Roosevelt, who was supposed to have made the first contribution.

Kallay thought war was a terrible thing and that he couldn't seem to understand why Great Britain, France and America wanted war so much. He seemed to think they were to be blamed of the situation, although he couldn't quite explain why. The only thing I could gather was that if everybody gave Germany what they wanted there would be no trouble. When I suggested giving them some of Hungary he bristled. He went on to tell me how everybody hated the Germans, but at the same time he couldn't see how Hungary could remain neutral; they would have to fight for the Germans even though they hated them.

He gave the same argument about the President's message that the Prime Minister did. From my conversation with him, I would say considerable propaganda is being circulated about Hungary regarding the President's message and the mythical government of Benes in America.

[111] Conversation with Count Bethlen

Budapest, May 12, 1939

Count Bethlen told me he had not retired from politics. On the contrary, he expected to be more interested in politics in the future than in the past. His decision not to test his seat in the House was due to the desire of the Regent that he enter the Upper House and that he had just been appointed.[296]

Count Bethlen said that it would not be so easy to predict what would happen in the next election as in past elections since this would be the first election under the secret ballot. While of course there were ways of influencing the voters and bringing pressure on them, still there were limits to the actual influence that could be exerted since under the secret ballot a man could promise one thing and actually vote another, and there was no way of telling whether he kept his promise or not. He, therefore, expected that a great many Opposition candidates would be elected, more than was generally supposed. I told him that I understood Eckhardt would suffer very much, and he said he didn't believe that for a minute. He thought Eckhardt would have more members in Parliament, certainly not any less.

Count Bethlen said Teleki had told him that Imredy had presented a list of 60 candidates to run on the Government ticket, but that Teleki refused 30 outright, and that after investigating the remaining 30 had accepted only 12. He had asked Teleki how many of these would be elected and Teleki replied "Not more than 8 of them." Also, Count Bethlen took occasion to say that Count Tisza had always found it very useful to have a good strong minority because this enabled him to resist many of the demands of Francis Joseph since he could always say that the minority was so strong that it would endanger his position if he tried to force such a demand upon Parliament. I rather judged from Count Bethlen's mentioning this that Teleki possibly has something of that kind in mind. In other words, the policy of the Government is to support many of the Opposition candidates.

Count Bethlen told me that Mikes, Bornemisza and many of the dissidents were going to run but that none of the Sztranyavszky group would run because they had no money. This also tended to confirm the conviction that there is some collusion between the Government and some of the Opposition candidates since you wonder where they would get the money to run.

Count Bethlen referred to Count Csaky's interview at Rome in regard to the President's message, and said it was perfectly ridiculous. He said, is the Foreign Minister's business to keep friendly with everyone and that nobody but a fool would think that in order to be friendly to one power he must repel another. Such a subservient policy was the worst possible one with the Germans, and certainly was not in keeping with Hungarian character. He said that Hungary would have to do everything possible to be neutral in the case of war and that the only thing he could see that would drag her into a war would be Rumania.

---

296 Regent Horthy appointed Bethlen member of the Upper House that same day.

Count István Bethlen hunting

I asked Count Bethlen if Germany promised Transylvania to Hungary in order to get permission to send German troops through to Rumania. This would not find great acceptance. He said no, he didn't think it would since he couldn't believe the Hungarian people were so simple as to become involved in a war on the side of Germany for such a forlorn prospect. He said one of the dangers for Hungary was the fact that the Army people were so much impressed by German might. He said they knew nothing about any other army and that they couldn't make any comparisons. However, he thought that the Army were not pro-German; in fact, they were very anti-German since they saw how Germany had intrigued against Hungary in Ruthenia and the way they prevented Slovakia from joining Hungary.

[112] Conversation with John Spisiak Slovak Minister

Budapest, May 22, 1939

The new Slovak Minister, Dr. Spisiak, called this morning and said that he had been asked by his Government to call on me for the purpose of seeing if *de facto* recognition could not be given them. He said he was not familiar with diplomatic usage; he didn't care whether it was *de facto* recognition or not; what they wanted was to be able to have commercial representatives in America and someone to validate documents so that commerce could go on, etc. He said so far as they were concerned they wouldn't mind recognizing any acts of the Czechoslovak Legation or Consulates in America, but naturally Germany wouldn't permit that. He said the Minister was a Slovak, and so it would be quite acceptable, but in their position this was impossible. He said they had no desire to create any difficulties or make trouble in any way, nor did they expect any political recognition or anything that would interfere with our attitude so far as Czechoslovakia was concerned, but merely some way to do business, and as far as he knew this would require *de facto* recognition, although if there was any way it could be done it was all right with them.

Dr. Spisiak told me that he had understood that the Germans had told Csaky and Teleki when they were in Berlin[297] that they would have to fight with Germany in case of a war with Poland, and that they naturally suspected there must be some reward offered by Germany, and he had no doubt that that reward was Slovakia. Of course, the Germans didn't tell them anything of the kind; on the contrary, they had offered several times to defend them against the Hungarians, but they refused the offer. Nevertheless, he said their position was quite unhappy so far as the political future was concerned since they had no idea what was going to happen to them, but for the moment they were quite satisfied since they had a measure of self-government. At least they could have their own schools and talk their own language.

Dr. Spisiak said that only part of their country was occupied by the Germans, and there the food situation was very bad because the German Army cleaned everything up. Elsewhere it wasn't so bad. Nevertheless, they would be content if the present situation would last. They would rather have the Germans than the Hungarians, even though the Hungarians permitted them to have a separate government as they have now.

Dr. Spisiak said that the difficulties with the Hungarians were all started and stirred up by the Germans; that the difficulties which had caused the Hungarians to bomb their airport and all the other things that happened had been done by Germans in Slovakia. He said it was simply the way they did things. As an example he cited the fact that the Germans had taken a Ford car full of dynamite, put it in a street in a town in Slovakia with a time fuse so that it blew up, and then they blamed this on the Communists and used it as an excuse to practically take over Bratislava.

---

297 Teleki and Csáky visited Berlin between April 29 and May 1, 1939.

Dr. Spisiak seemed to have no illusions whatever about the Germans, but still he said he preferred them to the Hungarians since the Hungarians were inhuman in their treatment of the Slovaks, whereas the Germans while taking their food and treating them brusquely, nevertheless treated them better than the Hungarians did. He said that if there was any attempt to give Slovakia to Hungary the Slovaks would fight, even if they knew it would do no good. However, he was under the impression that the Germans were double-crossing the Hungarians and that they wouldn't so easily turn over Slovakia to them, although he said he didn't know since the Germans likewise double-crossed the Slovaks whenever they chose. He said he knew at the same time that the Germans were coming to the Slovaks and offering them aid to fight the Hungarians, they had gone to the Hungarians and offered them help in fighting the Slovaks. In spite of all this, they would rather take their chances with the Germans.

[113] Conversation with Prime Minister Teleki
Budapest, May 27, 1939

1) The Prime Minister told me that he was very much concerned because he understood that negotiations were going on for the sale of American interests in the Ganz Company to Germany, and that since Germany's interests were entirely political he hoped that these shares would remain in American hands. He said that he would be embarrassed if anybody knew that he had made this request, but that it was for the interests of both his country and ours that they should not be sold to German interests. He said the sale to Germany would permit the Germans to bring in money for propaganda, and also increase Hungary's difficulties in keeping out German workmen. In fact, he said it would be a sad blow if this sale took place now.

The Legation understands that the stock belongs to ?? [sic]

2) The Prime Minister told me he expected the Nazis to get 40 seats although others thought less. He said an immense ammount of money from abroad had been put into the campaign in support of the National Socialist ticket. He expected a total opposition of about 90, but as majority of the Opposition is anti-German this would not be dangerous although he fervently hopes National Socialists would be much less than his estimate.[298]

---

298 In the elections of May 28–29, 1939, the opposition received altogether 77 seats in Parliament, the Arrowcross Party only 31.

[114] Conversation with Prime Minister Teleki

Budapest, September 23, 1939

Count Teleki was very friendly, and his attitude completely changed since the last time I saw him. He seemed to be willing to talk more or less openly about anything and was extraordinarily pleasant. He even accompanied me to the outer door of the reception room when I left.

Count Teleki told me it was impossible to tell what Hungary's policy would be two months from now or in any given situation which was not facing them at the present, but that at the moment and for the future so far as he knew now Hungary's policy was to guard in every possible way her neutrality. He thought it would be possible to stay neutral no matter what happened, but if Italy went to war he said he couldn't tell what effect it would have on Hungary until they were faced with the situation. He thought at the present moment Hungary's position was better than it had been because the conclusion of the war in Eastern Europe would minimize the danger for Hungary, even though it had brought them an undesirable neighbor. He didn't think there would be any fighting again, or at least very soon, in this part of the world, and if war was confined to the Western Front Hungary could go ahead in peace. He admitted the dangers due to demands Germany might make, but he didn't believe this would constitute a danger for Hungary. He is inclined to put the blame on the British and French for not giving more assistance to the Poles. He thought that the Polish High Command was dreadful, Ridj-Smigly[299] and all those surrounding him were legionnaires and more clever at politics than in warfare. He thought the French should have supplied some leadership and some airplanes and possibly a division of troops.

I asked him point-blank if it were true that Hungary would at the first opportunity attempt to regain Transylvania. He said that Hungary had unfinished business with Rumania which concerned Transylvania and which would have to be settled some day, either by peaceful means or by war, because present conditions would never be tolerated indefinitely by Hungarians. He said, however, that it might be 50 years before an opportunity arose that made it possible for Hungary to do something about it. The present moment, however, was not an auspicious one and that neither the heads of the Government nor the higher officers in the army had the slightest idea of making any move which would involve them in the war on either side, and to try and take Transylvania now would certainly put them in the war. Hungarians' one and only desire is to remain neutral, and nothing will be

---

299 Marshal Edward Rydz-Smigły (1886–1941), commander-in-chief of the Polish army.

done to jeopardize her neutrality. He said the younger officers in the army would like to go into Transylvania. He said that had no effect on the course of the Government. He didn't think the older officers in the army had any such thought or desire; he was very definite in his statements that this was not the moment to think of regaining Transylvania.

[115] Conversation with the Turkish Minister[300]
Budapest, September 30, 1939

The Turkish Minister said that he found an intense anti-German feeling to exist in Hungary, especially in high official circles and he felt that German aggression would be resisted. Hungary, he asserted, could continue to exist as an absolutely independent State only by virtue of a Franco-British victory. She now had two powerful neighbors to the north, to both of whom she felt unfriendly. However, they might prove to constitute a balance of power, neither being able to proceed to the South without the consent of the other. In that event, Hungary's situation was safer. However, Russia might agree to, or even encourage, Germany's invasion of Hungary as the beginning of a thrust to the South, to obtain concessions elsewhere or to cause Germany to become more involved. In this sense, Hungary's position became extremely delicate, and he felt that the situation in Hungary should be watched with great attention as developments here probably would afford a clue to the general situation.

In general, M. Unaydin found the international situation confusing and difficult of definite analysis, considering that unseen factors would have to become apparent before any correct estimate thereof could be made. The recent Russo-German agreement[301] was to him an enigma because it defied concrete evaluation. He did not believe Russia would cooperate fully in a military sense with Germany but, basing his observation on the definitive line of decision in Poland, he was inclined to believe that Russia's primary objective was to retrieve her ante-World War frontiers, especially since the acquisition of Estonian territory appeared to constitute her next desire.

Germany, in M. Unadin's opinion, stood to gain little in the long run from her association with Russia, and she stood the chance of coming absolutely under Russian hegemony. It was Russia's interest to see Germany defeated

---

300 Rusen Esref Ünaydin, Turkish envoy extraordinary and minister plenipotentiary in Budapest (from August 30, 1939).
301 The Molotov-Ribbentrop Pact was signed in Moscow on August 23, 1939.

by Great Britain and France, and therefore, she would afford no more material aid than was absolutely necessary, and he thought that Russia even might encourage Germany to proceed through Hungary into Yugoslavia with the hope of having her embroiled with Italy who would have to assist Yugoslavia and protect the Adriatic and her Northern frontier.

To the Turkish Minister, Italy remained an unknown factor. He was inclined to believe that she would practice opportunism, though it was a delicate task, and in the last analysis, he thought that it served Italian interests best for Germany to be defeated by the Allies, and that Italy would ultimately join them.

The Russian-German thesis, according to M. Unaydin, was that Poland, having disappeared as a State, the cause of the war was over and the onus for continuing hostilities now lay with the British and French. The latter rejected this theory and held to their original contention regarding the cause of the war — aggressive Nazism, which had to be destroyed. In consequence, no immediate peace could be envisaged. He thought that Great Britain and France ultimately would achieve a victory, especially if the war could be localized in the West, and he felt that an effective show of force by them would encourage South-East European States to rally to them, at least in a moral sense.

M. Unaydin said he knew nothing more regarding the Turkish-Russian conversations in Moscow than he had heard over the radio. The Russians, he said, since the inception of the Soviet-regime, had been particularly friendly with the Turks and had put aside all idea of conquering Turkey.[302] The latter's relations with Great Britain and France had become most harmonious, and were becoming increasingly so. Parenthetically, from the manner in which he linked these international relations, I felt that the Turkish Minister wished to give an impression that Turkey well might act as an intercessor between Russia and Great Britain and France.

[116] Conversation with M. Pipinelis Greek Minister
Budapest, October 4, 1939

The Greek Minister told me last night that before the war commenced he had a conversation with Count Csaky, in which Csaky told him there was no question in the world about Italy's immediately going to war if Germany

302 Reference to several earlier Russo-Turkish wars (the Crimean War 1853–56, the Russo-Turkish War 1875–78, World War I 1914–17). Russia relinquished all her territorial claims vis-à-vis Turkey in December 1917.

did. He knew this because Mussolini had told him so, and was very emphatic about it at the exact moment both countries would move. Since the war started, the Greek Minister said that one of his colleagues (he didn't say who) had been told by Csaky that he knew Italy would not go into the war at once, it was not surprising to him at all: Mussolini had told him that under no circumstances would they immediately go to war but that they would take their time and enter at the proper moment.

The Greek Minister also said that he had heard that Ciano[303] had promised on his last trip to Berlin that Italy would supply Germany with a number of submarines. He didn't think, however, it was so. He said a Hungarian journalist who has been over to Italy has seen Gajda,[304] and that Gajda told him no one in Italy wanted to go to war except Mussolini, that Mussolini was still sore at the British, and as he was always a revolutionary he naturally hated England, which he thought was holding Italy down and preventing her from becoming a great Power, and therefore, the destruction of the British Empire would be of enormous advantage. Gajda thought that despite the fact that no one else wanted to fight, if Mussolini decided for war, the Italians would support him.

[117] Conversation with Mr. de Kanya
former Minister of Foreign Affairs

Budapest, October 4, 1939

Mr. de Kanya said he didn't feel easy with the Russians on the frontier, particularly as he had no idea of how close the Russians and the Germans actually were. Pan-Slavism and pan-Germanism could well work hand in hand to mutual advantage and play havoc with this portion of the world — including Italy. His impression was that since neither Hitler nor Stalin ever kept their word neither of them could possibly trust the other very far and, therefore, he didn't believe their understanding was close, although the communique issued in Moscow seemed to indicate that it was, and probably next month would tell. Since the combination of the two isms would be disastrous for Italy — and he didn't believe Germany was willing yet to throw Italy over entirely — this was another reason for there being no definite understanding whereby the two movements could combine forces. He thought that the German-Russian rapprochement was not made as a result of Britain's

---

303 Ciano's visit to Berlin: October 1–2, 1939.
304 Virginio Gayda (1885–1944), Italian journalist, editor of *Giornale d'Italia*.

declaration of war but had been going on for some time. As far back as a year ago he had made up his mind that Germany and Russia were coming to an understanding, and he has no doubt this was all agreed upon, just waiting for the proper moment, and that Russian conversations with Great Britain and France took place long after they had definitely committed themselves to Germany.

de Kanya said that he had yesterday read a portion of MEIN KAMPF which somebody told him bore on the question of an alliance between Russia and Germany, and he found it very amusing because Mr. Hitler proved definitely that Germany never could be an ally of Russia, that it was absolutely impossible. He felt that a month would tell the story. Germany and Russia had made threats as to what action they will take in case peace proposals are refused. As they have been definitely refused it is now up to them to make good their threats. If they don't make them good in a month it will then prove that the German-Russian alliance is nothing except what can be seen on its face — that there is no understanding which would involve further cooperation between Germany and Russia — and the way was left open for a clash of interests which might bring Germany and Russia into antagonism: at least that is what he hoped.

de Kanya couldn't understand British and French policy of not making a serious war, and he didn't know why the Germans hadn't attacked France and England with airplanes. I told him Count Csaky's version, and he said as he had no knowledge of the feeling in France he couldn't say whether it was clever or not. The war, as it is being fought now, had him very much puzzled.

de Kanya thought Mr. Chamberlain's speech yesterday was exceedingly clever. He said he didn't consider most of his speeches clever at all, but he said he thought the one he made yesterday was a complete answer to Germany, and in a way which left Mr. Hitler holding the bag.

As for Hungary's position: He didn't believe she was in any danger at all; at least for the immediate future. Whatever understanding Germany and Russia had, certainly would not involve Hungary, that is, to the extent of her being occupied because Hungary was well in hand and there were more important things elsewhere. He thought Yugoslavia, Bulgaria, Rumania and Turkey would be the countries most concerned. Bulgaria and Yugoslavia, because they had always looked to Russia; Rumania, because she was a rich prize; and Turkey, because of Russian ambition to take Constantinople and to go to the Persian Gulf.

As things stood, Germany had Hungary in a position where she had to supply her with food, and he didn't think they would want Russia to take over Hungary. So if there is an understanding Hungary would fall into the German sphere of influence, and aside from being squeezed of foodstuffs and being put in a very delicate position, he thought at least during the progress of the war nothing would happen, as it would not profit Germany to enter it with her army.

Italy, Mr. de Kanya thought, would not go into the war on the side of Germany. He couldn't see it possible for her to reconcile her interests with the two isms.

[118] Memorandum

Budapest, November 6, 1939

Dr. Balogh,[305] who has just been to Belgrade, had a long conversation with the French Minister there. The latter said that a time would come — it is perhaps not very distant — when the Allies would be less tolerant of Hungary, Yugoslavia and the other Balkan States supplying Germany with food and other supplies.

Balogh also had some information to the effect that the Allies are looking for a way to "get at" Germany behind the Siegfried Line.[306] He has heard speculation about Weygand's[307] Army which is said to be building in Syria — possibly to be used to attack through the Balkans. Military circles may know more of this, if there is any substance to it at all.

There is increasing talk of change in Cabinet here. Specific names are now mentioned, but I have the feeling that most of my news is mere rumors and speculation.

Balogh said that Count Teleki was very much annoyed with the General Staff about what occurred in Transylvania.[308] Teleki threatened to resign if such a stupidity were repeated.

Bardossy, who is here from Bucharest, believes that Rumania is lost, a Russian demand on Bessarabia being virtually certain.

GGAjr:bpg[309]

---

305 Dr. József Balogh (1893–1944?), classical scholar, editor of *The Hungarian Quarterly* and *La Nouvelle Revue de Hongrie*.
306 German defense line from World War I, used by the withdrawing German army even toward the end of World War II.
307 French General Maxime Weygand (1867–1965), retired in 1935, commander-in-chief of the army from May 20, 1940; he couldn't stop the conquest of France.
308 A Hungarian conspiracy was revealed in Romania in early November. The Transylvanian minority plot was supported by Hungarian patriotic organizations. In a circular telegram of November 7, 1939, sent to all Hungarian envoys Foreign Minister Count Csáky hastened to declare that the Hungarian government had nothing to do with the case.
309 Dictated by second secretary Garret G. Ackerson of the U.S. legation in Budapest to stenographer "bpg."

[119] Conversation with Count Malagola

Budapest, November 6, 1939

Count Malagola said his delay in returning to Budapest was due to getting the necessary permissions, that he first had to fill out forms and send them to Florence, and because he had been born in Venice he had to send something over there. He finally decided to go down to the Foreign Ministry in Rome where he knew everybody. When he went there, everybody laughed heartily at the idea of his being held up for military service as they told him that at his age nobody cared whether he left the country or not. He said he spent a week in Rome and saw Ciano.

Malagola told Ciano he was returning to Budapest and that he didn't suppose anything would disturb him before he got back next summer, referring to the war, and Ciano smiled and said he didn't think so either. He said that the latest move in the Italian Cabinet took out German sympathizers, and since Ciano was now known to be very anti-German he felt that the possibility of Italy going to war with Germany was out. He agreed she might go to war with the Allies later, but he couldn't see the Axis functioning. He said that the alliance which Italy and Germany had, provided that Italy was not bound until 1943, that if either party went into war before that time the other party was not expected to participate. The alliance was made to impress the world with their friendship, but it was entirely in the future and not operative until 1943. He said that public sentiment in Italy was overwhelmingly against Germany, particularly since the Soviet pact. Futher, Italy was making money by being neutral, and a vast majority there wanted it to remain neutral. He said he talked to textile manufacturers and found those who were manufacturing woolens were making them for the British Army, while the Fiat company were making motors for the French. Nothing, practically, was going to Germany since they had no money to pay for purchases. Count Malagola said he had no commissions in connection with Yugoslavia or any other country at the present time.

[120] Conversation with Madame Ullein-Reviczky

Budapest, November 7, 1939

Madame Ullein-Reviczky[310] told me that lately her husband had given a tea at the Carlton Hotel for Italian and German newspapermen. After the invitations were issued, the Cabinet changed in Italy took place, and that as U-R construed this as anti-German he notified all the Italian newspapermen that Germans would also be present, and as a result none of them came. He didn't notify di Vinci because he thought, being a diplomat, he wouldn't want to come in any case. However, he happened to be in the hall when di Vinci came and told him that von Erdmannsdorff was there. de Vinci said nothing but went into a back room off the lobby and waited there until he saw von Erdmannsdorff leave, and then came in.

[121] Conversation with Dr. Tibor Eckhardt

Budapest, November 14, 1939

Dr. Eckhardt said that his trip to Belgrade was made at the request of Dr. Macek, the Croatian leader and Vice Premier of Yugoslavia.[311] While there he held a number of conversations with Dr. Macek and other peasant leaders and he found conditions between the Croats and the Serbs were not what they should be and that the Croats bitterly regretted the disappearance of the Austro-Hungarian Empire and the position they had therein. Dr. Macek's idea was to discuss the possibilities of a new Austro-Hungarian Empire after the war is finished, which some way or other he believes will have to be recreated and to which Croatia would like to belong.

Dr. Eckhardt said the Serbs were very sick of the Croats and he didn't think they would make much fight to keep them. However, Dr. Macek had in mind that Serbia and Bulgaria could be united in one country, and this being done, the Serbs would not mind losing Croatia. Dr. Macek said the Croats would never be happy tied up with the Balkans since their religion is Roman Catholic and their ideas western and not eastern, while Serbia was a

310 Antal Ullein-Reviczky (1894–1955), diplomat, international lawyer, adjunct professor at Debrecen University. Press chief in the foreign ministry 1939–41, and in the prime minister's office 1941–43, Hungarian minister to Stockholm 1943–44. His wife, Lovice Cumberbatch, was the daughter of a British diplomat, the consul at Istanbul.
311 Vladimir Maček (1879–1964), Croatian politician, leader of the Peasant Party, deputy prime minister of Yugoslavia 1939–41.

Greek Catholic country and proud of being Balkan. Dr. Eckhardt said that he believed there would be no difficulty in making an Adriatic bloc consisting of Italy, Greece, Albania, Yugoslavia and Hungary, but he did not know if there was any in process of formation.

Dr. Eckhardt said he knew nothing about any agreement between Italy and Yugoslavia to assist Hungary if the latter were attacked by Russia. He said there might be some such understanding, but he had never heard of it; nor had he ever heard of Italian assistance if Russia were to occupy Bessarabia and Hungary must occupy Transylvania. He didn't believe there was any such understanding. He didn't think Hungary would take any such step. Eckhardt agreed that Hungary was fortifying the frontier in Ruthenia but he thought the possibility of their holding back the Russian horde if they really tried to come through was nil.

[122] Conversation with Mr. de Winchkler head of MFTR[312]

Budapest, November 15, 1939

In conversation with the British Minister this morning, he told me the Regent had seen him on connection with the idea of Hungary buying some German boats but that, of course, they could not agree to that.

Mr. de Winchkler, former Minister of Commerce and President of the MFTR (Hungarian-owned Danube steamship company) was in today and told me they had for some time the idea of buying boats to be operated on the Mediterranean in connection with the Danubian boat line, that they had the capital in pounds to buy sufficient boats, that there had been an idea of buying German boats now in neutral ports, although it wasn't his idea, and he was not surprised when the British refused, even though the proposition was that these boats were to be chartered to British firms. The objection of the British was, of course, capital would be transferred to Germans and this they would not agree to.

Mr. de Winchkler now thought in view of the fact that American boats were shut off in coming to Europe there might be American boats he could buy. They only wanted small boats and their idea was to operate them as mentioned above in connection with the British under charter to British firms although sailing under the Hungarian flag. He wondered if any such

312 Magyar Folyam- és Tengerhajózási Rt. [Hungarian River and Sea Navigation Co.]. Winchkler was its chairman and general manager from 1936 to 1940.

arrangement would be possible and, if so, how he could get in touch with the people who had the boats, etc. I told him I would take up the matter with the Department to see what they had to say.

[123] Conversation with No. 1 — the Regent[313]
Budapest, November 15, 1939

1. No small country in Europe is safe from invasion, but Hungary has no fears of invasion in the near future. Germany can get more from Hungary as a neutral than she could if Hungary were to be invaded by German troops.

2. No request was ever made for permission for German troops to cross Hungary to attack Rumania. In fact, Germany had consistently cautioned Hungary not to make difficulties with Rumania.

3. No. 1 thought American public opinion was keeping Germans from going through Holland and Belgium.

4. He has reason to believe Germany and Russia had agreed to maintain peace in Southeastern Europe so Germany could get supplies from here.

5. Every action taken by Hungary since the war has been taken after approval of Italy. Italy was very insistent that Germans should not go through Hungary to attack Poland.

6. Axis still exists, but a German attack on Hungary would be tantamount to an attack on Italy. Such an attack might also force Yugoslavia on side of Allies. Hungary would resist with force any attempt to send troops through Hungarian territory.

7. Number 1 denied all rumors about his resigning or becoming Vice Regent and about a complete change of Cabinet. There may be small changes in the Cabinet from time to time.

8. Hungarian frontiers with Russia and with Slovakia being fortified.

---

313 No. 1 refers to Count Pál Teleki, as is clearly shown by the similarity of the following conversation, originally mistakenly placed further back in the volume than chronologically necessary. This is a brief sketch of the latter. The reference to "the Regent" does not make sense.

[124] Conversation with Prime Minister Teleki[314]

Budapest, November 15, 1939

I saw Count Teleki last night under circumstances which looked as though it might have been prearranged on his part. The day before yesterday Countess Teleki called up and asked me to come to tea yesterday afternoon. I assumed it was one of the large teas given by the Prime Minister's wife and was quite surprised when I arrived to find but a few ladies and one gentleman present. I talked to Countess Teleki for a while and in a few minutes Count Teleki entered. He made a point of saying that he hadn't intended to come but when he had heard I had come he came over. He sat down next to me and talked to me the entire time.

I asked Count Teleki for his opinion on the European situation and numerous other questions, and to my surprise found him the same as he was previous to becoming Prime Minister, quite willing to talk on any subject and answer any question. He told me that no small country in Europe was safe from invasion. This applied to Norway, Sweden, and Denmark as well as Hungary. However, Hungary had no particular fears at the moment since she felt for many reasons that she was less likely to be invaded than any other small country.

As far as he could see, there was only one reason why Hungary was in any danger at all, and that reason was that the German people required a shot in the arm now and then, so that if Germany made no progress on the western front it might be necessary to conquer some small country and keep up the flagging spirits of the people. However, there were still many small countries left besides Hungary which it would be more logical and more reasonable to conquer since there would be less risks involved and more motive. For example, Denmark, Holland, Belgium, Switzerland, and even possibly Sweden and Norway. While these countries might offer more resistance they would be of advantage in that they offered a way through to the enemy, a better military base or better control of the sea, etc. There would be absolutely no advantage in a military way taking over

Hungary since more food could be gotten from an independent Hungary than a conquered Hungary. There was no reason to believe that more oil could be gotten from a conquered Rumania than they were getting at present since not only would the oil wells be put out of commission and take some time to put them in order again, but there were other reasons, so any campaign in this direction would be unprofitable since Turkey in conjunc-

---

314 This conversation was originally mistakenly placed further back in the volume than chronologically necessary.

tion with the British would block them off from the Mosul oil fields[315] and there was no reason to go to war to get what they already were getting unless it was purely to obtain a cheap victory.

As far as he knew, up to this moment Germany had no thought of entering Hungary or Rumania. There had never been any request from Germany to permit German troops to cross Hungary to Rumania or any suggestion that they had any such request in mind. In fact, every suggestion that has been made has been to the contrary. Germany was constantly warning Hungary not to make difficulties with Rumania since they wished nothing to interrupt the flow of petrol. As he saw the situation, there were three things Germany could do: 1) to attack Britain directly, which in this kind of weather he thought would be most difficult and an invasion impossible 2) to go through Belgium and Holland; 3) to go through Switzerland. He barred out Switzerland because in his opinion it led to the wrong place. He said he knew the Germans were frightfully angry at Britain and were anxious to do everything they could to destroy her. Therefore, he didn't believe they would go through Switzerland because this would be an attack on France, for which the Germans have no interest at present. If a direct attack on Britain was impossible and they didn't go through Switzerland there was only one thing left, and that was to take Holland or Belgium, or both, in an endeavor to get near to Britain to form a base of attack. Of course there was still another alternative, a direct attack on the Maginot Line, and this the Germans might be compelled to make if none of the other three ways of attack were followed. He said there was no doubt in his mind that the only thing that held them back from going into Holland, and possibly Belgium, was American public opinion which the Germans were very anxious not to offend. Actually there had been no decision on the part of Germany as just what campaign they would pursue as there was divided counsel and they hadn't made a definite plan. Until they had made some such plan and given it a fair trial he thought the Germans' attention would be directed to the war and that no other small country than the three mentioned would be subject to any attack. If, however, the plan of campaign agreed upon proved a failure then for the reasons mentioned they might pick a quarrel with a country which could be conquered easily. Hungary would thus seem to be a reasonable choice. However, there were several reasons why Hungary was not such a likely choice as other small countries because (1) in his opinion every action taken by Soviet Russia was in preparation for a struggle with Germany and there could be no other reason for her bases in the Baltic, and no

---

315 Today Mosul is the third largest city of Iraq, next to the Tigris River. There are significant oil fields east and north of the city.

other reason for her position in Poland. He had reason to believe that both Russia and Germany had agreed that there would be peace in Southeastern Europe in order to enable Germany to get supplies from this section. While he felt that Russia would act towards Germany whenever she felt it safe for her to do so, it was someway off. He didn't, therefore, believe Russia would either take any action against Germany or German interests in this part of the world, and on the other hand, he didn't think Russia would permit Germany to go to the Black Sea if she could possibly help it. Therefore, any attack on Rumania would involve Russia. (2) Italy considered Hungary as her closest friend and supporter. Every action taken by Hungary since the war was taken after consultation with Italy and with her approval. While Hungary never had any intention of letting Germans go through to fight the Poles or anyone else, the Italians were very insistent that Hungary refuse any demands of this sort. While he did not think that Italy was going to war on behalf of Germany, still there was the Axis more or less functioning. Italy's position was still correct so far as the Axis is concerned. A German attack on Hungary would be almost equivalent to a German attack on Italy and would certainly and definitely put Italy in the Allies camp if it did not directly involve her in the war. Yugoslavia allied with Rumania would likewise be pushed definitely to the side of the Allies and possibly into the war. While the time has not yet come for the Yugoslavs to come to the defense of Hungary in case of invasion, she would have to do something if Hungary was invaded, and with the support of Italy and acting in conjunction with Italy would have considerable military strength.

For these reasons, Count Teleki believes it improbable that Germany would attack Hungary or Rumania under present circumstances and conditions. There is always the possibility that these conditions would change in such a way that Hungary would be in the same or worse position as any other country, or there was always the possibility that despite everything he had said Hungary would be invaded. Therefore, if he went back to his office and was told that Germany had made demands for sending troops through Hungary, or that Germany or Russia, or both, had actually invaded the country he would be surprised but not astonished since the head of a small country in Europe under present circumstances could expect almost anything even though his reason told him it was impossible.

Count Teleki complained because of the rumors which have started because he was sick. He said it is funny that after seven months as Prime Minister without a day's vacation, he couldn't take a week's rest without the town seething with rumors that he was going to resign, that he was going to become Vice Regent, and that the whole Cabinet was going to be changed. Ha said there was no truth in any of these rumors. There might be changes in the Cabinet from time to time but there was no thought of any definite

Count Pál Teleki in 1935

change, and he certainly had no intention of resigning. His illness was due to the grippe and he didn't feel at all well yesterday.

I have been puzzled in my mind as to why Count Teleki, all of a sudden, talked so freely. I know that he doesn't see either the French, German or British Ministers. The latter told me that Count Teleki had asked him not to come any more since every time he came the Germans wanted to know what it was, and O'Malley said he never got anything anyhow so he didn't care whether he called or not.[316] The French Minister told me that he had made one attempt but drew a blank and had no intention of going again as it was apparent he got nothing. The German Minister only recently told me even he didn't call on Count Teleki because he got nothing from him only stories about boy scouts, schools, etc. So far as I know, he has done no talk-

316 Cf. Montgomery's conversation with British minister O'Malley, November 15, 1939.

ing whatever. Therefore, I am curious to know why all of a sudden he starts talking to me after almost refusing to admit his name since he became Prime Minister.

I remember also my conversation with Count Csaky a few days ago. He struck me as quite changed and no longer talked of the Axis; in fact, he almost seemed anti-German. Therefore, I am wondering how this and Count Teleki's changed attitude can be accounted for. Is it because they are cut off from Britain and France, and want, therefore, to have the friendship of America with the idea what we know the Allies know, or that we will have something to say about the final peace, or just what is the reason. There is also another thing that comes to my mind, and that is the Red Cross. There has been some sort of a mixup for which the Hungarian Government are very apologetic, and Dr. Johan[317] called on me the other day on behalf of the Minister of the Interior and told me that Teleki had told the Minister that I should be seen and some explanation made. Just before that Countess Edina Zichy, whose son married Teleki's daughter,[318] suddenly asked me in for tea and there was only one other lady present who was connected with relief work, and the whole conversation was about the Red Cross, how it could be straightened out, etc. Therefore, it is possible that this is the cause of change in Teleki's attitude, although I don't believe it would cause him to talk like he did, nor could it have any effect on Csaky since this interview was before. It is certain that the conversation with me last night was sought for by Teleki since he told me so.

Teleki told me that Hungary would never give its consent to German troops crossing or entering Hungary, and that they would fight if they came, no matter how hopeless it might be. I suggested that it would be better to put up a phantom defense so as to keep them from destroying the country, but he was rather insistent that this would never do for Hungarians, that they couldn't hold up their heads if they didn't do everything possible to resist and drive out an invader no matter what the cost. He said anyone who looked at Czechoslovakia and Poland could see that it mattered very little so far as opposing them or not was concerned, but that no Hungarian could hold up his head if they were to do as the Czechs did, and they would never do it.

Incidentally, Count Teleki told me they were not only fortifying the Russian frontier but the German. This came about from the fact that my caddie came back to the golf course on a day's leave and told me that he was leaving to work on Count Szechenyi's place. Questioning him, I discovered that

---

317 Dr. Béla Johan (1889–1983), medical doctor, first Hungarian Rockefeller scholar (1922), director of the Hungarian Institute of Public Health (1925), secretary of state 1935–44.
318 Count Ferdinánd Zichy and Countess May Teleki.

he is in the engineering corps and that they are building fortifications on Count Szechenyi's place directed against Slovakia. In the conversation with Count Teleki, I mentioned with surprise that they were fortifying against the Slovaks since it was really against Germany. He told me that every frontier nowadays must be fortified and since the Germans were fortifying the frontier occupied by their supposed Allies, the Communists, there could be no objection to Hungary fortifying her frontier with Germany. However, there was a better reason since this frontier was actually Slovakia and there was no reason for Germany to object to the fortification of Slovak Frontier, since within the year there had actually been war between the two countries.

Count Teleki seemed perfectly calm and not the least bit nervous, and if he is disturbed by the international situation he showed no signs of it.

[125] Conversation with Mr. O'Malley British Minister
Budapest, November 15, 1939

The British Minister told me this morning that everything he had seen and heard since he had been here led to the same conclusions as those of Count Teleki. He saw no particular danger to Hungary for the moment. While there might possibly be in the spring, he agreed with Count Teleki that Hungary was in less danger than most of the small countries.

He explained Count Teleki's conversation with me by saying exactly the same thing had been done to him. The last time I saw him he told me Count Teleki had told him that he didn't want him to call because every time he did so it got in the papers and the Germans made a face about it, saying that he was not calling on him any more because he never got any information anyhow. However, not long ago Countess Teleki invited him to tea and he went up and found no one there but the Prime Minister who had proceeded to talk quite freely and fully contrary to any previous experience. In other words, paralleling both the circumstances and volubility of the Prime Minister in my case. He thought that both visits were the result of a growing conviction on the part of Hungarians that the war was going against the Germans and that it was better to be more friendly and more open with the Allied Powers, and also America since that country might have much to say about the events of the future whether she entered the war or not. He said it was true no such experience had happened to the French Minister but that this was natural because the Hungarians didn't trust the French but they did the British and Americans.

[126] Conversation with the Rumanian Minister

Budapest, November 15, 1939

The Rumanian Minister told me this morning that while he had heard in September from a newspaper man that Germany was about to come through Hungary to Rumania he had never particularly credited the rumor and had paid very little attention to it. Otherwise, he had no information whatever on the subject. His opinion was that there was an unwritten understanding between Germany and Russia to let the Southeastern portion of Europe remain neutral. On Germany's part this was to facilitate obtaining supplies and also to avoid another front which would bring in more enemies; on Russia's part, an unwillingness to come to conclusions with Germany at the present moment. However, he didn't believe that either Russia or Germany had any intention of permitting the other to enter Rumania without making every effort to stop it. He was certain that Russia had no thought of letting Germany come to the Black Sea or obtain possession of the oil fields, and likewise he was certain that Germany was not going to give over to Russia any portion of Rumania except possible Bessarabia. It is, therefore, not improbable that if either one made a move it would meet the other in Rumania and Rumania might become the scene of Russian-German hostility. However, he didn't believe that anything would be done now since the time is not propitious. Bessarabia was practically inundated at this time of the year and winter conditions made Transylvania and the Carpathian Mountains a formidable barrier although not insurmountable. Further, he believed that the attention of both Russia and Germany was directed elsewhere and for the moment there was no particular reason to think of Rumania. Later this might not be true.

He said that the German Minister told him yesterday that Mr. Clodius,[319] who left Budapest yesterday morning for Rumania, had told him that he expected more difficulties in dealing with Rumania because of British interference. Mr. Crutzesco, the Rumanian Minister, said that this might indicate future trouble but didn't think it amounted to much for the moment. As far as Russia was concerned, every move she made she indicated to Germany that she had one enemy in mind, that is, Germany. This is borne out by the statements of Mr. Molotov to the Turkish Foreign Minister. Mr. Molotov had scoffed at the ideas of Turkey being worried and said that Russia didn't care anything about small countries like Turkey — that they were only getting themselves in position for the inevitable struggle between Russia and Germany.

---

319 Karl von Clodius, deputy head of the department of economic policy in the German ministry of foreign affairs 1937–43.

[127] Conversation with Dr. Tibor Eckhardt

Budapest, November 16, 1939

Eckhardt said that he was very certain that the story about Hungary being invaded had been started by Italy in order to give Rome an opportunity to publicly state her interest in Hungary so that the Germans would be fully warned. He said that when he talked to Dr. Macek he had discussed with him the question of Serbian leaders. He found all of them in agreement that such a bloc could be formed and that he had submitted a written memorandum to Count Teleki on the subject. At the present time, Yugoslavia was just as much concerned about a German invasion of Hungary as Hungary itself, and any alliance which would bring Yugoslavia to Hungary's defense to enable Italian troops to cross Yugoslavia to aid Hungary was impossible because of the alliance between Rumania and Yugoslavia — which neither Italy nor Hungary wished to assume. Therefore, the suggestion of an Adriatic bloc offered a method of action which would leave Yugoslavia individually concerned with Rumania but the rest of the bloc pledged to mutual defense. He knew that Macek was friendly with the Italians, although he was very sore about the Albanian affair, but he didn't know whether Macek had made this suggestion at the instance of the Italians, but he believed it had great possibilities. This bloc would include Greece, Albania, Yugoslavia, Hungary, and Italy.

[128] Conversation with the Regent[320]

Budapest, November 16, 1939

The Regent was so worked up about Russia's entrance into Europe and what she might do in future and so little concerned about the possibility of Germany coming into Hungary that I had a difficult time getting much information out of him on the present-day situation.

The Regent believes that the Bolsheviks are only kidding Germany and that at the proper time they will cut her throat. He says they may be willing to give Germany supplies now but that they haven't much rolling stock and they cannot give much but when the time comes and she needs her most Russia won't give her a piece of bread. He says they are only awaiting an

---

320 This conversation was originally mistakenly placed further back in the volume than chronologically necessary.

opportunity to take everything they can and that the only salvation would be to settle the war somehow — Germany, England and France and everybody else including Hungary go against the Bolsheviks and drive them out of Europe.

He says he thinks there is an agreement between the Germans and the Bolsheviks regarding Central Europe but he doesn't think it amounts to anything on either side if there is some advantage in breaking it. He expects to see Russia take Bessarabia whenever she feels safe to do so but he doesn't think Germany will make any effort to go into Rumania even if the Russians take Bessarabia.

He says he is certain that the Russians covered the Rumanian frontier to keep Germany out and he doesn't think Germany would dare to make a move into Southeastern Europe without the consent of Russia, and he is certain Russia wouldn't voluntarily permit Germany to go into Rumania.

He told me definitely that Italy had promised Hungary military assistance in the event of an attack by Germany or Russia and he said they were negotiating with Yugoslavia for a similar guarantee but that the Yugoslav-Rumanian pact against Hungary interfered.[321] However, he thought some way would be worked out. I mentioned a Balkan bloc covering Greece, Albania, Yugoslavia, Italy and Hungary (as suggested by Tibor Eckhardt, although I didn't mention his name) and he said he hadn't heard of that but he seemed to think it offered possibilities since it got around Yugoslavia's guarantee to Rumania.

He told me Hungary had not the slightest intention of going into Rumania herself but that she would not look with equanimity on the Russians taking over Transylvania. However, he thought the Russians were more interested in Rumania proper since their old dreams aimed at getting a warm port which the possession of the Dardanelles would give them.

He said that the two men in the world who were the most powerful today and had the most influence were President Roosevelt and Mussolini. He commended the President's peace efforts, his support of Finland and all other things which he seemed to attribute to the fact that he was a sea-loving man. He said that he was very happy to see that the planes were not sinking battleships as he had been told they would.

He thought that the German story of British spies having engineered the bombing of the beer hall in Munich at which Hitler spoke was ridiculous. He said it was impossible even though they might have wanted to do so. He said you couldn't get away from the fact that someone high in the Nazi

---

321 Defense treaty between Romania and the Kingdom of the Serbs, Croats, and Slovenes, Belgrade, June 7, 1921.

ranks was responsible and he suggested that Mr. Himmler was very high up in the Nazi ranks.

The Regent said that Hitler's position was very difficult because he now had 23 million Poles, 11 million Czechs and Slovaks, millions of Catholics and Protestants and Jews, all of whom hated him, and it was a very difficult position to be in. It was hard enough to fight a war with the country behind you but it made many difficulties when such a large element of the population was against him.

He thought that if Blomberg had stayed in he might have controlled things but he didn't think much of the Army heads now, and he didn't believe there was much possibility of the Army taking charge. He couldn't see how it was all going to end, but he said it was a monumental stupidity because there was no reason for the war at all, and as matters now stood the Germans were worse off than they were when the war started, even if they got peace.

The Regent told me he had been wanting for some time to kick the Nazi sympathizers out of the Cabinet and suppress the Nazi party but Teleki always said to wait, and he said he is a very clever man so perhaps he is right. However, he got rid of one of them, Kunder,[322] who, he said is a terrible Nazi actually working for Germany, but he added I will get the rest of them in time. He said he would like to take steps against Imredy but Teleki says he is dropping lower and lower all the time and is killing himself. He told me again about how he thought Imredy such a great man when he put him in and that he went crazy, and he spoke again of the Jews, what a terrible thing he did to the Jews and how he (the Regent) did everything he could to minimize it.

He spoke of the Poles and said they never even had a chance because the Germans had long planned in advance their moves, every man knew where to drop his bomb and what to do, and when the order was given they didn't hesitate. They had their spies so that the Poles didn't even get started. He said they know everything.

---

322 Antal Kunder was minister of commerce and communications until October 27, 1939, and again in the Sztójay government of 1944. ˙

[129] Memorandum[323]

Budapest, November 17, 1939

The Regent told me that it was impossible for the small Governments in this part of the world to make any fair settlement among themselves because of the universal hatred engendered by centuries of warfare and so forth and so on. For example, he said that if God appeared to the King of Rumania and told him that unless he gave Transylvania back to Hungary, within two years Rumania would be wiped out, there would be nothing the King could do about it because if he tried to give Transylvania back to Hungary he would be put off the throne within twenty-four hours. The same thing held true in Hungary. Therefore, nothing could ever be really settled except by the big Powers capable of forcing a settlement and maintaining it. Since the different Powers each had their interests the only possible solution was a League of Nations, not as it was before with Costa Rica and other countries in the Western Hemisphere deciding the fate of a European nation, nor a League which was an adjunct to the British or French or any other Foreign Office, but a real League of European nations which would include every country in Europe and could have some authority. He told me that he of course was not in Mussolini's confidence to the extent of being told what his ideas were. He thought, however, that he was expecting or hoping that France would offer him Corsica, Tunisia or some other land and he didn't see why France didn't do it since Tunisia was largely Italian and France could afford to give it up, having plenty of other territory; and for the objects which would be achieved it would be worth it.

[130] Conversation with No. 2[324]

Budapest, November 22, 1939

1. Feared Munich bombing[325] (November 9th) would lead to purging of all sane and responsible officials left in German Government.

2. No. 2 not previously informed regarding Russo-German Pact; greatly surprised by it.

---

323 This conversation was originally mistakenly placed further back in the volume than chronologically necessary.

324 Probably Count István Bethlen. Montgomery refers to Bethlen's information elsewhere as well: „The details of happenings in the Upper House will be given me by Bethlen next week." (No. 79: November 28, 1940).

325 An assassination attempt on Hitler was carried out on the evening of November 8, 1939 in the Bürgerbräukeller in Munich. Despite some casualties, the attempt proved

3. Believes Army revolution in Germany now impossible as all leaders have been gotten rid of.

4. Investigation had proved that Hungarian Army was not involved in recent arming of Hungarians in Transylvania. Incident had been very unpleasant for Hungarian-Rumanian relations.

5. Believes Italy will remain neutral. Ciano has become very anti-German. However, the Axis will be kept in an effort to bar Soviets from domination in Balkans.

6. He is certain (i.e., No. 2) that Germans would go through Holland, Belgium eventually.

[131] Conversation with Mr. Jan Spisiak the Slovak Minister
Budapest, November 27, 1939

Mr. Spisiak says that Slovakia is an independent country and not a part of Germany, despite what anybody thinks. He says the German troops do not go into Slovakia except at such places as have been agreed upon between the two governments. He denies any concentration of troops in Slovakia at the present time and says on the contrary that Slovakia is free of troops; there are no Slovakian troops in the German Army; and his country is at peace with everyone. He admits that this as at the pleasure of Germany but he thinks the Germans want a sort of Exhibit A in the shape of a country which is under their protectorate and is enjoying a certain amount of independence. Mr. Spisiak is much worried about what is going to happen to his country when the war is over. He says very definitely that a victory for Germany would be a catastrophe for his country since he has no illusions as to what would then happen. He thinks this is equally true of Hungary and Rumania and perhaps Yugoslavia. He doesn't believe, though, that the Germans have any possibility of victory since he thinks their situation is somewhat desperate. He is not of the opinion that they will give up quickly; thinks the war will probably last two years more; and he is of the opinion that Hitler and his crowd will try to turn the country over to the Bolsheviks rather than be defeated. He says he is somewhat of a specialist, himself, on Russia, having studied that country for twenty some odd years and having spent some time there. He is of the opinion that Germany will not get many supplies from Russia. He thinks also that the Russians will make some sort of an offensive

---

to be essentially unsuccessful, and it has been alleged that it was arranged to bolster the popularity of the Führer as a propaganda trick of the Nazis. The explosion was said to have been committed by British agents.

militarily or otherwise, against Germany whenever the proper moment offers. At present he doesn't expect Russia to do anything in Rumania or Hungary because Germany is still in a position to resent it and would not permit it; further, he is under the impression that Italy is no strongly back of Hungary that it would be a dangerous move on the part of Russia to go into Hungary at all. He thinks that ultimately Yugoslavia, Italy, and Hungary will form a bloc for defense against Russia, and Germany too, for that matter. The Germans, though, he is certain, have no idea of going into Hungary although relations between Germany and Hungary are not at the moment very good. He says Hungary, Rumania and Yugoslavia are practically the hinterland of Germany and any invasion would so upset the economic balance of these countries that it would be disastrous for Germany and he considers an invasion of Hungary and other countries in Southeastern Europe would bring the war to a conclusion a year sooner because of its economic effect.

He talked about the Germans, and while they still have confidence in Hitler, they are very much puzzled and uncertain about the future and few of them can see just how they are going to win the war. He says the black-outs, food conditions and the situation generally are very depressing to the German people. As for his own country, he believes that their position is under- stood by the Allies and that after the war is over, should the Allies win as he expects, he hopes that they will give some consideration to Slova-kian wishes. One thing that Slovakia wishes above everything else is not to be united to Hungary. They would rather be with Poland, Austria, or Bohe-mia or anyone else, although they prefer to be an autonomous province of whatever country they might be in; they would rather be with any other country without autonomy than to be with Hungary with it. Naturally his country is much concerned as to what its ultimate destiny is, but there was nothing they could do but wait. He said that the relations between the Hun-garian and German Governments were not so good as they might be since the Germans knew that both the Regent and Count Teleki were very anti-German. In fact, he said that practically Csaky was the only pro-German left. He said it may be true that one or two Cabinet Ministers had German sympathies, but they were in positions where they made very little differ-ence and he thought that Csaky was not so pro-German as he had been and that in any case his influence was not as great as it might be.

He said that relations with Hungary were satisfactory, although not cor-dial. Hungary still considered them as dangerous because they thought Ger-man troops could go through Slovakia to Hungary. He admitted this to be true, although he denied there was any concentration of troops there now. He said actually they were a help to Hungary because the Hungarians could fortify and were fortifying the border with Slovakia on the grounds that they were afraid of the Slovaks whereas it was the Germans they feared and they couldn't very well fortify the German frontier without showing a lack of confidence in Mr. Hitler's guarantee of Hungarian independence. He said that Hungarians had confiscated a very large number of acres (I believe he mentioned 800,000)[326] of land from the Slovaks in the territory they had taken over, and that the Slovaks had in turn confiscated an equal amount of land from the Hungarians. The result was that they were having a conference in Budapest now and he felt that the matter would be ironed out.

He said that Slovakia was enjoying prosperity; there were no food restrictions. On account of the position of Finland, Sweden, etc., there was a great demand for her timber; her textile mills were working; and for the moment her situation was excellent. It is true the Germans were coming over in the nighttime and taking food, but even at that they were getting along very well.

He has just been appointed Minister to Bulgaria which he takes on in addition to his post here, and expects to go there shortly (Monday). He says they have Ministers in Rome, Moscow, Budapest, Bucharest, and now Sofia. He denies that Tiso is pro-German. In fact, he says he is not at all. He says that the situation in Bohemia is incredible, that the action of the Germans there leaves the Slovaks speechless because it is the only thing possible at the moment. Nevertheless, they sympathize with their Czech brothers.

He says he has just returned from Bratislava and was told there that the Gestapo had killed hundreds of students and professors and had closed the universities, even in places like Brno, where there had been no disturbances at all. He said he couldn't understand how the President and other officials of the so-called Czech Protectorate could remain in their positions, and neither could his Government. He thought they would resign or refuse to carry on, so they could only conclude that they were in some sort of position where this was impossible. He couldn't believe they would voluntarily remain as officials with the treatment which the Czechs were receiving at the hands of the Gestapo.

[132] Conversation with Mr. de Kanya
former Foreign Minister

Budapest, December 11, 1939

Mr. de Kanya told me that he had many friends in Germany, since he spent a good part of his life in Vienna and had been Minister in Berlin;[327] that he was constantly seeing various of these friends or hearing from them

---

326 368,000 hectars (1 acre = 0.46 hectares).
327 Kánya was Hungarian minister to Berlin between 1925 and 1933.

in an indirect way that all his information was to the effect that conditions in Germany were very bad indeed, and that the morale of the people was not too high.

He said that all in all most of his friends insisted that Germany was without doubt going to win the war; nevertheless, most of the time they talked in a manner which showed they hadn't the slightest bit of confidence in Germany's ability to even survive as a nation because they always indicated fears for Germany being cut up, turned Bolshevik, or other suggestions which were a little more frantic, and even told him confidentially they saw no way out. He said that only last week a very prominent German (he added, a man of good position who was conservative and trustworthy) told him that in his opinion if Mr. Hitler didn't do something either in the way of an offensive within six weeks, there would be a revolution, and that if this offensive didn't turn out to be a military success there would be a revolution anyhow. de Kanya said he could hardly believe this. Nevertheless, he doesn't believe, as Count Csaky and others do, that a revolution in Germany is impossible. He thinks that the Soviet move has disturbed a lot of Germans and that the more responsible elements are now thinking more or ways and means to protect themselves against the Soviets than they are of winning the war.

de Kanya says his German friends, without exception, pretend to believe that the French have no heart for the war that they are driven into it more or less by the British; and that they can separate the French from the British in time, after which they can finish off the British. The principal worry of most of them seems to be if they can hold off the Bolsheviks for this to happen.

de Kanya says some day he is going to give the story of his conversations with Hitler to the world. At the present time he cannot. When they are published, they will show that in every conversation he had with Hitler, Hitler never lived up to any promise he made. He said that conversation with Hitler was unilateral, since Hitler did all the talking. Every time he saw him he broke out in a lot of statements as to what he was going to do for Hungary, such as restoring the ancient kingdom; even in a small matter he definitely told him that Pressburg[328] belonged to Hungary, that he would see that the Hungarians got it; and that when the time came he ignored his promise entirely, as he had all the others.

de Kanya said that when the Regent went to Germany, Hitler spoke to him about the possibility of a war, and the Regent told him that it would be a mistake to go to war with England since due to her great sea power she was a very difficult country to defeat. He said Hitler instantly became furi-

---

328 Formerly Pozsony, today Bratislava.

ous and began to scream and yell at the Regent, and that right in the midst of his screaming the Regent held up his hands and told him in no uncertain terms that he was the Head of a State and he didn't expect to listen to any conversation addressed in such a tone and that unless he spoke to him in the language which one Head of a State used to another he would immediately return to Hungary. He said Hitler instantly caved in, and after that was very sweet to the Regent all the time he was there. Ribbentrop blamed de Kanya for this incident. He said de Kanya put him up to it, etc.

[133] Conversation with Prime Minister Teleki
Budapest, December 11, 1939

Hungary had no desire to go into another Austro-Hungarian Empire, nor to have a Hapsburg King. There was no possibility of a Hapsburg king in Hungary if it depended on the will of the people. One might be forced on them but he couldn't believe his throne would be secure.

As for a confederation either north or south, or in any direction, Hungary might fit into this provided it was a loose confederation in which every country was practically independent. Such a confederation might ultimately develop into an empire, but with the wave of nationalistic feeling that existed today he didn't believe that any force uniting all peoples would be successful and for that reason as well as for many others Hungary would not want to take part in it since she had enough experience of that kind and didn't care to repeat it. He felt that a settlement of the question of Transylvania along the lines he suggested would give Europe a certain amount of security against the Bolsheviks since the boundaries outlined were mountainous and could be more or less easily defended. Rumania was in no position to defend anything against the Bolsheviks or anything else.

He told me very confidentially that the Army knowing nothing about any army but the German Army had great admiration for that army and wanted to buy everything from Germany. Now they were in need of some aeroplanes and the Army proposed buying a number thereof from Germany. He didn't want to continue buying from Germany for several reasons: the main one because he didn't want to be dependent on Germany. He wanted to break the tie if possible and it occurred to him that instead of buying German aeroplanes they should buy American aeroplanes. He said he would take it up with the Regent; that the Regent was very enthusiastic about the idea. He was sure there would be terrible opposition from the Army because they couldn't believe that anybody but the Germans could have good aeroplanes and military equipment. He didn't know what the financial problem would be but it might be between the Army and the Ministry of Finance and that he might not be able to come through with it. However, he wanted to tell me about it so that if anything happened and they did place any orders I would know that they had this in mind. He asked me to keep this very confidential since he hadn't told the Army or anyone about it yet, and if it got out beforehand it would make it more difficult for him to do anything since if they would have the information they could prepare themselves with arguments, etc., whereas if he put it over the way he expected to he wouldn't have that opportunity.

1940

[134] Conversation with Prime Minister Teleki

Budapest, January 30, 1940

Count Teleki said he felt the Finnish situation[329] was extraordinarily important, that if the Finns could be helped and Russia held off, it would have an important bearing psychologically in Germany and would have considerable effect upon the duration of the war. A Russian victory, he considered, would be disastrous because it would bolster that element in Germany headed by Ribbentrop which promised great things from Russia. A Russian defeat, or at least holding the Russians off until Fall, would correspondingly effect the situation and by the elimination of Ribbentrop and others strengthen the hands of the conservative element which might then be in a position to make peace. For this reason he thought it of great importance that all possible help should be rendered Finland. A half battalion of picked Hungarians troops was leaving shortly via France and England, where they will be picked up on February 5 at Hull by a Finnish boat. These men are picked from a large number of volunteers, but none have been taken who have not had military experience, and most of them are specialists in various lines. A number of Hungarian volunteers have already gone throughout Germany; permission was granted small parties in civilian clothing to go through, but before the entire contingent had gone this permission was rescinded. They expect to send another half a battalion as soon as possible after the first. These men take no arms as the ammunition which the Finns have does not fit Hungarian guns and they will be armed on arrival. He thinks the Allies should take the Finnish situation seriously and give them all possible help, particularly aeroplanes which they need badly.

From the information he has, the situation in Germany is growing more desperate every day, and he thinks they must make some move. While he doesn't think they will attack Hungary, he doesn't dismiss the possibility. He does not believe that the Russians, in view of their Finnish debacle, will make any other ventures at least until the Finnish campaign is settled and doesn't believe in any case that Germany will permit them to attack Rumania.

---

329 The Soviet-Finnish war began on November 30, 1939.

Count Teleki says that while Hungary considers Rumania her enemy, he considers Soviet Russia a much greater one and that they will not take any step of any kind that may work out to the advantage of Russia. With the idea of forestalling any possible difficulties he has called to Budapest all of the various Hungarian leaders of Transylvania to impress upon them the importance of remaining quiet under present conditions and told them positively that Hungary has no intention of taking advantage of any Russian attack on Rumania, nor contrariwise making any attack to give the Russians an opportunity.

Count Teleki says that Hungary realized that she cannot withstand a German attack in force, but under no circumstances will they permit the Germans go through Hungary to Rumania, or to enter Hungarian soil for any purpose without resistance no matter how futile it may be. Germany has been putting great pressure on Hungary for oil, but has so far been refused. They are worrying considerably for fear that the British may attack Baku[330] and cut off oil which will greatly increase German pressure on Hungary. He says that he has no information which would enable him to form such an opinion, but he cannot believe the Germans will continue to hold out unless some action is taken to restore their enthusiasm. Therefore, he believes that by March or by April they will be compelled to do something. If this takes the form of an attack on the Maginot Line then this part of the world is safe, but he does not exclude the possibility that for the sake of an easy victory they might find some excuse for attacking Hungary or Rumania, even though it would be to their disadvantage since they will get more from both countries if they permit them to remain neutral. Hungary has complete plans for the destruction of factories, oil wells, and everything that would be of any possible use to the Germans, and this could be put into execution immediately in case of any German invasion whether for the purpose of occupying Hungary or attacking Rumania.

Hungary is not interested in becoming part of a new Empire including Austria or any other country. They may have achieved their independence and propose to keep it. They would be glad to join any economic confederation or any unit which permits them to keep their complete independence and will not take any chance on joining some empire where they would be in a minority and be overwhelmed by Germans or Slavs. He said there is little or no monarchist sentiment in Hungary and he felt that any schemes that the French might have in this connection would fail so far as Hungary is concerned.

He told me practically the same story about the revaluation of the pengo

---

330 Center of Soviet (Azerbaijan) oil production and export on the Caspian Sea.

in favor of Germany that Baranyai[331] told me. In addition, he confirmed that Mr. Baranyai wished to resign rather than to accede to German demands. He felt that the cession they made to Germany has not been important since it had no practical effect and it put them in a position to refuse something more important. He said that previously they had refused two major requests: one, that German troops be allowed to move through Hungary; two, that the treaty made by Germany with the Ruthenian Government prior to Hungary's taking it over and which gave Germany practically a monopoly on all mineral rights was repudiated despite German insistence for a period of eight months that it be recognized.

Count Teleki also said that Csaky's visit to Italy[332] was occasioned by the fact that the Italians got nervous for fear that the Hungarians would do something against Rumania which would give the Soviets an opportunity. Csaky had seen Ciano in Venice and assured him about Rumania. Csaky had given assurances that there was no intention to make any attack on Rumania regardless of what Russia did since such an attack would only benefit Russia. Hungary considers Rumania as an enemy, but she considers Russia as an infinitely greater one.

[135] Conversation with the Regent

Budapest, February 7, 1940

The Regent seemed to be in a very optimistic humor. He doesn't seem to worry at all about either Germany or Russia. He says by April 1st Hungary will be in condition so that anybody who attacks her will know it. He said that he had never thought that submarines would be able to do much damage since he himself had been quite successful in hunting them down, having sunk twenty-two submarines after he became Commander-in-Chief,[333] using a method devised by one of his young officers. He explained the method in detail; said he assumed that all this had been much improved now, so he never thought submarines would be the menace that some people feared.

He came to airplanes. He had nothing particular on this. He had been

---

331 Lipót Baranyai (1894-1970), Hungarian financial expert, member of the Hungarian Academy of Sciences, general manager (1936-38), subsequently president (1938–43) of the Hungarian National Bank.

332 Foreign Minister Count Csáky met Count Ciano in Venice on January 5–7, 1940.

333 Horthy became (the last) commander-in-chief of the Austro-Hungarian navy in 1918.

Regent Horthy and his wife in 1940

impressed by all the claims made as to what an airplane could do to a battleship and so forth. As far as he could see now, this had not been proven and he didn't believe that the airplane was going to settle the war. Both sides were more nearly equal now and what one gave the other could return.

He thought Mr. Hitler was not the man to quit voluntarily. He said most people who had a love for their country, if they saw they were in the way, they would retire but he did not think

Hitler in that category. He thought he wouldn't quit until he had to.

I had heard through his Chief of Cabinet that the British had sent an Admiral down here to discuss naval warfare with him so I asked him about it. He was very much pleased and impressed by the British action. He said he had merely asked some questions of the Minister and the next thing he knew there was an Admiral here who explained everything. He was very much pleased and flattered that they had so much confidence in him, and Mr. Hitler would be very glad to know what they told him. Everything was locked in his bosom and he wouldn't tell anybody. He said "I hope" then he stopped and put his hand over his mouth and said "I expect that the British will send their fleet through the Dardanelles and attack Baku. General Weygand isn't down there for nothing and that would be the way to stop the war." He explained that there is a railroad there that could be cut and also they could come back and menace Rumania so that she would have to think differently about the oil proposition. I said, "Wouldn't that endanger Hungary? Would not the Germans try to go through?" He said "We will risk it."

I spoke to him about Csaky's trip to Italy and he said this had been occasioned by the fact that somebody whose name he didn't mention but who he said was former Prime Minister of Rumania had gone over to Rome to ask the Italians to keep the Hungarians from attacking in case of a Russian attack. He said of course Hungary had no idea of making any attack at the present time except under one circumstance and that is if the Rumanians didn't resist the Russians or if their resistance was so feeble that the Russians started through Rumania proper into Transylvania in which case the Hungarians would go in to hold the passes to keep the Russians out of Hungary. However, he didn't believe the Russians were going to attack Rumania since he thought oil was too necessary for Germany to permit anything to happen which might upset oil deliveries.

He asked particularly about President Roosevelt — whether he was going to run for a third term — and again expressed his conviction that he simply must do it because the world needed him and he couldn't, he mustn't, quit until after the war was over.

[136] Conversation with Count di Vinci Italian Minister

Budapest, February 9, 1940

Count di Vinci said that he found the Foreign Office now extremely difficult. A year ago he could go to Csaky, Apor, Bessenyey, or de Kanya and get replies to almost any question; now he was utterly unable to get any information or even answers to simple questions from anybody but Csaky, and since Csaky is sick most of the time it made the situation difficult.

di Vinci said that not long ago Ciano telephoned in regard to some question which he considered rather ridiculous, but he couldn't answer without going to the Foreign Office. As Csaky was sick he called on Vornle, and to his astonishment Vornle said he didn't know. He, therefore, had to call on Teleki and asked if he could see him right away. When he asked Teleki about it Teleki was annoyed. He said, "Do you believe such silly rumors?" He told Teleki he didn't believe the rumor, but he added that as there was no one in the Foreign Office to give him a denial he had to come to him, and if he didn't get a story from him he would have to go to the Regent. His business was to supply answers if he could get them.

di Vinci said he hadn't seen Csaky lately. He saw him just after he returned from the Venice conference, but that since then Csaky had been sick and he hadn't seen him. He had asked to see him but Csaky sent word that if there was anything very important he could arrange it, but otherwise he wasn't well and would like to put it off. So since he had nothing important he hadn't tried to see him any more.

di Vinci considers the situation here serene for the moment and doesn't think the Germans are going to come in unless the situation changes materially. He says that Italy is doing everything she can to keep Hungary from attacking Rumania, but he doesn't believe that Hungary would anyhow since to do so would be aiding the Bolsheviks. However, he said there was a large sentiment in the Army and among others and the situation had to be watched, and it would be extremely silly for Hungary to do anything to involve herself in the international situation and he believed they wouldn't.

He spoke of the fact that American-Italian feeling was much better. He said Colonna had written[334] there had been a big change.

[137] Conversation with Dr. Tibor Eckhardt

Budapest, February 21, 1940

Eckhardt was very pessimistic in regard to Hungarian-German relations. He thinks that Germany is doing an enormous amount of work here and that they have succeeded in convincing many important people that Germany cannot lose the war and that this is bound to have considerable influence in case Germany should want to come through Hungary. He says to his own knowledge the Minister of War and the Chief of Staff not only believe that Germany is going to win the war but that Germany will invade the British Isles and take possession of them. Imredy is absolutely the tool of the Germans and can be depended upon to do his part at all times. Eckhardt says in his opinion that if the Germans demand a right of way across Hungary by the use of railroads or do anything of that nature there would be no question about Hungary resisting. However, he thinks that if Germany asked politely and as a friend for a right of way across Hungary or use of railroads to defend themselves against the British and the French a difficult situation would be created. The Regent and Teleki, he believes, will oppose it but it would be touch-and-go as to whether they could under such circumstances rally the Army to defense. He said that when King Charles came back the second time[335] the Minister of War and the Chief of Cabinet took a walk and that nobody could be found to stop Charles from entering Budapest. Bethlen appointed Gomboes who was an ex-Captain of the Army, gave him full power, and Gomboes took charge of the Army and threatened the officers with death if they didn't resist, and in this way Charles was stopped. A simi-

334 Former Italian minister to Budapest Prince Ascanio Colonna later became ambassador
   to Washington, D.C.
335 October 20 – November 1, 1921.

lar situation might come up if the Germans wanted to come in here and didn't put it in the nature of a demand. He didn't think that the Army would revolt against the Regent but it might be difficult to find anybody at the proper moment because they would all be scared to oppose Germany in such circumstances.

He said that Italy had been very much annoyed with Csaky's foreign policy and that they had unhesitatingly told the Hungarian Government so. The thing that annoyed them was his actions and remarks in connection with the Balkan Bloc and everything in connection with Rumania. They were anxious not to have any disagreements or any unpleasantness in the Balkans and considered his policy injudicious. Italy, therefore, had been in direct communication with Rumania and threatened to have King Carol come to Rome. It was the first time Italy had dealt directly with Rumania and the Government was said to be perturbed. Teleki sent for Bessenyey, and Apor, and as a result of this and Italy's displeasure Csaky gave his permission last Friday. However, Apor refused to take the position since he felt Csaky's policy had put Hungary in an awkward position and further, he felt his position vis-a-vis Germany was not good enough to give him any prospect of success. Therefore, nothing had been done and he thought it now probable that Csaky would continue.

[138] Conversation with Mr. Crutzesco the Rumanian Minister

Budapest, February 27, 1940

Mr. Crutzesco said that he personally had no doubt but that Yugoslavia would permit the passage of Italian planes over her territory were Russia to attack Rumania; and he believed that were Russia to attack Hungary and Italy desired to come to their aid she would like permit the Italians to cross Yugoslavia to come to Hungary. However, he did not think Italy would come to Hungary's assistance without an understanding with Germany: that is, if Hungary were attacked by the Soviets, Italian assistance would depend upon Germany's approval.

Mr. Crutzesco said that Germany did not veto Italian aid to Finland. Otherwise, he didn't think Italy would aid that country.

Mr. Crutzesco's idea is that Italy was trying to attain the leadership of the Balkan Bloc and that it was displeased at the Hungarians' reaction. He doesn't know anything about Italian displeasure because the Hungarian Minister at Moscow went to the Soviets in connection with the Venice meeting, but he is certain that Italy did not desire or approve the Hungarian

newspaper campaign against Rumania since Italy fully approved of everything that happened at Belgrade and does not want to antagonize either
Rumania or the Balkan Bloc.

Mr. Crutzesco said that on the 16th of February Mr. Ullein-Reviczky
made a call on the Yugoslav Minister and told him that Hungary would not
in future publish any articles against Rumania and tried to belittle the importance of the articles that were published, saying that they were only for
home consumption and that they meant nothing. As this date tallies with the
time that we understood the Italian reaction came, it fits in with the information we had.

Mr. Crutzesco hasn't any evidence or knowledge at all of improved
Turkish-Italian relations and doesn't know how this would affect Hungary.

Mr. Crutzesco read me running translations of telegrams which Gafencu[336]
sent him in reference to the meeting at Belgrade of the Balkan Bloc. These
all indicated great surprise at Hungarian reaction which apparently was quite
unexpected. They complained that nothing appeared in the papers concerning the sympathy expressed for Hungary, etc. One thing that struck me in
the telegrams was that he said the word "neutral" did not appear in their
communique because Turkey objected to the word, saying that they were
not neutral but non-belligerent.

Mr. Crutzesco seemed to have no idea at all of the agricultural situation
or what effect it would have. It seemed to be something new that there would
be any wheat shortage and he professed a lack of knowledge with respect to
the questions under that category. Mr. Crutzesco believes that the Hungarian
Army is pro-German, but he is under the impression that the Government
has it in control — at least as long as Italy is neutral. If Italy joined Germany he thought the situation might change quite materially.

Incidentally, Mr. Crutzesco told me that Csaky would never see him, and
although in the telegrams he read me Gafencu had instructed him to see Csaky
he had never been able to see him. However, Vornle had told him when he
called on him shortly after the appearance of the two articles concerning
Rumania, that Hungary would not publish any more articles if the Rumanian press didn't publish any articles about Hungary. He said that since that
time there had been no articles against Rumania except reprints of articles
from the foreign press about Rumania and little jabs here and there. Otherwise, this promise had been kept and the Rumanian press had been very
careful to print nothing about Hungary.

---

336 Grigore Gafencu (1892–1957), Romanian diplomat, journalist, politician, minister
   of foreign affairs 1938–40, Romanian minister to Moscow 1940–41.

[139] Conversation with former Foreign Minister de Kanya

Budapest, March 13, 1940

I called on Mr. de Kanya yesterday and told him of my conversation with Mr. Imredy on Monday, March 11. I said that this created a situation which was beyond my experience and, therefore, I came to him for advice; I didn't know quite how to handle the matter[337]

I told Mr. de Kanya I had written a letter to Count Csaky but that I hadn't sent it, first, desiring to discuss the matter with him. He was much astounded at the information I gave him, said there must be some mistake, had never heard of a Foreign Minister or anyone else in any responsible position doing anything of this sort, and was utterly unable to understand the reason if it was true. He read a copy of the letter I proposed to send to Csaky over three times, and finally said it was absolutely correct and the proper thing to do.

I told Mr. de Kanya I thought that Imredy had told the truth because otherwise he wouldn't have come to see me and use Csaky's name; I didn't think he would have that much gall. de Kanya admitted it was probably true, but he still couldn't comprehend it. He said if it was true Csaky no doubt would write back that Imredy was his former Chief as Prime Minister, a prominent member of the Government Party, etc., etc. He said that, of course, this made no excuse, but it was the only alibi he could think of for Csaky.

I said "What do I do then?" and he replied "Of course, you are perfectly free to send the correspondence to Count Teleki." I then said "And the Regent?" and he said "Yes, the Regent, too, if you want to." I said this certainly created a situation rather incredible, that I didn't see how I could go any more to the Foreign Minister under the circumstances. He said "Why not?" I replied that Count Csaky if he considered he was free to violate my confidence and l didn't feel free to violate his, then he had a rather unfair advantage. He said "Well, if it has developed that far and nothing done about it I should take a stenographer along when calling on Csaky, and if he doesn't let a stenographer come along when he talks then not to see him." I asked what Csaky could possibly have in mind, was he trying to force me to resign or be recalled. He said no, he couldn't believe that, and that it would be a mistake for me to do so, but he couldn't understand what the motive was behind it. He said of course that Csaky was young and that he had a great desire for public approval. He then referred to Csaky's reply to the interpellation in Parliament in connection with England and France, and said that

---

337 For a detailed background of this case see the introduction to this volume.

Kálmán Kánya and Count István Csáky in the late 1930s

was perfectly incredible, and said he couldn't think of anything more asi-
nine, but that it was due to the same thing, lack of experience and desire for
applause.

I asked him if it was true that Csaky had gotten in bad with Italy. He
said yes, there was no question about that, it was definitely true. I asked if it
was due to the articles on Rumania or about sending the Hungarian Minister
in Moscow to Molotoff to explain the Venice meeting. He said he didn't
know definitely as he had been sick, and particularly sick at that time, and
hadn't gone into particulars. He knew, however, that Italy was violently
worked up and he had thought it was concerning the attack on the Balkan
Bloc, but if Csaky had sent the Hungarian Minister to Molotoff it might
have been that.

I asked if he heard that Germany was likewise disturbed by Csaky's attack
on Rumania and threatened to invade Hungary. He said he hadn't heard that.

As I left he said, "Well, send your letter up right away, and in the meantime I will try to do something." He told me he was still feeling quite ill and
that while he had been out of the house to mass and on a few other occasions that he went against the advice of his doctor. He had hoped to come
up and have lunch with me and had been intending to call me up in connection with it, but he always felt too ill. He hoped now that by next week he
would be better and if so would call me up and arrange for lunch.

[140] Conversation with Mr. de Kanya

Budapest, March 22, 1940

Mr. de Kanya said that while it was not difficult for him to believe that there is no political significance in the reception of Archduke Otto by the President[338] — since he knew how casually these things were done in America — however, to a European the President can only have one personality: he cannot be President at one minute and a private individual the next. Since he is President whatever he does is official and will be given some official meaning, no matter how unofficial it may actually be.

The reception of Archduke Otto could only be interpreted by a European as an endorsement by the President, and through him the United States, of Archduke Otto's claim to the Hungarian throne. Since an overwhelming majority of Hungarians were opposed to Otto and had no intention of voluntarily making him king, this could not be considered friendly but not so disturbing. However, the fact that the visit was arranged under the auspices of Mr. Bullitt[339] was most disturbing. Mr. Bullitt, of course, was only on leave, but he is still Ambassador of the United States to France. It is well-known in Hungary that France has plans for a post-war readjustment in the Danubian Basin in which the restoration of Archduke Otto largely figures. The Hungarians are very much afraid that there will be an attempt to force Otto on the Hungarian throne, and this they will resist by force if necessary. They can only construe the reception given him in the United States under the auspices of Mr. Bullitt as support for the French plan. It doesn't matter what the reason for the visit was, or how Mr. Bullitt was there: there can be no other conclusion drawn and he suggested that I might better try to make no explanations as no one would believe them.

From hints that he dropped, I am under the impression that the reception of Otto is the reason for the special envoy being sent to America by Count Teleki.[340]

---

338 Otto von Habsburg was received by President Roosevelt at a "private audience" in March 1940 in the White House.
339 William Christian Bullitt (1891–1967), U.S. ambassador to Paris 1936–41.
340 Reference to the mission of Count Andor Teleki, nephew of Prime Minister Teleki, aiming at the estblishment of an official Hungarian fund of five million dollars. Andor Teleki delivered a letter dated March 17, 1940, from the prime minister to János Pelényi, Hungarian minister to Washington, D.C. The fund was withdrawn by the Hungarian government within a mere few days. Tibor Eckhardt left for the United States to start anti-Nazi political actions only a year later, on March 7, 1941, and arrived on August 8, 1941. His journey was supported and partially financed by Minister Montgomery.

[141] Conversation with Mr. Fisa
former Secretary of former Czech Legation[341]

Budapest, March 23, 1940

Mr. Fisa said that he is now in charge of the section in the Ministry of Interior at Prague which has to do with the adjustments of economic questions such as division of the national debt, occasioned by the partition of Czechoslovakia. In this capacity he makes frequent trips to Berlin, to Vienna, and to Bratislava. This is his second trip to Budapest. He is here with three Czechs and six Germans, and they are working under the direction of von Erdmannsdorff. He had lunch with von Erdmannsdorff on Tuesday, March 19. Mr. Fisa said that they knew very little in Bohemia about what was going on in the world, although he did listen to foreign broadcasts. However, he never knew how much of it was true since the German broadcast made such contrary claims they were completely at sea. As far as Bohemia is concerned, the situation remains the same as the last time he saw me, i. e. the Czechs are non-conforming 100%. They are going through the motions the same as he is, but any opportunity afforded they take advantage of.

He repeated what he told me in the last conversation that it would have been possible for the Germans by a policy of conciliation to have secured cooperation from the Czechs since nearly all of them are convinced that Czechoslovakia as had existed should not be reestablished, and if they received decent treatment from Germany, they might have been reconciled to become a part of the Reich. The Germans, however, made every possible psychological mistake, and now any hope of cooperation was forever gone. The Czechs were being careful since they realized that open rebellion was useless, but that does not mean that they are any more reconciled to German occupation than before.

The younger element among the Czechs were finished with Dr. Benes. They consider his policy to have been a failure and that he should retire and leave the way open for someone else. They hate the attacks that Csaky makes on him for that reason since they believe this is the only hope that can reestablish it. They wonder why Csaky is so foolish as to imagine that anything he could say against Benes would do anything but help him. The Czechs, particularly the younger element in Bohemia, realize that Czechoslovakia cannot and should not be reestablished as it was before. They wish to join some sort of a federation which would include Poland and Hungary, and possibly Austria if that country were separated from Germany, although

---

341 Peregrin Fiša was a former councilor at the Czechoslovak legation in Budapest (1938).

they are not certain but that Austria once having belonged to the Reich would not cause trouble if taken away. He thought, however, that if this federation were established on a Catholic basis Austria could be handled, although they were not certain.

They considered Hungary a very important part of any such federation and they would be willing to give her Slovakia provided Slovakia had reasonable autonomy in order to induce her to join. Also, they are prepared to accept a King since they now see this is the only way to hold the country together. They would prefer an English prince, but would accept an Italian one or even a Hapsburg if necessary. He says that the younger Czechs believe that only by such a federation could Germany be held back and the new countries have a reasonable chance of existence. He says that Germans who talk to him express great fear that in the event of defeat some such federation will be established since they are already thinking in terms of future expansion eastward, and southeastward, even if they lost this war, so they are concerned about the possibility of a federation or country shutting them off from the east and southeast.

For all materials of various kinds there is now just commencing to be a shortage. A rubber tire factory in Bohemia had to shut down for lack of material, and he thinks that for the next few months a number of other factories will begin to close.

Dr. Fisa says that there is plenty of food in Germany, and more in Bohemia than in Germany proper, but the variety is very limited and the quality is incredible. He says it is almost impossible to eat the food. However, life can be sustained and the people can even get fat since cake is one of the few things not rationed and people are now eating incredible quantities of it due to boredom with the rationed articles and quality.

He doesn't have any idea whether the Germans intend to make an offensive of some sort or not. He hears a lot about it but he doesn't think anybody knows anything or there have been any settled plans.

He is quite certain that Hungary will not be invaded very soon. He said the Germans loathe and detest the Hungarians and speak their minds very freely to him since they assume he likewise hates them. If it weren't for the fact that Germany realizes that an invasion of Hungary would disrupt her source of supplies he is certain Hungary would have been occupied long ago and believes that nothing would please the Germans more than to put the Hungarians in their place. Nevertheless, he believes that Hungary and the Balkan countries are safe from German attack as long as they can produce supplies and/or as long as the Germans think they can get more supplies by allowing them to remain neutral than they can by occupying it.

Dr. Fisa is worried, shared by all the younger people, because it is feared that the mistakes of the last twenty years will be repeated and that the man who are responsible for these mistakes will be forced down the throats of the Czech people, and that all they are going through now will be in vain.

[142] Conversation with Prime Minister Teleki
Budapest, April 9, 1940

Count Teleki said that he didn't know definitely what the subject of the Brenner talks[342] was, but he knew that nothing had happened which had changed Italian policy so far as the Soviets were concerned, or so far as Hungary was concerned. Italy was willing to make commercial agreements with Russians, but nothing else. This could not be said to be a change of policy. Any meeting, of course, strengthened the Axis in that if there was no meeting it would fall apart, so to that extent the meeting could be said to have strengthened the Axis.

As far as Hungary was concerned, it was not affected by the Brenner meeting since Italy did not agree to any spheres of influence. There was no definite plan for peace in Southeastern Europe except that for the moment the status quo must be maintained. He was fully in agreement with this idea, although Hungary was sacrificing her interests in not taking action against Rumania. He said that the proper time for Hungary to have done this was at the outbreak of the war since if she had to fight to obtain justice that was the best time to do it. Every day enabled the Rumanians with both German and Allied money to strengthen their position. Nevertheless, Hungary had waited and had no intention of doing anything until after the war. This was her contribution to the peace of Southeastern Europe.

Italy was prepared to go to the defense of Hungary to whatever extent she could. He said that since Yugoslavia would not permit the passage of troops there was no way for Italy to give Hungary military assistance. However, her position in the Balkans depended on Hungary; if she could not protect Hungary's independence her whole Balkan position would be lost. Therefore, he was sure it would do everything it could; he rather intimated that her moral position was stronger than military without saying so.

Hungary and Yugoslavia are becoming more friendly, but no one could tell how far this would develop or to what extent Yugoslavia might care to cooperate with Italy and Hungary, if at all.

There was no change in the status of Hungarian-Rumanian relations. Hungary expects to obtain all or a portion of Transylvania after the war, and

---

342 The meeting of Hitler and Mussolini at the Brenner Pass on March 18, 1940.

if she has to fight for it she will do so. She hopes, however, that in the general settlement that follows the war her just claims will be realized.

Count Teleki didn't know that the Vatican had any views in reference to Southeastern Europe except that it should be kept neutral if possible. The Pope was extraordinarily friendly to Hungary. He talked at length about the Pope, his personality, and said that Mr. Welles, was reported to have remarked that the best politician he had found in Europe was His Holiness the Pope.

The tightening of the British blockade system he felt would seriously affect Hungary. He expected during the next six weeks great pressure would be brought from both sides, and he was greatly worried about Hungary's ability to satisfy everybody. He said the British were more difficult to satisfy than the Germans since everything operated on navicerts, and it was a continuous job whereas the German agreements were made for a period of time. He said it took Quandt his entire time now to get the navicerts and there was always the fear that they wouldn't have enough raw material to operate their industries. He felt that the position of the neutrals would be very bad and he didn't know how Hungary could satisfy everybody. He thought the Germans would naturally retaliate and that the neutrals would be squeezed in between.

There is nothing new in Hungarian-Russian relations. They are just the same as they were.

He estimated at about 35% the damage caused by frost and floods, amounting to 30 million pengo. However, he said that a lot depended upon whether there was another flood when the ice began to melt in the Alps. If the present one got out of the way then they could take care of the water. If the melting started before the present flood was over it would be even worse then before. He said he was going to Szeged last night where he expected to see the flood on the Tisza river which would probably be at its crest this morning. He thought of course this would affect the economic situation but that they could stand it; if later floods did not add to the damage it would not be so bad. He didn't believe that flood damage would affect the German-Hungarian relations as he felt these could be ironed out. He thought the blockade was much more serious.

[143] Conversation of Mr. Travers with Dr. Ullein-Reviczky

Budapest, April 9, 1940

Dr. Ullein-Reviczky explained the situation as he saw it by telling me the story of an experience which he had some time ago. He said that he and another man stood directly behind a horse and that the horse could kick with either foot but that he was especially lucky because the horse had kicked with his left foot instead of his right; that he felt that the Baltic countries were standing behind the left foot and Hungary and the Balkans behind the right foot, and that Hungary thanked God that the horse had used the left foot.

He said that his trip to Germany had been very interesting and that the one thing that he had learned from it was that Germany is scared to death of Russia; that they kept asking him what he thought Russia would do and if there was any question of a Russian menace to Hungary. He said this had given them the idea of playing up to Russia and that in the next few days there would be appearing in several newspapers articles very friendly to Russia and that it may even be implied that Russia would guarantee Hungarian sovereignty against any large Power. He was taking it up with the Russian Minister and would try to get a friendly reply in the PRAVDA. At the same time they would tell Italy that this was not made against Italy and was only a game against Germany. He said that the Germans despised the Italians and knew that no matter what Germany did Italy would not fight against her. He said that he had implied when in Berlin that if there were any attack made on Hungary, Italy would come to Hungary's assistance but that the Germans sensed that.

He said the only thing that could save Hungary would be a two-faced game to try to prove to the Germans that they were friendly. He said it had been considered erecting fortifications on the German frontier, but that the Germans had stated that the first fort that was erected would cause Germany to enter Hungary.

In Berlin he saw no panic of any kind. The night life is especially gay; people get lots of things to eat but very little meat.

[144] Conversation with Count Teleki, Prime Minister

Budapest, April 9, 1940

I asked Count Teleki if he had seen the correspondence exchanged between Count Csaky and myself. He said he had, that he had talked to Count Csaky and that he thought the matter should be fixed up, and since he was a good friend of both he wanted to get us together and have the matter settled. He said he felt it was a misunderstanding, that Csaky was a little hasty because he was sick, etc., but intimated that it ought not to be taken seriously, this, that and the other. In other words, hush, hush.

I told Count Teleki I would not see Count Csaky until I heard from the Department, so we let it go at that. He said he agreed to that and that later he would take it up with me and see if he couldn't arrange a meeting. He didn't defend Csaky, but he didn't say he blamed him for anything, although he excused him on account of illness, etc.

[145] Conversation with Mr. de Barczy, Chief of Prime Minister's Cabinet

Budapest, April 13, 1940

Mr. de Barczy[343] told me that as far as he knew there had been no ultimatum, no demarche, no communication, and nothing from the German Government whatever in the last few days. He said he was certain he would know it because keeps the minutes of the Cabinet meetings and, therefore, attends the sessions; that they had a five or six hour session yesterday which Csaky attended and made a report, but there was no reference made to any such communications; and that Count Teleki had never mentioned it to him; and he couldn't understand but that if it had been received it would have been mentioned. He had vaguely heard about something concerning Danube boats but that he had paid no attention to it and thought it was more in connection with the possibility than with any actual demand for a through way.

As for the meeting of Bethlen and de Kanya, he said that caused comment only because it had taken place at this time. He said Count Teleki had been seeing Bethlen and de Kanya right along, and more particularly since his confidence in Count Csaky was not so great as it had been. However, there hadn't been a time since de Kanya left office when he wasn't in close touch with Teleki, and this is particularly correct since de Kanya is chairman of the Upper House Committee for Foreign Affairs. I asked about Imredy, who is chairman of the Lower House Committee for Foreign Affairs. He laughed and said no.

The conference of a few days ago as it happened was about affairs in general, and he presumed it concerned foreign affairs, but more particularly the Ruthenian situation or constitution. He said that at this moment Baron Perenyi[344] and a Ruthenian delegation were with the Prime Minister in connection with the plans for Ruthenians taking over on an autonomous basis,

---

343 István Bárczy (1882–1952) was secretary of state in the prime minister's office and responsible for the minutes of the cabinet meetings between 1921 and 1944.

344 Baron Zsigmond Perényi (1870–1946), minister of the interior 1919, MP 1927–33, guardian of the Crown 1933–1944, as such member, subsequently vice-president (1939–43) and president (1943–44) of the Upper House. He was a gubernatorial commissioner of the sub-Carpathian region in 1939-40.

but he said following that there would be a conference of former Prime Ministers to discuss the same matter, before it was put before Parliament. He said this was customary, that it was nothing that had not been done before, and that it was the usual procedure.

Barczy promised me that if he found anything of news of any kind he would let me know at once. He said in fact he would go down and see Count Teleki as soon as he was free to see if there was anything and that he would come and see me if there was. He said as soon as he heard anything of news, of any kind, he would call me up.

I feel rather confident that Barczy told me the truth and that there hasn't been anything that he knows about. It is quite possible that there are diplomatic conversations which Csaky knows about, and possibly Teleki, but they have not been presented to the Cabinet, as is always customary here, and that as any important problem shall be presented to a Crown Council it would seem as though nothing of any particular moment has happened.

[146] Conversation with the Greek Minister

Budapest, April 13, 1940

The Greek Minister was in to see me and told me that the Ministers of the countries represented by the Balkan Entente, Greece, Turkey, Yugoslavia, and Rumania had a meeting last night over the situation. All of them are very much alarmed, in fact, almost in a panic. They fear a German drive not only against Rumania but Yugoslavia also. The drive through Rumania they fear will go through to the Dardanelles and the one against Yugoslavia through to Salonika. They haven't anything to base their opinions on except the thousands of rumors with which Budapest is now full.

[147] Conversation with Mr. de Kanya

Budapest, April 18, 1940

Mr. de Kanya said that he was having difficulty getting any rest because the Diplomatic Corps seemed to be under the impression that he is still Foreign Minister and everybody was calling him up and coming to see him. He said for the last two weeks he had averaged two personal calls and five telephone calls a day from members of the Diplomatic Corps. Yesterday the Italian Minister called and he thought it was pretty thick since the Italians ought to be able to get information from the Foreign Office and he told the

Italian Minister so but he laughed and said nothing. Mr. de Kanya said that he did not try to keep in touch with foreign affairs although he was called in and consulted by Teleki on various things of major importance. He didn't like the idea of all these people calling upon him because it put him in a very peculiar position. Therefore, he tried to discourage them but when no result since they insisted on calling. He said that when he was called in by Teleki he was told things in confidence and he didn't feel he could reveal these to anybody since they were not his secrets and he is not a responsible officer of the Government. So, therefore, there was practically nothing he could tell his callers but they still seemed to come. He said in my case he felt a little differently since on account of my trouble with the Foreign Office,[345] Teleki had suggested that he better look after me a little bit. Therefore, he could tell me more than he could anybody else. I told him that this being the case I felt I was much better off not going to the Foreign Office than if I did call.

I asked him about the request to police the Danube and he said this was not put in the form of a demand but was put in the form of a suggestion. The Germans merely asked if the Hungarians didn't think it would be better if they took over the job and saved the Hungarians the expense. However, he said that Hungary and the other Danubian countries had come to an arrangement now whereby they would inspect cargoes and so forth on all Danubian shipments and the Germans had expressed satisfaction so that the matter was temporarily closed. He didn't think the Germans were coming into Hungary although he said there was no question in his mind but that the Germans who were now in Hungary, Rumania, Yugoslavia and other Danubian countries were the advance guard. He thought there were many more in Rumania than here. He estimated there were 2,000 in Hungary and said there was no question but that they were here to make trouble and help take over when they were ready. The Germans had told the Hungarians that they had no intention of doing anything in the direction unless the English invaded Rumania and tried to cut off the oil. The English had said they had no intention of invading Rumania unless the Germans did so; that is the way the situation stood. Thus both of them had a good excuse if they decided to make the invasion but he thought at present that neither one was anxious to do anything although no one knew when one or the other would decide it was an opportune moment, in which case they would accuse the other of the attempt.

Italy, he was quite certain, had no intention of going to war in the imme-

---

345 Cf. the conversation, with Kánya (March 13, 1940) and Teleki (April 9, 1940), as well as the introductory chapter by the editor.

diate future. He didn't think they were prepared. He said that in December Ciano had made the statement that it would take Italy three years to get ready for war. Therefore, he thought the violent Italian press campaign was an effort to divert part of the British fleet to the Mediterranean and thus help Germany in her Norwegian campaign. He said the majority of the Italian people hated the Germans and didn't want to go to war, as was also true of Ciano and the King. It was true that Mussolini hadn't forgiven the English for the sanctions and also felt that if the English won his position would be very insecure. Nevertheless, he didn't believe that unless a more favorable opportunity presented itself the Italians would make any move.

He said that Count Teleki had cracked the whip on the Party in the form of threatening to dissolve Parliament and that it had been very effective. There wasn't a peep now. He said it was very necessary and should have been done long ago. As far as Count Csaky was concerned, he said there were many reasons which I might guess why the Prime Minister didn't want to make a change. He had every intention of making the change at the first possible moment and if that possibility existed there would be a new Foreign Minister. In the meanwhile, he was not relying too much on the Foreign Office but was doing many things on his own.

He mentioned that he had sent an envoy to the United States[346] and I told him that I knew about it but that just today I had received word from the State Department that Pelenyi didn't know anything about it and I had understood that Count Teleki was to advise Pelenyi from Rome. He said he didn't know anything about that and didn't know a man had actually gone. All that he knew was that he was supposed to go and I presume he had gone. He didn't say what the purpose of the visit was.

[148] Conversation with the French Minister

Budapest, May 1, 1940

The French Minister told me yesterday that both Vornle and Csaky had told him that they had no doubt whatever that the Allies were intending to go into Norway but as usual they were too late and the Germans forestalled them. They thought the documentary proof which Mr. Ribbentrop had offered was authentic and that the Germans were fully justified in going into Norway. As far as Denmark was concerned, Count Csaky said that the Danes had

---

346 Count Andor Teleki.

agreed to the occupation of their country and, therefore, since the Danes had agreed, it was nobody else's business.

The French Minister asked him about the note addressed to the Danubian Powers concerning river police. Csaky said he had done this on his own initiative because he feared that the Germans might find this subject an excuse for intervention and he desired to forestall it. He said that in issuing the note he had been solely guided by the interests of the Danubian States and particularly of Hungary but that he couldn't do any more. As far as he was concerned, there was nothing more to be done.

[149] Conversation with Mr. Spisiak the Slovak Minister
Budapest, May 3, 1940

He told me that he had seen Csaky since his recent speech of outburst on Slovakia and that Csaky had told him that he made this speech against his will; that Sullo[347] had insisted that some such speech be made and that as Sullo was in opposition to him personally and criticized him severely always in Committee meetings he had to go in and make the speech. Personally he was for very good relations with Slovakia and that as far as the speech was concerned they need pay no attention to it; that everything would go on just as it had before. By everything was meant the different Commissions that are working here to settle the problems of land, etc., between the two countries.

Mr. Spisiak said they were going ahead and nothing had been changed. He didn't believe Csaky; that he just took advantage of the occasion to gain some personal popularity since he could not any longer attack Rumania or Yugoslavia and even had gotten into trouble on account of his attacks on Benes. Therefore, they considered it in the light of his attacks on Rumania — just a bid for personal popularity and of no importance otherwise.

I asked what the German Minister thought about it. He said he hadn't been to see the German Minister because the German Minister always took Csaky's side. He told the Slovak Minister that Csaky was the only friend they had in the Government and they must uphold him in every way. He, therefore, wanted the Slovak Minister to see that nothing happened in Slovakia that put Csaky in bad; and he knew if he went to him in the present instance he would get no comfort. He felt, however, that the Germans them-

---

347 Géza Szüllő (1873–1957), Hungarian landowner from the former Hungarian uplands (i.e., interwar Czechoslovakia), politician, member of the Upper House after 1938.

selves did not approve of it although there had been no word at all from Germany on the subject.

He said that Erdmannsdorff was not popular with the Germans and that there was always talk about him being replaced. He didn't think that Gleise von Horzterau[348] would replace him since he was on the General Staff in Berlin, but he wouldn't be surprised to see Erdmannsdorff changed since the Germans thought he was not rough enough with the Hungarians.

He spoke of the note of Csaky in regard to the mixed guards for the Danube River. He said he felt certain this was not something that Germany had asked but it was Csaky's own idea. The reason he felt sure that they had not acted with Germany in this matter was they never had had any advance information that Germany was asking for any such thing and that furthermore Germany had never replied to the note. He said that when Gleise von Horzterau was here last week he told a mutual friend that the Fuehrer did not want to destroy England or the British Empire. They wanted to win the war but they wanted to leave the British Empire strong to handle the Japanese.

Mr. Spisiak said in his conversations with Csaky, Csaky had repeatedly told him that Germany had already won the war; there was no question about the result. As far as Italy is concerned, Csaky told him no one knew what Italy would do. He thought she would come into the war ultimately because if Germany lost the fascist regime was finished, and he thought the fascists would get dragged into it if they possibly could. He said the campaign in Italy was not so much because of anti-English feeling on the part of the fascist leaders, but because they wanted to sell the idea to the Italian people that England was their enemy and must be destroyed — in other words, sell the war to the Italians.

Csaky also told him he didn't expect anything to happen here until the end of May. In the meantime, he considered it quite safe, I asked Mr. Spisiak what could happen except entry by the Germans and he laughed and said he couldn't think of anything else. I asked him about the German Army supposed to be in Slovakia and he claims that there is none there at all. His people told him there is a big army in Austria but he has no figures and wouldn't know what they were to do with it. He thinks it is probably ready for any emergency and that its best use at the present time is to threaten Hungary, Yugoslavia and Rumania so they can get trade treaties. He said Clodius was very well satisfied with his deal with Rumania.

---

348 Edmund von Glaise-Horstenau (1882–1946), Austrian historian and politician, a follower of the National Socialists who helped prepare the *Anschluß*, German general in Croatia after 1941.

[150] Conversation with The Regent, Admiral Horthy

Budapest, May 7, 1940

His Highness seemed in good health and spirits, although very much concerned about conditions. He said that he was in a terribly difficult position, and that he never knew from day to day what he would or could do. He thought that if the Allies wouldn't make any attack in the Mediterranean then Germany wouldn't move. He said that at the time he told me that Hungary would defend itself against Germany until the last peasant, conditions were quite different than they are now. As far as he was concerned, he was still of the same mind, but a leader couldn't go against his people; he had to take public opinion into consideration. If it were possible to make any sort of defense the situation would be different, but in the first place, the difficulties of Hungary's position militarily were very great, and in the second place, they didn't dare to make any preparations against Germany of even keeping an effective force on the border, so that any talk of defense was futile under such conditions. There might be a defense on the Tisza River, but this would mean that the Hungarian Army was standing in front of the Rumanian border to be shot down in defense of Rumania, and public opinion in Hungary would never stand for that. There appeared to be two choices: one, to let the Germans through to Rumania, and the other to make an effec-

The regent and Mrs. Horthy at Gödöllő
(with László Endre, deputy lord-lieutenant in the background)

tual resistance to German occupation. If such resistance could in any way
be effective he thought that there would be no question that they would
make such resistance even though they would have to make an inglorious
stand with a few troops and be swept out of the way. Therefore, he had to
take all these things into consideration. As things stood now if Germany
wanted to come through to Rumania there was nothing for Hungary to do
but consent. He doubted once the Germans ever got in here they would ever
get out, but at least in that way they might occupy some portion of the country, although he was not optimistic. His principal hope was that the Allies
would not attack, and in the meantime, that things would change for the
better, although he was somewhat discouraged. He said the oil wells are
going fine.[349] Count Teleki had just telephoned him that everything was
working efficiently; they were not losing any oil and that management was
excellent. He said that Germany had been putting pressure on them for oil
but they were not going to give in.

He said Rumania had managed her oil wells very badly, and as a result
thereof they would have no oil in five years. Hungary had no intention of
pushing her wells and wasting them for the future. He said nothing whatever about local politics.

I told the Regent that people in Belgrade seemed much upset, and he
said "Yes, the poor Yugoslavs, they are in a very difficult position, particularly since they don't seem to have any unity in their country."

I asked about Italy. He said that so far as he knew, Mussolini was the
only man in Italy who wanted to go to war and that he believed Mussolini
could not drag the Italians into the war. He said he considered the Pope the
greatest politician in Europe; he also thought highly of the King. So he hoped
these two would be able to keep Italy out of the war. From all he knew, he
was in no position to go to war and it would only cause a catastrophe for
this part of the world and certainly could do Italy no good.

Before I saw the Regent I talked to Captain Tost[350] who seemed to be
very much down.

Incidentally, one of the first things the Regent said to me was, "Do tell
me, is it true that the Germans have sunk a 30-thousand ton battleship with
bombs?" I said I didn't think it was true, I hadn't heard of it. He seemed
very much relieved. He then talked at length about the German flying force,
and American planes, and the war — always on the Allied side. I told him
that while I knew nothing about it, I was quite certain that Great Britain and

---

349 Hungarian oil production was started in 1937 at Budafa, in the oil fields of Zala
     County; Magyar-Amerikai Olajipari Rt (MAORT, the Hungarian-American Oil Co.)
     was established in 1938.
350 Lt. Col. Gyula Tost (1903–1944), an aide-de-camp of Regent Horthy.

France had no idea of attacking in the Mediterranean unless Italy got into the war, and I felt that the greatest danger was that Germany would attack in the Balkans to forestall some Allied action; also, that I didn't believe Great Britain would be ready for another year and that in the meantime they would fight more on the defensive than anything else. He seemed relieved at this idea.

He spoke of Hitler in terms of contempt and said everybody hated him. He told me again in detail how the Poles, the Czechs, and everybody else in this country had despised him, and said that if somebody came to him and said that Hungary would be better off if he would quit he would do so in a minute; however, no matter how much his country might suffer, Hitler would never quit.

The Regent said that as soon as the war is over he intended to select his successor and put him in and see that it didn't get in the wrong hands when he was going to retire. He said, further, if the proper moment came he was going to try to make a larger move for peace and he said he knew that the moment therefor hadn't come yet.

[151] Conversation with Prime Minister Teleki

Budapest, May 22, 1940

Count Teleki said that the present political situation in Southeastern Europe was quiet. Everybody was stunned and surprised by the German success and nobody had time to find themselves. There was no disposition at the moment for any country in Southeastern Europe to take any advantage of the situation and that time alone could tell how it would be affected.

As far as Hungary is concerned, he hadn't ever any idea of going into Slovakia or menacing Yugoslavia. The mobilization was for the purpose stated, i. e., the training of soldiers. They had picked this time for two reasons: one, that it was before the harvest, and the other afterwards. Since every country in Europe had mobilized it was quite apparent that the quicker that they got their army trained the better position they would be in, and, therefore, they chose this particular time. He said both Yugoslavia and Rumania had constantly had in the field more than their normal amount of soldiers and he couldn't see why Hungary doing likewise should be disturbing to anyone.

As far as Hungary is concerned, she wants peace in Southeastern Europe and will make no move until the war has been settled. There was no occasion for her doing so, and further it would be foolish to be precipitate.

Count Teleki said that he personally had been astonished at the case with which Germany had gone through Belgium and the French fortifications. He said he should not have been because he really knew the British and French had made every possible political mistake and he might have assumed that they would also make military mistakes; nevertheless, he was much surprised at what had happened. He thought these governments had not realized that the world was moving and that they had played home politics at the expense of their home security and the security of their empires. Now they were paying the price. He didn't give any indications of sympathy; nor did he seem to be particularly disturbed as to the future. I didn't bring up the subject of the possible outcome of the war, so that wasn't discussed.

I asked Count Teleki if Italy would enter the war and what would be the effect on Hungary. He threw up his hands and said he didn't know the answer to either question.

Count Teleki said that certain men were being released all the time and others called in. This was for many reasons, due to necessary adjustments, for example, people for certain lines of business being needed or people who were called up not being required. He said that they had mobilized because they couldn't have any sort of mobilization without it, but that the regular army had not been mobilized.

I asked Count Teleki about his visit to the oil fields, and whether he contemplated any changes in American managers, and he replied absolutely not. He found that the oil people were doing an excellent job both in management and otherwise, and that he couldn't see how anything could be made to improve their work.

Count Teleki didn't know anything about what Russia would do. He had heard the story about them not wanting the peace disturbed in the Balkans and he felt that was true, they didn't. He didn't know whether Yugoslav negotiations with Russia contemplated a defense pact, but he said of course Hungary would have to defend herself against Russia if she tried to come through Hungary but that he had no knowledge that she contemplated any such move. In fact, he felt reasonably sure that the Balkans would be stable for the time being.

[152] Conversation with Mr. de Kanya

Budapest, May 24, 1940

Mr. de Kanya said that while opinion here had shifted and German victory was considered almost inevitable, it wasn't pleasing to a great majority of the people. He even saw Csaky today and he was beginning to get worried. The Hungarians realized that German victory virtually would take away the independence of Hungary and this was not at all pleasing to Hungarians except of course a few who might profit and these were the worst type of Hungarians since this is the only type that had so far out and out identified themselves with the Nazi movement. He said a number of Nazis from Germany of high rank had called on him lately and discussed with him what should be done with Southeastern Europe. The assumption was that Germany had won the war and it was on this basis that they wished advice. They discussed something like a United States of the Balkans although not with a central Government. It would be more of a confederation under German leadership, Germany retaining the foreign policy and complete control, but each country retaining its independence. Germany would then promulgate a Monroe Doctrine[351] which would prevent any country not in Europe from having anything to say about any European country. This would shut out the British Empire, United States, and so forth.

Mr. de Kanya said that he doesn't believe that any settlement that could be arrived at after a German victory will last. He is certain that in 10 or 20 years there would be another war and that from that point of view he doesn't take any of this seriously but he doesn't expect to live 10 or 20 years and he would like to see Hungary an independent country during his lifetime. He is astonished at the ease with which the Germans have developed their offensive. He is wondering whether the French will hold out or whether there will be a revolution. He thinks the Blum Government[352] so sapped the strength of the French that they are incapable of the resistance they would have put up; he said it was perfectly incredible that while the Germans were working 12 hours a day the Blum Government introduced the 40-hour week and had everybody join the labor union with the idea of not working at all. It not only had prevented France from being really armed when she should be but it undermined the whole moral fiber of the French nation and certainly had its effect on the Army. He thought there was no question but that the Germans would invade England if they could. He didn't know what success they would have but hoped the English would hold out.

He said before the last war the British and French had wonderful diplomatic representation and their diplomatic work was perfect, but he was sorry to say that since the last war both France and England had been atrocious so far as their diplomatic work is concerned; they had not prepared for this war; their sacrifice of Poland was unnecessary and foolish; their

---

351 A principle declared by U.S. President James Monroe in 1823 which advised European powers against expansion in the Western hemisphere while warning the United States not to interfere in the matters of European states.
352 Subsequent Popular Front governments of French Socialist statesman Léon Blum in 1936–37, 1938.

dealings with Soviet Russia showed a lack of diplomatic skill; and they had been defeated in every diplomatic venture because they had stupid people and were not realists. He said the present French Minister here was so stupid that he would not talk with him because he couldn't carry on a conversation on diplomatic matters. O'Malley, he thought was a nice fellow but had done the stupidest things; the row he had with Teleki was occasioned by a demand that Hungary declare itself in favor of the Allies. He said O'Malley had been to England and it is possible received instructions to do something of this kind but if he knew the situation here he would have told them at once it was impossible; that Hungary couldn't think of declaring itself for the Allies.

He said the idea of Imredy coming back as Prime Minister at present was absurd. There was no possibility of such a thing happening under present conditions. In fact, he didn't think there would be any change of Government until after the war and whatever happened then would depend on the result of the war. Naturally if the Germans won they would have to take that into account very seriously but until that time he didn't expect anything to be done regardless of German success.

He said he didn't know anything about the mobilizing of two new Army Corps. As far as he knew, and he was certain it was correct, there was no motive in the past mobilization otherwise than announced.

Russia he thought was playing a very important part in this part of the world. He said that Ribbentrop before he got through with it would learn how stupid he had been in bringing Russia into Poland.

Mussolini, he said, knew well enough what it would mean if Germany obtained a dominant position in Europe. He didn't know what he would do but he thought the present German success might give him pause. He had no idea what Mussolini would do about the war but he said he had put it off and hadn't done anything but certainly knew what the situation would be if the Germans won. He might want to come in with them to get as much as he could or he might decide that it would be better to stay out or go in with the Allies rather than to risk Germany's dominating everything.

The same thing applied to Russia. They must know what it would mean if Germany becomes complete master of Europe and while they probably wouldn't dare openly to go against Germany they might certainly have something to think about.

[153] Conversation with Regent Horthy of Hungary

Budapest, May 25, 1940

The Regent was very much pleased when I presented him the picture of the President, which he opened at once as well as the letter. He said he would reply to it. His pleasure was evident, and he said again and again that he was very proud.

I asked the Regent what he thought of the military situation, and he replied that it was simply incredible, that he never would have believed it. It could only be compared both in its preparation and execution to Genghis Khan[353] who spent years preparing for attacks on other nations while they did nothing to defend themselves. He thought the situation of the British and Belgian armies in Belgium was precarious and he couldn't see how they were going to be saved.

The Germans talked of a new bomb which they would use at the right time, so deadly that it would kill everything within a mile. This had not yet been used, but he thought they intended to use it on England. He didn't believe that the Germans would attempt any invasion of England at once; rather that they would conduct an air campaign and depend upon the Fifth Column in England to make confusion in every possible way so that the way might be prepared for either surrender of England or ultimate invasion. He said that they claimed to have a large number of Communists and other sympathizers in England who are ready to act at the proper moment.

The Regent said that the situation of Italy was fast becoming precarious and that he thought Mussolini must be doing some thinking since the victory of the Germans was so overwhelming as to practically engulf Italy. He also thought that Soviet Russia must be becoming alarmed. He said that he expected them to attack Bessarabia since they now had it entirely surrounded by troops, and for this reason Hungary was calling up more troops in order to be in a position to do what she could to defend herself. He said that they expected to menace nobody. They never had any intention of doing anything while the war was on, and certainly under present conditions they wouldn't start anything. They didn't know, however, what was going to happen and it was only common sense to be better prepared for whatever eventuality developed.

He said that Hitler had no idea of war at all, that all this was being done by the General Staff, but that Hitler was getting all the credit so that he might be built up into some sort of a god. He said that the Germans tried out their tactics and implements of war in Spain and that they found many

---

353 Genghis Khan (1155 or 1167–1227), founder of the Mongolian empire.

things to correct; when these were corrected they decided to try them out on Poland. Hitler didn't think the Allies would go to war but they felt it necessary to try out their plans. After the Polish campaign they improved their technique again. In the meanwhile, the Allies did nothing, made no changes, and paid no attention to the lessons that should have been learned, and the Socialist Governments in Great Britain and France actually were cutting down and undermining the morale of the country while the Germans were working furiously in preparing to annihilate them. He said Hungary's position was one where her fate had gone out of her hands and there was nothing to do but wait and try to make the best of whatever happened.

[154] Conversation with Mr. Unaydin the Turkish Minister

Budapest, May 31, 1940

The Turkish Minister said that while the Allies now were suffering reverses, he felt that ultimately they would win the war. He pointed out some respects that the situation was better than it had been in the World War[354] when Germany had conquered Serbia and Rumania, and has as Allies Austria-Hungary, Bulgaria and Turkey. In consequence, she had full freedom of motion from the North Atlantic and the North Sea to the Persian Gulf. After Russia came into the war she acquired the Ukraine and then had complete freedom of motion as far as the Caucasus. With all this she had not had sufficient force ultimately to win.

Mr. Unaydin said that Hungary's four army corps mobilized. Two in the north and two in the south. He thought this was a measure taken to provide Germany or Italy with a corridor through Hungary in case of a Russian attack which Hungary would attempt to repel. However, he did not expect Russia to attack unless Italy or Germany took the initiative in South East Europe nor did he expect Russia to invade Bessarabia and thence Rumania because it would not be strategically of sufficient importance. Russia's objective would be Italy and to reach the Adriatic, and she would not proceed through Rumania and thence west through Bulgaria because this would be detrimental to the economic situation in the Balkans.

Mr. Unaydin felt that South East Europe was held in a state of equilibrium between Italy, Germany and Russia, and that while the situation was a

---

354 In World War I.

dangerous one he felt that none of the three countries wished to have it disturbed. He also thought that the Allies would make no move in the Balkans unless one of the three other Powers did it first.

He did not expect Italy to enter the war in the near future, and he considered an attempt to localize an attack on France to be impossible because immediately Italy did so the Allied fleets and the air forces would go into action and the war would extend to the whole Mediterranean, bringing in all the countries concerned.

Turkey, he said, was a strong and loyal ally of France and Great Britain and would act in concert with them. The Balkan Entente, also, was a reality and had more force than was apparent.

The Allied reverses in the west he found to have resulted from blunders of the high army commands. He did not hold Gamelin[355] directly responsible for this. He felt that the King of Belgium[356] had acted in a despicable manner and he seemed to feel that the French had been suspicious of him from the first. In consequence, they did not place their strongest forces on the Belgian battle line. The king, he said, either should have acted as did the King of Denmark,[357] asserting his country unable to withstand an attack and being unwilling to see the desolation war would bring and have capitulated in the beginning, or, failing this, have fought to the end.

Mr. Unaydin said history had shown that every major war was won at sea by the nation which was able to maintain supremacy there. He thought that while the Germans had a numerically superior air force, their planes were inferior to those of the Allies and that as Allied air strength grew they would obtain preponderance. In consequence, if the Allies could hold out for a brief time their situation would become increasingly better.

He spoke of the moral effect which the United States had had on the entire situation and the material aid which it had given the Allies, and he seemed to feel that the full American effort had not yet been made.

---

355 French General Maurice-Gustave Gamelin (1872–1958), commander-in-chief of the French army 1938–40, who was unable to stop the German attack on France and was therefore dismissed (May 19, 1940). The appointment of Gen. Weygand could not prevent the French collapse.

356 Leopold III (1901–1983), king of the Belgians 1934–[1940–]1950. Surrendered to the Germans in 1940 but did not go into exile, thereby making his claim to the throne fiercely debated. Ultimately abdicated in favor of his son, Baudouin I.

357 Christian X (1870–1947), king of Denmark 1912–47, became a symbol of national resistance under the German occupation.

[155] Conversation with Mr. Orlowski the Polish Minister

Budapest, June 8, 1940

The Polish Minister told me that John Makkai,[358] a Government Party M.P. and formerly a member of the Independent Farmers Party, but now connected with the MAGYARSAG right wing of the Government Party, had been sent to America to engage in 5th Column activities. Speaking to Mr. Travers, he said that his visa had been granted at the request of the Prime Minister's Office. The Polish Minister understood that he had long consultations with the German Minister before making his trip. Talking to Dr. Balog,[359] he confirmed that this man was going to America on behalf of Germany and said that so far as he knew Germany was paying his expenses either directly or indirectly. He said he had a very naive idea that he can make some speeches in America and that he had reviewed his speeches at the request of the F.O. They were very silly and as the man spoke very broken English the whole idea was fantastic. He didn't know what things of a secret nature he might have in his visit but as far as he knew the whole idea originated because Eckhardt was supposed to be having such a success and the Germans thought they should counteract it by sending another Hungarian to give the German side. He said that Teleki was aware of his mission and that he had approved, first, because pressure had been brought to bear upon him, and, second, because as he said he was a good man to get out of the country.

[156] Conversation with ex-Foreign Minister de Kanya

Budapest, June 19, 1940

Mr. de Kanya said that Hungary's position was a result of the unexpected weakness of the Allied Powers, that it was such that there was nothing left for her to do but to try in every way to play up to Germany. Hitler at this moment was the undisputed master of the European continent, and much as it distressed him and other Hungarians if Hungary was to exist and to get any satisfaction in the way of revision it would be at the will of Mr. Hitler.

---

358 János Makkai (1905–1994), journalist, author, politician, wrote for *Magyarság*, later *Új Magyarság*, MP for the NEP party after 1935.
359 Probably Dr. József Balogh.

Italy's entrance into the war had been a godsend for Hungary because if Italy hadn't entered the war Hitler would have done exactly as he pleased, whereas now Mussolini had considerable influence since he was the friend of Hungary, i.e. Hungary was his original child, so for his own consent he would have to be friendly to Hungary. Her position was not so desperate as it would have been if Italy hadn't entered the war.

He felt Teleki had done the right thing in playing up to Germany.[360] He admitted that his remarks about the Unknown Soldier, etc.,[361] were not such as he would have personally made, or would approve of, but nevertheless, he thought his policy had to be as pro-German as possible and he thought even if it might be that the wording came from some German source.

Mr. de Kanya was appalled at the stupidity of the Allied Powers, particularly England guaranteeing Poland, Greece, and Rumania and all those countries when they should have known that they weren't in any position to go to war with Hitler. He said he himself had told various Englishmen of prominence that they had better watch out for Hitler and that they were not ready to have any argument with him, but they always told him they were strong enough and he supposed they were stronger than he thought they were. Now that it was revealed that they had nothing behind all their guarantees he couldn't understand it.

Mr. de Kanya's opinion, however, was that the war would continue, that Germany would make every effort to capture the British Isles. He had no idea whether it would succeed. He thought the Germans felt it would, even though they knew it would be difficult. If the United States were to enter the war he could readily see the war lasting 15 or twenty years. Whether Germany could live within Europe he didn't know. He thought they could.

Mr. de Kanya said the Germans had every intention of going to war with Russia as soon as England was conquered, and that he felt that the Russians knew this and that was the reason they had taken over the Baltic States. He also thought it quite likely they would make another attack on Finland to take over that country and possibly try to take over Sweden. They were in a position to do this now if Germany were occupied elsewhere whereas later if the war were to settle down to a European blockade they would not be in such a position. He thought Imredy was pretty well finished for the moment

---

360 On the occasion of the occupation of Paris, Prime Minister Teleki delivered a speech in Parliament on June 17, 1940, and saluted "the German head of state and the German armed forces."

361 "The guard of the stigmatized of twenty years ago is standing in front of the hall of Versailles, but there is also a guard at the tomb of the unknown French soldier of the [First] World War as well as that of Napoleon, the greatest soldier-son of the French nation." (Count Pál Teleki; cf. the previous note.)

since he had made a fool of himself and people had gotten very tired of him. As to whether Germany would give Hungary anything he didn't know, but he thought if they didn't the feeling here would change considerably, even though there wasn't much they could do about it.

He realized that Italy was very vulnerable, but he was under the impression that she was stocked up with nine months supplies and that she would last that long without difficulty. He was interested in the reported demands of Germany for the French fleet and gold of all the countries it had taken over. He was wondering how they would get the fleet, and where they could make delivery even if the sailors wanted the ships delivered. Further, he understood that the gold was in America and England and he wondered how Germany expected to get it.

He said he had given out his interview praising Italy solely because he couldn't give out one in favor of Germany. Now that the pressure had been brought upon him to say something he agreed that he would make some pleasant gesture towards Italy but that he wouldn't towards Germany. He didn't write the interview but thought it was funny, but he signed it because it made no particular difference.

[157] Conversation with Mr. Crutzesco the Rumanian Minister

Budapest, July 6, 1940

The Rumanian Minister appeared very much concerned when I saw him last night. He said that he had seen Csaky several days ago and that Csaky had astonished him by saying that he had positive information that Rumania had plans to seize Eastern Hungary up to the Tisza river and that, therefore, Hungary had to mobilize. The Rumanian Minister said he asked Csaky whether at a time like this when they had lost a quarter of their territory and there appeared to be internal disturbances he thought they would attack a neighboring country to get more territory. Csaky insisted that they had positive information to that effect.

The Rumanian Minister said that the idea was perfectly ridiculous, that they had mobilized largely for internal reasons and that it had proved it was necessary because there were several attempts at revolution worked up by Communists and Iron Guards, and that if they hadn't mobilized there would have been much more trouble. Naturally, they had to place a good part of their troops on the Hungarian border to separate the Hungarian minority from Hungary. Otherwise there would be difficulty there. He thought Hungarian mobilization was an internal political move, and he couldn't see how they were going to demobilize without hurting the Government since the Nazis and opposition were trying to make all the capital they could out of the situation. He said he knew that Germany had told them not to go into Rumania and that, therefore, Hungary was in a very difficult position.

Mr. Crutzesco said that one of the things that was most peculiar was that his Yugoslav colleague, with whom he was in closest touch because of the relations between their two countries, had avoided him like a pest ever since the Russian ultimatum; that nearly all other Ministers, even the Slovak, had called on him, but that the Yugoslav not only failed to call but he had not heard a word from him.

Mr. Crutzesco also asked me what I thought of Michael Hadik.[362] He said Hadik was coming to him all the time saying terrible things about the Hungarian Government, things other Hungarians should not say, and he wondered whether Hadik was a spy or what his object might be.

[158] Conversation with Mr. de Kanya ex-Foreign Minister

Budapest, July 9, 1940

Mr. de Kanya said that Hungary was not trying to obtain territorial adjustment in Transylvania at the moment, since Germany stated positively there would be no adjustment until after the war and her new order had been established. What they were trying to do was to get a definite promise for a definite territorial revision and have this agreed to by Germany, Italy, and everybody concerned, and accepted by Rumania. So far the Germans have been very vague. They promised an adjustment after the war, but they never stated what the adjustment would be and Rumania has never accepted any adjustment, and that is what they are working on now.

I asked what good the promise would be even if made, and he replied, "Well, it would be if it were definitely settled than if left hanging in the air with only vague suggestions of territory" but that they had to fight that all out again after the war was over.

Mr. de Kanya said he had heard that Teleki and Csaky were going to Berlin[363] but he didn't know anything definite about it because he hadn't

---

362 Count Mihály Hadik (1907–1970), Liberal journalist, studied also in Britain, director of Globus and of Hornyánszky Co. from 1931, general manager of the Globus ΄concern 1941–44.

363 Teleki and Csáky discussed the settling of Hungarian-Romanian conflicts with Hitler and Ciano in Munich on July 10, 1940.

seen anybody about it for two or three days. He had no doubt that Ciano was arranging matters, and to a certain extent whether they made this trip or not would depend upon how successful Ciano was. He said he saw people from Germany quite frequently and that he had many friends there: they always called on him when they came to town and they always seemed to be coming. He was under the impression that the German people were becoming a little tired and discouraged; as they saw it they would have to fight England, and de Kanya thought that was not such an easy job as they thought. Then it was openly said that they were going to fight Russia. America was known to be very hostile, so many Germans thought that the time when they got finished with Russia they would have to fight America, so that the prospects ahead were for nothing but continuous war.

de Kanya said the new order in Europe that they expected to be established didn't sound so alluring to him. If it meant, as it undoubtedly did, that

*Kálmán Kánya on the terrace of his villa in
Balatonalmádi, 1940*

Germany was the complete master of the rest of Europe everyone would be held down by force of arms and he saw nothing but trouble ahead. As far as he was concerned, he would rather be dead than live under German hegemony. He said he wouldn't mind living under the British, although he liked the Germans better than the English and thought in many ways they were the greatest people in the world. He said he knew Hitler quite well and had read his book four or five times.[364] de Kanya said he was convinced Hitler would never be satisfied with anything less than world domination. It was all in his book, and although now and then he departed from his book he always came back to it.

de Kanya thought Hungary's position was very bad since if Germany won the war she would be a vassal of Germany whereas if England won it would be a war of exhaustion and the probabilities are that the Soviets would take over this part of the world so that it didn't look very rosy. He thought he would like to go to America and become an American.

[159] Conversation with Mr. Orlowski, Polish Minister

Budapest, July 25, 1940

Mr. Orlowski said that he saw Count Csaky several days ago and that he was very much worried about the situation in Rumania. He told him the Germans were also considerably worried. The reason the offensive against England had not taken place was that Hitler was sure that if he became involved with England, Russia would make further advances into Rumania and possibly take over the entire country.

Csaky said the Russians were intriguing and probably would not have much difficulty overthrowing the King and forming a new republic, which republic would later unite with Russia as had been done with the Baltic States. Hungary was also anxious that this didn't happen and therefore had to moderate her demands on Rumania so as to make it as easy for them as possible. The Prime Minister and Foreign Minister of Rumania had been called to Berchtesgaden[365] for the purposes of advising them to make a settlement with Hungary and Bulgaria so as to strengthen their position and enable Hungary and Bulgaria to unite with Rumania against the Russians.

---

364 Reference to *Mein Kampf* by Hitler.
365 Romanian prime minister Ion Gigurtu and foreign minister Mihail Manoilescu conferred with Hitler on July 26, 1940 in Salzburg, subsequently next day with Mussolini and Ciano in Rome.

Csaky was also very much upset because Orlowski told him that he understood the Germans were going to have a customs union with Hungary. This was apparently what Hungary fears and Csaky got very excited about the idea. He said it would be impossible for Hungary to do away with its manufacturing and be a peasant country. In this connection Csaky told Orlowski that Germany expected to take possession of Holland since the Dutch were actually Germans, and part of Belgium. The other half they expected to give to France in compensation for the territory they would have to take from France. France would then go into the group of secondary nations such as Italy and Spain. The manufacture of heavy goods in Europe would largely be concentrated in Germany, including part of Belgium taken over, and Bohemia. Other States would be expected to produce food products and small manufactured articles. They would not allowed to have any factories that could be turned into munitions factories. In that way Germany would control the entire manufacture of munitions and be able to hold down the rest of Europe for this reason.

[160] Conversation with the Rumanian Minister[366]

Budapest, August 6, 1940

Mr. Crutzesco told me that officially he knew absolutely nothing about any negotiations with Hungary in regard to Transylvania. Unofficially he knew that some such negotiations were contemplated and that Mr. Bossy[367] and Mr. Hiot[368] would come here for the purpose of conducting such negotiations. However, neither officially or unofficially did he know when they were coming, who would represent Hungary, or what the Rumanians had in mind so far as possible territorial concessions were concerned. He had never had any conversations with anyone connected with the Hungarian Government in regard to the Transylvanian question and he had no knowledge of what was in their minds unless the article in the PESTER LLOYD correctly summarized their intentions. If so, he regarded it as ridiculous and impossible. Rumania would never give up all that territory since it included a large majority of Rumanians, and there was no ethnological or any other basis for the line drawn. He said that negotiations were going on at the present time

---

366 Gheorghe Cruțescu, Romanian envoy extraordinary and minister plenipotentiary in Budapest.
367 Raoul Bossy, Romanian minister to Rome, earlier minister to Budapest.
368 Dinu Hiott, Romanian minister plenipotentiary.

with Bulgaria and he expects the results to be announced soon. The difference between the negotiations with Bulgaria and those with Hungary was that the Bulgarians were reasonable and even friendly, and involved only 200,000 people, whereas the Hungarian Government was unfriendly, unreasonable, and the question involved millions of people.

He emphasized that there was no thought of either with Bulgaria or Hungary of making an important change of frontiers, that whatever settlement there might be would only take place after the war was over. The Hungarians were keeping their army mobilized because they hoped for a revolution in Rumania and wanted to be ready to take advantage of such a situation if it came about.

[161] Conversation with the Rumanian Minister

Budapest, August 26, 1940

Mr. Crutesco said that he had been ill as a result of his trip to Rumania where he caught cold, and that any statement that he had been to the Foreign Office yesterday was totally untrue. Further, there was no conference of any kind with the German and Italian Ministers as stated on the radio. Also, there was no truth in the statement that the negotiations had at any time been broken off. The facts were that the Hungarians made demands for the greater portion of Transylvania. The Rumanians took the point of view that they could not discuss this until the question of the transfer of populations was agreed upon and the details solved, since any cession of territory would involve the transfer of populations.

The Hungarian delegation were compelled to return home for further instructions, and it was agreed that they should do so, and that there would be a further meeting this week. The Hungarians asked that this meeting be held in Hungary but the Rumanian Government had not yet agreed. They expect to know today. The only possible basis for a supposed conference was that Vornle had asked him to send someone up to discuss the place of meeting and his Secretary had gone up to see Vornle. Preceding him was the German Minister and as he came out the Secretary shook hands with him but had no talk with him whatever, and there was no Italian Minister present.

Crutesco said the Rumanians had proposed to the Hungarians that they both demobilize, but that the Hungarians had refused. He personally thought it would be a good idea to leave the whole thing to the armies to settle between themselves, as Rumania felt confident that she could defend her position. However, he didn't suppose Germany would agree to this.

Crutesco said he knew nothing of German pressure on Rumania, but he agreed it was certain that there had been some pressure. He didn't think, however, that there had been any definite wish as to what they wanted done as expressed by Germany. If they had said anything they simply advised the Rumanians to make some settlement. He was afraid that if no settlement was made and if things got worse the Germans would get tired of it and just take a map, draw a line and say that this is the new frontier.

He thought neither the Rumanians nor the Hungarians would be satisfied, so he hoped some settlement could be reached, but he said they were so far apart that it was difficult to see how this was possible without extensive negotiations. The Hungarian action in mobilizing and going through all the gestures of war didn't make for a pleasant atmosphere and didn't help the negotiations. In fact, it was a hindrance. The Rumanians had a certain amount of pride and they couldn't be put in a position of being bull-dozed by Hungarian tactics.

[162] Conversation with Dr. Eckhardt

Budapest, August 27, 1940

Mr. Eckhardt told me this morning that he had been out to see some of the labor camps where the Jews are confined. He said that no more than 10 percent of Jews were permitted in the Army, that is, in any single regiment. Since about one out of every three persons in Budapest was a Jew this had resulted in surplus of Jews in this and other districts. The younger people up to 10 percent had been used in the Army but the balance mostly had included all of the older ones and they were put out to compulsory labor. Presumably this all was to cover necessary labor such as digging fortifications, trenches, and all such things but they had not been used for this purpose at all. Most of those he saw were breaking rocks on the side of the road. Since practically none of them was used to manual labor what they did did not amount to anything and there was no particular use for the rock, so actually it was just a form of punishment and he was literally disgusted; thought it was absolutely inhuman, and it was simply a result of German pressure or attempts to play up to Germany.

I spoke to him about the confiscation of the Hatvany estate. He said this was done under the Jew Law and the Agricultural Expropriation Bill. The Jew Law provides that no Jews may own any agricultural land. The Agricultural Bill provides a method of payment which he thought was about 1/3 down and the balance in bonds. The price was to be fixed but they could appeal to the courts. I understood from other sources that in Hatvany's case he was allowed only 200 pengoes a hectare whereas he paid less than seven years ago 700 pengoes and further that the bonds which he got were due in 50 years and were of uncertain value.

[163] Conversation with Mr. Chorin
Budapest, August 27, 1940

Mr. Chorin, Head of one of the largest coal companies and also the Head of the Commercial Bank, told me this morning that the labor camps were entirely under control of the Army; that he had been to see Teleki about it and Teleki refused to have anything to do with it, saying it was just an Army matter. Actually the Army were drafting all sorts of people for these labor camps. For example, the Director General of the Gas Company,[369] one of the largest industrial concerns in Hungary, and incidentally a concern controlled by the Germans; as well as two of his Bank Directors have been drafted. In fact, he said he knew any amount of people of this sort including doctors, lawyers, and others who were not out breaking stones and working in mills, work to which they were not accustomed. They received no pay whatever, no clothes, no shoes, nothing. If their shoes wore out and they have no more, they have to go barefooted. Incidentally, he said that he saw Mr. Imredy the other day and Imredy was very much worked up about it. He said he was entirely opposed to this. His opposition, however, did not seem to be so much because of sympathy for the Jews but the idea of the Army being able to determine who was going into work camps and who wasn't he considered government by the Army rather than by civil authorities. Mr. Chorin said that actually the Government was getting away from the Jew Law all the time; that many of the things they were doing now were not provided for in the law. For instance, they were excluding Jews from work in certain types of business. There is no provision of this kind in the law. Incidentally, he said that doctors who were members of the Army and called into service are not permitted to do any work. They go to the hospitals, stand around all day and do nothing. Since some of these doctors are the best surgeons and the best doctors in Hungary, it seems rather silly not to let them practice their own profession for a living, or to have a profession if they are not going to use it.

---

369 Dr. Ede Véssei (1885–?), general manager of Budapest Székesfőváros Gázművei (Municipal Gas Works of Budapest) between 1932 and 1941 (by contract between 1932 and 1935).

On the subject of confiscation of estates, he said they were going to confiscate all estates belonging to the Jews. Some of them are the finest estates here. The pay as provided by the law he did not consider as amounting to confiscation. As a matter of fact, if they paid what the law provided they would pay less than the estates were worth, but not much less. However, he didn't believe they got any cash. He said the bonds were 3 percent, but the value was so uncertain that he was quite sure that I would not take them.

[164] Conversation with Mr. Crutesco
the Rumanian Minister

Budapest, August 31, 1940

The Rumanian Minister has just returned from Vienna after the conference,[370] which he considered disastrous for his country since Hungary had achieved far more than it had ever dreamed the Rumanians would be compelled to give. They, the Rumamians, had yielded because of the Russians on one side threatening them and the Hungarians on the other, the situation was too uncertain to permit them to refuse, particularly when they were offered the German guarantees for their frontiers, which was applicable against the Russians.

Mr. Crutesco said the Germans on the whole had been nice, but the Italians had been very nasty and had made everything difficult as possible for them. He said that there were about one million Rumanians in the territory to be ceded, which was about 42,000 square kilometers,[371] and the Hungarians were taking possession, or occupying, the new territory within fourteen days from yesterday, and the Rumanians were compelled to be out of the territory by that time. Eventual demobilization was contemplated but on account of the occupying of the territory, etc. it should be gradual. He said that the Germans he had talked to seemed to be profoundly discouraged, and he sat at the table next to a German and the latter had remarked a number of times that he didn't know what was going to happen, where they were going, and he could see nothing encouraging in the situation. He said the resistance of the British was very discouraging.

---

370 The Second Vienna Award, August 30, 1940: Northern Transylvania returned to
    Hungary, including Szeklerland, Kolozsvár [Cluj], and Nagyvárad [Oradea].
371 Actually 43,591 square kms.

[165] Conversation with Dr. Tibor Eckhardt

Budapest, September 9, 1940

Tibor Eckhardt told me yesterday that Count Bethlen was very much aroused about the Transylvanian award, that he had seen the Regent and had a three-hour talk with Teleki. He told Teleki that the acceptance of such an award was a betrayal of his countrymen. He condemned the whole procedure. He said that nothing should have been done until after the war was over, when a final settlement could have been made. Now they had not only gone to great expense in connection with mobilization, but they had accepted a settlement which was not satisfactory and they could hardly expect in the future any more than they had now, and since they had made such a settlement with one of the warring Powers, in the event the other Power should win they might lose everything.

Since Count Bethlen is a Transylvanian and one of the leading advocates of revision, his position is interesting; particularly so, as I have seen no one whose estates or home has been returned to Hungary by the new award while Count Bethlen did receive back what was left of his estate amounting to 2000 acres[372] of forest land. Apparently he would rather sacrifice this than to have to land returned.

Eckhardt also told me that Imredy was going to try to overturn Teleki before the Transylvanian deputies took their seats since that would give Teleki a large additional force. He said Imredy had about 43 of the National Union party and he expected the Opposition to join him but that he would be disappointed.

Eckhardt also said that when the troops went into Transylvania there were no cheers for anybody but Bethlen. Everywhere the cries were "Eljen Bethlen," and that Bethlen would have a big increase in prestige since he was a great hero in that part of the world.

[166] Conversation with Baron Thierry, Acting Chief of Political Section of the Foreign Office

Budapest, September 17, 1940

Baron Thierry[373] said different commissions were progressing favorably to settle up the various questions involved in the occupation of the part of Transylvania awarded to Hungary. It was true that the Rumanians had taken

---

372 1406 "hold" (1 acre = 0.703 cadastral "hold").

373 Baron Heribert Thierry, diplomat, councilor of the Hungarian legation at the Holy See, first secretary of the legation in Ankara in 1944.

all movable property, including that of the telephone company as well as cattle, and even window sashes, but it is expected that this will be ironed out by the various commissions.

Mr. Quinn of the telephone company telephoned this morning regarding compensation for the property of the Rumanian company taken over by the Hungarians, which was valued at 295 million gold lei, and he asked that the Hungarian Government recompense the American company rather than recompense the Rumanians for the seizure of this property. Thierry promised to let me know as soon as possible the attitude of the Hungarian Government in this matter. He indicated that it would take a long while for the commissions to iron out these problems and since the telephone company in reality was a Rumanian company its case would come within the purview of the general settlement.

I expect to do all possible at the Foreign Office, but I infer that since the telephone company is a Rumanian company it will be difficult if not impossible to get any settlement for the American company as such since undoubtedly this is the principal thing of value that the Hungarians have taken and it will be used to offset the claims against Rumania for property taken away by its nationals. Consequently, the telephone company will have to look to Rumania for compensation rather than to Hungary.

[167] Conversation with Baron Thierry, Acting Chief of Political Section of the Foreign Office

Budapest, September 17, 1940

Baron Thierry said the occupation of Transylvania was proceeding smoothly. While the Rumanian Army had taken everything movable including door knobs, doors and glass windows, it was expected that these would be adjusted by the various commissions now set up.

The political situation in Rumania now was stable. It would be bad for Hungary were it not so.

Baron Thierry did not know what Hungary would be able to do regarding foreign interests since these matters had to be taken up with various commissions which now were settling the Rumanian problems. Amongst these would figure the indemnification for property taken by Rumanians.

He promised to let me have a reply to the memorandum which I handed him this morning as soon as possible.

He claimed that the German-Hungarian minority treaty[374] made no change in the situation since everything included in it was covered by Hungarian law.

Baron Thierry knew nothing regarding the Jewish labor camps since these were in charge of the Army, but he understood the camps were being disbanded.

I told Baron Thierry that I understood Count Csaky to have said that no arbitration had taken place at Vienna and that Germany had refused to listen to a statement by either the Rumanian or Hungarian delegates, simply giving them a map showing the new frontier they would have to accept. (This was what Count Csaky had told the British Minister.) Thierry said this was not at all true. Hungary had gone to Vienna with no idea of seeking arbitration since the Germans always said that because of their past experience they would not act as arbitrators. When Hungarian delegates arrived at Vienna they stated their case, whereupon they both were told that Ribbentrop and Ciano would arbitrate the matter, providing the Hungarians and the Rumanians agreed in advance to accept the verdict. Since the Hungarian delegation had no power to make this agreement there was a delay until they could communicate with the Government in Budapest to obtain the necessary authority. When the agreement of both the Hungarian and Rumanian Governments to the Axis agreement was obtained, a map was produced showing the new frontier and the award thus made. Since both Governments had agreed in advance to accept the award, nothing else could be done. For the moment, Thierry considered Hungary was satisfied, although disappointed that she had not obtained what she wanted. He did not feel that the Hungarians had bound themselves forever, but under the present conditions and circumstances, revisionist ambition might be said to be satisfied.

[168] Conversation with Mr. MacMurray Ambassador to Turkey

Budapest, September 28, 1940

Mr. MacMurray[375] called on me yesterday and told me that sometime back Mr. Ottlik had been in Ankara and had a letter of introduction from Mr. Ackerson. When Mr. MacMurray arrived here he was invited to a good-

---

374 German-Hungarian agreement signed by foreign ministers Csáky and von Ribbentrop in Vienna on August 30, 1940, within the framework of the Second Vienna Award, on the condition of the German ethnic group in Hungary.
375 John V. MacMurray, U.S. ambassador to Ankara 1936–42.

bye party for the Ackersons by Ottlik (to which party I was not invited.) After dinner Mr. Ottlik took Mr. MacMurray off in a corner and told him how unfortunate it was that I was not on good terms with the Foreign Minister and said that Count Csaky would be very happy to have Mr. MacMurray call upon him to discuss the situation that existed between me and the Foreign Ministers.

Mr. MacMurray told Mr. Ottlik that he was here on leave and had nothing to do with the matter but that he would take it up with me, and if I wanted him to go and see the Foreign Minister he would do so; otherwise he would not.

As a result of the conversation Mr. MacMurray advised Mr. Ottlik that he did not care to call upon the Foreign Minister.

[169] Conversation with Dr. Eckhardt

Budapest, September 30, 1940

Dr. Eckhardt told me that he had received in great confidence from a competent source, which he was not at liberty to reveal, information to the effect that Germany had delivered a virtual ultimatum to Hungary demanding that the Mark be placed upon an equal basis with other currencies, and that in compliance the Hungarian Government was arranging to decrease the value of dollars and pounds, Swiss francs and other currencies, to bring the result desired by Germany. He said they chose this method rather than increase the value of the mark because they practically have no export business now, and if they made the mark more valuable it would simply mean they would get less from Germany and by decreasing the other currencies keeps the relations between the Pengo and the Mark the same.

Eckhardt is of the opinion that an economic crisis is fast developing in Hungary. He says that Weiss Manfred[376] had just dismissed 5000 men and he looks for a reduction in employment in textiles and other industries dependent upon exports to and imports from other countries than Germany. He says that textile mills are being converted to rayon[377] and that unless they can find some way to import cotton and raw material they will virtually disappear. He said that he discovered that when he was out in his own constituency the peasants who are dependent upon cotton goods are being told that they must take a certain amount of rayon. Eckhardt thinks that the

376 Ammunitions factory and industrial giant on Csepel Island founded by Manfréd and Berthold Weiss, south of Budapest.
377 Semi-synthetic textile based on viscose and its raw material.

situation is developing where Hungary will soon be little or no better off than the occupied territories.

In regard to the 3-Power Pact,[378] Eckhardt says it is quite evident that Germany and Italy believe that this will have the effect of lessening supplies to England since we will be frightened of being plunged into the war and want to keep everything for our own rearmament. Japan, he thinks, considers that since we are faced with a war on two oceans we won't dare to interfere with their plans for the Pacific. Since it is well known that Germany has feared American participation in the war, he regards this move as a sign of weakness on the part of the signatory Powers.

[170] Conversation with Mr. de Kanya ex-Foreign Minister

Budapest, October 1, 1940

Mr. de Kanya seemed very ill and looked very bad. He was very tired and I was permitted to stay only a few minutes. However, the first question he asked me was if I knew anything, and I said that all I knew was about the 3-Power pact. He said, "Oh, that!" Then he asked me what does it mean. I said that is what I wanted to find out from him. He replied, "I cannot understand it all. It looks just like a senseless gesture, but I don't see what the object is." I told him that I presumed the object was to make us stop sending supplies to the British, and he said, "You won't, will you?" and I said, "I don't think so." He then said, "I didn't think so, so there must be something other."

I said that I understood Hungary is going to join it, and he said "What?" I said that is what I hear, and he raised his hands in a gesture of resignation and let it go at that. Then I said, "I suppose we will have another signing here like the signing of the anti-Comintern pact," and all he said was, "I cannot believe that we will fool anybody. I don't think they themselves take it seriously, probably just to make the various peoples think they are doing something heroic." Then the nurse shooed me off.

---

378 The Tripartite Agreement was signed in Berlin by Germany, Italy, and Japan on September 27, 1940.

[171] Conversation with Baron Thierry at F. O.

Budapest, October 11, 1940

Baron Thierry told me he knew nothing about the demonstration[379] or what it meant, but that the Prime Minister, who in his speech referred to being compelled to take some action, had not meant military action; that the Prime Minister had referred to a clause in the Vienna Award which was to the effect that if the Rumanians and Hungarians were unable to agree on the various matters in connection with the transfer of the territory the Germans and Italians would arbitrate. Teleki meant that the Hungarians would have to ask for arbitration.

I called Baron Thierry's attention to the fact that there was very little difference between Germany and Rumania at the present time and that it looked strange that the negotiations had been broken off by Rumania under the circumstances, and I asked how they expected anything from Germany and Italy in view of the fact that the Germans were now running Rumania and may have broken off the negotiations, and it looked like Rumania would get the best of it. He professed ignorance of this; that they had the impression the Germans were running things in Rumania, but he didn't know what it meant.

Baron Thierry didn't know anything about Yugoslavia and had not heard that Germany has asked her to join the Axis, or that any such article had appeared in the German papers. He said positively Hungary had no agreement with Italy or Germany in connection with Yugoslavia and had no offer from Yugoslavia for revision, and that neither Germany nor Italy had made any suggestion which would involve revision or any attack by Hungary on Yugoslavia.

The press campaign against Rumania, he said, was merely leading up to the asking for a new arbitration. Rumanian-Hungarian negotiations had been broken off by the Rumanians.

Baron Thierry knew that Szalasi had made a speech giving his program.[380] He said he didn't know anything about it, that it was internal affairs and that he hadn't paid much attention to it.

I asked about the anti-American press campaign, and particularly about the letter I wrote Csaky to which I never had any reply. He said this was a matter for the press department and that he could say that the whole matter had been satisfactorily explained by the Hungarian Minister at Washington

---

379 A miners' strike began in Salgótarján on October 7, 1940, and lasted for several weeks.

380 Ferenc Szálasi delivered an "inaugural" program speech in the "House of Fidelity" (VI. Andrássy út 60.) upon his release from prison on October 7, 1940.

to the State Department, including the attack on President Wilson. I told him that I heard Imredy was back of this, but he said he heard nothing about it, that it was a local matter and the press section should handle it.

Baron Thierry said that the Hungarian-German agricultural agreement had been received by him but that he had not looked at it and that he didn't know very much about it at this moment. He said that so far as they know, no German troops had passed through Hungary. He would guarantee that they had not passed down the Danube in boats, hidden. He said that he probably thought they had because he said the Hungarian Legation at Berlin had been suddenly called upon for 6000 visas and he assumed it was for use of the troops in coming down to Rumania, but that there had been no request as such for troops, and as far as he knew, nobody came in any civilian clothing.

[172] Conversation with Dr. Tibor Eckhardt

Budapest, October 21, 1940

Eckhardt told me this morning that he felt that German troops in Rumania were merely the advance guard who were preparing bases for German against British colonies. He thought the British had been wrong in not agreeing to give Dardanelles to Russia since this would have prevented Germany from coming through. Now, however, it was too late. If the Germans took Constantinople it would make an enormous impression in Moslem countries, and if they succeeded in crossing the Dardanelles, as he thought they would and attack the Near East, Egypt and menace the British colonies in Africa, it would help the German people to stand the bombing and offset the disappointment at their failure to occupy England. He said he had it directly from Germany that the Army had given up hope for the present of occupying England but that Hitler hadn't. Therefore, there would be no attempt at present, the bombing would continue, and if later it looked as though such an attempt was feasible it would take place. In the meantime, the German Army would be occupied in the Balkans and Northern Africa.

He did not believe that Germany would take the rest of France because this would mean that the British and the Americans would take over the French colonies. Germany wanted to keep the French colonies and would do nothing that would prejudice French possession, for the moment. Ultimately he expects France and Britain to be at war. He thinks at present both sides are withholding action since both are trying to win over the French colonial troops. The British don't want to attack the French for that reason, and the French don't want to start war on Britain until they have the situation in the colonies better in hand. The French he thinks are being entirely guided by Germany.

Dakar[381] menaces British communication around Africa, but the British cannot do anything about it for the reason mentioned. They don't want to start action against France for fear of prejudicing their position in the colonies.

[173] Conversation with Mr. Tibor Eckhardt et al about going to America

Budapest, November 8, 1940

Mr. Chorin who was in to see me lately told me that he and others were urging Tibor Eckhardt and Count Bethlen to leave the country and go to England and America. In the first place both of these men would be put in concentration camps if the Germans came in; second, there should be someone in both England and America capable of explaining the Hungarian point of view and interpreting what is happening here so that these Powers would understand the real situation in Hungary; further, should the Germans take possession of the country another Government could be set up in America or England, the Hungarians in the meanwhile (in America) give lectures, etc., and could give a true idea of the war feelings of Hungary and enemy propaganda counteracted. I asked him if he was prepared to finance such a business, thinking that would end his interest in the matter. To my surprise, he said he was.

I mentioned the matter to Eckhardt, and he apparently knew nothing about it. He said he didn't want to leave the country as long as the Regent was in power. When I called on de Kanya the other day de Kanya brought the subject up, and said he was very strongly in favor of it; and he had talked to one of the Cabinet Ministers, who was also in favor of the idea, and that if he were able to he would go and see the Prime Minister and the Regent about it. I told him that Eckhardt didn't seem to know anything about it and wasn't very strong about the idea. He said to have me see Eckhardt for him. I did this.

Yesterday Eckhardt came to see me and I told him de Kanya was very insistent that he should leave the country with Bethlen, for no other reason than to save themselves from the concentration camp, that he would be able

---

381 The troops of the British navy and the Free France movement unsuccessfully tried, under General Charles de Gaulle, to take Dakar in French West Africa (today the capital of Senegal) on September 22–25, 1940.

to do much for Hungary in America and England if the country was occupied by the Germans, as he felt was quite probable.

Yesterday Eckhardt came to see me again, and I told him I was going to see the Regent and asked if he wanted me to mention the matter to the Regent. My interest in the matter is purely to consolidate the anti-German feeling and to give individual assistance to those who are on the anti-German side.

[174] Conversation with H.S.H. The Regent

Budapest, November 8, 1940

The Regent received me with his face wreathed in smiles and almost jumped up and down with apparent joy in telling me how happy he was over the reelection of President Roosevelt. He said he and Madame Horthy had sat up to the early hours of the morning of Wednesday trying to get the election results and that they were both terribly disappointed because they got nothing. However, now that the election was assured they were very happy because they believed in everything President Roosevelt stood for, and he felt that his reelection was the first bright thing that happened in many months and meant so much to the entire world.

The Regent told me he wanted to write a personal letter of congratulation to the President and asked me if I would send it in the pouch. In the meantime he said he would be pleased if I would wire the President that he was delighted at his election. I said to him, "I don't know, you know our codes are broken down and somebody may decode the message." He said "I don't care if they do."

After disposing of the election the Regent told me that he had something very interesting to tell me in great confidence. He didn't want it repeated to anyone. He said that a man who had been a liaison officer with him in the last war and was now one of the high ranking German Admirals[382] had been to Budapest lately and had asked for permission to call. As he was at Godollo he sent word for him to come down there and do some shooting. The man accepted with pleasure, and they had a very fine hunt. He said that he purposely said nothing to him about the war because he didn't want the man to think he invited him down there for the purpose of pumping him. As the man was a rather silent man and said very little, he was therefore sur-

---

382 Most probably Adm. Wilhelm Franz Canaris (1887–1945), head of the German *Abwehr*, and a participant and martyr of the assassination attempt on Hitler on July 20, 1944

prised when after the hunt the man said, "Admiral, you know the navy has-
n't changed at all in Germany. All the other forces are different, but the
navy is just the same as before the war. We must be grateful to Hitler for the
fact that he has done so much for the navy, but we and Japan both have
made one very serious mistake, that is, not with the navy, but our Governments and the Japanese Government thought that the air arm could take the
place of the Navy. That has proved to be a great mistake. The British navy
is still intact; it is a wonderful navy. It is just as true now as it was in the last
war, that the Power that commands the sea will win the war." The Regent
said he didn't say anything but he was naturally pleased at this statement
because it agreed with his own ideas.

I spoke to the Regent about Eckhardt and Bethlen going to America and
England. I told him the idea and he thought it might be a good one. He said
he would speak to the Prime Minister about it. I then brought up the subject
of our Military Attache[383] and told him all about it, and said that if the Foreign
Office would tell us the truth we wouldn't have to go rooting around for
information. He said he didn't know why the F.O. didn't tell us the truth, he
couldn't understand it. I told him something of my position vis-a-vis the
Foreign Minister, and asked him if he received copies of the letters of our
correspondence. At first he said no, and then when I called it to his attention
he said he had and remembered it, but said Csaky is just afraid of the Germans, absolutely frightened by them and does all these things because he is
so scared. I didn't contradict him, but I told him Csaky was making my position rather difficult. The Regent said to me, "Anything that happens now, no
matter what, come to me." I said, "I cannot come to Your Highness." He
said, "Then call up Captain Tost to take the matter up with me." He said, "I
am still here; in fact, more in charge than appears on the surface. We had to
let the German troops come through,[384] for after all they said they were coming through to protect the oil fields, but we absolutely refused to let them
make a base here, and I don't intend to do it. Further, I am going to kick the
Nazis out of Parliament." I said, "What will Germany say to that?" He said,
"I don't care, I am going to do it now or later. In fact, I wouldn't have them
in Parliament at all because that would be the simplest solution. In times
like this Parliament is dangerous, but I don't want to ape the dictators. I

383 U.S. military attaché Richard C. Partridge witnessed the passage of a German military train near Szolnok, Hungary. He was accused of treason but Horthy's personal
intervention helped smooth the case, which ended in a Hungarian apology. (J. F.
Montgomery, *Hungary the Unwilling Satellite,* 143–44)
384 On September 30, 1940, the Hungarian government agreed to the crossing of Hungary by German "study" troops heading towards Romania.

don't want to have them think I am going to have their form of government. I am going to have a Parliament, but am going to kick the Nazis out."

The Regent told me that he had issued a new order to the Army that no one was to engage in politics in any form, upon penalty of immediate dismissal, that every officer had to sign a statement acknowledging the receipt of this order, and he felt that this would have a decided effect, particularly as he had dismissed a lot of officers who had engaged in politics.[385]

[175] Conversation with Mr. Barany[a]i President of the National Bank

Budapest, November 8, 1940

Mr. Baranyi[386] [sic] told me that they were very nervous for fear something would happen that would cause our Government to shut off credits. He said this would be disastrous for Hungary and that it would have a great effect on Hungarian sympathies, and from that point of view, would be bad for England. Hungary is not for Germany despite appearances, and people wouldn't like to be punished for something they couldn't help, particularly when they are independent. He said that he himself would be in favor of it if the Germans actually had control of Hungarian finances, but at this moment, they hadn't and he hoped that we wouldn't be too quick about taking any action. In other words, that we would be sure that the situation was such as demanded action before we ever did anything. For fear of some such action he was transferring some gold, amounting to 10 or 15 million pengo, from the United States to Argentina. He told me that he didn't know how long Hungary could stand the pace and he was very pessimistic about conditions here, and conditions in Europe. He saw no possibility even if the war stopped tomorrow of Europe recovering very quickly and felt that the center of everything would move to America. He felt that America would become the actual head of the British Empire and that Europe power would become third-rate as compared to America. He said if he wasn't a Hungarian and didn't have a duty to his country he would try to go to America and get a job, at anything, in order to be there because he felt that conditions here were going to be absolutely such that no one could contemplate them with equanimity.

---

385 On October 28 German agent Otto Braun complained to his bosses in Berlin that high-ranking pro-German officers, including Lt. Gen. Barabás and Lt. Col. Juhász, had been dismissed in Hungary. Cf. *Wilhelmstrasse,* 546.

386 Lipót Baranyai (1894–1970), president of the Hungarian National Bank.

[176] Conversation with Mr. Charonov the Soviet Minister

Budapest, November 16, 1940

Mr. Charonov[387] said that he had no information concerning the Molotov-Hitler conversations.[388] However, he was certain that the occupation of Turkey or of the Dardanelles was not the subject of the conversation. He felt that there wasn't any probability of Hungary being occupied by the Germans since it was not necessary, and they were doing very well as it was.

He felt certain that the situation here would not change, although he did think there might be airports established in Hungary before the war was over. I said this would mean that the British would bomb Hungary. He thought that might be true, but it wouldn't mean that they would bomb Budapest since the airports would be located elsewhere and there would be no reason to bomb Budapest.

He said he had information from German sources that they were not backing Szalasi any more, but Imredy. I told him that as long as the Regent was alive and in power Imredy would never be Prime Minister, and he said the Germans had told him that, and that they didn't expect any change which would bring Imredy to power, but only that he would be the leader of the German forces in Hungary.

[177] Conversation with the Regent

Budapest, November 22, 1940

The Regent said that they had received word from the Germans a few days ago to the effect that they would like to have them adhere to the 3-Power Pact, and they had asked what this involved. They were told that it meant no commitments of any kind in case of war. It only meant that they would be in the scene for the new order in Europe and would be participant in any peace conference, etc. With this understanding they agreed to adhere. However, when they were called to Vienna a few days ago they feared that some demand was to be made. The demand they feared most was that the Germans were preparing for on offensive this way and to want bases in Hungary. This they could not admit since they considered that would involve

---

387 Nikolai Charonov, Soviet envoy extraordinary and minister plenipotentiary in Budapest.
388 Soviet foreign minister Vyacheslav Molotov conferred in Berlin as of November 12, 1940.

the loss of sovereignty and Hungary would in no case sign anything which involved her sovereignty.

However, when they got to Vienna[389] there was nothing whatever said about any offensive in the Balkans, nor was any request made for bases. On the contrary, they were told again that this did not involve Hungary in any war and that, further, apparently as an added inducement, they were told that the committee which was investigating Rumanian atrocities in Transylvania was going to back up the Hungarian claims in toto, since it made no difference to them one way or the other; as nothing was involved they adhered to the pact and they would have signed anything else, no matter what it was, if it did not involve their sovereignty.

Hitler had told Teleki that he considered Mussolini very foolish to start a war entirely unprepared[390] and that Germany under no circumstances, would be of any help. He said that the Italians had lost face and they would have to redeem themselves. If the Germans came in and helped them then all the Balkans and other countries would consider the Italians as worth nothing and the loss of prestige would be harmful to the Axis. Since Italy had enough troops to finish the job they would have to finish it themselves.

They learned at Vienna that Molotov came to Berlin under pressure and that his visit produced no satisfactory results. Hitler wanted Russia to attack Persia, but Russia didn't seem to want to. Hitler wouldn't allow Russia to attack European Turkey or occupy the Dardanelles, and the troops in Rumania are there not only to guard the oil fields but to prevent any such move.

The Regent said that the Germans complained bitterly about the supplies from Russia and said that nearly everything they ordered was delayed because something broke down or wouldn't work. They would like very much to send in their own technicians but the Russians wouldn't allow it.

Germany is very anxious for peace. They say that they have plenty of food to last forever and they have all the material they need. They can build as many planes and ships as the United States and England together, and while there is an admission that the British fleet still controls the seas they said that the present situation can continue indefinitely and, therefore, the only sensible thing to do is to make peace. The President of Portugal[391] has agreed to act as intermediary with England, and either has initiated peace proceedings or expects to do so. Germany, it is alleged, will offer Britain wonderful peace terms.

The Regent said that Mussolini was in a bad fix. He had gone into the

---

389 Hungary signed the Tripartite Agreement in Vienna on November 20, 1940.
390 Italy invaded Greece on October 28, 1940.
391 António de Oliveira Salazar (1889–1970), prime minister of Portugal 1932–68, foreign minister before and during World War II.

Greek war with only one good division in Albania. The rest were nothing at all. The good division had smashed the line and gone on, expecting to be followed by the rest of the Army but they found themselves completely alone. The Greek troops cut them off and captured or cut to pieces the entire division. The Regent has a very low opinion of Italian troops, and said that his experience in the last war[392] was that they couldn't do much fighting. He said he knew personally of one instance of an Italian advance being stopped by Hungarian troops merely jumping out of their trenches and yelling, whereupon the Italians fled without one shot being fired.

The Regent said it was a mistake to consider Major Partridge's action as spying. He visualized a spy as one who broke in the middle of the night and did something he was not supposed to do. Major Partridge had done only what a Military Attache is supposed to do, and what he himself had done when he was a Naval Attache. A spy was something entirely different and that we could consider the incident closed and never have happened.

The Regent told me that in two weeks they expected to kick the Nazi Party out, that they were now in a better position to do so than before.

The Regent was much pleased with the letter[393] and thanks from the President, and said that aside from his love for the President he would have considered his defeat a world calamity as men like him were needed today as never before.

[178] Conversation with No. 79[394]

Budapest, November 28, 1940

No. 79 informed me that the debacle of Italy, according to Csaky, makes it necessary for Hungary to reorient herself; otherwise she would be entirely at the mercy of Germany. Therefore, Csaky said, that if Hungary and Yugoslavia should stand together there would be no danger of Hungary becoming involved in the war, and Italy's present loss of prestige makes it necessary that these relations should be improved, and Csaky thought that shortly this matter would be taken care of. He assured the committee that there was no possibility of Hungary attacking Yugoslavia since there was no obligation of any kind in a military way involved in the adherence to the pact. He

---

392 In World War I.
393 The reply of President Roosevelt to the congratulations of Regent Horthy.
394 Probably Tibor Eckhardt. This assumption is supported by the very detailed presentation of his own speech in Parliament.

did not believe Yugoslavia would sign and adhere to the 3-Power Pact, but the fact that Hungary did would make no difference in their getting together and Yugoslavia and Hungary becoming more friendly.

Eckhardt in his speech in the Lower House Committee on Foreign Affairs opposed the signing of the Protocol to the Pact: 1, because Hungary now has become dependent; for 1000 years she stood on the policy of independence, never becoming involved voluntarily with any other country. There were times when she became involved because of association with the Austro-Hungarian Empire, but it was not of her own free will. Since the war they definitely remained independent. With regard to the Pact it was the first time they ever signed anything which involved them with any other nation in such a way that they became dependent; 2, the Pact is unilateral, giving Hungary obligations of an uncertain and probably dangerous character, but giving her nothing in return; 3, Germany speaks of her lebensraum,[395] but Hungary also has its lebensraum. The inclusion of Slovakia and Rumania in the Pact excludes Hungary from the possibility of ever having her own lebensraumwhich Germany says is necessary for any nation to live; 4, In principle Hungary has always minded its own business. Now it is committed in the struggle for world domination; 5, The fact that Hungary has not been given the right to vote, such as Italy, Japan and Germany have, the only the right of consultation means they have accepted the Fuhrer idea which Hungary has never done, and it doesn't mean that they are equal partners with Germany, Italy and Japan, but simply theoretically they will be told before something id done, although they wouldn't have any right to any decision, even though it affected Hungary adversely; 6, The signing of the protocol to the pact would make a bad impression in America, and he was convinced that America would have a great deal to say after the war, and if she had nothing to say about the peace treaties at least it would be the only nation in the world with any money, and the whole of Europe would be dependent upon their good-will.

Csaky, in replying, said that Hungary's position was difficult because of the war, and he thought it was better that Hungary be consulted in everything rather than be in a position where they had no chance to give their ideas and state their side, and since no military obligations were involved they could not see but what they were better off being in with the most powerful neighbors, even though it is only a mater of consultation than they would be if they had no rights whatever. He said that it was not a fact that the Pact gave Hungary no rights but only obligations. He said that Germany

---

395 *"Lebensraum"* – living space, the territory befitting Germany, in German National Socialist rhetoric.

and other signers had agreed to defend Hungary against attack. Eckhardt asked "Against whom?", but there was no reply.

Csaky did not say anything about Hungary's lebensraum, but he said that Hungary was not a partner of Rumania and Slovakia and had no obligations to them whatever. It was for this reason that separate pacts were signed as Hungary would not sign a pact which brought them in as a partner with Rumania and Slovakia.

Csaky said that the pact was an empty frame without content and had no military agreement. Parenthetically, General Werth told Bethlen that Hungary had no agreement of any sort in a military way in connection with the pact and was not bound to attack Yugoslavia or any other country because Germany did.

In the Lower House Committee, Eckhardt, Rassay, Zilinsky and Payer[396] spoke against the pact. The only ones who spoke in favor were the Imredy and Nazi groups. No one in the Government Party said a word, and they seemed more sympathetic with the objectors than with the Imredy and Nazi groups. Imredy's argument was that the Government should have adhered to the pact long ago and then they would have gotten the whole of Transylvania.

In the Upper House the only one who spoke in favor of the pact was Ottlik.[397] Bethlen, Szullo[398] and Baron Pronay[399] spoke against it. The details of happenings in the Upper House will be given me by Bethlen next week.

Csaky in addressing the Lower House seemed subdued and not very cocky. He admitted that one of the great dangers of the pact was its effect in America because he thought that the friendship of America would be very important after the war.

Teleki did not appear in the Lower House, but he did in the Upper. He, however, did not say a word but looked down all the time and gave the impression that he was rather ashamed.

Csaky, incidentally, for the first time read his whole speech and his replies. They apparently having been gone over by Teleki in advance. In Csaky's speech he said that the situation in the Balkans had improved and that nothing would happen here and gave assurances that Hungary would not be in the war under any circumstances. Otherwise, his speech is substantially as reported in the papers.

---

396 Endre Bajcsy-Zsilinszky (1886–1944), anti-Nazi politician, MP; Károly Peyer (1881–1956), leader of the Social Democrats.
397 György Ottlik.
398 Géza Szüllő (1873–1957).
399 Baron György Prónay (1887–1968), retired secretary of state, member of the Upper House.

Incidentally, my informant told me that the Hungarian Government was in no way bound by the pact since the Hungarian constitution provided ratification by Parliament. Therefore, the present Government were bound so long as they were in office, but Hungary itself was not bound. He didn't know why the Germans had overlooked this since it was very plain in the constitution, unless it was because they did not like to be put in a position of asking Parliament to approve something when they are against Parliamentary procedure.

[179] Conversation with Mr. de Kanya

Budapest, December 18, 1940

Mr. de Kanya told me yesterday that there had actually never been any demand on the part of Germany to put troops in terminals and stations. It was merely a tentative suggestion that such permission would facilitate the movement of troops, more in the nature of a sounding with a view to seeing whether the Hungarian Government was still as determined to refuse as before. There was no indication given that it was to be immediate.

Mr. de Kanya said he had seen a number of people connected with the Government and had discussed matters with them, and as far as he could find out, there is not the slightest thing to indicate that the Germans had any idea of a movement in this direction in the near future. It looked to him as though they were beginning to get worried about England and that their main concentration for the moment was on the possibility of invasion. He did not believe they intended to go to Italy's aid or occupy any more countries until the question of invasion was settled either by making an attempt or concluding that it was impossible. The Germans were now saying that the war would not be won in Egypt but in Britain. The fact that Britain had not been conquered was becoming more embarrassing to the German Government every day in view of their repeated declarations. He believed that the Germans were discovering that the occupation of countries against their will had its disadvantages and he did not believe they would at this period of the war think of making any offensive which required taking in more territory.

The Italian debacle was a calamity for Hungary since Italy was her main supporter and since she could more or less balance between the two her position was not so bad. With Italy's poor showing[400] the situation vis-a-vis Germany was very much different.

Mr. de Kanya's information was to the effect that the Italians were now

---

400 In the Italian-Greek war.

blaming everything on Ciano. He had heard that Ciano was supposed to have said in reference to the Greek war that this was his war. Mr. de Kanya said the idea that Ciano could start a war on his own was fantastic to anyone who knew the situation at that time. Nothing could happen without Mussolini's approval. He thought that these stories were being circulated with the idea of throwing Ciano overboard. He was very much afraid that the whole regime would go, and what he feared especially was what would follow.

[180] Conversation with Baron Ullmann

Budapest, December 19, 1940

Baron Ullmann[401] called on me yesterday and told me that the control of the Credit Bank was in danger because the stock held by the Schneider Munitions Corporation was about to be taken over by the Dresdener Bank. He said that while this block of stock was only a small percent of the total holdings of the stock outstanding, nevertheless being a solid block (whereas the other stock ownership was widespread) it could have a great deal to say in the management of the Bank, if not control. As the Credit Bank itself controls industries which constitute practically 45% of the industrial life of Hungary and through which ever village and hamlet in Hungary is reached, should the Germans obtain this stock they would be in a position to have indirect control of all these companies and institutions as well as to put Germans into the management of all these various companies.

He said there was a certain amount of stock held in England and a little while back he had gone to the British Minister and suggested that the British Treasury take control of this stock and appoint someone in Hungary as their agent. This had been done. However, should the Schneider stock be sold the British holdings were not sufficient to checkmate them without help from the Hungarian Government. If the Government were willing to influence shareholders in Hungary then the Hungarian stock plus the British stock could completely control the Bank, but not only was the Government at the present time unwilling to make the slightest gesture in that direction but they would even be frightened of the suggestion. The President of the Credit Bank, Dr. Fabinyi,[402] was utterly paralyzed with fright and could not be induced to make any sort of move.

---

401 Baron György Ullmann, executive director of Magyar Általános Hitelbank (General Credit Bank of Hungary).

402 Dr. Tihamér Fabinyi (1890–1953), lawyer, minister of finance 1935–38, member of the Upper House, president of Magyar Általános Hitelbank [General Credit Bank of Hungary] 1938–44.

The manner in which the Germans are about to acquire the stock is interesting and has a bearing on Baron Ullmann's errand to me. The managing director of the Schneider company is a prisoner in German hands. He was recently taken to Berlin under armed guard and there was introduced to sign a bill of sale transferring the stock in the Credit Bank to the Dresdener Bank in exchange for Marks (the kind issued for France). On the strength of this they tried to obtain the stock from the Schneider company but have not yet actually obtained possession of the shares since Marshall Petain[403] has refused to approve the sale.

Baron Ullmann's hope now is that the Marshall will continue to hold out and with that in mind he was anxious that our Government do something to strengthen the Marshal's hand. If this could not be done he was anxious at least to get word to the Hungarian Minister at Vichy, Count Khuen-Hedervary, whom he thought might do something. I told him that such a request coming from the Regent, the Prime Minister or the Foreign Minister, or any official, I could transmit but I couldn't see how I could do so from a private citizen. He then wondered if it would be sufficient if the President of the National Bank asked me because he said he wouldn't dare to go near Count Teleki because he knew not only would Teleki do nothing but he would be furious with him. He wouldn't go to the Regent because the Prime Minister would get mad when he heard about it, and probably would take it out on him. Therefore, the only person he would dare approach would be the President of the National Bank.

---

403 Marshal Henri-Philippe Pétain (1856–1951), French "head of state " of the German puppet regime of the "Vichy republic."

1941

[181] Conversation with Foreign Minister Bardossy

Budapest, February 13, 1941

László Bárdossy, March 28, 1941

Mr. Bardossy told me how sorry he was that I was leaving since we were old friends and he had hoped that we could work well together and he knew we would. I told him I understood that the Foreign Office had been instrumental in getting me home. He said he had heard the story, but, so far as he knew, there was no truth whatever in such a story. He said that he had made an investigation in the Foreign Office and if there was any request or intimation of that kind it did not appear on the records and nobody in the Foreign Office knew anything about it at all. I said, "Maybe Csaky did it himself. He often did things that other people knew nothing about." He said, "Of course, he might, but how could he? He would have to write to the Minister in Washington." I told him that I thought it might possibly have been done through another diplomat who came here, and he said he thought it was funny that anyone would pay attention to a request made in such a manner, but if it had been done at all he was glad that it was done that way since it would mean that an American was also involved and not only a Hungarian. He had lots to say about Csaky, uncomplimentary, and repeated what Ullein told me a few days ago, that he thought Csaky's mind had been affected by his illness. While we were talking about Csaky, the Prime Minister came up and said "What are you fellows so deep in conversation about?" and Bardossy replied, "We were just panning Csaky," whereupon Teleki said "Oh," and nothing else.

Memorandum for the Minister:

Please endeavor to obtain information from the Russian Minister as to whether he will be able to extend any special and urgent passport facilities for American citizens should occasion arise for us to leave via Russia. We desire this information not only for diplomatic officers and fasmilies, but also other Americans, including American newspaper correspondents.

HKT/w[404]

[182] Conversation with Prime Minister Count Teleki

Budapest, February 13, 1941

Count Teleki told me at lunch the other day that every morning when he got up he pinched himself to see if he was still here, and then he said, "Well, thank God, another 24 hours have gone by and nothing has happened." Every 24 hours, he said, that passed by was just that much gained. He had no idea what was going to happen. He wouldn't be surprised at anything. He couldn't see any use of having a lot of theories as to whether the Germans would take over the country or what they would do. He just had to be prepared for the worst, and if it didn't happen he would be grateful.

I told him that I understood the German Minister was calling on the Regent and I supposed he must want something. He replied, "Want something? They want something all the time. Not a day goes by but von Erdmannsdorff doesn't call on somebody and want something." He refused 90% of all requests but he always had to give him something, so little by little they get more and more. If the war lasts long enough they will gradually get everything except, we hope, there will be something left when the war finishes, although they may come some day and take the rest in one gulp. However,

---

404 Dictated by Howard K. Travers to "w."

Opening the session of the Hungarian Parliament,
June 15, 1939:
Minister Montgomery arrives at Kossuth Lajos Square
with his daughter, Ms. Jean Riddell

they were as diligent as they could be in putting up as stiff a resistance as possible. For example, he said, about two weeks ago they had trouble getting enough engines, or possibly there was engine trouble he said. Anyhow when the troops got to the border there was no engine to pull the train, so the commander proposed that they unload their equipment, get in it, and go on to Rumania that way. The Hungarian officer in charge told him that he was sorry, but his instructions were to let the trains through but not troops and if they started to walk the troops the Hungarian frontier guards would have to fire on them no matter what happened. That was the orders they had. Teleki said this officer was on very good terms with the Germans and told them in a nice way. Nevertheless, they waited for the train and didn't try to march across. He said this was an illustration that they did go to extremes if necessary to protect their sovereignty, but that they were always compelled to make concessions and couldn't refuse everything. Now and then they had to give them something, but as they made so many requests and were always after the same thing over and over again it was a difficult situation.

He told me emphatically that the story that he had made any request in connection with me was absolutely untrue, and he couldn't understand how such a thing could have originated, that he was terribly sorry to see me go as he considered me one of his oldest friends and a good friend of Hungary.

APPENDIX

CHRONOLOGY OF EVENTS
1933–1941

1933

January 30:	Adolf Hitler becomes chancellor of Germany
February 4:	Kálmán Kánya appointed Hungarian foreign minister
February 27:	Reichstag fire
March 4:	Franklin D. Roosevelt 32nd President of the United States; New Deal starts
March 19:	Rome Pact signed by Italy, Britain, France, and Germany
March 27:	Japan leaves League of Nations
May 12:	Federal Emergency Relief Administration provides $500 million for victims of U.S. depression
May 13:	Hungarian prime minister Gyula Gömbös distances himself from Hungarian National Socialist movement in Parliament
May 18:	Tennessee Valley Authority established for comprehensive redevelopment of Tennessee Valley region
June 15:	Organization of Hungarian National Union Party (NEP) starts
June 17:	Gyula Gömbös visits Adolf Hitler in Berlin
July 13:	Extension of prerogatives of regent of Hungary (Act XXIIII:1933)
July 23–26:	Prime Minister Gömbös and Foreign Minister Kánya visit Mussolini in Rome
September 14–16:	Kálmán Kánya's visit to Paris
October 14:	Germany leaves disarmament conference and League of Nations
November 16:	U.S. provides diplomatic recognition to Soviet Union
December 5:	Amendment XXI abolishes prohibition in U.S.

1934

January 14:	Prime Minister Gömbös openly criticizes Hungarian National Socialist leader Count Sándor Festetics
January 26:	German-Polish treaty of friendship and non-aggression
February 6:	Soviet-Hungarian diplomatic relations established
February 7:	Austrian chancellor Dollfuss discusses potential Austrian–Hungarian–Italian alliance in Budapest

February 9:	Balkan Pact (an alliance of Yugoslavia, Romania, Turkey, and Greece) signed in Athens to maintain European status quo
February 17:	Great Britain, France, and Italy declare necessity to maintain the sovereignty and territorial integrity of Austria
March 17:	Rome Protocol on political and economic cooperation of Italy, Austria, and Hungary
April 4:	Romanian prime minister Titulescu sharply attacks Rome Protocol of March 17
April 24:	Tibor Eckhardt withdraws in Parliament from demanding universal suffrage and secret ballot
May:	Eckhardt and Gömbös agree on Smallholders' Party supporting the prime minister vis-à-vis Count István Bethlen
June 14:	Austrian chancellor Dollfuss visits Budapest
July 25:	Nazi coup in Vienna, Dollfuss murdered
August 2:	Field Marshal Paul von Hindenburg, president of Germany, dies
August 10:	Austrian chancellor Schuschnigg visits Budapest
August 19:	Hitler asserts personal rule, becomes Führer of Germany
September 18:	Soviet Union enters League of Nations
October 9:	Murder in Marseille: Alexander I, king of Yugoslavia, and French foreign minister Louis Barthou assassinated
October 20:	Gömbös discusses anti-Czechoslovak cooperation in Warsaw
November 6, 8:	Gömbös negotiates with Mussolini in Rome and with Schuschnigg on the Semmering
December 5:	Franco-Soviet agreement on an "Eastern Locarno"

1935

January 13:	Plebiscite returns Saar to Germany
February 8:	Hungarian Communist Mátyás Rákosi sentenced to lifelong prison term
March 15:	Hitler repudiates military restrictions imposed by Treaty of Versailles and restores conscription in Germany
April 6–7:	Parliamentary elections in Hungary
April 11:	Victorious Entente powers (Great Britain, France, and Italy) declare common front against Germany in Stresa
May 4:	Foreign ministers of Italy, Austria, and Hungary negotiate in Venice; Kálmán Kánya rejects plan of a Danubian Pact
May 24:	Prussian prime minister Hermann Göring visits Budapest
June 18:	In Anglo-German naval agreement, Germany agrees that her navy will not exceed one-third of tonnage of Royal Navy
August 14:	Social Security Act in U.S.

September 15:	Nuremberg Laws give a racial definiton of Jews, and prohibit marriage and sexual relation between Jews and Gentiles
October 2:	Italian troops invade Ethiopia
October 20:	Tibor Eckhardt calls for cooperation against dictatorial tendencies of Prime Minister Gyula Gömbös
October 24:	Count István Bethlen attacks Gyula Gömbös and his government in Parliament
November 28:	Prime Minister Gömbös and Foreign Minister Kánya confer in Vienna
December 13:	Eduard Beneš follows Tomáš G. Masaryk as president of Czechoslovakia

1936

January 1:	In a newspaper declaration on New Year's Day, Count István Bethlen calls upon opposition to fight against dictatorship
February 16:	Popular Front wins elections in Spain
March 7:	German troops enter Rhineland, demilitarized by the Treaty of Versailles
March 11:	Unpublished in Hungarian press, Horthy greets Hitler on occasion of remilitarization of Rhineland
March 13–14:	Austrian chancellor Kurt von Schuschnigg discusses relationship of Austria and Hungary to Little Entente in Budapest
March 21–24:	Italian, Austrian, and Hungarian prime ministers and foreign ministers confer in Rome, signing 2nd Treaty of Rome
April 3:	Austria discontinues obeying military clauses of Treaty of St. Germain and introduces universal conscription
April 22:	Foreign Minister Kánya declares to German, Italian, and Polish governments that Hungary wishes to reestablish her military parity
May 9:	Annexation of Ethiopia by Italy
June 6–8:	Meeting of Supreme Council of Little Entente in Bucharest
June 11:	German foreign minister Baron von Neurath in Budapest
July 17–18:	Spanish Civil War starts
August 1–16:	Olympic games in Berlin: a propaganda success for Nazi Germany
August 22:	Regent Miklós Horthy visits Hitler at Berchtesgaden
August 24:	Germany introduces compulsory conscription
September 19:	Foreign Minister von Neurath visits Budapest again
October 6:	Prime Minister Gyula Gömbös dies in Munich, the government resigns
October 10:	Italian foreign minister Count Ciano, Prussian prime minister Göring, and Austrian chancellor Schuschnigg arrive in Budapest for the funeral of Gömbös; new Hungarian goverment formed by Kálmán Darányi
October 17:	Count István Bethlen calls for a fight against dictatorships at memorial dinner of Ferenc Deák Society

November 1:	Mussolini proclaims Rome-Berlin Axis
November 3:	Franklin Delano Roosevelt reelected
November 13:	Italian foreign minister Count Ciano visits Budapest to prepare visit of Regent Horthy to Rome
November 18:	Germany and Italy acknowledge government of Franco in Spain
November 23:	Regent Horthy, accompanied by Prime Minister Darányi and Foreign Minister Kánya, visits Rome
November 24:	Germany and Japan sign Anti-Comintern Pact
December 1:	Pan-American Congress opens in Buenos Aires; President Roosevelt introduces his peace program; Regent Horthy arrives in Vienna

1937

January 20:	Inauguration of F. D. Roosevelt
January 21:	Yugoslav initiative for Yugoslav-Hungarian treaty of friendship
January 22:	Czechoslovak and Romanian initiatives for treaty of non-aggression with Hungary; Foreign Minister Kánya refuses both proposals
January 23:	Hungary's answer to the Yugoslav initiative is positive, provided that a number of preconditions are met
March 14:	*Mit brennender Sorge:* encyclical by Pope Pius XI condems persecution of the Catholic Church in Germany
March 31:	Yugoslavia rejects the Hungarian proposals of January 23
April 6:	German minister von Mackensen pays farewell visit to regent of Hungary after alleged involvement in attempted coup
April 15:	Budapest police take Ferenc Szálasi, leader of National Socialist Party of the National Will, into custody
April 23:	Ferenc Szálasi sentenced to three months in prison
May 1:	President Roosevelt signs U.S. Neutrality Act
May 3:	Austrian president Miklas in Budapest
May 19–22:	King Victor Emanuel III of Italy and queen visit Hungary
June 14:	In his address at Szentgotthárd, Tibor Eckhardt, leader of Smallholders' Party, speaks out against planned extension of prerogative of regent
July 1:	Lower house of the Hungarian Parliament unanimously accepts extension of regent's prerogative
July 7:	Japan attacks China without declaration of war
September 2:	Wagner-Steagall Act to ease housing shortage in U.S.
September 14:	Hungarian government recognizes Franco government
September 21:	Hungarian defense minister Vilmos Rőder visits Berlin, accompanied by commander-in-chief and chief of staff

September 25–29:	Mussolini visits Hitler
October 1:	Field Marshall Pietro Badoglio, Italian chief of staff, in Budapest
October 23:	Austrian chancellor Schuschnigg in Budapest
November 6:	Italy joins Anti-Comintern Pact
November 20–29:	Hungarian prime minister Darányi and foreign minister Kánya on official visit to Germany
November 29:	Ferenc Szálasi sentenced to ten months in prison
December 11:	Italy leaves League of Nations; Hungarian defense minister Vilmos Rőder visits Rome

1938

January 9:	Signatories to Agreement of Rome meet in Budapest
February 4:	Joachim von Ribbentrop appointed foreign minister of Germany; German armed forces placed under personal control of Hitler
February 4-10:	Regent Horthy, accompanied by Hungarian prime minister and foreign minister, visits Poland to discuss "horizontal axis" of Poland, Hungary, Yugoslavia, and Italy
February 10:	Address by Count István Bethlen in Hungarian Parliament: opposes solution of Jewish question and reorganization of political life along German lines
March 2:	Hungarian foreign minister Kánya in Vienna
March 12:	German troops invade Austria
March 13:	Anschluß: Austria declared part of German Reich
April 3:	Radio address of Regent Horthy: *Anschluß* does not jeopardize independence of Hungary
April 15:	Letter by President Roosevelt to Hitler and Mussolini on protection of 31 nations against aggression
April 24:	Germans in Sudetenland demand full autonomy
May 11:	Regent Horthy visits Adolf Hitler in Kiel to participate at exercise of German fleet
May 12:	Darányi government steps down
May 14:	Béla Imrédy appointed prime minister of Hungary
May 25:	Eucharistic Congress starts in Budapest
May 29:	1st Jew Bill (XV:1938) declared
June 14:	General Wilhelm Keitel, head of German armed forces, visits Budapest
July 6:	Ferenc Szálasi sentenced to three years in prison
August 20–26:	Regent Horthy, accompanied by Hungarian prime minister, foreign minister, and minister of defense, visits Germany
August 20–29:	Conference of Little Entente countries and Hungary in Bled (Yugoslavia)

September 15:	Hitler-Chamberlain meeting in Berchtesgaden
September 20:	Hungarian prime minister Imrédy and foreign minister Kánya in Germany
September 22:	Hitler meets Chamberlain in Bad Godesberg
September 29–30:	Munich Agreement attaches Sudetenland to Germany
October 5:	President Beneš of Czechoslovakia resigns
November 2:	First Vienna Award: southern Slovakia returned to Hungary
November 9–10:	*Kristallnacht:* pogrom in Germany
November 28:	Foreign Minister Kálmán Kánya resigns
	(in office since February 4, 1933)
December 10:	Count István Csáky appointed Hungarian foreign minister
December 19:	Italian foreign minister Count Ciano visits Budapest

1939

February 3:	Arrowcross bombing at the synagogue in Dohány utca, Budapest
February 15:	Prime minister Béla Imrédy resigns, as demanded by regent
February 16:	Count Pál Teleki appointed prime minister of Hungary
February 24:	Hungary joins Anti-Comintern Pact
February 25:	Hungarist Movement as well as Hungarist Party outlawed by Hungarian interior minister
March 8:	Foundation of Arrowcross Party officially announced in Hungary
March 14:	Father Jozef Tiso declares establishment of an independent Republic of Slovakia
March 15:	German troops invade Bohemia and Moravia, Hungarian troops start retaking sub-Carpathian region
April 11:	Hungary leaves League of Nations
April:	*The Grapes of Wrath* by John Steinbeck published
May 5:	2nd Jew Bill (IV:1939) announced
June:	King George VI and Queen Elizabeth visit President Roosevelt
July 24:	Prime Minister Teleki tells Hitler and Mussolini that Hungary does not intend to engage in war against Poland
August 8:	Hungarian foreign minister Count Csáky visits Hitler at Berchtesgaden
August 18:	Csáky confers in Rome
August 19:	Tibor Eckhardt reelected as leader of Smallholders' Party (head of party since 1932)
August 23:	Ribbentrop-Molotov Pact: German-Soviet non-aggression treaty
September 1:	German attack on Poland
September 3:	British and French declaration of war on Germany

September 5:   U.S. declares neutrality

September 28:   Warsaw taken by Germans

September 30:   Partition of Poland and establishment of the new German-Soviet borders; all British expeditionary forces in France

November 3:   Cash and Carry: President Roosevelt modifies Neutrality Act of May 1937, allowing Britain and France to purchase American weapons

November 30:   Soviet Union invades Finland ("Winter War")

1940

January 5–7:   Csáky and Ciano confer in Venice

January 17:   Tibor Eckhardt resigns, Zoltán Tildy elected acting chairman of Smallholders' Party

March 12:   Peace Treaty of Moscow signed: Finnish territory ceded to Soviet Union

March 17:   Prime Minister Pál Teleki deposits $5 million in U.S. to establish a Hungarian government-in-exile (withdrawn)

March-May: Murder at Katyn: mass execution of captured Polish officers by Soviets

May 10:   Germany attacks Netherlands, Belgium, and Luxembourg; Winston Churchill replaces Neville Chamberlain as British prime minister

May 12:   German attack on France

May 29–June 3:   Evacuation of British troops from Dunkerque

June-September: Battle of Britain

June 10:   Italian declaration of war on Britain and France

June 14:   German troops enter Paris

June 16:   Marshall Pétain becomes French prime minister

June 17–23:   Soviet Union occupies Baltic states

June 18:   General Charles de Gaulle establishes French National Committee of Resistance in London

June 22:   French armistice signed at Compiègne

June 27:   Soviet troops invade Bessarabia

July 1:   New French government formed at Vichy

July 10:   Marshal Pétain "head of the French state;" Teleki and Csáky confer with Hitler in Munich

August 2:   Bessarabia annexed by Soviet Union

August 3:   Baltic states annexed by Soviet Union

August 23:   Beginning of Blitz: German terror bombing of British cities

August 30:   Second Vienna Award: northern Transylvania returned to Hungary

September 16:   Selective Service Act in U.S.; Ferenc Szálasi amnestied in Hungary

September 27: Germany, Italy, and Japan sign Tripartite Agreement in Berlin

October 21: Former Hungarian prime minister Béla Imrédy announces establishment of Party of Hungarian Renewal

October 28: Italy invades Greece

November 5: Franklin D. Roosevelt elected U.S. president for third term

November 12: Soviet foreign minister Vyacheslav Molotov in Berlin

November 20: Hungary joins Tripartite Agreement

December 12: Hungarian-Yugoslav "treaty of eternal friendship" concluded in Belgrade

1941

January 27: Hungarian foreign minister Count István Csáky dies

February 4: Diplomat László Bárdossy appointed foreign minister

March 7: Tibor Eckhardt leaves for U.S. with a political mission (arriving on August 8, 1941)

March 11: U.S. Congress votes for Lend-Lease Act

April 2: German army starts invading Yugoslavia through Hungary

April 3: Hungarian prime minister Count Pál Teleki commits suicide, Foreign Minister László Bárdossy appointed prime minister

April 6: Germany attacks Yugoslavia and Greece

April 17: Yugoslavia surrenders

April 18: Vichy government leaves League of Nations

May 27: National state of emergency in U.S.

June 22: Germany invades Soviet Union

June 26: Hungary declares state of war with Soviet Union

August 14: Atlantic Charter: Roosevelt and Churchill declare common peace terms

December 7: Pearl Harbor: Japan attacks the U.S.; state of war exists between Great Britain and Hungary

December 8: U.S. declares war on Japan

December 11: Germany and Italy declare war on U.S.

December 12: Hungary declares state of war with U.S.

BIOGRAPHICAL NOTES

ACKERSON, Garret G. (?-?), U.S. diplomat, 2nd secretary of U.S. legation in Budapest.

ALBRECHT, Archduke (1897–1955), pro-Nazi member of the Habsburg family in Hungary, cooperated with the Hungarian Arrowcross movement and acted as informer for the SS during World War II.

ALEXANDER I (1888–1934), king of Yugoslavia 1921–34, murdered in Marseille.

APOR, Gábor, Baron (18891969), Hungarian diplomat, permanent deputy of foreign minister after 1935, minister to Holy See from 1939.

BAKACH-BESSENYEY, György, Baron (1892–1959), Hungarian diplomat, head of political section of foreign ministry 1934–38, subsequently minister to Belgrade (1938–41), Vichy (1941–43), and Bern (1943–44).

BÁRDOSSY, László (1890–1946), Hungarian diplomat and politician, minister to Bucharest 1934–41, foreign minister 1941–42, prime minister 1941–42, executed as a war criminal.

BENEŠ, Eduard (1884–1948), foreign minister of Czechoslovakia 1918–35 (and prime minister 1921–23), president of Czechoslovakia 1935–38, 1946–48.

BETHLEN, István, Count (1874–1946), Transylvanian landowner and Hungarian statesman, prime minister 1921–31.

BLOMBERG, Werner Eduard Fritz von (1878–1947) German general, field marshal from 1936, minister of war 1933–38.

BOSSY, Raoul (1894–?), Romanian minister to Budapest 1936–39, and Berlin 1941–43.

CAROL (Charles) II (1893–1953), king of Romania 1930–40, son of Ferdinand I. Forced to abdicate because of his relationship with Madame (Magda) Lupescu in 1925. Returned in 1930, proclaimed his dictatorship in 1938, and founded Front of National Resurrection under his own leadership. Forced to abdicate again in 1940 for his son, Mihai (Michael); went into exile.

CHAMBERLAIN, Arthur Neville (1869–1940), British statesman, son of Joseph Chamberlain, half-brother of Sir Austen Chamberlain, Conservative MP 1918–40, member of several British governments 1922–37, prime minister 1937–40. Leading figure in policy of appeasement vis-à-vis Nazi Germany.

CHORIN, Ferenc, Jr., Dr. (1879–1964), Hungarian industrialist, general manager, later chairman of coal-mining plant Salgótarjáni Kőszénbánya Rt, president of Federation of Hungarian Industrialists (GYOSZ) 1928–42, member of Upper House of Hungarian Parliament.

CIANO, Galeazzo, Count (1903–1944), Italian Fascist leader, son-in-law of Benito Mussolini, foreign minister 1936–43, executed for rebelling against the Duce.

COLONNA, Ascanio Prince (1883–?), Italian diplomat, minister to Stockholm and Budapest (1932–36), ambassador to Washington.

CRUŢESCU, Gheorghe (1890–1950), Romanian minister to Budapest 1939–41.

CSÁKY, István, Count (1894–1941), Hungarian diplomat, chief of cabinet of foreign minister 1935–38, foreign minister 1938–41.

DARÁNYI, Kálmán (1886–1939), Hungarian politician, lord lieutenant, minister of agriculture 1935–38, prime minister 1936–38, speaker of the House 1938–39.

DOLLFUSS, Engelbert (1892–1934), Austrian Conservative statesman, leader of Christian Socialist Party, minister of agriculture 1931–32, chancellor 1932–34, murdered by Nazis.

ECKHARDT, Tibor, Dr. (1888–1972), Hungarian politician, lawyer, MP, founding president of *Ébredő Magyarok Egyesülete* [Union of Awakening Hungarians] 1923–, leader of Hungarian National Independence Party (Defenders of the Race), acting vice-president of *Magyar Revíziós Líga* [Hungarian Revisionist League] from 1928, chairman of Smallholders' Party 1932–1940, Hungary's permanent delegate to League of Nations; left Hungary for United States in 1941.

EDEN, Sir Anthony (1897–1977), British MP after 1923, minister for League of Nations affairs 1935, foreign minister 1935–38, 1940–45, 1951–55, prime minister 1955–57.

GÖRING [Goering], Hermann (1893–1946), German Nazi politician, president of the Reichstag, Prussian minister of interior, Prussian prime minister, head of Luftwaffe, the German air force, *Reichsmarschall*; committed suicide in Nürnberg.

GÖMBÖS, Gyula (1886–1936), Hungarian officer and statesman, captain in the general staff, chairman of Hungarian National Defense Union (MOVE), leader of Hungarian National Independence Party (Defenders of the Race) 1923–28, army general after 1930, minister of defense 1929–36, prime minister 1932–36.

GRIGORCEA, Vasile (1883–1949), Romanian diplomat, minister to Budapest (1928–36), later London.

HABSBURG, Otto von, Dr. (b. 1912–), archduke and royal Hungarian prince, heir to throne of Austria-Hungary, son of Charles IV, King of Hungary (= Charles I as Emperor of Austria).

HITLER, Adolf (1889–1945), leader of German National Socialist Workers' Party 1920–1945, dictator of Germany 1933–45, chancellor 1933–34, "Führer and Chancellor" 1934–45.

HODŽA, Milan (1878–1944), MP in Hungarian Parliament 1905–18, member of Czechoslovak Parliament 1918–38, Czechoslovak prime minister 1935–38.

HÓMAN, Bálint (1885–1951), historian, director, subsequently president of Hungarian National Museum, university professor of history, member of Hungarian Academy of Sciences, minister of religion and education 1932–38, 1939–42.

HORTHY, Miklós (1868–1957), Hungarian naval officer and statesman, aide-de-camp of Emperor-King Franz Joseph I 1909–1914, vice-admiral and last commander-in-chief of Austro-Hungarian navy. Regent of Hungary 1920–44.

HORY, András (1883–1971), Hungarian diplomat, minister to Belgrade (1924–27), Rome (1927–33), later Warsaw (1935–39), permanent deputy of foreign minister 1934–35.

IMRÉDY, Béla (1891–1946), director and later president of Hungarian National Bank, minister of finance 1932–35, prime minister 1938–39, minister without portfolio for economic affairs 1944, executed as a war criminal.

KÁLLAY, Miklós (1887–1967), lord lieutenant, minister of agriculture 1932–35, foreign minister 1942–43, prime minister 1942–44.

KÁNYA, Kálmán (1869–1945), Austro-Hungarian minister to Mexico 1913–19, general secretary of Hungarian foreign ministry 1920–25, Hungarian minister to Berlin 1925–33, foreign minister 1933–38.

KERESZTES-FISCHER, Ferenc (1881–1948), lawyer in Pécs, lord lieutenant of county of Baranya, city of Pécs, later county of Somogy, interior minister 1931–35, 1938–44.

Kobr, Miloš (?–?), Czechoslovak minister to Budapest 1933–39.

MACKENSEN, Hans Georg von (1883–1947), son of Field Marshal August von Mackensen and son-in-law of German foreign minister von Neurath. German minister to Budapest 1933–36, secretary of state for foreign affairs 1936–38, ambassador to Rome 1938–43.

MALAGOLA Cappi, Count (?–?), Italian diplomat.

MANIU, Iuliu (1873-1953), Romanian politician, member of Hungarian Parliament 1906–10, leader of Romanian National Peasant Party after 1926, prime minister 1928–30 and 1932–33.

MUSSOLINI, Benito (1883–1945), Italian Fascist leader, prime minister 1922–1943, dictator of Italy as the Duce.

NEURATH, Konstantin Freiherr von (1873–1956), German diplomat, ambassador to Rome (1922–30) and London (1930–32), foreign minister 1932–38. *Reichsprotektor* of Bohemia and Moravia after German occupation of Czechoslovakia.

ORŁOWSKI, Leon (1891–1976), Polish diplomat, minister to Budapest 1936–40, went into exile in U.S.

OTTLIK, György (1889–1966), Hungarian diplomat, journalist, associate member of Hungarian delegation to League of Nations 1927–34, editor of *Budapesti Hírlap* (1934–35), *La Nouvelle Revue de Hongrie* (1935–39), and *Pester Lloyd* (1937–44).

PAUL, Prince (1893–1976), regent of Yugoslavia 1934–41

ROSENBERG, Alfred (1893–1946), German Nazi politician, editor of Nazi Party paper *Völkischer Beobachter,* author of racist *Der Mythus des 20. Jahrhunderts; Reichsminister* responsible for occupied eastern territories during World War II.

SCHUSCHNIGG, Kurt von (1897–1977), Austrian statesman, minister of justice (1932), subsequently of education (1933), in Dollfuss government; chancellor of Austria 1934–38.

SZÁLASI, Ferenc (1897–1946), Hungarian army officer in the general staff, leader of Arrowcross Party from 1940, imprisoned between 1938–40, "Leader of the Nation" after October 15, 1944, executed as a war crimial.

TELEKI, Pál, Count (1879–1941), Hungarian geographer, cartographer, and statesman; university professor of geography, member of Hungarian Academy of Sciences, member of several Hungarian governments; prime minister of Hungary 1920–21, 1939–41; committed suicide.

TISO, Josef (1887–1947), leader of Slovak People's Party, Slovak prime minister 1938–39, subsequently president 1939–45, executed as a war criminal.

TITULESCU, Nicolae (1883–1941), Romanian diplomat, foreign minister 1927–28, 1932–36.

TRAVERS, Howard Karl (1893–1976), U.S. diplomat, 1st secretary of U.S. legation in Budapest.

VÖRNLE, János (1890–?), Hungarian diplomat, permanent deputy of foreign minister 1938–41, minister to Ankara 1941–1944.

DIPLOMATIC REPRESENTATIVES
IN BUDAPEST
1933–1941

(Dates indicate Letter of Credence presented)

Argentina   *(formerly in Berlin)*
Eduardo LABOUGLE
    Envoy Extraordinary and Minister Plenipotentiary
    (August 20, 1932)
Félipe CHIAPPE
    Chargé d'Affaires ad interim
    (1938–39)
José Manuel LLOLBET
    Envoy Extraordinary and Minister Plenipotentiary
    (March 7, 1939)

Austria   Baron Leopold HENNET
    Envoy Extraordinary and Minister Plenipotentiary
    (November 10, 1932)
Baron Odo NEUSTÄDTER-STÜRMER
    Envoy Extraordinary and Minister Plenipotentiary
    (February-November 1936)
Eduard BAAR-BAARENFELS
    Envoy Extraordinary and Minister Plenipotentiary
    (January 4, 1937–March 13, 1938)

Belgium   Count Jacques de LALAING
    Envoy Extraordinary and Minister Plenipotentiary
    (April 2, 1935–1941)

Brazil   *(Residence formerly in Vienna)*
Souza-Leao S. de GRACIE
    Envoy Extraordinary and Minister Plenipotentiary
    (October 15, 1935)
Octavio FIALHO
    Envoy Extraordinary and Minister Plenipotentiary
    (May 2, 1939)

Bulgaria   Ivan POPOV
    Chargé d'Affaires ad interim
    (October 9, 1933)
Stoil C. STOILOV
    Chargé d'Affaires, subsequently
    Envoy Extraordinary and Minister Plenipotentiary
    (April 28, 1935)

Dimitru TOSHEV
Envoy Extraordinary and Minister Plenipotentiary
(May 11, 1940)

Chíle *(residence formerly in Vienna)*
Don Ricardo AHUMADA
Chargé d'Affaires ad interim
(1935–36)
Fernando Garcia OLDINI
Minister Resident
(May 30, 1936)
Enrique SERRANO
(1941–43)

Croatia Ivo de GAJ
Envoy Extraordinary and Minister Plenipotentiary
(March 10, 1942–1944)
Alfred RUKARINA
Chargé d'Affaires ad interim
(1944)

Czechoslovakia Miloš KOBR
Envoy Extraordinary and Minister Plenipotentiary
(April 20, 1933–March 15, 1939)

Denmark
and Iceland *(residence in Rome)*
J. C. W. KRUSE
Envoy Extraordinary and Minister Plenipotentiary
(February 23, 1933)
Otto WADSTED
Envoy Extraordinary and Minister Plenipotentiary
(February 28, 1940)
L. B. BOLT-JÖRGENSEN
Envoy Extraordinary and Minister Plenipotentiary
(October 20, 1941–1944)

Egypt Ahmed KADRY EL Bey
Envoy Extraordinary and Minister Plenipotentiary
(February 3, 1936)
Dr. Mourad SID AHMED Pacha
Minister
Mohamed Soliman EL HOUT bey
Chargé d'Affaires
Abdel Kerim SAFWAT
Chargé d'Affaires
(April 13, 1940–1942)

Estonia Jaan MÖLDER
  Chargé d'Affaires ad interim
  (1935)
  Richard JOFFERT
  Chargé d'Affaires ad interim
  (1936–1937)
  Johann LEPPIK
  Envoy Extraordinary and Minister Plenipotentiary
  (May 24, 1937)

Finland Onni TALAS
  Envoy Extraordinary and Minister Plenipotentiary
  (March 13, 1931)
  Aarne WUORIMAA
  Envoy Extraordinary and Minister Plenipotentiary
  (July 8, 1940–1944)

France Louis de VIENNE
  Envoy Extraordinary and Minister Plenipotentiary
  (1927)
  Gaston MAUGRAS
  Envoy Extraordinary and Minister Plenipotentiary
  (December 10, 1934)
  Pierre GUERLET
  Envoy Extraordinary and Minister Plenipotentiary
  (January 28, 1939)
  Count Robert de DAMPIERRE
  Envoy Extraordinary and Minister Plenipotentiary
  (September 11, 1940)
  Christian de CHARMASSE
  Envoy Extraordinary and Minister Plenipotentiary
  (1943)
  Jules BRÉVIÉ
  Envoy Extraordinary and Minister Plenipotentiary
  (June 10, 1943–1944)

Germany Hans von SCHOEN
  Envoy Extraordinary and Minister Plenipotentiary
  (May 26, 1926)
  Hans Georg von MACKENSEN
  Envoy Extraordinary and Minister Plenipotentiary
  (December 7, 1933)
  Otto von ERDMANNSDORFF
  Envoy Extraordinary and Minister Plenipotentiary
  (May 11, 1937)
  Dietrich von JAGOW
  Envoy Extraordinary and Minister Plenipotentiary
  (July 31, 1941)

Edmond VEESENMAYER
Envoy Extraordinary and Minister Plenipotentiary,
Plenipotentiary of the Reich
(March 18, 1944)

Great Britain
(The British Empire) Sir Patrick William Maule RAMSAY
Envoy Extraordinary and Minister Plenipotentiary
(December 9, 1933)
Sir Geoffrey George KNOX
Envoy Extraordinary and Minister Plenipotentiary
(October 28, 1935)
[later Sir] Owen St. Clair O'MALLEY
Envoy Extraordinary and Minister Plenipotentiary
(May 16, 1936–December 7, 1941)

Greece
Demetrios SICILIANOS
Envoy Extraordinary and Minister Plenipotentiary
(January 2, 1933)
Panayotis PIPINELIS
Envoy Extraordinary and Minister Plenipotentiary
(September 28, 1936)
Pericles SKEFERIS
Envoy Extraordinary and Minister Plenipotentiary
(February 12, 1940–1942)

Holy See
Mgr. Dr. Angelo ROTTA,
Archbishop of Thebes, Papal Nuncio
(May 13, 1930–1944)

Iran
(residence in Rome)
Ananchiravan Khan SAPAHBODY
Envoy Extraordinary and Minister Plenipotentiary
(August 21, 1935)
Mohamed SAED
Envoy Extraordinary and Minister Plenipotentiary
(February 19, 1938)
Mosapha ADLE
Envoy Extraordinary and Minister Plenipotentiary
(October 29, 1938)

Iraq
(residence in Rome)
Dr. Muzahim ELPATCHADJI
Envoy Extraordinary and Minister Plenipotentiary
(?–?)

Italy
Prince Ascanio COLONNA
Envoy Extraordinary and Minister Plenipotentiary
(October 6, 1932)

Count Luigi Orazio V<small>INCI</small> G<small>IGLIUCCI</small>
Envoy Extraordinary and Minister Plenipotentiary
(December 21, 1936)
Giuseppe T<small>ALAMO</small>
Envoy Extraordinary and Minister Plenipotentiary
(March 16, 1940)
Filippo A<small>NFUSO</small>
Envoy Extraordinary and Minister Plenipotentiary
(January 8, 1942)
Raffaelo C<small>ASERTANO</small>
(December 9, 1943–1944)

Japan   *(residence formerly in Vienna)*
Matsukichi M<small>ATSUMAGO</small>
Envoy Extraordinary and Minister Plenipotentiary
(March 25, 1933)
Masayuki T<small>ANI</small>
Envoy Extraordinary and Minister Plenipotentiary
(July 20, 1936)
Tsutomu S<small>UAVA</small>
Chargé d'Affaires ad interim
(1938)
Kojiro I<small>NOUE</small>
Envoy Extraordinary and Minister Plenipotentiary
(October 4, 1939)
Toshitaka O<small>KUBO</small>
Envoy Extraordinary and Minister Plenipotentiary
(February 6, 1941–1944)

Latvia   *(residence in Warsaw)*
Nicolas A<small>BOLTINS</small>
Chargé d'Affaires ad interim
(1935–36)
Dr. Mikelis V<small>ALTERS</small>
Envoy Extraordinary and Minister Plenipotentiary
(June 4, 1936)
Ludvigs E<small>KIS</small>
Envoy Extraordinary and Minister Plenipotentiary
(September 24, 1938–1940)

Lithuania   *(residence in Warsaw)*
Dr. Jaulys Jurgis Š<small>AULYS</small>
Envoy Extraordinary and Minister Plenipotentiary
(May 20, 1932–1940)

Manchukuo Lu I-<small>VEN</small>
Envoy Extraordinary and Minister Plenipotentiary
(October 4, 1940–1944)

Mexico
(residence in Rome)
Manuel C. TELLEZ
Envoy Extraordinary and Minister Plenipotentiary
(November 7, 1934)
Eduardo VASCONCELOS
Envoy Extraordinary and Minister Plenipotentiary
(1936)
Gustavo VILLATORO
Chargé d'Affaires ad interim
(1937–40)
Manuel MAPLES ARCE
Chargé d'Affaires ad interim
(1940)

The Netherlands
L. G. van HOORN
Envoy Extraordinary and Minister Plenipotentiary
(February 17, 1933)
R. C. T. Roosmale NEPVEU
Envoy Extraordinary and Minister Plenipotentiary
(June 21, 1937–1940)

Norway
(residence in Berlin)
Arne SCHELL
Envoy Extraordinary and Minister Plenipotentiary
(February 26, 1923–1940)

Order of Saint John
of Jerusalem
Prince Don Carlo CAFFARELLI
Envoy Extraordinary and Minister Plenipotentiary
(June 14, 1935)

Paraguay
(residence formerly in Vienna)
Gustavo A. WIENGREEN
Envoy Extraordinary and Minister Plenipotentiary
(July 15, 1935–1942)

Poland
Dr. Stanislaw LEPKOWSKI
Envoy Extraordinary and Minister Plenipotentiary
(June 21, 1931)
Leon ORŁOWSKI
Envoy Extraordinary and Minister Plenipotentiary
(June 4, 1936–1940)

Portugal
José da COSTA CARNEIRO
Envoy Extraordinary and Minister Plenipotentiary
Carlos de Almeida Afonseca de SAMPAIO CARRIDO
Envoy Extraordinary and Minister Plenipotentiary
(1939–44)

*The diplomatic corps at the opening of the new session of Parliament,
Budapest, June 15, 1939*

Romania   Vasile GRIGORCEA
                  Envoy Extraordinary and Minister Plenipotentiary
                  (November 7, 1928)
             Raoul BOSSY
                  Envoy Extraordinary and Minister Plenipotentiary
                  (December 21, 1936)
             Gheorghe CRUŢESCU
                  Envoy Extraordinary and Minister Plenipotentiary
                  (November 3, 1939)
             Eugene FILOTTI
                  Envoy Extraordinary and Minister Plenipotentiary
                  (June 28, 1941–1944)

Slovakia   Jan SPISIAK
                  Envoy Extraordinary and Minister Plenipotentiary
                  (May 23, 1939–1944)

Spain   Carlos ARCOS y CUADRA
                  Chargé d'Affaires ad interim
                  (1933–37; unoccupied in 1937)

Count Carlos de BAILÉN
    Chargé d'Affaires
    (1938)
Miguel Angel de MUGUIRO y MUGUIRO
    Envoy Extraordinary and Minister Plenipotentiary
    (May 19, 1938–1944)

Sweden

(residence formerly in Vienna)
Ulf Torsten UNDÉN
    Envoy Extraordinary and Minister Plenipotentiary
    (October 11, 1928)
Carl Joan DANIELSSON
    Envoy Extraordinary and Minister Plenipotentiary
    (November 4, 1942–1944)

Switzerland

(residence formerly in Vienna)
Dr. Maximilien H. J. JAEGER
    Envoy Extraordinary and Minister Plenipotentiary
    (May 12, 1925)

Turkey

Erkin BEHIC
    Envoy Extraordinary and Minister Plenipotentiary
    (December 10, 1928)
Rusen Esref ÜNAYDIN
    Envoy Extraordinary and Minister Plenipotentiary
    (August 30, 1939)
Sevket Fuat KECECI
    Envoy Extraordinary and Minister Plenipotentiary
    (October 21, 1943–1944)

**Union of Soviet
Socialist Republics**

(residence formerly in Vienna)
Adolf PETROVSKI
    Envoy Extraordinary and Minister Plenipotentiary
    (April 9, 1934)
Alexander BEKZADIAN
    Envoy Extraordinary and Minister Plenipotentiary
    (December 24, 1934)
Nikolai CHARONOV
    Envoy Extraordinary and Minister Plenipotentiary
    (September 24, 1939–June 23, 1941)

United States of America

John Flournoy MONTGOMERY
    Envoy Extraordinary and Minister Plenipotentiary
    (August 1, 1933 – March 1941)
Herbert Claiborne PELL
    Envoy Extraordinary and Minister Plenipotentiary
    (May 20, 1941–December 1941)

Yugoslavia   Jovan DUČIĆ
            Envoy Extraordinary and Minister Plenipotentiary
            (February 25, 1932)
            Alexandar VUKČEVIĆ
            Envoy Extraordinary and Minister Plenipotentiary
            (February 22, 1934)
            Svetozar RAŠIĆ
            Envoy Extraordinary and Minister Plenipotentiary
            (October 20, 1938–April 10, 1941)

Sources

Magyarország tiszti cím- és névtára 1933–41.

László Zsigmond, ed., *Magyarország és a második világháború.*
   (Budapest: Kossuth, 1961), 507–511.

László Zsigmond, ed., *Diplomáciai iratok Magyarország külpolitikájához 1936–1945*
   (Budapest: Akadémiai Kiadó, 1962–1982),
   Vol. I (ed. Lajos Kerekes, 1962), 745–752; Vol. II. (ed. Magda Ádám, 1965), 909–916;
   Vol. III (ed. Magda Ádám, 1970), 713–719; Vol. IV (ed. Gyula Juhász, 1962), 807–812;
   Vol. V (ed. Gyula Juhász, 1982), 1269–1275.

Pál Pritz, *Magyarország külpolitikája Gömbös Gyula miniszterelnöksége idején 1932–1936*
   (Budapest: Akadémiai Kiadó, 1982), 282–283.

List of the Members of the Diplomatic Corps at Budapest
   September 1940. MS, J. F. Montgomery Papers

BIBLIOGRAPHY

Archival Sources

John Flournoy Montgomery Papers
Sterling Memorial Library, Yale University

John Flournoy Montgomery Collection
Országos Széchényi Könyvtár, Budapest, Hungary

József Balogh Papers, Fond 1
Országos Széchényi Könyvtár, Budapest, Hungary

Published Primary Sources

Andorka, Rudolf. *A madridi követségtől Mauthausenig: Andorka Rudolf naplója*
   [From the Madrid Legation to Mauthausen: The Diary of Rudolf Andorka].
   Budapest: Kossuth, 1978.

Bandholtz, Maj. Gen. Harry Hill. *An Undiplomatic Diary.*
   Edited by Fritz-Konrad Krueger.
   New York: Columbia University Press, 1933.

Ciano, Galeazzo. *Ciano's Diary 1939–1943.*
   Edited by Malcolm Muggeridge. London: William Heinemann, 1947.

Foreign Relations of the United States. Diplomatic Papers, 1935–41.
   Washington: United States Government Printing Office, 1952–58.

Gergely, Jenő, Ferenc Glatz, and Ferenc Pölöskei, eds. *Magyarországi pártprogramok
   1919–1945* [Hungarian Party Programs, 1919–1945]. Budapest: Kossuth, 1991.

Horthy, Miklós. *The Confidential Papers of Admiral Horthy.*
   Edited by Miklós Szinai and László Szűcs. Budapest: Corvina, 1965.

Horthy, Admiral Nicholas. *Memoirs.* London: Hutchinson, 1956;
   New York: Robert Speller and Sons, 1957.

Hory, András. *Bukaresttől Varsóig* [From Bucharest to Warsaw].
   Edited by Pál Pritz. Budapest: Gondolat, 1987.

Ickes, Harold L. *The Secret Diary of Harold L. Ickes: The First Thousand Days
   1933–1936. New* York: Simon and Schuster, 1953.

Long, Breckenridge. *The War Diary of Breckenridge Long: Selections from the Years
   1939–1944.* Edited by Fred L. Israel. Lincoln: University of Nebraska Press, 1966.

Montgomery, John Flournoy. *Hungary, The Unwilling Satellite.*
New York: Devin-Adair, 1947. Reprint. Morristown, NJ: Vista Books, 1993.

Nixon, Edgar B., ed. *Franklin D. Roosevelt and Foreign Affairs.*
Cambridge: Harvard University Press, 1969. Vols. I–III.

O'Malley, Sir Owen. *The Phantom Caravan.*
London: John Murray, 1954.

Ránki, György, Ervin Pamlényi, Loránt Tilkovszky, and Gyula Juhász, eds.
*A Wilhelmstrasse és Magyarország: Német diplomáciai iratok Magyarországról
1933–1944* [The Wilhelmstrasse and Hungary: German Diplomatic Papers on
Hungary, 1933–1944]. Budapest: Kossuth, 1968.

Roosevelt, Eleanor. *This I Remember.* New York: Harper & Brothers, 1949.

Roosevelt, Nicholas. *A Front Row Seat.*
Norman: University of Oklahoma Press, 1953.

Szegedy-Maszák, Aladár. *Az ember ősszel visszanéz...*
[Looking Back as the Fall Comes]. Vols. I–II. Budapest: Európa, 1996.

Zsigmond, László, ed. *Diplomáciai iratok Magyarország külpolitikájához 1936–1945*
(DIMK) [Diplomatic Papers on Hungarian Foreign Policy]. 5 vols. Budapest:
Akadémiai Kiadó, 1962–1982.
Vol. I, Lajos Kerekes, ed., 1962; Vol. II, Magda Ádám, ed., 1965;
Vol. III, Magda Ádám, ed., 1970; Vol. IV, Gyula Juhász, ed.,
1962; Vol. V, Gyula Juhász, ed., 1982.

Zsigmond, László, ed. *Magyarország és a második világháború* [Hungary and World
War II]. Budapest: Kossuth, 1961.

Literature

Buell, Raymond Leslie. *Isolated America.* New York-London: Knopf, 1940.

Dallek, Robert. *Franklin D. Roosevelt and American Foreign Policy, 1932–1945.*
New York: Oxford University Press, 1979.

De Santis, Hugh. *The Diplomacy of Silence. The American Foreign Service, the Soviet
Union, and the Cold War, 1933–1947.* Chicago-London: The University of Chicago
Press, 1980.

Dombrády, Lóránd. *Hadsereg és politika Magyarországon 1938–1944* [The Army and
Politics in Hungary, 1938–1944]. Budapest: Kossuth, 1986.

Dreisziger, N. F. "'Bridges to the West': The Horthy Regime's Reinsurance Policies in
1941," in *War & Society,* 7 (May 1989), 1–23.
Dreisziger, Nándor, ed. *Hungary in the Age of Total War, 1938–1948.* New York:

Columbia University Press, 1998.

Fenyo, Mario D. *Hitler, Horthy, and Hungary: German-Hungarian Relations 1941–1944*. New Haven and London: Yale University Press, 1972.

Flynn, John T. *The Roosevelt Myth*. Rev. ed. New York: Devin-Adair, 1956.

Gergely, Jenő. *Eucharisztikus Világkongresszus Budapesten/1938* [Eucharistic World Congress in Budapest, 1938]. Budapest: Kossuth, 1988.

Gergely, Jenő. *Gömbös Gyula. Politikai pályakép* [Gyula Gömbös, a Political Biography]. Budapest: Vince, 2001.

Gergely, Jenő and Pál Pritz. *A trianoni Magyarország* [The Hungary of Trianon, 1918–1945]. Budapest: Vince, 1998.

Gergely, Jenő, Ferenc Glatz, and Ferenc Pölöskei, eds. *Magyarországi pártprogramok 1919–1944* [Party Programs in Hungary, 1919–1944]. (Budapest: Kossuth, 1991.

Glatz, Ferenc. *Nemzeti kultúra – kulturált nemzet (1867–1987)* [National Culture, Cultured Nation, 1867–1987]. Budapest: Kossuth, 1988.

Juhász, Gyula. *A háború és Magyarország 1938–1945* [The War and Hungary, 1938–1945]. Budapest: Akadémiai Kiadó, 1986.

Juhász, Gyula. *Magyarország külpolitikája* , 1919–1945 [Hungarian Foreign Policy, 1919–1945]. 3rd ed, Budapest: Kossuth, 1988.

Juhász, Gyula. *Uralkodó eszmék Magyarországon 1939–1944* [Ruling Ideas in Hungary, 1939–1944]. Budapest: Kossuth, 1983.

Kanawada, Leo V., Jr. *Franklin D. Roosevelt's Diplomacy and American Catholics, Italians, and Jews.* Ann Arbor, Michigan: UMI Research Press, 1982.

Kennan, George F. *American Diplomacy 1900–1950*. Chicago, Illinois: University of Chicago Press, 1951.

Lackó, Miklós. *Nyilasok, nemzetiszocialisták 1935–1944* [Arrowcross Members, National Socialists, 1935–1944]. Budapest: Kossuth, 1966.

L. Nagy, Zsuzsa. „Amerikai diplomaták Horthy Miklósról, 1920–1944" [American Diplomats on Miklós Horthy, 1920–1944]. *Történelmi Szemle*, 3–4 (1990), 173–196.

Macartney, C. A. *October Fifteenth: A History of Modern Hungary, 1927–1945.* Edinburgh: Edinburgh University Press, 1956.

Ormos Mária. *Franciaország és a keleti biztonság 1931–1936*
[France and Eastern Security, 1931–1936].
Budapest: Akadémiai Kiadó, 1969.

Ormos, Mária. *Hitler.* Budapest: T-Twins, 1993.

Ormos, Mária. *Magyarország a két világháború korában (1914–1945)*
[Hungary in the Era of the Two World Wars (1914–1945)].
Debrecen: Csokonai, 1998.

Ormos, Mária. *Mussolini: Politikai életrajz.*
[Mussolini, a Political Biography]. Budapest: Kossuth, 1987.

Parmet, Herbert S., and Marie B. Hecht. *Never Again: A President Runs for a Third Term.* New York: Macmillan, 1968.

Pritz, Pál. *Magyarország külpolitikája Gömbös Gyula miniszterelnöksége idején 1932–1936* [Hungary's Foreign Policy under Prime Minister Gyula Gömbös].
Budapest: Akadémiai Kiadó, 1982.

Pritz, Pál. *Magyar diplomácia a két háború között. Tanulmányok*
[Hungarian Diplomacy between the Two Wars: Studies].
Budapest: Magyar Történelmi Társulat, 1995.

Ránki, György. *Emlékiratok és valóság Magyarország második világháborús szerepéről* [Hungary's Role in World War II: Memoirs and Reality]. Budapest: Kossuth, 1964.

Romsics, Ignác. *Bethlen István: Politikai életrajz*
[István Bethlen, a Political Biography]
Budapest: Magyarságkutató Intézet, 1991.

Romsics, Ignác. *Hungary in the Twentieth Century.*
Budapest: Corvina/Osiris, 1999.

Sakmyster, Thomas. *Hungary's Admiral on Horseback:*
Miklós Horthy, 1918–1944. New York: Columbia University Press, 1994.

Shirer, William L. *The Rise and Fall of the Third Reich:*
A History of Nazi Germany. New York: Simon and Schuster, 1960.

Sipos, Péter. *Imrédy Béla és a Magyar Megújulás Pártja*
[Béla Imrédy and the Party of Hungarian Renewal].
Budapest: Akadémiai Kiadó, 1970.

Sipos, Péter and István Vida. "The Policy of the United States towards Hungary during the Second World War." *Acta Historica Acad. Sci. Hung.,* (1983), 79–110.

Stuart, Graham H. *American Diplomatic and Consular Practice.*
New York: Appleton-Century-Crofts, 1936 (1st ed.), and 1952 (2nd ed.).

Thayer, Charles W. *Diplomat.* New York: Harper & Brothers, 1959.

Tilkovszky, Loránt. *Teleki Pál – legenda és valóság*
[Pál Teleki: Legend and Reality]. Budapest: Kossuth, 1969.

Contributions by the Editor

Frank, Tibor. "Literature Exported: Aspects of *The Hungarian Quarterly* (1936–1944)."
Studies in English and American, Budapest: L. Eötvös University, 4 (1978): 255–282.

Frank, Tibor. "Luring the English-Speaking World: *Hungarian History* Diverted."
The Slavonic and East European Review 69 (January 1991): 60–80.

Frank, Tibor. "Editing as Politics: József Balogh and *The Hungarian Quarterly.*"
The Hungarian Quarterly, 34 (Spring 1993): 5–13. Reprinted, with notes added, in
Ethnicity, Propaganda, Myth-Making.

Frank, Tibor. "Isolationism and US Immigration Policies: The Case of Pre-War
Hungary." In *From Theodore Roosevelt to FDR: Internationalism and Isolationism
in American Foreign Policy,* edited by Daniela Rossini, 131–146. Keele: Keele
University Press, 1995.

Frank, Tibor. "Diplomatic Images of Admiral Horthy: The American Perception of
Interwar Hungary, 1919–1941." In *Images of Central Europe in Travelogues and
Fiction by North American Writers,* edited by Waldemar Zacharasiewicz, 192–211.
Tübingen: Stauffenburg Verlag, 1995.

Frank, Tibor. "Unlikely Friendship: U.S. Minister John F. Montgomery and Hungary's
Regent Miklós Horthy." In *The Fabric of Modern Europe: Studies in Social and
Diplomatic History,* edited by Attila Pók, 183–199. Nottingham: Astra Press, 1999.

Frank, Tibor. *Ethnicity, Propaganda, Myth-Making: Studies on Hungarian
Connections to Britain and America, 1848–1945.* Budapest: Akadémiai Kiadó, 1999.

Frank, Tibor. "Treaty Revision and Doublespeak: Hungarian Neutrality, 1939–1941."
In *European Neutrals and Non-Belligerents during the Second World War,* edited by
Neville Wylie, 150–173. Cambridge: Cambridge University Press, 2002.

Frank, Tibor, ed. *Roosevelt követe Budapesten: John F. Montgomery bizalmas politikai
beszélgetései 1934–1941.* [Roosevelt's Minister to Budapest: The Confidential
Political Conversations of John F. Montgomery, 1934–1941]. Budapest: Corvina,
2002.

LIST OF ILLUSTRATIONS

Photos in this volume come partly from the album of Minister John F. Montgomery, donated by the minister's family to the Hungarian National Széchényi Library in Budapest. These pictures are reproduced here courtesy of Ms. Jean Montgomery-Riddell and are marked "A". All other photographs (marked "B") were selected from the photo collection of the Hungarian National Museum, which kindly granted permission to publish them. Wherever it was possible, I added the name of the photographer. Unfortunately this proved to be impossible in the case of the minister's pictures that were glued into his album.

INDEX

Page numbers in italics refer to footnotes. The index does not include the list of diplomatic representatives in Budapest, the bibliography, and the list of illustrations.